Adult- Gero and Family
Nurse Practitioner

Certification Practice Questions

Includes Answers and Explanations

Adult- Gero and
Family Nurse Practitioner

Certification Practice Questions

Includes Answers and Explanations

Amelie Hollier, DNP, FNP- BC, FAANP

Advanced Practice Education Associates, Inc.
118 Abigayles Row
Scott, LA 70583 U.S.A.

Printed in the United States of America.

NOTICE:

The author, reviewers, and publisher of this book have taken extreme care to insure that the information contained within this book is correct and compatible with standards of care generally accepted at the time of publication. Sources were used which were believed to be complete and accurate. If by human error or changes in standards of care, the information contained herein is not complete or is not accurate, the author, reviewers, publisher, or any other party associated with this publication cannot accept responsibility or consequences from application of the material contained within. Readers and users of this publication are encouraged to check the information with other sources. **If you are unwilling to be bound by the above, please contact the publisher.**

ISBN 978-1-892418-18-0

Author

Amelie Hollier, DNP, FNP-BC, FAANP

Dr. Hollier is a nationally certified family nurse practitioner. She is President and CEO of Advanced Practice Education Associates (APEA). She is in clinical practice in Lafayette, Louisiana at Our Lady of Lourdes Regional Medical Center. She has co-authored and authored seventeen books for primary care providers. Amelie travels extensively throughout the United States presenting certification review courses for nurse practitioners and presenting pharmacology and primary care topics to professional APRN groups. Amelie received her Doctorate of Nursing Practice from University of Tennessee-Memphis and was inducted as a Fellow in AANP in 2007.

Advanced Practice Education Associates, Inc. is an educational organization committed to helping nurse practitioners and nurse practitioner students advance professionally and educationally through review courses, continuing education programs, books, and other educational offerings.

Acknowledgements

This book would have been impossible without the never-ending patience, encouragement, confidence, and support of my family. Thank you all!

I am especially grateful to Jeanie Doucet, Lisa Puckett, Sonia Guidry and Christopher Rush for everything they did to help get this book to print. It is an honor and a privilege to work with you.

A special thank you to Julie Siracusa for sharing her artistic gift in the design of the cover of this book.

This book is dedicated to my family both young and old.

Amelie Hollier

Preface

Adult-Gero and Family Nurse Practitioner Certification Practice Questions contain review questions and practice examinations intended to assist future family, adult, and adult-gero nurse practitioners to prepare for national certification examinations. Nurse practitioner students will also find it invaluable for evaluation of their knowledge level. A chapter on study skills and test-taking strategies is also included to maximize the test-taker's potential for success.

The author's recommendation for the most effective use of this book is to first review a specific subject area independently, then answer the questions that correlate with that subject. If it is determined that certain topics are unfamiliar, then these areas may need further attention. After sufficient reading and review in all areas, a practice exam can be taken. The practice examinations will help to determine strengths and weaknesses in both knowledge and clinical application.

Adult-Gero and Family Nurse Practitioner Certification Practice Questions contain multiple choice, competency-based, questions intended to test the student's knowledge and ability to apply that knowledge in clinical situations. Content areas covered in the exams are health promotion, disease prevention, diagnosis and management of acute and chronic illnesses across the life span, the research process, and professional issues.

The test items in this book were written by a practicing, certified, family nurse practitioner.

A variety of current resources, from clinical practice, educational, and research literature, were used in the development the items and rationales.

A sincere effort has been made to provide readers with current, accurate, and comprehensive information. If the reader has any questions or comments, the author welcomes communication via e-mail at *questions@apea.com*.

Updates to this edition will be posted at www.apea.com/updates.php.

Contents

Study Skills

Plan ahead. Determine the total content that needs to be reviewed, and then allow yourself adequate time to prepare. Develop a reasonable study schedule *now* in order to avoid cramming. Research has demonstrated that short daily study periods are more productive than marathon cramming sessions. Divide the content into small sections that are not overwhelming. Set your study goals, and then set out to accomplish those goals. An effective way to achieve daily goals is to use an index card on which the tasks to complete are listed. The most important point to make is this: *Don't procrastinate!*

Outline the content to be learned. Use the practice questions in this book to familiarize yourself with the content. There will be areas identified that need very little further review, and areas identified that need extensive study. Begin by skimming and scanning all material for the session of study, then delve deeper. Remember to focus mainly on major concepts, avoiding becoming bogged down by details.

Decide how much time you can spend each day or week. Consider what time of day you study best. Pay attention to your biological clock. At the end of each study session, take a little time to summarize what you have learned, including important concepts.

Be versatile. Use a variety of resources, allowing all of your senses to help you learn. There are books, videotapes, computer programs, review tests, audio tapes, review courses, review books, and journals available. Organize a weekly study group with a few classmates. Hearing information and explaining to another (audio-learning) is a valuable adjunct to hearing and writing information (visual learning). Discover what method of learning works best for you, and enjoy the process.

A **quiet atmosphere** with minimal distractions facilitates concentration. Find a quiet place to study.

New information must be reviewed continually in order to build strong memory traces. The more frequently information is recalled, the more firmly it becomes etched in the memory.

Motivate yourself. Remember your personal goal, whether it is personal fulfillment, a more successful future, a career change, or something more altruistic in nature. Goals serve as incentives for work. The desire to reach a goal is a powerful motivator.

Test-Taking Strategies

Develop the ability to relax. After you have prepared for an examination, you do not want anxiety to impair your performance. Get enough rest the night before the test. Relaxation exercises such as deep breathing, progressive muscle relaxation, and guided imagery, can have positive effects.

Develop your test-taking skills through practice. Remember, the items are designed to test your knowledge and ability to apply the knowledge. Ask yourself what the purpose of the question is, and answer with that purpose in mind.

Practice. Use the sample tests. Read question stems carefully, becoming aware of the specific information requested, and identifying key words. Develop the habit of looking out for negative stems, which can be tricky. Examples of negative stems are "EXCEPT," "NOT," "LEAST," "INCORRECT," and "FALSE."

After you first read a question, try to answer it without looking at the multiple-choice options.

Evaluate each answer choice as if it were a "True-False" question. If the answer is true, include it in your options. If it is false, eliminate it. Eliminate obvious distractors, leaving fewer options from which to identify the correct answer. Again, beware of negative stems where the correct answer choice is the option that is *false.*

Base your answers on principles of nursing practice for the general population, unless the stem specifies otherwise.

If a particular item has you stumped, **make an educated guess** and move on. You can return to it later, if time allows. Attempt every question, but keep moving on. Pace yourself. Remember, there is no penalty for wrong answers. Guess if you have no idea, but answer every question.

Allow ample time to arrive on time at the test site. It is a good idea to make a practice run to the test site if you are not familiar with the area.

Listen to all instructions, and **read** all directions.

Try to **avoid becoming distracted** by those who finish the test before you. Work at your own pace. Finishing the examination first is not the objective.

Be aware of pitfalls. One major pitfall is the tendency to rely on past experience. Although certification examinations are practice-based, all practitioners may not follow standards of nursing practice.

Record your answers carefully. If you skip a question, be sure to mark the question so that you can come back to it.

Think positively! Maintain confidence. Continue to put forth your best effort and don't give up.

Check your work. After the test, as you review your answers, try not to make changes unless you are reasonably certain your original response was incorrect. Research has shown that when in doubt, the first answer choice is most likely to be the correct response.

We hope that this book will help future advanced practice registered nurses to meet the challenge of transition from student to practitioner. The challenge to constantly maintain current knowledge, enabling us to provide continuous expert nursing care, should never end.

Further Reading

Hargrove-Huttel, R., & Colgrove, K. (2008). *Pharmacology Success: A Course Review Applying Critical Thinking to Test Taking*. Philadelphia: F.A. Davis.

Kesselman-Turkel, J., & Peterson, F. (2004). *Test-Taking Strategies* (2nd ed.). Madison, WI: Univ of Wisconsin Press.

Korchek, N., & Sides, M. B. (2002). *Nurse's guide to successful test taking* (4th ed.). Philadelphia: Lippincott.

Nugent, P., & Vitale, B. (2008). *Fundamentals Success: A Course Review Applying Critical Thinking to Test Taking* (2nd ed.). Philadelphia: F.A. Davis.

Rooney, R., & Lipuma, A. (1992). *Learn to be the master student: How to develop self-confidence and effective study skills.* Silver Springs, CO: Maydale.

Shain, D. (1995). *Study Skills and Test-Taking Strategies for Medical Students: Find and Use Your Personal Learning Style* (2nd ed.). New York: Springer.

NOTE TO STUDENTS:

A special format has been created to assist with studying. The answers and explanations to the following items can be found on the reverse side of the question page. Merely fold the answer page back onto the question page and the answers will line up on the same line as the questions.

Adult and Adult-Gero students should concentrate on the following sections:

- Subject-specific categories
- Adult Exams
- Geriatrics

Family students should concentrate on the following sections:

- Subject-specific categories
- Family Exams
- Pediatrics

Cardiovascular Disorders

1. According to the National Heart, Lung and Blood Institute, which characteristic listed below is a coronary heart disease (CHD) risk equivalent; that is, which risk factor places the patient at similar risk for CHD as a history of CHD?

a. **Hypertension**
b. **Cigarette smoking**
c. **Male age > 45 years**
d. **Diabetes mellitus**

2. A patient will be screened for hyperlipidemia via a serum specimen. He should be told:

a. **to fast for 12-14 hours.**
b. **to fast for 6-8 hours.**
c. **that black coffee is allowed.**
d. **a non-fasting state will not affect the results.**

3. A 65 year-old male patient has the following lipid levels:

Total cholesterol 240 mg/dL
LDL 140 mg/dL
HDL 35 mg/dL
Triglycerides 129 mg/dL

What class of medications is preferred to normalize his lipid levels and reduce his risk of a cardiac event?

a. **Niacin**
b. **Fibric acids**
c. **HMG Co-A reductase inhibitor**
d. **Bile acid sequestrants**

4. Which test listed below may be used to exclude a secondary cause of hyperlipidemia in a patient with elevated lipids?

a. **CBC**
b. **TSH**
c. **Urine culture and sensitivity**
d. **Sedimentation rate**

1. *d.*

In determining whether a patient should be treated for hyperlipidemia, a patient's risk factors must be determined. After assessing fasting lipids, specifically LDLs, CHD equivalents must be identified. These are diabetes, symptomatic carotid artery disease, peripheral artery disease, abdominal aortic aneurysm, and multiple risk factors that confer a 10 year risk of CHD > 20 percent. Major CHD risk factors are elevated LDL cholesterol, cigarette smoking, hypertension, low HDL cholesterol, family history of premature CHD [in male first degree relatives (FDR) < 55 years; female FDR, 65 years], and age (men ≥ 45 years, women ≥ 55 years). Patients with 2 or more risk factors should have a 10 risk assessment performed and treated accordingly.

2. *a.*

Serum total and HDL cholesterol can be measured in fasting or non-fasting individuals. There are very small and clinically insignificant differences in these values when fasting and not. The primary effect of eating on a patient's lipid values is on the triglyceride levels. The maximum effect of eating on triglyceride levels occurs at 3-4 hours after eating, but there may be several peaks during a 12-hour period. Therefore, the most accurate triglyceride levels will be obtained following a 12-hour fast.

3. *c.*

The only medication class that reduces elevated lipid levels and has proven efficacy in reducing risk of cardiac events, even for primary prevention, is a HMG Co-A reductase inhibitor, a statin. Statin therapy has been shown to reduce overall mortality due to cardiovascular deaths. The statin should significantly reduce his total cholesterol and LDL values.

4. *b.*

Patients who have dyslipidemia should be screened for diabetes, renal disease, and hypothyroidism. Nephrotic syndrome can produce remarkably elevated cholesterol levels. Therefore, measurements of glucose, creatinine, and thyroid stimulating hormone should be performed when evaluating dyslipidemia. Sedimentation rate is a measure of non-specific inflammation and so is not helpful in this situation. Specifically, hypothyroidism can produce marked lipid abnormalities.

5. In order to reduce lipid levels, statins are most beneficial when taken:

- **a. once daily in the AM.**
- **b. always with food.**
- **c. with an aspirin in the evening.**
- **d. in conjunction with diet and exercise.**

6. A patient taking atorvastatin for newly diagnosed dyslipidemia complains of muscle aches in his upper and lower legs for the past three weeks. It has not improved with rest. How should this be evaluated?

- **a. Stop the atorvastatin immediately.**
- **b. Check liver enzymes first.**
- **c. Order a CPK level.**
- **d. Ask about nighttime muscle cramps.**

7. Which hypertensive patient is most likely to have adverse blood pressure effects from excessive sodium consumption?

- **a. 21 year-old Asian American male**
- **b. 35 year-old menstruating female**
- **c. 55 year-old post menopausal female**
- **d. 70 year-old African American male**

8. A patient with poorly controlled hypertension and history of myocardial infarction 6 years ago presents today with mild shortness of breath. He takes quinapril, ASA, metoprolol, and a statin daily. What symptom is NOT indicative of a heart failure exacerbation?

- **a. Fatigue**
- **b. Headache**
- **c. Orthopnea**
- **d. Cough**

9. A patient with newly diagnosed heart failure has started fosinopril in the last few days. She has developed a cough. What clinical finding can help distinguish the etiology of the cough as heart failure?

- **a. It is dry and non-productive.**
- **b. It is wet and worse with recumbence.**
- **c. It is purulent and tachycardia accompanies it.**
- **d. Shortness of breath always results after coughing.**

5. ***d***

Statins are used to reduce elevated levels of lipids in conjunction with modifications in diet and exercise. The timing of statin dosing and indication with food (or not) is different for each statin. Most patients who take statins are also candidates for aspirin as primary or secondary prevention, but aspirin does not improve statin tolerance. Statins are correctly taken once daily.

6. ***c***

This patient has a complaint of myalgias that could be associated with statin use. This patient should be assessed for rhabdomyolysis. This is done by measuring a CPK level. If this value is elevated, atorvastatin should be stopped immediately. Liver enzymes would not assess for the etiology of myalgias. They assess tolerance of statins in the liver. Nighttime muscle cramps are not associated with statin use.

7. ***d***

Two groups of patients typically experience adverse blood pressure effects from consumption of sodium greater than 2000 mg daily. Those patients considered to be most sodium sensitive are elderly patients and African American patients. Thus, choice d is the best choice listed.

8. ***b***

Fatigue is a common symptom in cardiac patients that can represent a worsening of many cardiac diseases such as coronary artery disease, heart failure, valvular dysfunction. Orthopnea and cough, especially nocturnal, are classic symptoms of worsening heart failure.

9. ***b***

The cough associated with fosinopril an ACE inhibitor, is dry, non-productive and may be described as annoying. Its severity does not change with position or time of day. A cough associated with heart failure is wet, worse when lying down, and is usually described by patients as "worse at night". Choice c is often associated with fever and probably reflects an infectious process like pneumonia.

10. A patient with shortness of breath has suspected heart failure. What diagnostic test would best help determine this?

- a. **Echocardiogram**
- b. **B type natriuretic peptide (BNP)**
- c. **EKG**
- d. **Chest x-ray**

11. Which class of medication is frequently used to improve long-term outcomes in patients with systolic dysfunction?

- a. **Loop diuretics**
- b. **Calcium channel blockers**
- c. **ACE inhibitors**
- d. **Thiazide diuretics**

12. Ramipril has been initiated at a low dose in a patient with heart failure. What is most important to monitor in about one week?

- a. **Heart rate**
- b. **Blood pressure**
- c. **EKG**
- d. **Potassium level**

13. Which medication listed below could potentially exacerbate heart failure in a susceptible individual?

- a. **Metoprolol**
- b. **Furosemide**
- c. **Metformin**
- d. **Acetaminophen**

14. A 75 year-old patient with longstanding hypertension takes a combination ACE inhibitor/ thiazide diuretic and amlodipine daily. Today his diastolic blood pressure and heart rate are elevated. He has developed dyspnea on exertion and peripheral edema over the past several days. These symptoms demonstrate:

- a. **primary renal dysfunction.**
- b. **development of heart failure.**
- c. **failure of HCTZ.**
- d. **dietary indiscretions.**

10. *b*
BNP is a hormone involved in regulation of blood pressure and fluid volume. When the BNP level is 80 pg/mL or greater, the sensitivity and specificity is 98% and 92%, favoring a diagnosis of heart failure. Alternatively, BNP levels less than 80 pg/mL strongly suggest that heart failure is not present (Some US institutions use 100 pg/mL). Other conditions may cause elevated BNP levels: thoracic and abdominal surgery, renal failure, and subarachnoid hemorrhage. Consequently, careful assessment of the patient is prudent. Echocardiograms mechanically evaluate the heart and establish an ejection fraction. If <35-40%, then CHF can usually be diagnosed. Ejection fractions do not always correlate with patient symptoms. EKG evaluates the electrical activity of the heart. Chest x-ray can indicate heart failure but a BNP is a more sensitive measure.

11. c
ACE inhibitors are commonly used in patients with systolic dysfunction because they reduce morbidity and mortality, i.e. these medications alter prognosis. They also improve symptoms of fatigue, shortness of breath, and exercise intolerance. Loop and thiazide diuretics improve symptoms, but do not alter long-term prognosis with heart failure. Beta blockers should be used in conjunction with ACE inhibitors and diuretics, but not as solo agents. Beta blockers can potentially worsen heart failure, so their use in patients with heart failure should be monitored carefully.

12. *d*
ACE inhibitors work in the kidney in the renin angiotensin aldosterone system and can impair renal excretion of potassium in patients with normal kidney function. In patients with impaired renal blood flow and/or function, the risk of hyperkalemia is increased. Common practice is to monitor potassium, BUN, and Cr at about one week after initiation of an ACE inhibitor and with each increase in dosage.

13. *a*
Metoprolol is a cardioselective beta blocker that decreases heart rate. A patient with heart failure will compensate for heart failure by increasing heart rate to maintain cardiac output (CO). Metoprolol impairs the patient's ability to increase heart rate when needed to maintain cardiac output (CO=stroke volume x heart rate). Consequently, the use of beta blockers in patients with heart failure should be monitored carefully. Furosemide may actually improve shortness of breath in a patient with heart failure. Metformin and acetaminophen have no direct effect on cardiac output in a patient with heart failure.

14. *b*
The symptoms of increased heart rate in the presence of dyspnea on exertion and peripheral edema are symptoms of heart failure. Longstanding hypertension is a major risk factor for development of heart failure. Dietary indiscretion, like sodium/ fluid excess may produce peripheral edema, but should not produce dyspnea and peripheral edema in the absence of heart failure.

15. A medication which may produce exercise intolerance in a patient with hypertension is:

 a. **hydrochlorothiazide.**
 b. **amlodipine.**
 c. **metoprolol.**
 d. **fosinopril.**

16. A 40 year-old African American patient has blood pressure readings of 175/100 and 170/102. What is a reasonable plan of care for this patient today?

 a. **Start low dose thiazide diuretic.**
 b. **Start an ACE inhibitor twice daily.**
 c. **Initiate low dose HCTZ and candesartan.**
 d. **Initiate amlodipine, beta blocker, or ACE inhibitor.**

17. A patient with hypertension describes a previous allergy to a sulfa antibiotic as "sloughing of skin" and hospitalization. Which medication is contraindicated in this patient?

 a. **Ramipril**
 b. **Metoprolol**
 c. **Hydrochlorothiazide**
 d. **Verapamil**

18. Which item below represents the best choice of anti-hypertensive agents for the indicated patient?

 a. **Beta blocker for a 38 year-old diabetic patient**
 b. **ACE inhibitor for a patient on a K^+ sparing diuretic**
 c. **Beta blocker in a 46 year-old patient with migraines**
 d. **Diuretic in a patient with history of gout**

19. A patient has had poorly controlled hypertension for more than 10 years. Indicate the most likely position of his point of maximal impulse (PMI):

 a. **5th Intercostal space (ICS) mid-clavicular line (MCL).**
 b. **8th ICS MCL.**
 c. **5th ICS, left of MCL.**
 d. **6th ICS, right of MCL.**

15. *c*
Metoprolol is a cardioselective beta blocker. It will produce bradycardia that is responsible for exercise intolerance. As a patient exercises, a concomitant increase in heart rate allows for an increase in cardiac output. If the heart rate is not able to increase because of beta blocker influence, neither can the cardiac output. The patient will necessarily slow down his physical activity. Choices *a* and *d* have no direct effect on heart rate. Amlodipine is a calcium channel blocker that does not decrease heart rate.

16. *c*
This patient has Stage 2 hypertension based on JNC VII's classification of hypertension. Stage 2 hypertension should be treated initially with 2 medications and life style modifications. Based on this, choice *c* is the best response. A single medication is unlikely to decrease his blood pressure to a normal range.

17. c
This patient's allergy to "sulfa" sounds like Stevens Johnson Syndrome, a potentially life-threatening allergic reaction. Hydrochlorothiazide has a sulfonamide ring in its chemical structure, generally referred to as "sulfa". This sulfonamide ring can initiate an allergic reaction in patients with sulfa allergy. Since the patient's allergic reaction to sulfa was so serious, other sulfonamide medications should be completely avoided until consultation with an allergist. The other medications can be used without concern in the presence of a patient with a sulfa allergy because there is no sulfonamide component.

18. c
Beta blockers may be used as prophylactic agents in patients with migraine headaches, thus, serving to treat hypertension and as prophylaxis for migraine headaches in this patient. Beta blockers may mask the signs and symptoms of hypoglycemia in patients with diabetes. They should be used with caution, but used when indicated. ACE inhibitors decrease potassium loss and so should not be routinely used in patients who are on potassium sparing diuretics because hyperkalemia may result. Diuretics can produce hyperuricemic states due to fluid loss. Therefore, they should be avoided in patients with gout.

19. c
The PMI or apical impulse is produced when the left ventricle moves anteriorly and touches the chest wall during contraction. This is normally found at the 5th intercostal space, mid-clavicular line. Certain conditions and diseases like heart failure, cardiomyopathy may account for this; or left ventricular hypertrophy from prolonged hypertension can displace the apical impulse. The displacement usually occurs left and laterally from its usual location. Thus, 5th ICS, left of mid-clavicular line. Conditions like pregnancy may displace the apical impulse upward and to the left.

20. Which laboratory abnormality may be observed in a patient who takes lisinopril?

a. **Decreased INR**
b. **Decreased calcium level**
c. **Increased potassium level**
d. **Increased ALT/AST**

21. A patient with hypertension has taken hydrochlorothiazide 25 mg daily for the past 4 weeks. His blood pressure has decreased from 155/95 to 145/90. How should the nurse practitioner proceed?

a. **Wait 4 weeks before making a dosage change.**
b. **Increase the hydrochlorothiazide to 50 mg daily.**
c. **Add a drug from another class to the daily 25 mg hydrochlorothiazide.**
d. **Stop the hydrochlorothiazide and start a drug from a different class.**

22. Which study would be most helpful in evaluating the degree of hypertrophy of the atrium or ventricle?

a. **Chest x-ray**
b. **Electrocardiography**
c. **Echocardiography**
d. **Doppler ultrasound**

23. The valve most commonly involved in chronic rheumatic heart disease is the:

a. **aortic.**
b. **mitral.**
c. **pulmonic.**
d. **tricuspid.**

24. A patient has an audible diastolic murmur best heard in the mitral listening point. There is no audible click. His status has been monitored for the past 2 years. This murmur is probably:

a. **mitral valve prolapse.**
b. **acute mitral regurgitation.**
c. **chronic mitral regurgitation.**
d. **mitral stenosis.**

20. c
Lisinopril is an ACE inhibitor. This medication causes retention of potassium. A potassium level should be measured about one month after initiating therapy and after each dose change. The other laboratory values are not specific to changes that can take place when a patient takes an ACE inhibitor.

21. ***c***
Although we do not know this patient's age, race, or target blood pressure, it still exceeds the minimum threshold of 140/90 mm Hg. It is not acceptable to continue the current dose. Increasing the hydrochlorothiazide to 50 mg daily will not result in a decrease in blood pressure, only an increase in potassium loss. Adding a drug from a different medication class is a good choice because the combined effects of antihypertensive medications nearly always produce a decrease in blood pressure and both drugs can be maintained in low doses to minimize side effects.

22. ***c***
Echocardiography is of greatest value when evaluating valves, chamber size, cardiac output, and overall function of the myocardium. It is noninvasive and allows specific measurement of chamber size and thickness of the myocardium. The chest film is important in identification of chamber enlargement, but its primary importance is in assessment of the pulmonary vasculature. Electrocardiography (ECG) provides information about the heart's conduction system and identifies cardiac rhythm, though ventricular enlargement can be identified on ECG. Doppler ultrasound identifies intracardiac flow velocities and can assist in quantifying the severity of regurgitation or stenosis.

23. ***b***
The mitral valve has a propensity for disorders secondary to rheumatic heart disease. Rarely is the pulmonic valve involved, but the aortic and tricuspid valves follow in descending order of involvement. Following an episode of rheumatic fever, which occurs infrequently in the US today but is common in developing countries, the valves can become stenotic or regurgitant. This is a major cause of valvular disease in the US seen primarily in immigrants.

24. ***d***
Mitral valve prolapse (MVP) is an unlikely etiology since MVP is a systolic murmur. Additionally, the question states there is no audible click, and a mid to late systolic click is characteristic of MVP. Acute mitral regurgitation (MR) develops usually after rupture of the chordae tendineae, ruptured papillary muscle after myocardial infarction, or secondary to bacterial endocarditis. Symptoms of failure appear with abrupt clinical deterioration in the patient. There would not be a 2-year course for this patient. Dilation of the left atrium and ventricle is typical in chronic MR since both chambers are affected from regurgitant blood flow across the diseased valve, but, MR is a systolic murmur, not diastolic. This is mitral stenosis (MS) because MS produces the only diastolic murmur listed in the question.

25. A 28 year-old has a Grade 3 murmur. Which characteristic indicates a need for referral?

   a. **A fixed split**
   b. **An increase in splitting with inspiration**
   c. **A split S2 with inspiration**
   d. **Changes in intensity with position change**

26. A 25 year-old patient has aortic stenosis (AS). The etiology of his AS is probably:

   a. **congenital.**
   b. **rheumatic.**
   c. **acquired calcific.**
   d. **unknown.**

27. The most common arrhythmia resulting from valvular heart disease is:

   a. **atrial fibrillation.**
   b. **paroxysmal supraventricular tachycardia.**
   c. **ventricular fibrillation.**
   d. **heart block.**

25. a

A split is created because of closure of valves. For example, an S2 is created by closure of the aortic and pulmonic valves. Normally these split with inspiration and almost never with expiration. Splits should never be fixed. This indicates some pathology like an atrial septal defect, pulmonic stenosis, or possibly mitral regurgitation. In any event, this patient needs initial evaluation with an echocardiogram because fixed splits are always considered abnormal.

26. *a*

In someone younger than 65 years of age, the most likely cause is congenital. The aortic valve usually consists of three cusps, but some individuals are born with a bicuspid aortic valve. Rheumatic heart disease is the second most common cause of aortic stenosis in this age group, but the incidence has decreased drastically in the last many decades because of the use of antibiotics to treat Streptococcal infections. In more than 90% of patients older than 65 years, acquired calcifications appear on a normal tricuspid valve and produce aortic stenosis.

27. *a*

The most common arrhythmia seen in all forms of valvular disease is atrial fibrillation. It is usually seen in patients with organic heart disease. Paroxysmal supraventricular tachycardia is one of the most common arrhythmias but often occurs in patients with no underlying heart disease. It is usually caused by reentry in the AV node and not by valvular heart disease. Ventricular fibrillation and heart block are more likely to represent disease in the conduction system of the myocardium.

Dermatologic Disorders

1. **A patient is diagnosed with tinea pedis. A microscopic examination of the sample taken from the infected area would likely demonstrate:**

    a. **hyphae.**
    b. **yeasts.**
    c. **rods or cocci.**
    d. **a combination of hyphae and spores.**

2. **Which test is NOT suitable to diagnose shingles if the clinical presentation is questionable?**

    a. **Tzanck preparation**
    b. **Polymerase chain reaction (PCR)**
    c. **Direct fluorescent antibody (DFA)**
    d. **Complete blood count (CBC)**

3. **The most common form of skin cancer is:**

    a. **squamous cell carcinoma.**
    b. **basal cell carcinoma.**
    c. **malignant melanoma.**
    d. **cutaneous carcinoma.**

4. **The nurse practitioner examines a patient who has had poison ivy for 3 days. She asks if she can spread it to her family members. The nurse practitioner replies:**

    a. **" yes, but only before crusting has occurred".**
    b. **" yes, the fluid in the blister can transmit it."**
    c. **"no, transmission does not occur from the blister's contents."**
    d. **"no, you are no longer contagious. "**

5. **A low potency topical hydrocortisone cream would be most appropriate in a patient who has been diagnosed with:**

    a. **psoriasis.**
    b. **impetigo.**
    c. **cellulitis.**
    d. **atopic dermatitis.**

1. ***a***

Under microscopic exam, hyphae are long, thin and branching, and indicate dermatophytic infections. Hyphae are typical in tinea pedis, tinea cruris, and tinea corporis. Yeasts are usually seen in candidal infections. Cocci and rods are specific to bacterial infections.

2. ***d***

Herpes viruses are the causative agents in shingles, chickenpox, genital herpes, and oral fever blisters. Diagnosis is usually made on clinical presentation. However, in questionable cases, lab tests may be employed. A Tzanck preparation is a rapid test used to diagnose infections due to herpes viruses. Cells taken from a blister's fluid are smeared on a slide and stained with a Wright's stain or the fluid can be used for other methods of testing. DFA is the most common test employed for shingles diagnosis because it can be rapidly performed and offers results in about 90 minutes. PCR may be performed on skin scrapings, serum or blood for herpetic diagnosis. CBC may indicate a patient with a viral infection, but is non-specific for herpetic infections.

3. ***b***

Skin cancers are divided into two major groups: non-melanoma and melanoma skin cancer. Basal cell carcinoma is considered non-melanoma skin cancer and is the most common form of skin cancer in the US. It is most common in 40-60 year-olds, but can be found in any age if the skin is regularly exposed to sunlight or ultraviolet radiation. Basal cell carcinoma grows slowly and if not treated can spread to surrounding areas of tissue or bone.

4. ***c***

The skin reaction seen after exposure to poison ivy (or any other skin irritant), takes place because of contact with the offending substance. In the case of poison ivy, the harmful exposure occurs from contact with oil from the plant. The eruptions seen are NOT able to transmit the reaction to other people unless oil from the plant remains on the skin and someone touches the oil. The fluid found in the blisters is NOT able to transmit poison ivy to anyone, only the oil from the plant can do that. After oil has touched the skin, some time must pass for the reaction to occur. Therefore, reaction times vary depending on skin thickness and quantity of oil contacting the skin.

5. ***d***

Low potency steroid creams are almost never potent enough to treat psoriasis. These require higher potency steroid preparation or systemic agents. Impetigo is a superficial bacterial infection and a steroid cream would be contraindicated. Cellulitis is an infection of the subcutaneous layer of the skin and requires an oral or systemic antibiotic. Atopic dermatitis is a chronic inflammatory disorder of the skin that involves a genetic defect in the proteins supporting the epidermal layer. A patient with atopic dermatitis would be the most appropriate (of those listed above) to use a low potency topical steroid cream.

6. A skin lesion fluoresces under a Wood's lamp. What microscopic finding is consistent with this?

a. **Clue cells**
b. **Herpes simplex**
c. **Hyphae**
d. **Leukocytes**

7. Which chronic skin disorder primarily affects hairy areas of the body?

a. **Seborrheic dermatitis**
b. **Atopic dermatitis**
c. **Contact dermatitis**
d. **Hydradenitis suppurativa**

8. A 16 year-old male has nodulocystic acne. What might have the greatest positive impact in managing his acne?

a. **Retin-A® plus minocycline**
b. **Benzoyl peroxide plus erythromycin**
c. **Isotretinoin (Accutane®)**
d. **Oral antibiotics**

9. Patients with atopic dermatitis are likely to exhibit:

a. **itching.**
b. **asthma and allergic bronchitis.**
c. **nasal polyps and asthma.**
d. **allergic conjunctivitis and wheezing.**

10. A patient will be taking oral terbinafine for fingernail fungus. The NP knows that:

a. **this will cure her infection 95% of the time.**
b. **a topical antifungal will work just as well when the nail matrix is involved.**
c. **terbinafine is a potent inhibitor of the CYP 3A4 enzymes.**
d. **toenail fungus resolves faster than fingernail fungus after treatment.**

6. ***c***

A Wood's lamp emits ultraviolet light when turned on. If an area fluoresces under Wood's lamp illumination, a fungal (and sometimes bacterial) infection should be suspected. The test is most effectively performed in a darkened room so the fluorescence can be more easily identified. Deodorant, soap, and make-up may also fluoresce. About one-third of hyphae fluoresce.

7. ***a***

Seborrheic dermatitis causes flaking of the skin, usually the scalp. In adolescents and adults, when it affects the scalp, it is termed dandruff. When this occurs in young children or infants, it is termed "cradle cap". The exact cause is unknown; however it has a propensity for hairy areas of the body such as the scalp, face, chest, and legs. It appears greasy and flaky. This may be seen in patients with Parkinson's disease.

8. ***c***

Nodulocystic acne is the most severe form of acne vulgaris. Nodules and cysts characterize this disease. They can be palpated and usually seen on the skin, although, they actually are under the skin's surface. They develop when the follicle wall ruptures and leaks pus and cell contents in the dermis. The contaminated material infects adjoining follicles and the nodule develops. Isotretinoin is the only known effective treatment.

9. ***a***

Atopic dermatitis is diagnosed on clinical presentation and includes evidence of prutitic skin. It is recurrent and often begins in childhood. For decades the "atopic triad" has been used to refer to patients with atopic dermatitis, asthma, and allergic rhinitis. This has recently been called in to question. A similar triad, known as Samter's triad, consists of asthma, aspirin sensitivity, and nasal polyps. Samter's triad is not the same as the atopic triad.

10. ***c***

Most oral antifungal agents inhibit the 3A4 enzymes in the cytochrome P450 system. This is why they must be used with extreme caution (or not used) in patients who consume medications that need 3A4 enzymes for metabolism. And, liver enzymes must be monitored in patients who take oral antifungal medications and discontinued if elevations are >2.5 times the upper limits of normal. There is no oral agent that has a 95% cure rate for fingernail fungus (tinea unguium). This can be a difficult infection to clear even if oral antifungal agents are utilized. A topical antifungal agent typically will not clear the infection if the nail matrix is involved. There is anecdotal evidence that menthol ointments or bleach may cause resolution when used topically. Generally, resolution of fingernail fungus occurs more rapidly than toenail fungus because toenails grow at slower rates than fingernails.

11. A patient reports that he found a tick on himself about one month ago. He reports that there is a red circle and a white center near where he remembers the tick bite. He did not seek treatment at the time. Today he complains of myalgias and arthralgias. What laboratory test can be used to help diagnose Lyme disease?

- **a. CBC**
- **b. Lyme titer**
- **c. ELISA**
- **d. Skin scraping**

12. A "herald patch" is a hallmark finding in which condition?

- **a. Erythema infectiosum**
- **b. Pityriasis rosea**
- **c. Seborrheic keratosis**
- **d. Atopic dermatitis**

13. A patient presents with plaques on the extensor surface of the elbows, knees, and back. The plaques are erythematous and there are thick, silvery scales. This is likely:

- **a. plaque psoriasis.**
- **b. guttate psoriasis.**
- **c. atopic dermatitis.**
- **d. Staph cellulitis.**

14. The American Cancer Society uses an ABCDE pneumonic to help patients develop awareness of suspicious skin lesions. What does the "B" represent?

- **a. Bleeding**
- **b. Black**
- **c. Border**
- **d. Benign**

15. A skin lesion which is a solid mass is described as a:

- **a. macule.**
- **b. papule.**
- **c. vesicle.**
- **d. bullae.**

11. ***c***
A detailed history should always precede testing for Lyme Disease. The red circle with the white center is likely erythema migrans (EM). EM is the characteristic skin lesion of Lyme Disease (and other illnesses) and usually occurs within one month following the tick bite. Many learned authorities including the Infectious Diseases Society of America conclude that individuals should not be screened/tested for Lyme disease unless they have a high probability of having Lyme disease. In this case, historical features coupled with physical exam support the diagnosis, and thus screening. The most common initial serologic test for screening is an ELISA. If it is positive, it should be confirmed with a Western blot. Unfortunately, there are a large number of false positives and so a confirmation should be performed.

12. ***b***
Pityriasis rosea (PR) is a self-limiting exanthematous skin disorder characterized by several unique findings. It is more common in young adults. A characteristic finding is the "herald" or "mother" patch found on trunk. This looks like a ringworm and precedes the generalized "Christmas tree" pattern rash. The lesions associated with the rash are salmon-colored and oval in shape. Most cases clear in 4-6 weeks, but the plaques may last for several months.

13. ***a***
Plaque psoriasis is seen initially in young adults and is characterized as described above. The thick, silvery scale is pathognomic and is usually asymptomatic, though, some patients will complain of pruritis. A clinical finding that will help establish a diagnosis is pitting of fingernails. This is found in about 50% of patients with psoriasis. The plaques are commonly distributed on the scalp, extensor surface of the elbows, knees, and back. This is a chronic skin disorder.

14. ***c***
The pneumonic is helpful when looking at skin lesions, but is primarily used for patient education. The "A" represents asymmetry (asymmetrical lesions are worrisome), "B" is border (irregular borders), "C" is color (colored lesions have more melanin imparted to them and may be associated with malignant melanoma), "D" is diameter (larger than a pencil eraser is concerning), and "E" represents enlarging or elevated (lesions which are actively enlarging are growing; elevated lesions are concerning).

15. ***b***
A papule is an elevated solid mass up to 1.0 cm. in diameter. A macule is flat and small; like a freckle. A vesicle is filled with a serous fluid and less than 1.0 cm in diameter. A bullae is fluid filled and larger than 1.0 cm in diameter.

16. A patient was burned with hot water. He has several large fluid filled lesions. What are these termed?

- a. Vesicles
- b. Bullae
- c. Cysts
- d. Wheals

17. The lesions seen in a patient with folliculitis might be filled with:

- a. blood.
- b. pus.
- c. fluid.
- d. serous fluid.

18. Impetigo is characterized by:

- a. honey-colored crusts.
- b. silvery scales.
- c. marble-like lesions.
- d. wheals with pus.

19. The best way to evaluate jaundice associated with liver disease is to observe:

- a. blanching of the hands, feet, and nails.
- b. the sclera, skin, and lips.
- c. the lips, oral mucosa, and tongue.
- d. tympanic membrane and skin only.

20. Which of the following lesions never blanches when pressure is applied?

- a. Spider angioma
- b. Spider vein
- c. Purpura or petechiae
- d. Cherry angioma

21. A 60 year-old patient is noted to have rounding of the distal phalanx of the fingers. What might have caused this?

- a. Coronary artery disease
- b. Hepatic cirrhosis
- c. Lead toxicity
- d. Iron deficiency anemia

16. *b*
Bullae are fluid filled lesions that are greater than 6 mm in diameter. These are common in patients who have a superficial partial thickness burn. Vesicles are also fluid filled, but they are smaller than 5 mm in diameter. A cyst is enclosed in a sac that can contain fluid or gelatinous material. Wheals are erythematous, irregular raised areas on the skin. All of these are termed primary lesions.

17. *b*
Folliculitis is a superficial inflammation of hair follicles usually caused by bacteria. As a superficial infection, it involves only the epidermis. When this occurs, there are usually numerous pustular lesions. The composition of pus is dead white cells and other cellular debris.

18. *a*
Impetigo is a superficial bacterial infection of the skin characterized by honey-colored crusts. Another form of impetigo is characterized by the presence of bullae. These infections are treated with topical antibiotics, good hygiene, and frequent hand washing. It is usually caused by *Staphylococcus* or Group A *Streptococcus*.

19. *b*
Looking at the sclera allows the examiner to see jaundice most easily and reliably. Jaundice may also appear in the palpebral conjunctiva, lips, hard palate, undersurface of the tongue, tympanic membrane, and skin. Jaundice in adults is a result of liver disease usually, but can be due to excessive hemolysis of red blood cells. In infants the usual cause is hemolysis of red blood cells as is seen in physiologic jaundice.

20. *c*
Blanching with pressure over spider angiomas always occurs. Spider veins and cherry angiomas usually blanch with pressure. Purpura and petechiae never blanch with pressure. Purpura and petechiae represent an extravasation of blood under the skin. This will not blanch. This is usually observed in patients with thrombocytopenia or trauma.

21. *b*
Rounding of the distal phalanx describes clubbing. Clubbing of fingers is most often associated with chronic hypoxia as seen in cigarette smokers and patients with COPD or lung cancer. Other causes are cirrhosis, cystic fibrosis, pulmonary fibrosis and cyanotic heart disease.

22. A patient is found to have koilonychia. What laboratory test would be prudent to perform?

a. **Liver function tests**
b. **Complete blood count**
c. **Hepatitis B surface antigen**
d. **Arterial blood gases**

23. Which of the following antibiotics may increase the likelihood of photosensitivity?

a. **Amoxicillin**
b. **Cephalosporins**
c. **Fluoroquinolones**
d. **Macrolides**

24. A patient has used a high potency topical steroid cream for years to treat psoriasis exacerbations when they occur. She presents today and states that this cream "just doesn't work anymore." What word describes this?

a. **Rebound effect**
b. **Tachyphylaxis**
c. **Tolerance**
d. **Lichenification**

25. A patient has seborrheic dermatitis. Which vehicle would be most appropriate to use in the hairline area to treat this?

a. **Solution**
b. **Cream**
c. **Powder**
d. **Foam**

26. Which of the following areas of the body has the greatest percutaneous absorption?

a. **Sole of the foot**
b. **Scalp**
c. **Forehead**
d. **Genitalia**

22. *b*
Koilonychia is the term that describes spoon shaped nails. Spoon shaped nails may be present in patients with long-standing iron deficiency anemia. A CBC should be performed to assess for anemia. The most common symptoms of iron deficiency anemia are weakness, headache, irritability, fatigue, and exercise intolerance.

23. *c*
Many medications can produce a phototoxic reaction when a patient is exposed to sunlight. Antibiotics are especially notable for this. Common antibiotics associated with photosensitivity are tetracyclines, sulfa drugs, and fluoroquinolones. Other common medications that increase photosensitivity are hydrochlorothiazide, diltiazem, selective serotonin reuptake inhibitors, antihistamines, ibuprofen, and naproxen.

24. *b*
Tachyphylaxis is the word used to describe a gradual and progressively poorer clinical response to a treatment or medication. This is particularly true of topical glucocorticoids, bronchodilators, nitroglycerine, and antihistamines when they are overused. The rebound effect describes a condition where initial clinical improvement occurred, but worsening now has occurred. Lichenification refers to a thickening of the skin. Drug free intervals are important to prevent tachyphylaxis.

25. *d*
Seborrheic dermatitis affects the hairy areas of the body. In hairy areas of the body, foams are specifically used because they spread easily and are transparent. Lotions can be used in hairy areas because they provide a cooling, drying effect and are transparent. Lotions are the weakest of all vehicles. Creams and powders could be used, but patients prefer other vehicles and so compliance is less with these.

26. *d*
Genitalia have the highest percutaneous absorption across the entire body. This is important because low potency creams will act with greater potency in this area. Always start with low potency creams in the genitalia. The sole of the foot has the lowest percutaneous absorption followed by the scalp, forehead, and genitalia. Therefore, the sole of the foot will require more potent vehicles to enhance absorption.

Endocrine Disorders

1. **A female patient has the following characteristics. Which one represents a risk factor for development Type 2 diabetes?**

    a. **Dyslipidemia**
    b. **History of gestational diabetes**
    c. **Hypertension**
    d. **Exposure to cigarette smoke**

2. **A diagnosis of Type 2 diabetes mellitus can be made:**

    a. **if risk factors plus a family history of diabetes are present.**
    b. **with an Hgb A1C of 7% or greater.**
    c. **if glucose values of 110, 119, and 115 are observed on different days.**
    d. **following fasting glucose values of 126 and 130 on different days.**

3. **Ideally, a patient should have a fasting glucose that is:**

    a. **between 60-100 mg/dL.**
    b. **less than 126 mg/dL.**
    c. **less than 100 mg/dL.**
    d. **repeated in a non-fasting state.**

4. **Undiagnosed diabetes may present as:**

    a. **recurrent vaginal candidiasis.**
    b. **chronic halitosis.**
    c. **varicose veins.**
    d. **paresthesias in the upper extremities.**

5. **A 38 year-old male patient, thought to be in good health, presents to a primary care clinic. On routine exam the patient's fasting blood sugar is 242 mg/dl. A repeat value after eating is 288 mg/dL. Which of the following is least helpful in the initial evaluation of this patient?**

    a. **Blood pressure**
    b. **Non-fasting lipids**
    c. **Hgb A1c**
    d. **Microalbuminuria**

1. *b*

History of gestational diabetes conveys an 83% chance of developing Type 2 diabetes (within 17 years of delivery). Dyslipidemia and hypertension are not risk factors for diabetes, though they are commonly seen in conjunction with diabetes. A family history of Type 2 diabetes as well as obesity, significantly increase the risk of developing diabetes. Sedentary lifestyle promotes weight gain and so, increases risk of Type 2 diabetes.

2. *d*

Type 2 diabetes can be diagnosed under 4 circumstances: In the instance of a glucose value $\geq$ 126 (and confirmed on subsequent day), a glucose value greater than 200 mg/dL with symptoms of "the 3 P's", an A1C $\geq$ 6.5% (and confirmed on a different day), or 2 hour plasma glucose > 200 mg/dL during an oral glucose tolerance test. Choice *c* indicates a patient with pre-diabetes.

3. *c*

The ideal screening glucose is done during a fasting state and should be less than 100 mg/dL. Abnormal values should always be repeated. If a patient is non-fasting and the glucose value is less than 125 mg/dL, most authorities consider this to be normal.

4. *a*

Candida is part of the normal vaginal flora. However, when glucose levels rise, Candida dramatically increases in numbers. Patients can present with recurrent vaginal candidiasis since the vagina offers an ideal environment to grow yeast. The other choices listed above do not relate to elevated glucose levels or diabetes. Diabetic paresthesias typically present in the lower extremities.

5. *b*

Lipids should be done a non-fasting state. Triglycerides are especially sensitive to non-fasting states and will give an abnormally elevated value if performed in a non-fasting patient. Since triglycerides are frequently elevated in patients with elevated glucose levels, a fasting level should be performed. Initially, a blood pressure, fasting lipids, and microalbuminuria are critical to assessing this patient's diabetic status.

6. The most appropriate screen for diabetic nephropathy is:

a. **creatinine clearance.**
b. **microalbuminuria.**
c. **BUN/Cr.**
d. **serum creatinine.**

7. What is the earliest detectable glycemic abnormality in a patient with Type 2 diabetes?

a. **Postprandial glucose elevation**
b. **Nighttime hyperglycemia**
c. **Fasting glucose elevation**
d. **Abnormal Hgb A1C**

8. Which choice best describes the most common presentation of a patient with Type 2 diabetes?

a. **Acute onset of hyperglycemia with other symptoms**
b. **Hyperlipidemia and presence of retinopathy**
c. **Insidious onset of hyperglycemia with weight gain**
d. **Microalbuminuria**

9. A 65 year-old diabetic has been on oral anti-hyperglycemic agents and is still having poor glycemic control. His AM fasting glucoses range from 140s-160s. You decide to add insulin. He weighs 127 kilograms. What should the NP order as an initial starting dose?

a. **10 units long-acting insulin at bedtime**
b. **30 units long-acting before breakfast**
c. **5 units intermediate insulin at bedtime**
d. **20 units short-acting insulin at breakfast**

10. A patient presents with consistently elevated blood glucose before his evening meal. What choice below represents an insulin change that would improve his evening glucose?

Current regimen:
AM: 22u intermediate-acting insulin, 12u short-acting insulin
PM: 10u intermediate-acting insulin, 8u short-acting insulin

a. **24u intermediate-acting insulin in AM**
b. **14u short-acting insulin in AM**
c. **12u intermediate-acting insulin in PM**
d. **10u intermediate-acting insulin in PM**

6. ***b***
Microalbuminuria literally means "small amounts of protein in the urine". This is a sensitive and early measure of kidney disease in diabetics. It is an appropriate screen for undiagnosed diabetic nephropathy. Microalbuminuria is screened annually in Type 2 diabetics who are at least 12 years of age. If microalbuminuria is positive, it should be re-assessed in 3-6 months. Many false positives can occur. However, if it is positive after repeating once or twice, it is likely a true positive.

7. ***a***
The earliest glycemic abnormality is postprandial glucose elevation. Early in the pathogenesis of diabetes, glucose levels increase to abnormal levels after eating. Over the next few hours, if the patient does not eat, the glucose levels will fall to a normal range again via many different physiologic mechanisms. This may occur for months or years before glucose levels become consistently elevated and are not able to return to normal despite long periods of fasting. Once glucose levels are elevated and remain elevated, patients usually experience symptoms such as fatigue, thirst, frequent urination, and hunger.

8. ***c***
Most patients with type 2 diabetes mellitus are asymptomatic at presentation. They are identified because of screening and identification of risk factors. Hence, diabetes usually has an insidious onset and is associated with weight gain, especially in adults and adolescents after puberty. An acute onset is typical of patients with type 1 diabetes. Microalbuminuria develops after several years of having diabetes.

9. ***a***
According to American Diabetes Association (ADA) consensus algorithm for initiation and adjustment of insulin therapy (ADA, 2009), an intermediate or long-acting insulin should be started at bedtime or morning as a once daily dosage. A prudent starting dose is either 10 units insulin or 0.2 units per kilogram (approximately 25 units of insulin).

10. ***a***
This patient's blood sugar is consistently elevated before the evening meal. This indicates that he needs more AM intermediate-acting insulin on board. A prudent increase in insulin dose involves 2-3 unit increases at a time. He is taking 22 units of intermediate-acting insulin in the AM. His dose should be increased to 24 or 25 units in the AM followed by blood sugar checks for 3 days after the insulin change (blood sugar checks before dinner). If he is not at goal, then the AM intermediate-acting insulin can be increased by an additional 2-3 units until blood sugars are at goal, or the patient becomes symptomatic with low blood glucose values.

11. Mr. Smith, an overweight 48 year-old male with undiagnosed type 2 diabetes mellitus presents to your clinic. Which symptom is least likely associated with type 2 diabetes mellitus?

a. Fatigue
b. Constipation
c. Athlete's foot
d. Impetigo

12. Mr. Jones, a patient with type 2 diabetes, brings his obese 15 year old son in to see the nurse practitioner. You examine the 15 year-old son and identify acanthosis nigricans. This probably indicates:

a. undiagnosed diabetes.
b. insulin resistance.
c. familial skin changes.
d. poor hygiene.

13. A patient with newly diagnosed Type 2 diabetes asks what his target blood pressure should be. The most correct response is:

a. about 130/90.
b. in the low 140s over the 90s.
c. less than 130/80.
d. the systolic should be in the 120s-130s.

14. The most appropriate time to begin screening for renal nephropathy in a patient with Type 2 diabetes is:

a. at diagnosis.
b. one year after diagnosis.
c. 2-3 years after diagnosis.
d. 5 years after diagnosis.

15. A diabetic patient with proteinuria (approximately 1 g/d) has been placed on an ACE inhibitor. How soon can the anti-proteinuric effect of the ACE inhibitor be realized in this patient?

a. 6-8 weeks
b. 3 months
c. 6 months
d. 3-5 years

11. ***b***

Fatigue is a common early symptom of diabetes. Athlete's foot could represent peripheral fungal infections related to sustained elevations in glucose. Impetigo, though not common in adults, could represent a superficial bacterial infection related to elevated glucose levels. Constipation could be due to many factors, but not specifically diabetes. Conversely, the three factors most closely associated with diabetes are fatigue and infections.

12. ***b***

Acanthosis nigricans (AN) has been associated with insulin resistance. While the majority of cases are benign and associated with obesity, AN is also associated with certain GI tumors (unlikely in a 15 y/o). However, in a 15 year-old this is particularly important since AN in children and adolescents is often a predictor of development of type 2 diabetes. It is also associated with type 2 diabetes in adults. AN is prevalent on the flexor surfaces of the axillae and neck. The lesions are slightly elevated and have a velvety appearance.

13. ***c***

The 2012 American Diabetes Association's target blood pressure for "most patients with diabetes" is less than 130/80 mm Hg. Less than 130/80 means that the systolic blood pressure should be ***in the 120s*** **at the highest and the diastolic blood pressure should be** ***in the 70s*** **at the highest.**

14. ***a***

Patients with type 2 diabetes should be screened for renal nephropathy at the time of diagnosis. "Serum creatinine should be measured at least annually in all adults with diabetes regardless of the degree of urine albumin excretion" according to American Diabetes Association. Nephropathy develops in about 30% of patients with diabetes. Diabetic nephropathy is defined as the presence of diabetes and more than 300 mg/d of albuminuria on at least 2 occasions separated by 3-6 months.

15. ***a***

The effect can be realized as early as 6-8 weeks after starting an ACE inhibitor or ARB. The ACE inhibitor should be titrated upward so that urinary protein is less than 500 mg/d or the patient exhibits deleterious symptoms from ACE or ARB use. A second agent can be added if the ACE or ARB reaches maximum dosage, but goal proteinuria has not been achieved. Monitor the patient's serum creatinine and potassium levels with dose changes because both can increase to unacceptable levels when drugs affecting the renin-angiotensin-aldosterone system are used.

16. A recently diagnosed patient with type 2 diabetes presents today with fever and burning with urination. She is diagnosed with a urinary tract infection (UTI). Her urine dipstick is positive for protein. Which statement is correct?

a. **This patient has microalbuminuria secondary to diabetes.**
b. **The finding of protein is an incidental finding.**
c. **The proteinuria is related to the UTI.**
d. **No specific conclusions can be drawn about the proteinuria.**

The next two questions apply to the following patient.

A 55-year-old female patient with diabetes has these fasting lipid values:

Total cholesterol 200 mg/dL
HDL 45 mg/dL
LDL levels of 120 mg/dL
Triglyceride 309 mg/dL

17. According to American Diabetes Association (ADA) which patient lipid value(s) meet(s) the goal for this patient?

a. **Total cholesterol only**
b. **Total cholesterol, HDL, LDL**
c. **LDL only**
d. **None are at goal**

18. This patient's Hgb A1c was measured. It is 9.2%. What is the relationship between Hgb A1c and this patient's lipid values?

a. **There is no specific relationship.**
b. **Elevated lipids will increase as Hgb A1c increases.**
c. **Hgb Alc decreases as triglycerides decrease.**
d. **Hgb A1c will decrease as HDL values increase.**

19. Hyperthyroidism may affect the blood pressure:

a. **by producing an increase in systolic and diastolic readings.**
b. **by producing a decrease in diastolic blood pressure.**
c. **when the heart rate is increased.**
d. **with unpredictable results.**

16. ***d***
No conclusion can be drawn from this particular finding of proteinuria. Transient proteinuria can be found in the setting of fever, during the course of UTI, after intense exercise, poor glycemic control, and other systemic conditions. A diagnosis of microalbuminuria must be made after two positive screens on dipstick at least 3-6 months apart.

17. ***d***
This patient has diabetes. Her target lipid values according to American Diabetes Association should be HDL > 50 mg/dL (> 40 mg/dL for males), LDL < 100 mg/dL, triglycerides < 150 mg/dL. The ADA does not have a recommendation for total serum cholesterol specific for patients with diabetes, but, total cholesterol should be less than 200 mg/dL for the general population according to NCEP (National Cholesterol Education Program).

18. ***c***
Two known factors specifically contribute to elevated Hgb A1c levels: elevated glucose values (measured with a Hgb Alc) and excessive alcohol consumption. Diabetic patients with elevated triglyceride levels and elevated Hgb A1c levels can usually expect to have improved triglyceride levels as Hgb A1c levels begin to normalize.

19. ***a***
A common effect of hyperthyroidism on blood pressure is an increase in both systolic and diastolic readings over the patient's usual readings. In fact, hyperthyroidism is a common endocrine cause of secondary hypertension. Other endocrine causes of secondary hypertension are pheochromocytoma, Cushing's syndrome, and neuroblastoma. It is very common to measure a resting heart rate of greater than 100 bpm in patients who have untreated hyperthyroidism.

20. Which laboratory abnormality very commonly accompanies hypothyroidism?

a. **Hypernatremia**
b. **Polycythemia**
c. **Dyslipidemia**
d. **Hypoprolactinemia**

21. What is the most sensitive laboratory assay for screening and identifying the vast majority of ambulatory patients with primary hypothyroidism?

a. **TSH only**
b. **TSH and T4**
c. **TSH, T4, and T3**
d. **TSH and TRH (thyrotropin releasing hormone)**

22. A 45 year-old female patient has a screening TSH performed. Her TSH value is 13 mU/L. It was repeated in one week and found to be 15 mU/L. What explains this finding?

a. **Subclinical hypothyroidism**
b. **Hypothyroidism**
c. **Transient hypothyroidism**
d. **Hyperthyroidism**

23. A patient with a past history of treatment for hyperthyroidism is most likely to exhibit:

a. **a euthyroid state.**
b. **hypothyroidism.**
c. **hyperthyroidism.**
d. **subclinical hypothyroidism.**

24. When the serum free T4 concentration falls:

a. **the TSH falls.**
b. **the TSH rises.**
c. **there is no relationship between T4 and TSH.**
d. **T3 falls.**

20. ***c***

Hypothyroidism adversely affects lipid metabolism. A finding of elevated lipids, specifically dyslipidemia, is common when TSH values exceed 10 mU/L. Consequently, patients with dyslipidemia should also have a TSH evaluated. Dyslipidemia should not be treated until the TSH decreases to 10 mU/L or less. Other abnormal laboratory findings associated with hypothyroidism are hyponatremia, hyperprolactinemia, hyperhomocysteinemia, anemia, and elevated creatinine phosphokinase.

21. ***a***

TSH assays have become ultra sensitive and so diagnosis of hypothyroidism can take place at a very early stage. Therefore, measurement of thyrotropin releasing hormone (TRH) is no longer necessary. Primary hypothyroidism accounts for 95% of patients with hypothyroidism. There are 2 reasons to order a TSH and T4 in ambulatory patients for screening; if pituitary or hypothalamic disease is known or suspected, or if the patient is receiving medications or has specific diseases that can affect TSH secretion. Examples of drugs and disorders that can increase TSH secretion are metoclopramide, amiodarone, adrenal insufficiency, pituitary adenoma, and generalized thyroid hormone resistance. In hospitalized patients, TSH should not be used as a sole means to evaluate thyroid disease because many different factors in seriously ill euthyroid patients can affect TSH secretion.

22. ***b***

This patient has hypothyroidism because her TSH exceeds 5 mU/L. Common symptoms associated with hypothyroidism include fatigue, weight gain, dry skin, cold intolerance, constipation, menstrual irregularities, and hair and nails that break easily. The diagnosis should be easily realized since the TSH is elevated on two occasions.

23. ***b***

Hypothyroidism is the most likely result when a patient has been treated for hyperthyroidism because treatment typically destroys the gland's ability to produce thyroid hormone (T3 and T4), in the future. Radioactive iodine or drugs can be used to inhibit synthesis of thyroid hormone.

24. ***b***

As a patient's T4 concentration falls (although still within normal range), the anterior lobe of the pituitary gland responds by secreting TSH. TSH finds its way to the thyroid gland and causes an increase in T4 secretion. In this manner, T4 concentrations remain within a normal range and help maintain a euthyroid state in the patient.

25. A 30 year-old female patient who complains of fatigue has a screening TSH performed. Her TSH value is 8 mU/L. What should be done next?

- a. **Begin thyroid supplementation.**
- b. **Repeat the TSH and add T4.**
- c. **Begin supplementation and repeat the TSH in 4-6 weeks.**
- d. **Measure the T4 and consider repeating the test in a month.**

26. A patient with hypothyroidism has been in a euthyroid state for several years. On screening, her TSH is elevated. The most likely cause of this is:

- a. **change in laboratory's method of measuring TSH.**
- b. **substitution of levothyroxine for a generic medication.**
- c. **aging.**
- d. **taking extra doses of T4.**

27. In order to determine how much T4 replacement a patient needs to re-establish a euthyroid state, the nurse practitioner considers:

- a. **the TSH value.**
- b. **the patient's T4.**
- c. **the patient's body weight.**
- d. **the patient's gender.**

25. *b*

TSH values rise and fall continuously. Consequently, TSH levels are repeated and an average is usually calculated. A diagnosis of hypothyroidism can be made after a second abnormal TSH unless the initial value is very elevated and the patient is symptomatic. When an elevated TSH is discovered, it should be repeated and a serum free T4 can be measured. Depending on these results, a diagnosis of thyroid disease can be made.

26. *b*

Generic medications for levothyroxine can have varying bioavailabilities. It is not uncommon to have fluctuations in TSH levels if brand names or generics are substituted for each other. Although there can be only subtle differences between T4 formulations, patients should attempt to use the same manufacturer, whether generic or not. Many learned authorities recommend brand name because less variation in TSH levels occur from prescription to prescription.

27. *c*

Replacement is based on body weight and is usually calculated in kilograms. The patient's weight is calculated in kilograms and multiplied by 1.6 to determine the replacement needed in one day. This is the amount that should be prescribed provided the patient is otherwise healthy, is less than 50 years old, and has no evidence of underlying cardiac disease.

Eye, Ear, Nose, Throat Disorders

1. **A patient is diagnosed with otitis externa. He complains of tragal pain, otic discharge, otic itching, and fever. What is the cardinal symptom of otitis externa?**

    a. **Tragal pain**
    b. **Otic discharge**
    c. **Otic itching**
    d. **Fever**

2. **What symptom triad is most commonly associated with infectious mononucleosis?**

    a. **Fever, lymphadenopathy, pharyngitis**
    b. **Fatigue, fever, pharyngitis**
    c. **Body aches, fever, splenomegaly**
    d. **Headache, lymphadenopathy, tonsillar exudates**

3. **What medication should always be avoided in patients with mononucleosis?**

    a. **Clindamycin**
    b. **Ibuprofen**
    c. **Amoxicillin**
    d. **Topical lidocaine**

4. **The most common complication of influenza is:**

    a. **cough.**
    b. **bacterial pneumonia.**
    c. **viral pneumonia.**
    d. **bronchitis.**

5. **An older adult has cerumen impaction in both ears. His hearing is diminished. This type of hearing loss is:**

    a. **sensorineural.**
    b. **conductive.**
    c. **presbycusis.**
    d. **cholesteatoma.**

1. ***a***
Otitis externa is "swimmer's ear". This is a superficial infection usually caused by *Pseudomonas* in the external canal. Fever, a typical systemic symptom is inconsistent with otitis externa since the infection is superficial. The other symptoms listed are typical of patients who are diagnosed with otitis externa. However, the cardinal symptom is tragal pain.

2. ***a***
The triad includes fever, lymphadenopathy, and pharyngitis. Fatigue commonly accompanies mononucleosis ("mono"), but this is not part of the triad. Approximately 50% of patients with mono have splenomegaly. Body aches are probably the effect of fever, but do not characterize the disease. The etiologic agent of mononucleosis is the Epstein Barr virus. It is often spread by intimate contact between susceptible contacts. It is spread via saliva and has been called "the kissing disease".

3. ***c***
A generalized rash may be seen in patients with mononucleosis (mono) who are given amoxicillin or ampicillin at the time of the acute phase of the illness. The rash does not represent an allergic reaction, but instead probably represents a reaction between the Epstein Barr virus and the penicillin molecule. The rash is usually described as maculopapular and may be pruritic. The rash has also been described with other beta-lactam antibiotics, azithromycin, cephalexin and levofloxacin.

4. ***b***
Pneumonia is the most common complication of influenza; bacterial pneumonia is the most common form. *Streptococcus pneumoniae* is the most common bacterial pathogen. 25% of deaths associated with influenza are related to pneumonia. Clinical presentation of pneumonia as a complication of influenza is characterized by worsening of symptoms after an initial period of improvement for 1-3 days. Fever, cough, purulent sputum predominate. Cough is a symptom of influenza, not a complication. Bronchitis might be part of the differential of influenza, however, fever is uncommon in bronchitis.

5. ***b***
A conductive hearing loss is one in which sound cannot enter the external canal or, the middle ear. This is produced when something, fluid, cerumen, or a foreign body prevents sound from entering the ear. A sensorineural hearing loss involves the inner ear or 8th cranial nerve. Presbycusis is the term used to describe hearing loss associated with aging. Hearing loss associated with presbycusis is usually more significant in the 6th decade. Cholesteatoma is a middle ear tumor.

6. A 70 year-old patient has begun to have hearing loss. She relates that her elderly parents had difficulty hearing. Which complaint below is typical of presbycusis?

   a. **Inability to hear consonants**
   b. **Asymmetrical loss of hearing**
   c. **Inability to hear low pitched sounds**
   d. **Pulsatile noise in the ear**

7. Which statement about serous otitis media is correct?

   a. **This usually needs treatment with antibiotics.**
   b. **This can be diagnosed with pneumatic otoscopy.**
   c. **Serous otitis media can produce a sensorineural hearing loss.**
   d. **Otitis media and serous otitis are frequently associated with fever.**

8. Acute otitis media can be diagnosed by identifying which otic characteristic(s)?

   a. **Decreased mobility of the tympanic membrane (TM)**
   b. **Middle ear effusion and erythema of the TM**
   c. **Opacity and erythema of the TM**
   d. **Marked redness of the TM**

9. On routine exam, a 15 year-old patient's tympanic membrane (TM) reveals a tiny white oblong mark just inferior to the umbo on the surface of the TM. The patient has no complaints of ear pain and gross hearing is intact. What is this?

   a. **A variant of normal**
   b. **Scarring of the tympanic membrane**
   c. **A cholesteatoma**
   d. **A foreign body**

10. What clinical finding necessitates an urgent referral of the patient to an emergency department?

   a. **A fiery red epiglottis**
   b. **Sudden onset of hoarseness**
   c. **Purulent drainage from the external canal**
   d. **Tragal tenderness**

6. *a*

Presbycusis is age related hearing loss. The significance of this patient's parental hearing loss is important for history. Presbycusis is influenced by genetics as well as noise exposure, medications, and infections. Loss of ability to hear speech in crowded rooms or noisy area, inability to understand consonants, and loss of high-pitched sounds is typical. Hearing loss is symmetrical. Asymmetrical hearing loss is a red flag regardless of the age at which it occurs. Tinnitus is common and is an annoying sensation associated with presbycusis. A pulsatile noise in the ear raises suspicion of a tumor or arteriovenous malformation.

7. *b*

Serous otitis media (SOM) is also called otitis media with effusion (OME) or "glue ear". OME occurs when there is fluid (non-infectious) in the middle ear. This prevents normal mobility of the tympanic membrane and creates a conductive hearing loss. Pneumatic otoscopy is the primary non-invasive diagnostic method because it has a high sensitivity and specificity. It may be present before otitis media develops, or it may follow resolution of otitis media. OME is far more common than otitis media and is not associated with systemic symptoms like fever. Acute otitis media (AOM) describes infected fluid in the middle ear.

8. *b*

The diagnosis of acute otitis media (AOM) requires the finding of a middle ear effusion (MEE) AND a sign of acute inflammation, such as distinct fullness or bulging of the tympanic membrane (TM), ear pain, or marked redness of the TM. MEE is characterized by the presence of middle ear fluid (bubbles or an air fluid interface) or finding of TM abnormalities (opacity, impaired mobility, or color change). The other finding that constitutes a diagnosis of AOM is the finding of acute, purulent otorrhea that is not due to otitis externa. This characterizes a ruptured TM from otitis media.

9. *b*

A white, chalky mark on the surface of the TM reflects scarring of the tympanic membrane (TM). This can occur secondary to TM rupture or tympanostomy tube placement. The normal color of the TM is pink or pearly gray so this is not a variant of normal. A cholesteatoma is an abnormal growth found in the middle ear or mastoid, not on the surface of the TM. Foreign bodies typically reside in the external canal.

10. *a*

A finding of a fiery red epiglottis signals epiglottitis. Since airway obstruction can be rapid with epiglottitis, immediate referral to an emergency department is warranted. Sudden onset of hoarseness does not signal a specific emergency situation. Purulent drainage from the external canal may signify a ruptured tympanic membrane or otitis externa. Tragal pain is significant of otitis externa.

11. A teenager with fever and pharyngitis has a negative rapid strept test. After 24 hours, the throat culture reveals "normal flora". Which conclusion can be made?

- **a. The pharyngitis is not secondary to Strept.**
- **b. The pharyngitis is secondary to a bacterial pathogen but not Strept.**
- **c. The pharyngitis is of undetermined etiology.**
- **d. The patient has mononucleosis.**

12. A 45 year-old patient describes a spinning sensation that has occurred intermittently for the past 24 hours. It is precipitated by position changes like rolling over in bed. During these episodes, he complains of intense nausea. Which symptom is most characteristic of vertigo with a peripheral etiology?

- **a. The length of duration of symptoms**
- **b. Sensation of spinning**
- **c. Precipitation with position change**
- **d. Nausea**

13. A patient presents to a nurse practitioner clinic with paroxysmal sneezing, clear rhinorrhea, nasal congestion, facial pain. Which symptom below is NOT associated with allergic rhinitis?

- **a. Sneezing**
- **b. Rhinorrhea**
- **c. Nasal congestion**
- **d. Facial pain**

14. Which of the following is most likely observed in a patient with allergic rhinitis?

- **a. Exacerbation of symptoms after exposure to an allergen**
- **b. Nasal congestion and sneezing**
- **c. Post nasal drip and sore throat**
- **d. Worsening of symptoms during a sinus infection**

15. A 30 year old male has been diagnosed with non-allergic rhinitis. What finding is more likely in non-allergic rhinitis than allergic rhinitis?

- **a. Older age of symptom onset**
- **b. Male gender**
- **c. Post nasal drip**
- **d. Sneezing**

11. ***c***

The patient has a *preliminary* culture that indicates the presence of normal flora, i.e. no finding of pathogenic organisms like beta hemolytic Strept. A final culture result generally takes longer than 24 hours to complete. It is premature to make a diagnosis at 24 hours with this culture report. The only conclusion that can be made at this time is "pharyngitis of undetermined etiology". He should be treated symptomatically with antipyretics and analgesics until a final culture is available to help with formulation of a diagnosis.

12. ***c***

Vertigo may have either a peripheral or central (brainstem or cerebellum) etiology. The most common form of peripheral vertigo is benign paroxysmal positional vertigo (BPPV). It is usually due to calcium debris in the ear's semicircular canals. Vertigo is a symptom, not a disease. It is characterized by the sensation of moving, having objects around the patient move, or a tilting/swaying sensation. Spinning sensation is a typical description of a patient with BPPV. During acute attacks of vertigo, regardless of the etiology, nausea and vomiting are common. Attacks can be transient and last for days to weeks.

13. ***d***

Facial pain is not associated with allergic rhinitis. In conjunction with nasal congestion, it is most likely a sinus infection. Patients with allergic rhinitis and nasal congestion are more likely to develop acute and chronic bacterial sinusitis because untreated allergic rhinitis results in impaired mucus flow. This increases the risk of infection. Symptoms of bacterial sinusitis include nasal congestion, purulent post-nasal drip or rhinorrhea, facial pain and maxillary tooth pain. There is no symptom that can differentiate bacterial from viral sinusitis.

14. ***a***

Allergic rhinitis is usually diagnosed on clinical presentation and history. The diagnosis is appropriately made when allergic rhinitis symptoms are reproducible after exposure to the suspected allergen, like pollen. Nasal congestion, sneezing, post-nasal drip and sore throat are not exclusive to allergic rhinitis. Finally, sinusitis does exacerbate allergic rhinitis symptoms.

15. ***a***

Non-allergic rhinitis, often called vasomotor rhinitis, is very common in the US. It is typically diagnosed and differentiated from allergic rhinitis by history. Although both conditions may co-exist in patients, non-allergic rhinitis typically has onset after age 20 years. Allergic rhinitis typically presents prior to age 20 years. The most common symptoms associated with non-allergenic rhinitis are nasal congestion and post-nasal drip. It is predominantly reported in females. Common precipitants of non-allergic rhinitis symptoms can occur with exposure to spicy foods, cigarette smoke, strong odors, perfumes, and alcohol consumption. This is frequently treated with topical azelastine.

16. Most commonly, epistaxis occurs:

- a. in women.
- b. at Kiesselbach's plexus.
- c. in the posterior septum.
- d. in patients on anticoagulants.

17. A 70 year-old patient in good health is found to have a large, white plaque on the oral mucosa of the inner cheek. There is no pain associated with this. What is a likely diagnosis?

- a. Cheilitis
- b. Aphthous ulcer
- c. Sjogren's syndrome
- d. Leukoplakia

18. A patient has been diagnosed with acute rhinosinusitis. Symptoms began 3 days ago. Based on the most likely etiology, how should this patient be managed?

- a. Amoxicillin with clavulanate
- b. Decongestant and analgesic
- c. Azithromycin and decongestant
- d. Levofloxacin

19. Which of the following symptoms is more indicative of a bacterial sinusitis than viral?

- a. Yellow nasal discharge
- b. Worsening of symptoms after initial improvement
- c. Nasal congestion and rhinorrhea
- d. Facial pressure

20. A patient who is otherwise healthy states that he woke up this morning and has been unable to hear out of his left ear. The Weber and Rinne tests were performed. What is the primary reason for doing this?

- a. To assess for progressive hearing loss.
- b. It is nearly useless and should not be performed.
- c. It can help identify malingerers.
- d. It helps differentiate conductive from sensorineural hearing loss.

16. *b*

Most nosebleeds occur in men; 80% occur anteriorly. Kiesselbach's plexus is the most common site for any epistaxis to occur because this site represents the anastomosis of branches of three primary vessels: the ethmoidal artery, the sphenopalatine artery, and the facial artery. Anticoagulants place patients at very high risk for nose bleeds, but they do not constitute the majority of patients with nose bleeds.

17. *d*

The etiology of this white plaque is unclear from the given information, but it cannot be cheilitis. This affects the lips. It cannot be an aphthous ulcer because this is painful. Sjogren's syndrome does involve the mucous membranes but manifests itself as dry mouth, not a plaque or lesion. The differential diagnosis for a white oral plaque should include oral leukoplakia, a premalignant lesion. This is often related to HPV, human papilloma virus. Risk factors include smokeless tobacco. Others in the differential include oral hairy leukoplakia (seen almost exclusively in patients with HIV), squamous cell carcinoma, and malignant melanoma. It may also be a completely benign growth, but this can only be established after biopsy.

18. *b*

The vast majority of patients who have acute rhinosinusitis have a viral infection. In fact, 2% or fewer cases of acute rhinosinusitis are due to bacteria. When bacteria are the causative agents, *Streptococcus* and *Staphylococcus* are common pathogens. Since the most likely pathogen is a virus, symptomatic treatment should occur unless a red flag such as fever, facial pain, purulent drainage, etc. is present. Typically, conservative measures should be used for 7-10 days prior to antibiotic use. In clinical practice, patients typically request antibiotics sooner than 7-10 days.

19. *b*

There are no specific signs or symptoms that can clearly differentiate viral from bacterial sinusitis, including discolored nasal discharge. Facial pressure is present in both viral and bacterial infections, but facial pain is more likely to be associated with bacterial infection. However, rhinosinusitis symptoms lasting greater than 7 days and purulent nasal discharge, unilateral facial pain or maxillary tooth pain, and worsening of symptoms after initial improvement are suggestive of bacterial infection.

20. *d*

The Rinne and Weber tests can help differentiate conductive from sensorineural hearing loss. Once it is determined that the patient's hearing loss is conductive or sensorineural, the differential can be better developed. Common causes of conductive hearing loss are cerumen impaction, otitis externa, tympanic membrane rupture. Common causes of sensorineural hearing loss are presbycusis, Meniere disease, acoustic neuroma.

21. A patient stated that his ears felt stopped up. He pinched his nose and blew through it forcefully. The nurse practitioner diagnosed a ruptured left tympanic membrane. What would indicate this?

a. **Bright red blood in the left external canal**
b. **Pain in the left and right ears**
c. **Clear fluid in the left external canal**
d. **Absence of hearing in the left ear**

22. A patient describes a sensation that "there is a lump in his throat". He denies throat pain. On exam of the throat and neck, there are no abnormalities identified. What is the most likely reason this occurs?

a. **Factitious sore throat**
b. **Lymphadenitis**
c. **Globus**
d. **Esophageal motility disorder**

23. A patient with a bacterial sinusitis cannot spread this to others via:

a. **hand contact.**
b. **droplets.**
c. **fomites.**
d. **urine or stool.**

24. A patient diagnosed with Strept throat received a prescription for azithromycin. She has not improved in 48 hours. What course of action is acceptable?

a. **The patient should wait another 24 hours for improvement.**
b. **The antibiotic should be changed to a first generation cephalosporin.**
c. **A different macrolide antibiotic should be prescribed.**
d. **A penicillin or cephalosporin with beta lactamase coverage should be considered.**

25. A patient has been given amoxicillin for 8 days for sore throat. Today, the patient has developed a pruritic full body rash and diagnosed with penicillin allergy. What describes the skin manifestations of penicillin allergy?

a. **The rash will be fine and papular.**
b. **There will be hives.**
c. **There will be large, splotchy, non-pruritic areas.**
d. **The rash will not blanch.**

21. *a*
This patient ruptured his tympanic membrane (TM) traumatically from excessive pressure when he pinched his nose and blew out through it at the same time. It is common to find bright red blood (not clear fluid), but not active bleeding, in the external canal of the affected ear. He may experience pain in the affected ear, but this alone would not be indicative of a ruptured TM. Hearing may be diminished in the affected ear but should not be absent. Patients usually describe hearing as muffled.

22. *d*
The term used to describe the sensation of "a lump in my throat", or the feeling that there is a foreign body in the throat, is globus. It is not associated with sore throat or pain. The most common cause of globus is GERD or other disorders of the upper esophageal tract. If there is no actual foreign body or abnormality, then other etiologies may be psychologic or psychiatric disorders.

23. *d*
Bacterial infections of the upper respiratory tract can be transmitted by direct contact with fomites, secretions, or by respiratory droplet. Fomites are inanimate objects where bacterial or viral particles live and are easily transmitted to others who touch the fomite. A doorknob is a common example. Infectious particles remain pathogenic for varying lengths of time depending on the organism, environment, and the fomite. Bacterial and viral particles are denatured once present in the digestive system and are no longer able to produce upper respiratory infection via stool or urine.

24. *d*
The patient should demonstrate improvement after 48 hours if an antibiotic with the appropriate antimicrobial spectra was prescribed. A macrolide would be a poor choice because there are high rates of Strept resistance to macrolide antibiotics. In light of this, strong consideration should be given to an antibiotic with different antimicrobial spectra. Since Strept was diagnosed and azithromycin was ineffective, the prescriber should consider that the causative agent has macrolide resistance and could be beta lactamase producing. An antibiotic with beta lactamase coverage should be considered. Choice d provides this coverage.

25. *b*
The usual skin manifestation associated with an allergic reaction is hives. It is urticarial and of rapid onset. Hives are intensely pruritic, well circumscribed, raised, and erythematous. Penicillin is known to be allergenic and should be stopped immediately in these circumstances. An antihistamine should be administered.

26. A patient reports a penicillin allergy. What question regarding the allergy should the nurse practitioner ask to determine whether a cephalosporin can be safely prescribed?

a. **Have you ever taken a cephalosporin?**
b. **How long ago was the reaction?**
c. **What kind of reaction did you have?**
d. **What form of penicillin did you take?**

27. Which medication listed below is considered ototoxic?

a. **Digoxin**
b. **Aspirin**
c. **Ramipril**
d. **Metoprolol**

26. *c*
The most important question to ask the patient is "what kind of reaction did you have?" Unfortunately, many patients who report penicillin allergy are not actually penicillin allergic. About 2-10% of patients who are penicillin allergic have cephalosporin allergy too. Cephalosporins should never be prescribed for penicillin allergic patients if the patient reports hives or an anaphylaxis after having taken penicillin.

27. *b*
Many medications are ototoxic in patients who are otherwise healthy. Some patients are at increased risk (for ototoxicity) when they consume ototoxic medications if they have impaired renal function. Renal impairment makes excretion of the ototoxic drug more difficult and ototoxicity becomes more likely. Hearing loss secondary to use of the following medications should always be assessed: aspirin, aminoglycosides, vancomycin, erythromycin, loop diuretics (like furosemide), the anti-malarial medications, sildenafil (tadalafil, vardenafil) and cisplatin. ACE inhibitors, digoxin, and beta blockers are not associated with ototoxicity.

Gastrointestinal Disorders

1. **A 24 year-old male has recently returned from a weekend camping trip with friends. He has ulcerative colitis and history of migraine headaches. He reports a two-day history of headache, nausea, and vomiting with weakness. Which of the following is *least likely* as a possible cause?**

    a. **Migraine headache**
    b. **Exacerbation of ulcerative colitis**
    c. **Acute gastroenteritis**
    d. ***Norovirus***

2. **A 26 year-old female with low-grade fever and nausea has pain at McBurney's point. The most appropriate action by the NP is to:**

    a. **order a CBC and pregnancy test.**
    b. **order an abdominal ultrasound.**
    c. **refer her to the emergency department.**
    d. **order an abdominal CT.**

3. **A 56 year-old male patient has been diagnosed with an inguinal hernia. What symptom would make the nurse practitioner suspect an incarcerated hernia?**

    a. **Swelling**
    b. **Change in skin color**
    c. **Constipation**
    d. **Pain**

4. **A patient with a suspected inguinal hernia should be examined:**

    a. **in the prone position.**
    b. **standing.**
    c. **side-lying.**
    d. **with patient squatting.**

5. **A patient has been diagnosed with Hepatitis A. The most common reported risk factor is:**

    a. **drinking contaminated water.**
    b. **homosexual activity.**
    c. **international travel.**
    d. **eating contaminated food.**

1. ***b***
The patient presents with headache, nausea and vomiting. His symptoms could be due to migraine headache or acute gastroenteritis. Norovirus is a common cause of gastroenteritis. An exacerbation of ulcerative colitis would produce lower GI symptoms (diarrhea, flatulence, or bleeding), not nausea, vomiting, and headache.

2. ***a***
Patients with appendicitis usually have pain at McBurney's point, the painful area in the lower right quadrant of the abdomen. However, because this patient is of child bearing age, pregnancy is part of the differential and must be ruled out. Once pregnancy status is determined, patient disposition can be managed. If pregnancy is ruled out, then workup for appendicitis can proceed. CT scan of abdomen has very high sensitivity and specificity for appendicitis (95 and 94% respectively) and so it is the gold standard for diagnosis of appendicitis.

3. ***d***
A hernia is a weakened area in the muscle where loop of bowel protrudes through the abdominal wall. Normally, hernias are not frankly painful, though they may be tender. A painful hernia should be suspected as one that has become incarcerated or strangulated. Incarceration means that the hernia cannot be reduced; it is trapped. A strangulated hernia means that it is incarcerated and ischemia is present. A strangulated hernia is a surgical emergency. Emergency surgery should be performed within 4-6 hours to prevent loss of bowel.

4. ***b***
The patient should be examined while he is standing. He should be asked to bear down, cough, or strain during the exam. Though hernias are far more common in males, they can be found in females too. In males, the patient should be asked to stand. The examiner should put his 2nd or 3rd finger through the scrotum and into the external ring. When the patient is asked to cough, a "silky" feel will butt up against the examiner's finger, and the hernia can be easily felt.

5. ***c***
Traveling internationally is the most common risk factor. Hepatitis A (HAV) is spread via the fecal-oral route (and is highly contagious), though most people have no recollection of eating or drinking contaminated food/drink. Mexico, Central and South America are countries with the highest reported rates of HAV. Other risk factors are contact with infected family or close contacts and homosexual activity among men. Hepatitis A has declined since vaccination in the US has become widespread.

6. Most patients who have acute hepatitis A infection:

- a. develop fulminant disease.
- b. become acutely ill.
- c. have a self-limited illness.
- d. develop subsequent cirrhosis.

7. A patient has the following laboratory value. What is the clinical interpretation? Hepatitis A: (+) IgG

- a. He has hepatitis A.
- b. He has immunity to hepatitis A.
- c. He has no immunity to hepatitis A.
- d. More data is needed to interpret this.

8. A patient has been diagnosed with Hepatitis B. The most common reported risk factor is:

- a. drinking contaminated water.
- b. eating contaminated food.
- c. exposure to blood.
- d. sexual exposure.

9. Most patients who have acute hepatitis B infection:

- a. are females.
- b. are acutely ill.
- c. have varied clinical presentations.
- d. develop subsequent cirrhosis.

10. A patient has the following laboratory value. What does this mean? Hepatitis B surface antigen (+)

- a. He has acute hepatitis B.
- b. He has immunity to hepatitis B.
- c. He has no immunity to hepatitis B.
- d. More data is needed.

11. A patient has a positive hepatitis B surface antibody. This means:

- a. he has acute hepatitis B.
- b. he has chronic hepatitis B.
- c. he is immune to hepatitis B.
- d. he needs immunization to hepatitis B.

6. ***c***

Clinical presentation of patients infected with hepatitis A virus (HAV) is very variable. However, most adult patients have a self-limited, uncomplicated course. There may be mild, flu-like symptoms or there may be a more acute and severe clinical manifestation. Rarely does HAV result in hepatic failure unless there are other complicating illnesses like HIV or hepatitis B or C. In children, most are asymptomatic.

7. ***b***

This patient is immune to hepatitis because he has a positive immunoglobulin G (IgG). This signifies immunity secondary to: (1) past infection, or (2) immunization. A negative IgG signifies absence of immunity to Hepatitis A and susceptibility if exposed.

8. ***d***

Hepatitis B is transmitted by blood and body fluids. While exposure to infected blood or blood products would significantly increase risk of infection in unvaccinated people, this is much less likely than becoming infected via sexual exposure or IV drug use. Hepatitis A is transmitted via fecal oral routes. Choices a and b implicate hepatitis A as the etiologic agent.

9. ***c***

Most patients with Hepatitis B (70%) have sub-clinical hepatitis. Development of cirrhosis is rare following Hepatitis B infection unless other systemic factors are present, such as ethanol abuse, HIV infection, Hepatitis C infection, etc. There is no predilection for this disease by gender. When patients are symptomatic, they typically develop nausea, jaundice, and flu-like symptoms with fever, body aches, and fatigue.

10. ***a***

A positive hepatitis B surface antigen means that this patient has acute hepatitis B. The first serologic marker to be positive is the surface antigen. It can become positive as soon as 3-4 weeks after exposure to hepatitis B.

11. ***c***

The hepatitis B surface antibody indicates immunity to hepatitis B virus. Specifically, if this patient comes in contact with hepatitis B virus, he will not become infected with hepatitis B. The presence of hepatitis B surface antibody indicates immunity from immunization or actual infection. It also indicates recovery if the patient was infected.

12. A patient has a positive anti-HCV test. This means:

- **a. he has hepatitis C.**
- **b. he has immunity to hepatitis C.**
- **c. he does not have hepatitis C.**
- **d. more data is needed.**

13. An 83 year-old patient is diagnosed with diverticulitis. Where is her pain typically located?

- **a. Epigastric area**
- **b. Right or left lower quadrant**
- **c. Left lower quadrant**
- **d. Right lower quadrant**

14. GERD (gastroesophageal reflux disease) and physiologic reflux have similar characteristics. However, physiologic reflux:

- **a. can produce mucosal injury.**
- **b. rarely occurs at nighttime.**
- **c. occurs only postprandial.**
- **d. is always asymptomatic.**

15. A patient asks for advice about a medication that will produce rapid relief if he is having heartburn symptoms. What should the nurse practitioner respond?

- **a. Calcium carbonate**
- **b. Ranitidine**
- **c. Omeprazole**
- **d. Sucralfate**

16. The relationship between duodenal ulcer disease and *H. pylori* infection is:

- **a. distant.**
- **b. very unlikely.**
- **c. possible.**
- **d. very likely.**

12. ***d***
The anti-HCV test is a screening test. A patient who has a positive screen for hepatitis C may have the disease, but more data is needed to determine this. Once the screen is positive, a confirmatory test should be performed. The confirmatory test is the RIBA (recombinant immunoblot assay). If it is positive, it indicates past or current infection with hepatitis C. If negative, the RIBA indicates that the screen was a false positive.

13. ***c***
Diverticular disease is more common in older adults. About 70% of patients diagnosed with diverticulitis have left lower quadrant pain. Pain may be present for several days prior to the acute episode. In addition to left lower quadrant pain, bloating and cramping are commonly described by these patients. Diverticulitis occurs secondary to perforations of a diverticulum.

14. ***b***
GERD is usually associated with symptoms that produce injury to the mucosa. This rarely occurs in physiologic reflux. Characteristics typical of physiologic reflux are that it occurs primarily post-prandial (like GERD), are usually asymptomatic, rarely occur nocturnally, and are usually short-lived. In contrast, GERD usually occurs nocturnally, especially when there is lower esophageal sphincter disease.

15. ***a***
Antacids, like calcium carbonate, produce the most rapid change in gastric pH and thus, the most rapid relief of symptoms. However, the increase in pH lasts 20-30 minutes and so, may provide only "short-lived" relief. H2 blockers, like ranitidine, and proton pump inhibitors, like omeprazole, may take many hours before relief is realized and so are not the best choices for immediate relief of symptoms. Sucralfate does not affect gastric pH or acid output. Instead, it forms a viscous, adhesive substance that adheres to the surface of gastric and esophageal ulcers.

16. ***d***
H. pylori **is a gram negative organism that is a major etiologic factor in development of duodenal ulcer disease, gastric adenocarcinoma and lymphoma of the stomach. Only about 10-15% of patients with** ***H. pylori*** **infection actually develop duodenal ulcer disease, but this is the largest contributor to duodenal ulcer development. Other etiologic factors in duodenal ulcer development are NSAID overuse and smoking.**

17. A patient with gall bladder disease has classic symptoms. Which symptom below is NOT classic of gallbladder disease?

- a. **Intense, dull pressure in the mid abdomen**
- b. **Pain that radiates into the chest, back, or right shoulder blade**
- c. **Pain that worsens after a fatty meal**
- d. **Pain that occurs when the stomach empties**

18. Which of the following would be usual in a patient with biliary colic?

- a. **Presence of gallstones on imaging studies**
- b. **Presence of gallstones and unpredictable abdominal pain**
- c. **Positive Murphy's sign only**
- d. **Pain in upper abdomen in response to eating fatty foods**

19. A 42 year-old patient was diagnosed with ulcerative colitis many years ago. What part of his routine health screenings should be stressed by the nurse practitioner?

- a. **He should be screened at age 50 with a colonoscopy.**
- b. **Tetanus immunization should be given every 5 years.**
- c. **Pneumococcal vaccine should be administered by age 50.**
- d. **He should have a colonoscopy every 1-3 years.**

20. The relationship between colon polyps and colon cancer is:

- a. **polyps eventually all become malignant.**
- b. **polyps have a slow progression to colon cancer.**
- c. **polyps have a rapid progression to colon cancer.**
- d. **polyps have no relationship to colon cancer.**

21. A fecal occult blood test (FOBT) obtained during a rectal examination:

- a. **should be adequate for screening of colorectal cancer.**
- b. **will usually detect the presence of polyps.**
- c. **is adequate to screen for rectal cancer only.**
- d. **is inadequate to screen for colorectal cancer.**

22. Which characteristic *does not* describe hemorrhoids?

- a. **Bleeding**
- b. **Burning**
- c. **Itching**
- d. **Carcinogenic**

17. *d*
The pain associated with cholecystitis is usually constant and may or may not occur in relation to meals, but, it rarely occurs after the stomach has emptied (takes several hours) or with fasting. Initial pain is usual after a fatty meal. The pain is usually in the upper right quadrant but is nearly as common in the mid abdomen. The pain can mimic a myocardial infarction and so it must be treated as cardiac pain until proven otherwise. The pain is usually caused by contraction of the gallbladder after a meal. The contraction may force a stone or sludge against the gallbladder outlet. Discomfort can last for several hours.

18. d
Biliary colic refers to discomfort produced by contraction of the gallbladder. This occurs in response to eating. Typically, pain occurs in the upper right quadrant or chest, peaks in an hour after eating, and then remains constant and finally subsides over the next several hours. A positive Murphy's sign is elicited when the gallbladder wall is inflamed. It can be elicited by palpating the gallbladder just beneath the liver as the patient takes a deep breath.

19. *d*
A history of ulcerative colitis or Crohn's disease is associated with an increased risk of colorectal cancer. Recommendations vary according to organization, but generally, screening with annual colonoscopy should take place 8-10 years after diagnosis in patients with pancolitis. Screening should take place for 15 years after diagnosis in patients with colitis involving the left colon. Colonoscopy should be repeated every 1-3 years.

20. *b*
Colon polyps are usually very slow growing and take a long time to progress to cancer. This is the reason that a colonoscopy does not need to be repeated annually. While not all polyps grow slowly, this is the usual progression.

21. *d*
This is not adequate to screen for colorectal cancer. Fecal occult blood tests have a much higher sensitivity if three consecutive stool specimens are used (applying 2 samples per card for each specimen). A single specimen is inadequate for screening purposes. Since polyps do not usually bleed, the fecal occult blood test is not a good screen for polyp identification.

22. *d*
Hemorrhoids are vascular structures in the anal canal. The classic symptoms of hemorrhoidal disease are bleeding, itching, burning. They are not carcinogenic; nor are they found with greater prevalence in patients with colorectal cancer. They are of equal prevalence in men and women. The most common age is 45-65 years.

23. A 70 year-old patient states that he had some bright red blood on the toilet tissue this morning after a bowel movement. What is the most likely cause in this patient?

a. **Hemorrhoids**
b. **Diverticulitis**
c. **Colon cancer**
d. **Colon polyp**

24. A 50 year-old with a history of consumption of 3-4 alcoholic drinks daily and weekend binges has elevated liver enzymes. Which set of enzymes is most representative of this patient?

a. **AST= 200, ALT= 75**
b. **AST= 100, ALT = 90**
c. **AST=100, ALT=200**
d. **AST= 30, ALT= 300**

25. A 37 year-old has routine blood work performed during an annual exam. He is found to have elevated liver enzymes. On exam he has a tender, enlarged liver. How should the nurse practitioner proceed?

a. **Repeat the liver enzymes today.**
b. **Order a hepatitis panel.**
c. **Have patient return in one week for recheck.**
d. **Order a CBC.**

26. A patient had an acute onset of right upper quadrant pain that has lasted for the past 3 days. He has low-grade fever. Which lab test(s) will be elevated if he has pancreatitis?

a. **CBC**
b. **Serum amylase**
c. **ALT and AST**
d. **CRP**

27. What choice below is most commonly associated with pancreatitis?

a. **Gallstones and alcoholism**
b. **Hypertriglyceridemia and cholecystitis**
c. **Appendicitis and renal stones**
d. **Viral infection and cholecystitis**

23. ***b***
Nearly 1 in 3 patients in this age group with acute lower gastrointestinal bleeding have bleeding secondary to diverticulitis. Nearly 1 in 5 have colorectal cancer or polyps, though, polyps usually do not bleed. Regardless of the etiology, this patient needs referral for a colonoscopy to identify the cause of bleeding. He is at high risk for colon cancer because of his age. The appropriate recommendation is referral to gastroenterology for colonoscopy.

24. ***a***
The normal AST/ALT ratio in healthy subjects is 0.8. In patients with alcoholic hepatitis, the usual ratio (AST:ALT) is 2:1. When the ALT is very elevated, infectious hepatitis must be considered. Normally, both AST and ALT are less than 40 IU/L. The level of elevation does not correlate with the degree of damage in the liver and has no prognostic value in patients with non-acute liver disease.

25. ***b***
The differential for a patient with elevated liver enzymes can reflect many different etiologies. Since the liver is tender and liver enzymes are elevated, a likely etiology is hepatitis. The size and consistency of the liver should be ascertained. The spleen should be assessed. If it is palpable, it is enlarged also. Hepatitis panel should be performed and strong consideration given to referral to gastroenterology. Repeating liver enzymes might be considered if the rest of the exam was normal and the lab values were the only thing abnormal. The results of a CBC will not change the differential. The patient's abnormal labs and exam make this urgent and waiting a week will delay diagnosis and possible treatment.

26. ***b***
Serum amylase levels begin to rise 6-12 hours after pancreatic insult and remain elevated for 3-5 days. The other tests described may be abnormal but are not specific for pancreatitis.

27. ***a***
In adults, the most common causes of acute pancreatitis are gallstones and alcoholism. Pancreatitis in women is more often due to gallstones; in men, due to alcoholism. Hypertriglyceridemia can precipitate pancreatitis, but a serum amylase measurement may be normal. This can be a difficult diagnosis to make. The other conditions listed are not associated with pancreatitis. However, viral infections of the pancreas can produce pancreatitis.

Hematology Disorders

1. **A 26 year-old female has thalassemia minor. What should be limited in her diet to avoid hepatotoxicity?**

    a. **Vitamin C**
    b. **Vitamin B12**
    c. **Folic acid**
    d. **Multi-vitamin with iron**

2. **Leukemia may have varied clinical presentations. Which characteristic would be unusual to find in a patient with leukemia?**

    a. **Thrombocytopenia**
    b. **Hepatosplenomegaly**
    c. **Severe anemia**
    d. **Sickle shaped cells**

3. **A female patient has been diagnosed with Glucose-6-phosphate dehydrogenase deficiency (G6PD). What should be done to prevent lysis of red cells in this patient?**

    a. **Avoid aspirin and sulfa drugs**
    b. **Minimize iron consumption in her diet**
    c. **Receive immunizations timely**
    d. **Consume adequate amounts of water daily**

4. **Which anemia is described as a macrocytic anemia?**

    a. **Folic acid deficiency anemia**
    b. **Thalassemia**
    c. **Iron deficiency anemia**
    d. **Sickle cell anemia**

5. **Which anemias are described as microcytic, hypochromic anemias?**

    a. **Vitamin B12 and iron deficiency anemia**
    b. **Folic acid and iron deficiency anemia**
    c. **Iron deficiency anemia and thalassemia**
    d. **Sickle cell anemia and anemia of chronic disease**

1. ***d***

A patient with thalassemia minor has a disease characterized by over production of one chain of the hemoglobin molecule. Beta thalassemia patients usually require no specific therapy. These patients are asymptomatic, but may be chronically, mildly anemic. They should avoid iron overload by supplementation, but, generally, are able to safely take iron when iron deficiency anemia and thalassemia co-exist.

2. ***d***

Leukemia is characterized by a failure of the bone marrow. The bone marrow produces red cells, white cells, and platelets. Clinical presentation reflects deficiency of one or more of these cell types and may be identified on CBC. Therefore, patient symptoms vary at presentation. Hepatosplenomegaly may be observed in a patient with leukemia. Sickle shaped cells are seen in patients with sickle cell anemia (SCA) and would not be observed in a patient with leukemia unless he also had SCA.

3. ***a***

G6PD deficiency is an X-linked disorder. This means it is carried on the X chromosome. Both male and female infants may exhibit this. G6PD is the most common enzymatic disorder of red blood cells in humans. These patients should avoid certain substances like aspirin, sulfa drugs, and fava beans because consumption can precipitate lysis of red blood cells. Timely immunizations and adequate daily water consumption are beneficial to all patients but not specifically those with G6PD.

4. ***a***

Folic acid and Vitamin B12 deficiency anemias are characterized by macrocytic red cells. Thalassemia and iron deficiency anemias are microcytic anemias. Sickle cell anemia is characterized by sickle-shaped red cells; hence the name, sickle cell anemia.

5. ***c***

Iron deficiency anemia is characterized by small (microcytic), pale (hypochromic) red cells. Thalassemia is a microcytic, hypochromic anemia also. There is a strong familial component. Folic acid and Vitamin B12 deficiency anemias are characterized by macrocytic red cells. Sickle cell anemia is characterized by sickle-shaped red cells. Hence, the name sickle cell anemia.

6. A 65 year-old male is being treated with oral medications for hypertension, hyperlipidemia, diabetes, and osteoarthritis. The most likely reason for his iron deficiency anemia is oral treatment for:

a. **hypertension.**
b. **hyperlipidemia.**
c. **diabetes.**
d. **osteoarthritis.**

7. A patient is being treated for iron deficiency anemia. Iron is better absorbed:

a. **with food.**
b. **on an empty stomach.**
c. **with a food rich in vitamin C.**
d. **in the evening.**

8. What choice below can be attributed to the two most common causes of iron deficiency anemia in adults?

a. **Bleeding in the gastrointestinal tract and through loss of bone mass**
b. **Aging and menses**
c. **Poor diet and lack of adequate iron intake**
d. **Gynecologic losses and bleeding in the gastrointestinal tract**

9. Lead toxicity can be associated with:

a. **folic acid deficiency anemia.**
b. **anemia of chronic disease.**
c. **sideroblastic anemia.**
d. **vitamin B12 deficiency.**

10. An example of a macrocytic anemia is:

a. **iron deficiency anemia.**
b. **pernicious anemia.**
c. **anemia of chronic disease.**
d. **sideroblastic anemia.**

11. A patient is found to have an anemia. The patient's MCH is normal. The patient's anemia can be described as:

a. **macrocytic.**
b. **normocytic.**
c. **macrochromic.**
d. **normochromic.**

6. ***d***

Osteoarthritis is often treated with analgesics and non-steroid anti-inflammatory drugs (NSAIDs). NSAIDs can be associated with GI bleeding, especially when they are taken chronically. This patient should be screened for blood in his stool. The other diseases listed, as well as the treatments for them, are not associated with iron deficiency anemia.

7. ***b***

Iron is better absorbed on an empty stomach. This is the most efficient way to absorb iron. However, it is poorly tolerated on an empty stomach and many times patients have to eat something in order to tolerate oral forms of iron. If this is the case, it should be taken with a food rich in vitamin C since this enhances iron absorption. Time of day does not affect iron absorption.

8. ***d***

The most common body systems associated with blood loss are the gynecologic (GYN) tract and the gastrointestinal (GI) tract in patients of all ages. In women of menstruating age, the GYN tract is a common source of blood loss, especially when menses is heavy. The GI tract is more likely to be the source of blood loss when adults are iron deficient, especially if they possess risk factors for iron deficiency anemia, such as chronic aspirin or NSAID use.

9. ***c***

Sideroblastic anemia occurs when iron is unable to be incorporated into the hemoglobin molecule despite there being adequate amounts of iron available. An iron deficiency anemia results. This can be due to an inherited enzyme deficiency, it can be acquired (as in the case of lead toxicity), or of it can be of idiopathic origin. Lead can produce a sideroblastic anemia because it prevents iron from being incorporated into the heme portion of the hemoglobin molecule. Sideroblasts may be visible on blood smear. They represent an accumulation of iron in the cell's mitochondria.

10. ***b***

A macrocytic anemia indicates that size of red blood cells is larger than expected, hence, the prefix, macro. Iron deficiency anemia produces a microcytic anemia. Anemia of chronic disease can produce a microcytic or normocytic anemia, but usually a normocytic anemia is evident. Sideroblastic anemia produces a microcytic anemia.

11. ***d***

The MCH, mean corpuscular hemoglobin, indicates the degree of hemoglobin incorporation into red cells. If this is normal, it is described as a normochromic anemia. If the MCH is decreased, the anemia is described as a hypochromic anemia. When the MCH is increased, the anemia is described as hyperchromic. Macrochromic does not describe red blood cells. Macrocytic and normocytic describe SIZE of red cells and is indicated by the MCV.

12. A patient is found to have an anemia. The patient's MCV is normal. The patient's anemia can be described as:

a. macrocytic.
b. normocytic.
c. macrochromic.
d. normochromic.

13. A 75 year-old patient who has multiple chronic diseases has been in very poor health for a decade. What type of anemias is he most likely to exhibit?

a. Iron deficiency and folic acid
b. Folic acid and pernicious
c. Iron deficiency and anemia of chronic disease
d. Thalassemia and Vitamin B12

14. An obese 78 year-old male with poorly controlled hypertension and diabetes has a normocytic, normochromic anemia. This anemia is likely:

a. iron deficiency.
b. associated with chronic disease.
c. pernicious anemia.
d. folic acid deficiency anemia.

15. A 70 year-old male has lymph nodes in his axillary and inguinal areas that are palpable but non-tender. He states that he feels well today. What should be included in a differential diagnosis for this patient?

a. Leukemia
b. Lymphoma
c. Asymptomatic lymphadenitis
d. Cat-scratch disease

16. A patient with pernicious anemia may be observed to have:

a. darkening of the skin.
b. joint aches.
c. glossitis.
d. thrombocytopenia.

12. *b*
The MCV, mean corpuscular volume, indicates the size of the red cells. If this is normal, it is described as a normocytic anemia. If the MCV is decreased, the anemia is described as a microcytic anemia. When the MCV is increased, the anemia is described as macrocytic. Macrochromic does not describe red blood cells. Normochromic describes the degree of hemoglobin incorporation into red cells and is indicated by the MCH.

13. *b*
Having multiple chronic illnesses does increase the likelihood of having folic acid deficiency. Pernicious anemia, secondary to vitamin B12 deficiency, is commonly seen in older patients with chronic illnesses too. Many patients have both concurrently. Patients with folic acid deficiency and/or vitamin B12 deficiency are more likely to be elderly, in poor health, and have poor diets. Both may also be seen in patients who consume excessive amounts of alcohol. Nothing in history indicates this as the etiology.

14. *b*
This is classic anemia of chronic disease. This is especially evident when chronic diseases are poorly controlled. It is most frequently characterized by a normocytic, normochromic anemia. Iron deficiency anemia is microcytic, hypochromic. Pernicious anemia, associated with B12 deficiency, and folic acid deficiency anemia are both macrocytic anemias.

15. *b*
Lymphoma is malignancy of the lymphatic system. Hodgkin and Non-Hodgkin lymphomas are examples. In older patients, non-Hodgkin lymphoma is considerably more common. It is characterized by enlarged lymph nodes and may be accompanied by fever, cough, night sweats, and fatigue. Asymmetric adenopathy is most common in Hodgkin lymphoma; in non-Hodgkin lymphoma, adenopathy is disseminated.

16. *c*
Glossitis is an inflammation of the tongue with a change in its usual color. It may be tender also. This is commonly observed in patients who have B12 deficiency anemia (pernicious anemia). The tongue can appear pale, bright red, or swollen. Glossitis is not seen in all patients with pernicious anemia, but this finding should prompt the healthcare provider to assess B12 and folate levels. Pernicious anemia is not associated with any of the other choices in this question.

17. A patient has CBC results that indicate a microcytic, hypochromic anemia. The nurse practitioner should suspect:

   a. **pernicious anemia.**
   b. **iron deficiency anemia.**
   c. **vitamin B12 deficiency.**
   d. **sickle cell anemia.**

18. An older adult has suspected B12 deficiency. Which of the following lab indices is most indicative of a B12 deficiency?

   a. **Increased MCV**
   b. **Increased MCH**
   c. **Decreased hematocrit**
   d. **Thrombocytosis**

19. A 66 year-old African American male complains of pain in his trunk, especially his ribs. Cardiovascular disease is ruled out. He has a normocytic, normochromic anemia with hypercalcemia. The differential diagnosis should include:

   a. **multiple myeloma.**
   b. **lymphoma.**
   c. **leukemia.**
   d. **parathyroid disease.**

20. Which white cell should be present in the greatest number in a patient who is healthy today?

   a. **Neutrophils**
   b. **Basophils**
   c. **Eosinophils**
   d. **Lymphocytes**

21. A patient is having an allergic reaction to seafood. Which white cell will probably be increased?

   a. **Neutrophils**
   b. **Lymphocytes**
   c. **Eosinophils**
   d. **Basophils**

17. ***b***
Iron deficiency anemia is characterized by a microcytic, hypochromic anemia. Pernicious anemia, caused usually by a vitamin B12 deficiency, is a macrocytic anemia. Sickle cell anemia is characterized by sickle shaped cells.

18. ***a***
A vitamin B12 deficiency can produce an anemia called pernicious anemia. This is most commonly found in older adults and is characterized by macrocytosis, an increased MCV. In other words, the red cells are larger than expected. An increased MCH may be seen in a B12 deficiency, but this is unusual. A decreased hematocrit will be seen in most anemias, but this is not specific to a B12 deficiency. Thrombocytosis refers to an increased number of platelets in the blood stream.

19. ***a***
Multiple myeloma is a neoplastic proliferation in the bone marrow that results in skeletal destruction. It is more common in older patients; the average age of diagnosis is 66 years. Common clinical findings are pain in the long bones, especially those of the trunk and back. Accompanying findings are anemia, usually normocytic/normochromic, hypercalcemia, and renal insufficiency. Parathyroid disease can produce increased calcium levels, but it is not associated with pain in the trunk.

20. ***a***
Neutrophils usually comprise 60-70% of white cells in a patient who has no infection. Other names for neutrophils are "polys", also known as polymorphonuclear leukocytes; or "segs", also known as segmented neutrophils. Any of these terms may be used because they all refer to the same white cells.

21. ***c***
In a CBC, the white cell that increases during an allergic reaction is the eosinophil. Generally, the percentage of eosinophils in a normal CBC is 2-4%. Increases in eosinophils are observed in patients with allergic reactions as well as patients with parasitic infections.

22. Which disease listed below can be associated with lymphocytosis?

a. **Mononucleosis**
b. **Strept throat**
c. **Iron deficiency anemia**
d. **Hemolytic anemia**

23. Thrombocytopenia may present as:

a. **fatigue.**
b. **fever.**
c. **purpura.**
d. **a butterfly rash.**

24. What hallmark finding is associated with both B12 and folate deficiencies?

a. **Glossitis**
b. **Macrocytosis**
c. **Memory loss**
d. **An MCV < 80fL**

25. Which adult female patient has an anemia?

a. **Hgb = 14.4**
b. **Hct = 35.2**
c. **Hgb = 13.5**
d. **Hct = 40.1**

26. The laboratory identifies metamyelocytes in a 50 year-old patient who had a CBC performed. What might be an expected finding in this patient?

a. **Splenomegaly**
b. **Elevated liver function studies**
c. **Decreased uric acid level**
d. **Decreased platelet count**

22. *a*

Lymphocytosis refers to an increased number of circulating lymphocytes. These are usually the predominant white cell in viral infections, especially mononucleosis. Lymphocytes are not increased in patients with anemias. Bacterial infections, like streptococcal disease, would likely be characterized by decreased lymphocyte counts.

23. *c*

Thrombocytopenia refers to a decreased number of circulating platelets. By definition, this occurs when fewer than 150,000 platelets/microL are present. This occurs gradually. The first evidence of this is usually seen in the skin and may occur as bruising, petechiae, or purpura. Gums may bleed easily with tooth brushing. Platelet counts less than 60,000/microL can bring about bleeding with minor trauma. Spontaneous bleeds can occur when the platelet count is less than 10,000/microL. Fatigue and fever are not specific to thrombocytopenia. A butterfly rash may be associated with lupus.

24. *b*

Both of the anemias associated with these two conditions produce a macrocytosis, an increase in the size of the RBC. Glossitis is common in patients with a vitamin B12 deficiency. Memory loss is not a hallmark finding, though, changes in cognition may be associated with B12 deficiency. Choice D indicates a microcytic anemia.

25. *b*

An anemia may be diagnosed when the hemoglobin OR hematocrit is less than the expected value for age and gender. Expected values are determined by population norms, which are established by the laboratory that does the testing. Generally, in an adult female, a hemoglobin < 12.0 or hematocrit < 36% constitute anemia.

26. *a*

The finding of metamyelocytes is an ominous one. These represent immature white cells that are usually present only in the bone marrow. The examiner should consider a diagnosis of leukemia. A definitive diagnosis can only be made after a bone marrow aspiration and examination. Many adult patients are asymptomatic for months before diagnosis. Splenomegaly and hepatomegaly are common because of an excess of neutrophils produced by a diseased bone marrow.

27. A patient had a splenectomy after an automobile accident 3 months ago. Patients who are asplenic are:

a. **at an increased risk of hepatomegaly.**
b. **more susceptible to bacterial infection.**
c. **at risk for bleeding disorders.**
d. **more likely to exhibit anemia.**

28. A measure of the degree of variation in red cell size is indicated by:

a. **RDW.**
b. **MCHC.**
c. **MCV.**
d. **MCH.**

27. *b*
Any patient who is asplenic is at an increased risk of bacterial infection, especially by encapsulated organisms. The spleen is responsible for removal of aging RBCs and bacteria. When it is absent, a patient is more susceptible to infection, particularly *Streptococcus pneumoniae*. The spleen is a major lymphopoietic organ and plays a major role in humoral immunity responsible for rapid response to infection. Thus, the need for review of the patient's immunization status. A pneumococcal immunization is prudent in a patient who is asplenic.

28. *a*
RDW is the RBC distribution width, a measure of the variation in red cell size. This is reported on a CBC.

Men's & Women's Health

1. **A nurse practitioner identifies filamentous structures and many uniform, oval shaped structures during a microscopic exam of vaginal discharge. These are probably:**

    a. **bacteria.**
    b. **sperm.**
    c. **hyphae and yeast.**
    d. **Candida albicans.**

2. **"Hot flashes" that occur during menopause are thought to be related to:**

    a. **low estrogen levels.**
    b. **low progesterone levels.**
    c. **fluctuating progesterone levels.**
    d. **fluctuating estrogen levels.**

3. **Three of the following interventions are appropriately used to prevent osteoporosis after menopause. Which one is not?**

    a. **Limited alcohol intake**
    b. **Performance of weight-bearing activities for 40 mins. at least 5 days/week**
    c. **Estrogen replacement therapy**
    d. **Adequate calcium & vitamin D intake**

4. **A 16 year-old female is diagnosed with primary dysmenorrhea. She has taken over the counter ibuprofen in 800 mg increments every 8 hours during menses for the past 3 months with minimal relief of symptoms. What intervention will provide greatest relief of dysmenorrhea symptoms?**

    a. **Flurbiprofen during menses**
    b. **Combined oral contraceptives**
    c. **Daily multivitamin with B12 supplementation**
    d. **30 minutes of regular exercise daily**

5. **A 50 year-old female believes that she is "menopausal". She complains of "hot flashes" and has not had menses in 12 months. Which of the following test results may be helpful for confirmation of menopause?**

    a. **Increased thyroid stimulating hormone**
    b. **Decreased follicle stimulating hormone**
    c. **Hypoestrogenemia**
    d. **Increased follicle stimulating hormone**

1. ***c***

Filamentous structures likely describe hyphae. Typically, hyphae are the mechanism that allows fungal growth. The uniform oval shaped structures are likely yeast. These can range in size but are usually large and unicellular. Visualization of hyphae and yeast should prompt an immediate diagnosis of a fungal infection. Candida albicans is a specific fungus, often found in vaginal secretions. Since there are many fungi that can produce hyphae and yeast, it is not possible to diagnose Candida albicans specifically.

2. ***d***

Low estrogen levels alone do not produce hot flashes. Female first graders are known to have low estrogen levels but do not have hot flashes. The fluctuation in estrogen levels produces vasomotor symptoms referred to as "hot flashes".

3. ***c***

Prevention of osteoporosis may be optimized by elimination of risk factors and engaging in interventions that maximize bone density. Good nutrition from infancy throughout adulthood is a major component of good bone health. Others include engaging in weight-bearing exercises, adequate intake of calcium and vitamin D, smoking cessation, limiting alcohol consumption to moderate amounts, and avoidance when possible of medications that may decrease bone density (corticosteroids, anticonvulsants). Osteoporosis occurs at accelerated rates in women who are post-menopausal. The lack of estrogen can produce rapid bone loss due to bone resorption. Estrogen replacement is not used to prevent or treat osteoporosis.

4. ***b***

NSAIDs and hormonal contraceptives represent the mainstay of pharmacologic treatment for dysmenorrhea. NSAIDs produce an 80-86% response rate when used for dysmenorrhea. The general recommendation is that when one agent (NSAIDs or hormonal contraceptives) does not produce relief of symptoms, the other agent should be tried. Hence, the best choice is oral contraceptives. Both agents should be considered for women who are symptomatic with one agent only.

5. ***d***

Follicle stimulating hormone (FSH) begins to rise during menopausal transition. This stage of menopause begins with variation in menstrual cycle length and ends 12 months after the final menses. If the patient is older than 45 years and menstrual cycle dysfunction has been ruled out, menopause should be considered. Possibly the best approach to diagnosing menopause is to ask and observe clinical manifestations. An elevated FSH is not necessary to make a diagnosis of menopause but is commonly done in clinical practice. Diagnosis entails a review of her symptoms. Specifically, changes in bleeding patterns, hot flashes, sleep disturbances, and genitourinary symptoms are characteristic of menopause.

6. **A patient who is scheduled for pelvic exam with PAP smear should be advised to avoid douching, sexual intercourse, and tampon use before her exam. For how long should she be advised to avoid these activities for optimal evaluation?**

    a. **24 hours**
    b. **48 hours**
    c. **36 hours**
    d. **One week**

7. **A 54 year-old female presents with a small to moderate amount of vaginal bleeding of recent onset. She has been postmenopausal for approximately 2 years. What diagnosis is *least* likely?**

    a. **Endometrial carcinoma**
    b. **Ovarian cancer**
    c. **Endometrial hyperplasia**
    d. **Uterine polyps**

8. **A 20 year old female reports that her grandmother and mother have osteopenia. What should she be encouraged to do to reduce her risk of osteopenia?**

    a. **Aerobic exercise, weight loss, low fat diet**
    b. **Smoking cessation, weight bearing exercise**
    c. **Calcium supplementation, vitamin A, C & D intake**
    d. **Optimal caloric intake, vitamin D supplementation**

9. **A diagnosis of osteoporosis can be made when:**

    a. **an x-ray indicates fragility fractures.**
    b. **bone mineral density is 2.5 standard deviations below the mean.**
    c. **T-score greater than 2.5.**
    d. **DXA scan indicates fragility fracture index.**

10. **The recommended time to initiate screening for cervical cancer in women is:**

    a. **prior to becoming sexually active.**
    b. **at age 18 years.**
    c. **at age 21 years.**
    d. **3 years after first sexual intercourse.**

6. *b*
The general recommendation is to avoid these activities and any vaginal medication for 48 hours prior to PAP smear. Douching and tampon use can remove superficial cells which are the ones collected and used as representative samples on PAP smear. Sexual intercourse should be avoided because there can be specimen contamination by the male partner and semen can make the smear thick and difficult to read. With vaginal medications or creams, either can serve as a barrier to epithelial cell sampling.

7. *b*
Ovarian cancer may present as an adnexal mass, pelvic or abdominal symptoms and a variety of others. Postmenopausal bleeding (PMB) is a very uncommon presentation of ovarian cancer, but can present this way. In women with PMB, other causes of uterine pathology should be evaluated before considering ovarian pathology. In early menopause, the most common etiology is atrophy of the endometrium or vaginal mucosa. This patient is postmenopausal for approximately 2 years. Other common causes of PMB are polyps, fibroids, and endometrial hyperplasia.

8. *b*
Cigarette smoking accelerates skeletal bone loss. The mechanism is unknown, but, it may be due to increased metabolism of estrogen. Therefore, smoking cessation is important in prevention of osteopenia as well as other diseases and conditions. Exercise should occur at least 30 minutes three times per week to maintain bone density. This has also shown to decrease incidence of hip fractures in older women. Walking increases hip and spine density. Vitamin D (at least 1000 IU per day) and calcium intake (1200-1500 mg per day) should accompany weight bearing exercise and smoking cessation.

9. *b*
Osteoporosis can be diagnosed with a bone mineral density test (BMD). The technique used is a dual energy x-ray absorptiometry (DXA). This is the most common clinical tool used to diagnose osteoporosis. Osteoporosis can also be diagnosed when there is a fragility fracture. This can be identified on x-ray. In an absence of trauma, a fragility fracture may indicate osteoporosis, multiple myeloma or other diseases. BMD that is 2.5 or more standard deviations below the young adult mean (or T-score of -2.5 or less) constitutes a diagnosis of osteoporosis.

10. *c*
Prior to 2009, the recommendation for cervical cancer screening was by age 18 years or 3 years after first sexual intercourse. American Cancer Society (ACS) and American College of Obstetricians and Gynecologists (ACOG) have updated this. The current recommendation for cervical screening is age 21 years. Cervical cancer is considered extremely rare in patients younger than 21 years.

11. A female patient is 35 years old. She has never had an abnormal PAP smear and has had regular screening since age 18. If she has a normal PAP smear with HPV testing today, when should she have the next cervical cancer screening?

a. **One year**
b. **2-3 years**
c. **3 years**
d. **5 years**

12. The primary risk factor for development of breast cancer in women of average risk is:

a. **age.**
b. **smoking history.**
c. **number of live births.**
d. **exposure to estrogen.**

13. A patient who is 35 years old has identified a small, discrete mass in one breast. How should this be evaluated?

a. **Ask whether the mass changes at the time of menses.**
b. **Order a mammogram and ultrasound to assess the mass.**
c. **Have her return 3-10 days after next menses.**
d. **Order a mammogram 3-10 days after next menses.**

14. A localized tumor in the prostate gland associated with early stage prostate cancer is likely to produce:

a. **urinary hesitancy.**
b. **low back pain.**
c. **urinary frequency.**
d. **an absence of symptoms.**

15. Hematuria is not a common clinical manifestation in:

a. **early prostate cancer.**
b. **benign prostatic hyperplasia.**
c. **bladder cancer.**
d. **renal cancer.**

11. ***d***
American College of Obstetricians and Gynecologists recommends screening for women over age 30 years no more frequently than every 5 years if both tests are negative and adequate screening has taken place. If she had been screened with PAP only, the recommendation for screening would be in 3 years. US Preventive Services Task Force recommends screening this patient in 5 years. Human papilloma virus (HPV) testing in combination with cervical cytology has been shown to be more sensitive than cytology alone. However, HPV alone is not recommended as a lone screening modality. Finally, HPV testing is more specific in women over age 30 years.

12. ***a***
Age is the most important risk factor for developing breast cancer in women of average risk. Breast cancer is more common in older women and has a higher mortality rate when discovered. Nearly 85% of breast cancer occurs in women who are 50 years of age or older. Exposure to estrogen and genetic factors are important risk factors but do not contribute to development of breast cancer as greatly as age does in women of average risk. Hence, the reason for diligent annual screening in women who are 50 years of age and older.

13. ***b***
Clinical evaluation of a breast mass begins with a good history of the mass and a physical exam of the breasts, lymph nodes, neck, and chest wall. While asking about whether the mass changes with menses is a good question in history, a mammogram should be the first radiographic assessment in females with breast complaints who are over age 30. This patient is 35 years old. An ultrasound is used for evaluation of a focal abnormality in a breast, especially if it has been identified on a mammogram. In this patient, both are prudent since there is a discrete, palpable mass. Re-assessing the mass 3-10 days after next menses may be appropriate for a female younger than age 30 depending on her history and physical exam.

14. ***d***
Localized tumors associated with early stage prostate cancer usually produce no symptoms or clinical manifestations. Occasionally, localized tumors produce UTI symptoms, nocturia, daytime voiding frequency, and diminished force of urinary stream. These symptoms are common with benign prostatic hypertrophy (BPH). An uncommon manifestation of prostate cancer is hematuria.

15. ***a***
Localized tumors confined to the prostate gland are rarely associated with hematuria. In fact, localized tumors in the prostate gland rarely produce symptoms or any clinical manifestations. This fact strengthens the importance of screening for prostate cancer using digital rectal exam (DRE) and measurement of prostate specific antigen (PSA). Hematuria is commonly seen in benign prostatic hyperplasia, bladder cancer and renal cancer.

16. Digital rectal exam may be performed to assess the prostate gland. Which term does NOT describe a prostate gland that may have a tumor?

a. **Nodular**
b. **Asymmetrical**
c. **Boggy**
d. **Indurated**

17. A 40 year-old male has been diagnosed with acute bacterial prostatitis. His prostate specific antigen (PSA) is elevated on diagnosis. How soon should his PSA be rechecked?

a. **2-3 days**
b. **1 week**
c. **2 weeks**
d. **4 weeks**

18. A 50 year-old male comes to the nurse practitioner clinic for evaluation. He complains of fever 101F, chills, pelvic pain, and dysuria. He should be diagnosed with:

a. **acute bacterial prostatitis.**
b. **chronic bacterial prostatitis.**
c. **urinary tract infection.**
d. **non-bacterial prostatitis.**

19. Which of the following medications should be avoided in a 65 year-old male with benign prostatic hyperplasia (BPH)?

a. **Doxazosin**
b. **Ciprofloxacin**
c. **Pseudoephedrine**
d. **Propanolol**

20. What is the recommendation of American Cancer Society for screening an average risk 40 year-old Caucasian male for prostate cancer?

a. **Digital rectal exam**
b. **Serum prostate specific antigen (PSA)**
c. **Digital rectal exam and PSA**
d. **He should be screened starting at age 50 years**

16. ***c***
A boggy prostate describes a gland that is edematous and tender, such as is seen in a patient with bacterial prostatitis. The other terms indicate an abnormality that could represent a prostate gland tumor.

17. ***d***
Prostate infection or inflammation can cause a sharp rise in PSA values. Elective PSA should be deferred for four weeks after an episode of bacterial prostatitis. Checking prior to this time will likely result in an elevated serum PSA level and unnecessary testing and worry for the patient.

18. ***a***
Acute bacterial prostatitis should always be considered first in a male patient who presents with these symptoms. He may be expected to have cloudy urine and symptoms of obstruction, like dribbling. Chronic bacterial prostatitis presents with a more subtle presentation such as frequency, urgency, and low-grade fever. Urinary tract infection is far less common in men than women and is usually associated with anal intercourse or being uncircumcised. Nonbacterial prostatitis presents like chronic prostatitis except that urine and prostate secretion cultures are negative.

19. ***c***
Nasal decongestants like pseudoephedrine should be avoided in men with BPH. These will increase the urge to urinate. Urinary frequency is a bothersome symptom of males with BPH. Medications that are known to impair urination are muscle relaxants, narcotics, tricyclic antidepressants such as amitriptyline, and medications with anticholinergic properties such as antihistamines.

20. ***d***
American Cancer Society recommends initial prostate screening of an average risk male at age 50 years with PSA testing with or without digital rectal exam. If the initial PSA is $<$ 2.5 ng/mL, the screen can be repeated in 2 years. If the PSA is $\geq$ 2.5, annual screening should take place.

21. What is the recommendation of American Cancer Society for initial screening of an African-American male for prostate cancer?

a. **Digital rectal exam starting at age 40 years**
b. **PSA starting at age 45 years**
c. **Discussions starting at age 40-45 years**
d. **He should be screened starting at age 50 years**

22. A 25 year-old male patient is training for a marathon. He reports an acute onset of scrotal pain after a 10 mile run. He has nausea and is found to have an asymmetric, high-riding testis on the right side. What should be suspected?

a. **Sports hernia**
b. **Epididymitis**
c. **Testicular torsion**
d. **Prostatitis**

23. A 22 year-old male who is otherwise healthy complains of scrotal pain. His pain has developed over the past 4 days. He is diagnosed with epididymitis. What is the most likely reason?

a. **His age**
b. **Infection with chlamydia**
c. **Underlying hydrocele**
d. **Urinary tract infection**

24. Noninfectious epididymitis is common in:

a. **soccer players.**
b. **truck drivers.**
c. **marathon runners.**
d. **men who wear "boxers".**

25. A common presentation of an inguinal hernia is:

a. **groin or abdominal pain with a scrotal mass.**
b. **an abdominal mass without pain.**
c. **scrotal and abdominal masses.**
d. **abdominal pain and scrotal erythema.**

26. Hesselbach's triangle forms the landmark for:

a. **inguinal hernia.**
b. **femoral hernia.**
c. **abdominal hernia.**
d. **umbilical hernia.**

21. ***c***
American Cancer Society guidelines recommend beginning screening discussion at age 40-45 years for males at high risk for developing prostate cancer (e.g. a first degree relative with prostate cancer before age 65 or African American race). The reason for "screening discussions" is to keep males involved in individual decision making. The PSA threshold is 4.0 ng/mL. Testing is discouraged for males with less than a 10 year expected survival. US Preventive Services Task Force does not recommend screening.

22. ***c***
The most serious cause of acute scrotal pain is testicular torsion. The most common age group for this to occur is adolescents; however, almost 40% of torsion occurs in males greater than age 21. This is more common after minor testicular trauma or after strenuous exercise. This is an urgent urological referral. The other choices listed do not produce acute scrotal pain in conjunction with these physical findings.

23. ***b***
Several factors predispose males to epididymitis. In men under age 35, the most common cause of epididymitis is infection with *Chlamydia trachomatis.* In older men, urinary tract pathogens are more typical. In pre-pubertal boys, bicycle riding and heavy physical exertion are most common. In pre-pubertal boys, consideration should be given to congenital abnormalities.

24. ***b***
Noninfectious epididymitis occurs when there is reflux of urine into the epididymis from the ejaculatory ducts and vas deferens. This can cause ductal obstruction and acute inflammation without infection. This can occur if males spend a lot of time sitting. Truck drivers are particularly susceptible because they spend many uninterrupted hours sitting when they are driving. Other typical risk factors are vigorous exercise that involve heavy lifting or upper body workouts; especially sit-ups or abdominal crunches.

25. ***a***
An inguinal hernia is characterized by herniation of bowel or omentum into the scrotum. It typically presents with scrotal pain and a scrotal mass or scrotal swelling. Abdominal or groin pain with a scrotal mass is a common presentation. Bowel sounds may be audible in the scrotum.

26. ***a***
Direct inguinal hernias occur through Hesselbach's triangle. The inguinal ligament, the rectus muscle, and the epigastric vessels form the triangle. When there is a weakness in the floor of the inguinal canal, a hernia can result. Inguinal hernias are the most common groin hernias in men and women. Repair of this is the most common surgical procedure performed in the US.

Neurological Disorders

1. A patient diagnosed with cluster headaches:

   a. usually has scotomas.
   b. can be diagnosed with an imaging study.
   c. should eliminate triggers like nicotine and alcohol.
   d. may exhibit nuchal rigidity.

2. An elderly patient has an audible carotid bruit. He has a history of hypertension, hyperlipidemia, and a myocardial infarction 5 years ago. The finding of a bruit indicates that the patient:

   a. probably will have a stroke.
   b. has more than triple the risk of stroke compared to individuals who do not have a carotid bruit.
   c. is more likely to die from cardiovascular disease than cerebrovascular disease.
   d. probably has a significant carotid artery lesion.

3. Mini mental status exam helps to identify patients who have symptoms of:

   a. cognitive impairment.
   b. depression.
   c. behavioral changes.
   d. stroke.

4. A 26 year-old patient with long history of chronic sinusitis presents today with temperature of 103.2 F, headache, and stiff neck. Which finding below should make the nurse practitioner suspect meningitis?

   a. Positive Kernig's and Brudzinski's signs
   b. History of HIV
   c. Photophobia
   d. Decreased cervical range of motion

5. Which of the following would NOT be part of the differential diagnosis for an 84 year-old patient with dementia symptoms?

   a. Tumor
   b. Cerebral hemorrhage
   c. Cerebral infarct
   d. Normal aging process

1. ***c***
Cluster headaches are extremely painful headaches but are not as common as migraine or tension headaches. The headaches occur in cyclical patterns, hence the name "cluster". The cycle lasts about 2-12 weeks. A single attack may last 30-90 minutes, but can last up to 3 hours. Patients do not exhibit fever or nuchal rigidity. These symptoms may characterize meningitis. Lifestyle measures like avoiding alcohol, nicotine, and high altitudes may help prevent a headache . Avoiding afternoon naps, bright lights, and glare during a headache cycle, may prevent a subsequent headache from occurring. Scotoma refers to an area of diminished vision in the visual field.

2. ***c***
In asymptomatic individuals, carotid bruits are a poor predictor of carotid artery stenosis or stroke risk. Even when a bruit is identified and the patient has a stroke, the majority of strokes will occur in an area other than the carotid artery. Individuals with a carotid bruit have double the risk of stroke compared to individuals without an audible bruit. In patients with significant carotid artery stenosis, only 50% have an audible carotid bruit. The value of a carotid bruit is that it is a good marker of generalized atherosclerosis. When it is identified, disease in other vessels should be evaluated. Statistically, patients with an audible carotid bruit are more likely to die of cardiovascular disease than cerebrovascular disease.

3. ***a***
The mini mental status exam (MMSE) is the most widely used screening tool in primary care to evaluate cognitive impairment. The exam helps healthcare providers evaluate 6 areas: orientation, short-term memory-retention/recall, language, attention, calculation, and constructional praxis. It does not diagnose Alzheimer's disease but is used to assess cognition as described above.

4. ***a***
These two tests demonstrate nuchal rigidity. Brudzinski's sign refers to spontaneous flexion of the hips during attempted passive flexion of the neck. Kernig's sign refers to the inability to allow full extension of the knee when the hip is flexed 90 degrees. In addition to the finding of nuchal rigidity, headaches, fever, and altered mental status characterize acute, bacterial meningitis.

5. ***d***
Changes in cognition are not associated with the aging process, though 50% of adults over age 90 have some form of dementia. All patients should have some type of imaging to rule out tumor, infection, hemorrhage, infarct, etc. Experts are unable to agree on which neuroimaging studies are most valuable.

6. A family member of a newly diagnosed Alzheimer's disease patient asks how long the patient will have to take donepezil, an acetylcholinesterase inhibitor, before learning whether it is beneficial or not. You reply:

a. **4 - 8 weeks.**
b. **about 12 weeks.**
c. **6 - 12 months.**
d. **at least one year.**

7. An elderly patient with organic brain syndrome is at increased risk of elder abuse because she:

a. **lives in a nursing home.**
b. **has multiple caregivers.**
c. **is incontinent of stool and urine.**
d. **has declining cognitive function.**

8. A 68 year-old smoker with a history of well controlled hypertension, describes a syncopal episode which occurred yesterday while mowing his lawn. Today, he has no complaints. Initially, the NP should:

a. **perform a complete neurological and cardiac exam with auscultation of the carotid arteries.**
b. **order a 12 lead ECG, carotid ultrasound, and perform a physical exam.**
c. **order a CT of the brain, blood clotting studies, and cardiac enzymes.**
d. **check blood pressure in 3 positions, order a 12 lead ECG, and schedule an exercise stress test.**

9. Which cranial nerve is assessed by administering the Snellen test?

a. **II**
b. **III**
c. **IV**
d. **VI**

10. The Snellen chart is used to assess:

a. **near vision.**
b. **distant vision.**
c. **color vision.**
d. **peripheral vision.**

6. *c*

The ideal time to evaluate the efficacy of an acetylcholinesterase inhibitor (Ach-I) is 6-12 months of use. The evaluation should include caregiver feedback, repeat mental status assessments, ability to perform activities of daily living, healthcare provider's assessment, side effects, and cost. If Ach-I is stopped, it can be restarted at a later date.

7. *d*

Elders are at increased risk of abuse because of their decline in cognitive function. Caregiver strain, stress, and depression occur at higher rates than in the general population. According to the National Center of Elder Abuse, family members are likely to be abusers of the infirmed elderly. Healthcare providers should remain alert to signs of elder abuse and caregiver stress.

8. *a*

The event described is syncope. Syncope is a brief and sudden loss of consciousness that occurs with spontaneous recovery. This is a significant event but especially in a smoker with hypertension. The initial assessment of this patient must start with an examination of the patient's cardiac and neurological systems. Based on the findings and tentative diagnosis of syncope, coupled with the patient's history of the event, other tests might be ordered to evaluate arrhythmias, stroke, transient ischemic attack, myocardial infarct, carotid stenosis, etc. A referral to specialty care is indicated after initial workup by the nurse practitioner.

9. *a*

The Snellen chart is used to assess vision. Cranial nerve II, the optic nerve, must be intact for intact visual acuity. Cranial nerves III, IV, and VI are responsible for eye movement, not vision.

10. *b*

The Snellen eye chart was named after Dr. Hermann Snellen. The Snellen fractions, 20/20, 20/30, etc. are measures of sharpness of distant vision. Actually, 20/20 is not normal vision; it is a reference standard. Average acuity in a population is 20/15 or 20/10 (hence the reason there are 2 lines beneath the 20/20 vision line). When visual acuity is assessed, each eye is covered and assessed independently; termed monocular.

11. A person with 20/60 vision:

  a. is legally blind.
  b. will have difficulty reading a newspaper.
  c. will be unable to see the big “E” on the eye chart.
  d. has better vision than someone with 20/80 vision.

12. A 72 year-old patient with a relatively benign medical history complains of new onset headache associated with abrupt onset of visual disturbances. Her sedimentation rate is elevated. Her neuro exam is otherwise normal. What is the most likely reason for her symptoms?

  a. Stroke
  b. Migraine headache
  c. Brain tumor
  d. Temporal arteritis

13. Which finding below is typical in a patient with Bell’s palsy?

  a. Facial pain that is bilaterally symmetrical
  b. Unilateral numbness of the cheek
  c. Facial numbness and sagging of eyelid bilaterally
  d. Loss of hearing on the affected side

14. A patient is diagnosed with carpal tunnel syndrome. Which finger is not affected by carpal tunnel syndrome?

  a. Thumb
  b. Second finger
  c. Fourth finger
  d. Fifth finger

15. A 70 year-old patient exhibits a “pill rolling” tremor. This likely indicates:

  a. intention tremor.
  b. alcohol withdrawal.
  c. Parkinson’s disease.
  d. benign essential tremor.

11. ***d***

Using the Snellen nomenclature for describing visual acuity (example 20/80), the first number represents the test distance. In most cases this is 20 feet. The second number represents the distance at which the average eye can see the letters on a specific line of the chart. In other words, the examinee can see at 20 feet what an average eye (20/20) can see at 80 feet. 20/80 is a measure of distant vision, not near vision; choice b does not apply to this example. The big "E" represents 20/200 vision. 20/200 is considered legally blind by most standards.

12. ***d***

Giant cell arteritis, also known as temporal arteritis, is most likely in this patient based on the results of the exam and lab. This is best diagnosed by temporal artery biopsy. Temporal arteritis is a chronic vasculitis of the medium and large vessels. A biopsy can be performed on the same day as it is suspected. Generally, patients have complaints of new onset headaches, abrupt onset of visual disturbances, jaw claudication, unexplained fever or anemia, and an elevated sedimentation rate. The average age of diagnosis is 72 years. She should be referred to neurology for evaluation today.

13. ***b***

Bell's palsy is a weakness or temporary paralysis of cranial nerve VII. It is usually idiopathic and nearly always unilateral. It is unusual to experience pain associated with Bell's palsy; it is infrequently reported. Typical symptoms include numbness on the affected side, sagging eyebrow, and possible inability to blink the eye on the affected side. If the patient is unable to blink, the eye should be lubricated to keep it moist. Bell's palsy may take weeks before it completely resolves.

14. ***d***

Carpal tunnel is an entrapment neuropathy of the median nerve at the wrist due to inflammation of the wrist tendons, transverse carpal ligament, and/or surrounding soft tissue. Compression of the median nerve produces paresthesias in the thumb, index finger, middle finger, and the radial side of the ring finger. The fifth finger is not affected.

15. ***c***

Parkinson's disease is an idiopathic neurodegenerative movement disorder characterized by 4 prominent features: bradykinesia, muscular rigidity, resting tremor, and postural instability. The pill rolling tremor is the presenting sign in 50-80% of patients with Parkinson's disease. Approximately 30% of patients do not present with tremor of any type.

16. A 60 year-old patient has anosmia. Which cranial nerve must be assessed?

a. **I**
b. **II**
c. **V**
d. **X**

17. What cranial nerve is responsible for hearing?

a. **II**
b. **III**
c. **V**
d. **VIII**

18. A 70 year-old patient is concerned and comes into the clinic with complaints of headache, slurred speech, and onset of symptoms within the last 60 minutes. When the patient is examined, her complaints are confirmed by the examiner. What is the likely etiology of this event?

a. **Migraine headache**
b. **Alcohol intoxication**
c. **Stroke**
d. **Bell's palsy**

19. A patient who is 82 years old is brought into the clinic. His wife states that he was working in his garden today and became disoriented and had slurred speech. She helped him back into the house, gave him cool fluids, and within 15 minutes his symptoms resolved. He appears in his usual state of health when he is examined. He states that although he was scared by the event, he feels fine now. How should the nurse practitioner proceed?

a. **Prescribe an aspirin daily.**
b. **Re-examine him tomorrow.**
c. **Send him to the emergency department.**
d. **Order an EKG.**

20. A patient reports a history of transient ischemic attack (TIA) 6 months ago. His daily medications are lisinopril, pravastatin, and metformin. After advising him to quit smoking, what intervention is most important in helping to prevent stroke in him?

a. **Auscultation of carotid arteries at each visit**
b. **Taking a baby aspirin daily**
c. **Assessing hemoglobin A1C every 3-6 months**
d. **Encouraging smoking cessation at each visit**

16. ***a***
Anosmia refers to the inability to smell. Cranial nerve I is the olfactory nerve and is not usually tested. However, cranial nerve I lesions do occur. Anosmia would be a clinical manifestation of this. If CN I is assessed, the examiner uses a familiar smell like coffee or peppermint and asks the examinee to identify the smell. The inability to do this with a familiar smell is termed anosmia.

17. ***d***
Cranial nerve VIII is responsible for hearing. Cranial nerve II is the optic nerve and is responsible for vision. Cranial nerve III is partly responsible for eye movement. Cranial nerve V is the facial nerve and is responsible for sensation of the face. It is tested by a light touch on the patient's forehead.

18. ***c***
Migraine headache can produce headache and numbness of the face. However, migraine risk decreases as age increases and is unlikely of new onset in this 70 year-old patient. Stroke increases as age increases. Bell's palsy is accompanied by facial numbness and sometimes slurred speech occurs if the upper lip is affected, but, headache does not accompany Bell's palsy. Alcohol intoxication might be considered, but, stroke must be ruled out. When headache accompanies stroke, it is often hemorrhagic stroke, but ischemic stroke can cause headache too.

19. ***c***
This patient likely suffered a transient ischemic attack. He needs urgent evaluation with head CT and/or MRI, ECG, lab work (CBC, PTT, lytes, creatinine, glucose, lipids and sedimentation rate); possible magnetic resonance angiography, carotid ultrasound, and/or transcranial Doppler ultrasonography. He is at increased risk of stroke within the first 48 hours after an event like this one. On initial evaluation, the most important determination to be made is whether the etiology of the stroke or TIA is ischemic or hemorrhagic. After this determination, treatment can begin. Unfortunately, this determination cannot be made in the clinic. The patient needs urgent referral to a center where this evaluation and possible treatment can be performed.

20. ***b***
Antiplatelet therapy, usually aspirin, inhibits the enzyme cyclooxygenase and reduces thromboxane A2 production, which stimulates platelet aggregation. Risk of ischemic stroke is reduced. The dosage of aspirin needed to prevent an event is debatable. Most studies found that 75- 150 mg daily was as effective in preventing stroke as was higher doses. Lower doses of aspirin are associated with less GI toxicity and subsequent side effects.

21. An elderly patient is at increased risk of stroke and takes an aspirin daily. Aspirin use in this patient is an example of:

a. primary prevention.
b. secondary prevention.
c. tertiary prevention.
d. primary or secondary.

22. Which of the following criteria is attributed to migraine headache without aura?

a. Pain is episodic during the headache
b. Pain lasts 4-72 hours
c. There are underlying neurologic abnormalities
d. Vascular abnormalities are visible with imaging

23. Which headache listed below is more likely to be triggered by food?

a. Cluster
b. Migraine
c. Tension
d. Vascular

24. Most patients with migraine headache symptoms do not need imaging for diagnosis. Which finding in a patient with migraine headache symptoms would compel the examiner to order an imaging study?

a. First occurrence with typical migraine symptoms
b. Nausea and photophobia
c. Rapidly increasing frequency of headache
d. Fully reversible speech disturbance

25. A 62 year-old female patient presents to the clinic with very recent onset of intermittent but severe facial pain over the right cheek. She is diagnosed with trigeminal neuralgia. What assessment finding is typical of this?

a. Pain is much worse with sticking her tongue out
b. Pain is better with light touch over the affected area
c. Pain is relieved with NSAIDs
d. Pain may be triggered with touch of the right cheek

21. *a*
Primary prevention refers to an action that has the potential to prevent an event prior to its occurrence. Secondary prevention refers to an intervention demonstrated to help prevent a second occurrence of a deleterious event; or may refer to an intervention designed for early detection. Tertiary prevention is an action designed to prevent additional deleterious events from occurring.

22. *b*
In order to meet International Headache Society criteria for a migraine headache without aura, the following 5 criteria must be met: 1) headache lasts between 4-72 hours, 2) headache has at least 2 of the following characteristics: unilateral location, pulsating quality, moderate to severe in intensity, aggravated by routine activity, 3) during the headache at least one of the following occurs: nausea and/or vomiting, photophobia or phonophobia, 4) at least 5 attacks occur which fulfill these criteria, and 5) there is no underlying disease.

23. *b*
Migraine headaches are more likely to be triggered by food than tension headaches or others. Common food triggers are alcohol, chocolate, aged cheeses, nuts, nitrates, nitrites, and caffeine.

24. *c*
Fully reversible speech disturbance in conjunction with migraine type symptoms likely represents a typical aura. Nausea and photophobia are typical with migraine headaches. A normal neurological exam in conjunction with typical migraine symptoms, even on first occurrence, does not compel the examiner to order an imaging study. A headache with rapidly increasing frequency, history of lack of coordination, localized neurologic symptoms, headache that awakens the patient from sleep all increase the likelihood that a neurologic abnormality exists. Any of these findings should compel the examiner to order an imaging study. The study most likely to be ordered is a CT scan or MRI with and without contrast. However, an MRA maybe ordered depending on the suspected underlying abnormality.

25. *d*
Trigeminal neuralgia is a common cause of severe facial pain. It is described by patients as electric or shocking pain. Triggers for pain are light touch to the affected area, chewing, cool breeze on the cheek, and smiling or grimacing. It is more common in older adults.

26. A patient complains of severe facial pain on the right side of her face. She states that her symptoms have gotten worse over the past 48 hours. Which diagnosis below is NOT part of the differential diagnosis?

   a. **Bell's palsy**
   b. **Trigeminal neuralgia**
   c. **Tooth abscess**
   d. **Shingles**

26. *a*

Bell's palsy does not produce pain. It usually produces symptoms over several hours. Common symptoms include sagging eyebrow, an impaired eye blink or the inability to blink the eye on the affected side, mouth drawn up on the affected side. The facial nerve, Cranial Nerve VII, is affected in patients who present with Bell's palsy.

Orthopedic Disorders

1. What joints are least commonly involved in osteoarthritis?

   a. **Fingers**
   b. **Wrists**
   c. **Hips**
   d. **Knees**

2. An x-ray report of a patient's painful right knee indicates "joint space narrowing". What does this mean?

   a. **The patient is aging**
   b. **Gout is present**
   c. **This is a normal finding**
   d. **Loss of cartilage has occurred**

3. Which symptom can be used to rule out a fracture?

   a. **Degree of pain**
   b. **Extent of mobility**
   c. **Degree of swelling**
   d. **No symptom can rule out a fracture**

4. A long distance runner is diagnosed with a tibial stress fracture. Which statement is true about the injury?

   a. **The pain worsens with rest.**
   b. **The patient should be casted for 6 weeks.**
   c. **Plain x-rays will confirm the diagnosis.**
   d. **Rest and an alternative activity are recommended.**

5. What is the most prevalent skeletal problem in the United States?

   a. **Osteoarthritis**
   b. **Stress fractures**
   c. **Osteoporosis**
   d. **Gouty arthritis**

1. *b*

Osteoarthritis (OA) is characterized by destruction of the articular cartilage. The fingers, knees, hips, and spine are most commonly affected. OA is more common in men before age 45 years, but is more common in females after age 55 years. Often osteophytes form in the diseased joints. The most commonly involved joints are found in the fingers.

2. *d*

In the knee, joint space narrowing indicates a loss of articular cartilage and usually worsening osteoarthritis. As cartilage wears away, the meniscus becomes displaced and the space normally found in the joint becomes narrowed. This is referred to as "joint space narrowing". This can occur as a result of osteoarthritis but is seen in rheumatoid arthritis, ankylosing spondylitis, and in some connective tissue disorders.

3. *d*

A fracture of a bone generally results in swelling, pain, and decreased mobility due to swelling and/or pain. Fractures are not asymptomatic events, but no single symptom can rule a fracture out. Fractures are usually the result of trauma, but tumor, osteoporosis, and cancer should be considered if history suggests this.

4. *d*

Stress fractures are an example of an overuse injury. These occur in patients who are engaged in repetitive physical activities. These commonly occur in the feet and shins, though it is usually unilateral. X-rays usually do not demonstrate stress fractures, so history and exam are important. Treatment involves resting the injured joint. Engaging in an alternative exercise (termed, cross-training) that does not stress the fractured area, is recommended. One example of cross training is swimming. Casting and crutches are reserved for use when conservative treatments are not effective.

5. *a*

Osteoarthritis (OA) is the most common form of arthritis and the most common skeletal abnormality listed above. Risk factors for OA are known to be advancing age, female gender, obesity, and joint injuries. Joint injuries or fractures from earlier decades will increase the likelihood of OA in the affected joint.

6. Which of the following tests, if positive, is part of the criteria for systemic lupus erythematosus (SLE)?

   a. **Antinuclear antibody (ANA)**
   b. **Rheumatoid factor**
   c. **Elevated liver function studies**
   d. **Erythrocyte sedimentation rate (ESR)**

7. A 75 year-old patient has osteoarthritis and pain. Which of the following medications increases the risk of a GI related ulceration?

   a. **Celecoxib**
   b. **Warfarin**
   c. **Tramadol**
   d. **Amitriptyline**

8. A 16 year-old male plays trumpet in the school marching band. He has had marching practice every day for the last week. Today he complains of pain in his left midfoot. The foot is neither swollen nor red. What is the most likely diagnosis in the differential?

   a. **Strain**
   b. **Bursitis**
   c. **Stress fracture**
   d. **Tendonitis**

9. A patient presents with right shoulder pain (7/10 on the pain scale) after an acute shoulder injury yesterday. He fell against a brick wall while working at his home. He reports pain that radiates into his upper arm. How should this be managed?

   a. **Immobilize the right shoulder for 3 days**
   b. **Rest, ice, and naproxen for one week**
   c. **Order an x-ray of the right shoulder**
   d. **Prescribe physical therapy for the patient**

10. A 50 year-old patient reports acute pain in his lower back that started 2 weeks ago after working in his yard. The pain radiates into his right leg intermittently. He has been managing his pain with over the counter NSAIDs. There are no red flags in his history or exam. When should consideration be given to imaging studies?

   a. **Now**
   b. **At 4 weeks**
   c. **At 8 weeks**
   d. **There is no need**

6. ***a***
The criteria for diagnosis of lupus have been established by the American College of Rheumatology. It includes 11 criteria: malar rash, discoid rash, sun-related rash, painless oral ulcerations, joint pain or swelling involving two or more joints, inflammation involving the heart or lungs, renal disorder, a non-specified neurological disorder (seizures or psychosis), CBC abnormalities such as anemia, leukopenia, or thrombocytopenia, immunologic disorders (another positive autoimmune test such as an anti-phospholipid antibody test), or positive ANA. Having 4 or more of these criteria either at one time or over time can constitute a diagnosis of SLE. An elevated sedimentation rate is a very non-specific measure of inflammation.

7. ***a***
Celecoxib is an NSAID. All NSAIDs increase the risk of upper and lower GI ulcerations. Other lower GI complications include perforation, stricture, anemia, and hypoalbuminemia. Warfarin does not increase the risk of ulceration, but if ulceration occurs, the risk of bleeding is greatly increased. Neither tramadol nor amitriptyline is considered ulcerogenic.

8. ***c***
This is a stress fracture and commonly occurs with an abrupt increase in activity, especially marching. A stress fracture of the metatarsals is commonly called a "march" fracture because it is frequently seen in soldiers who march. This occurs because of an increase in weight-bearing loads on the metatarsals. Stress fractures occur more commonly in patients with flat feet. Stress fractures of the 2nd, 3rd, and 4th metatarsals account for 90% of metatarsal stress fractures.

9. ***c***
An x-ray is generally the initial test used to evaluate trauma that results in acute pain. An x-ray could demonstrate fracture of the clavicle or humerus, or dislocation. It would not be helpful for evaluation of most soft tissue injuries. No other interventions are appropriate until fracture and dislocation have been ruled out.

10. ***b***
Imaging studies are usually not indicated for uncomplicated acute low back pain. The probable precipitant, working in his yard, is a common cause of low back pain. As long as pain is of less than 4 weeks duration and there are no red flags in history or exam, radiologic tests can be delayed. Radiologic studies should be considered initially in selected patients with history of cancer, age greater than 50 years, significant trauma or neurologic deficits, or pain inconsistent with history.

11. A 65 year-old female complains of left medial knee pain. She has been told that she has arthritis in this knee. Where would the pain be located?

a. **Medially, radiating into the upper thigh**
b. **Medially, along the joint line**
c. **About an inch above the medial knee joint line**
d. **About an inch below the medial knee joint line**

12. A 60 year-old patient who is otherwise healthy, presents with acute onset of right knee pain. She denies injury but reports that she walked up a lot of steps yesterday. She is diagnosed with prepatellar bursitis. What is a common finding?

a. **Limping and erythema about the anterior knee**
b. **Swelling and pain to touch of the anterior knee**
c. **Posterior knee pain, anterior knee edema, and redness**
d. **Tenderness to touch of the tibial tubercle**

13. A 55 year-old male patient describes severe pain at the base of his left first toe. He is limping and says he can't remember hurting his toe. Which symptom below suggests something other than gout?

a. **Pain**
b. **Elevated sedimentation rate**
c. **Erythema**
d. **Fever**

14. An 80 year-old patient is very active but presents today with posterior hip pain for the past week. Which of the following is *least* likely part of the differential diagnosis?

a. **Osteoarthritis**
b. **Sacroiliac joint disease**
c. **Lumbar radiculopathy**
d. **Herpes zoster**

15. A 75 year-old female, who knits daily, has a positive Finkelstein test. What is her likely diagnosis?

a. **Gamekeeper's thumb**
b. **De Quervain's tenosynovitis**
c. **Osteoarthritis of the thumb**
d. **Trigger thumb**

11. ***b***

The classic pain pattern described by patients with arthritis in the medial aspect of the knee is along the joint line. This is also the common presentation for patients who have tears to the medial collateral ligament, medial meniscal tears, or fracture of the tibial plateau. Pain located immediately below (within 2-4 cm.) the joint line may be anserine bursitis.

12. ***b***

Prepatellar bursitis is often precipitated by an increase in activity involving the knee, such as was given in history by this patient. If it was infectious in origin, erythema would be present, but based on this patient's history and absence of risk factors, that is less likely. Prepatellar bursitis is characterized by swelling and inflammatory changes anterior to the patella, no symptoms posteriorly. The patient probably will limp due to pain. Tenderness to touch of the tibial tubercle is characteristic of Osgood Schlatter disease, but, is common in an under 19 years age group.

13. ***d***

This presentation is classic for gout except that gout is not associated with fever. This presentation coupled with fever should prompt the examiner to suspect septic arthritis. If this is the presentation, this patient should have a joint tap (or refer to an orthopedic surgeon). Synovial fluid will be aspirated and sent to the laboratory for evaluation. The fluid will contain white cells and bacteria if infection is present.

14. ***a***

The most common presentation of osteoarthritis of the hip involves anterior hip pain, not posterior hip pain. Posterior hip pain is the least common pain pattern associated with the hip. This should raise suspicion of pain referred from another area, such as the SI joint, the lumbar area, or herpes zoster. Anterior hip pain, typical of osteoarthritis, radiates into the groin.

15. ***b***

De Quervain's tenosynovitis represents inflammation of the extensor and flexor tendons in the thumb. It is 8x more common in women than men and may accompany pregnancy, trauma, or some systemic diseases like rheumatoid arthritis. The classic finding in de Quervain's tenosynovitis is a positive Finkelstein test. Pain can radiate up the forearm. The probable precipitant is this patient's daily knitting.

16. Which symptoms are most commonly found in a patient with rheumatoid arthritis?

- **a. Morning stiffness, positive rheumatoid antigen and antinuclear antibody**
- **b. Fever, symmetrical joint involvement, normal sedimentation rate**
- **c. Asymmetrical joint involvement, male gender, pain**
- **d. Nodular lesion on the elbow, negative sedimentation rate, positive antinuclear antibody**

17. The "get up and go" test in an elderly patient is used to evaluate:

- **a. risk for falls.**
- **b. lower extremity strength.**
- **c. mental acuity.**
- **d. driving safety.**

18. A 75 year-old has pain from osteoarthritis in her right knee. What intervention is considered first line to treat her pain?

- **a. Exercise**
- **b. Acetaminophen**
- **c. Ibuprofen**
- **d. Tramadol**

19. What medication is recommended by American College of Rheumatology as a first line agent for a patient who has been unsuccessful with non-pharmacologic interventions for osteoarthritis pain?

- **a. Naproxen**
- **b. Acetaminophen**
- **c. Ibuprofen**
- **d. Tramadol**

20. An adolescent athlete has injured his ankle playing basketball. He has right ankle pain, ecchymosis, significant edema, and he is unable to bear weight at the time of the clinical exam. Which diagnosis is *least* likely?

- **a. An avulsion fracture**
- **b. Grade I sprain**
- **c. Grade II sprain**
- **d. Grade III sprain**

16. *a*
Rheumatoid arthritis is a difficult diagnosis to make because there are many factors to evaluate and none are consistently positive in all patients. Clinical clues that should cause the examiner to suspect rheumatoid arthritis are symmetrical peripheral polyarthritis, morning stiffness lasting greater than one hour, the presence of rheumatoid nodules, bone erosions on x-ray, positive sedimentation rate as an early phase reactant, positive rheumatoid antigen, and positive antinuclear antibody. None of these characteristics are positive in all patients and other autoimmune rheumatic diseases can be part of the differential.

17. *a*
The "get up and go" test is used to evaluate musculoskeletal function. The patient is asked to rise from a seated position in an armchair, walk across the room, turn around, and return to the chair. This test evaluates the patient's gait, balance, leg strength, and vestibular function. It should be assessed in patients who report a fall or who present after a fall but who appear without injury.

18. *a*
American College of Rheumatology recommends exercise as first line treatment for osteoarthritis. Since osteoarthritis is a chronic condition, medications are not the initial intervention for pain relief. Non-pharmacologic interventions like heat and exercise are always attempted initially. When initial interventions are unsuccessful, they are continued and medications are added. Relief of pain is the primary indication for use of medications.

19. *b*
Osteoarthritis is a chronic condition and non-pharmacologic interventions should be tried initially. When these do not bring about relief of pain, or bring incomplete relief of pain, medications should be considered. Initially, acetaminophen up to 650 mg four times daily can be tried. Hepatotoxicity must be monitored, but is not common using this dose. Unfortunately, acetaminophen is less effective at pain relief than NSAIDs like ibuprofen or naproxen. However, these are associated with greater risk and so should not be used if a medication associated with less risk brings relief. This is especially true in an elderly patient.

20. *b*
Ankle sprains are generally graded based on clinical signs. A grade I sprain results from minimal stretching or small tears in the ligament. There is mild tenderness and edema, and the patient is able to bear weight. A grade II sprain is more significant. The clinical signs are more severe stretching and tearing of ligament(s) with moderate pain, edema, tenderness, and ecchymosis. Weight bearing is painful, but the patient can walk. A grade III sprain is the most severe. It involves complete tear of a ligament. There is joint instability, severe pain, edema, tenderness, and ecchymosis. Patients usually are unable to bear weight due to pain. An avulsion fracture could produce the same symptoms described above. This patient needs an x-ray to rule out fracture.

21. The Ottawa ankle rules help the examiner determine when:

a. **an inversion ankle injury has occurred.**
b. **an anterior talofibular fracture has occurred.**
c. **x-rays are needed with a suspected ankle sprain.**
d. **referral to orthopedics should occur.**

22. When should functional rehabilitation occur once a patient has had an ankle or knee sprain?

a. **The day of the injury**
b. **About 5 days post-injury**
c. **2-3 weeks after injury**
d. **When the patient's pain level allows**

23. Management of a sprained ankle includes:

a. **x-rays.**
b. **rest, ice, compression, elevation.**
c. **anti-inflammatory medications.**
d. **activity as tolerated.**

24. What does a positive anterior drawer test demonstrate with an injured knee?

a. **Injury to the lateral meniscus**
b. **Instability of the anterior cruciate ligament**
c. **Stability of the posterior cruciate ligament**
d. **Stability of the lateral knee**

25. Which diagnosis is the *least* likely cause of extrinsic shoulder pain?

a. **Angina**
b. **Hepatobiliary disease**
c. **Pneumonia**
d. **Gout**

21. ***c***
The Ottawa ankle rules have been extensively tested on adults and pediatric patients who present with acute ankle pain. They direct the examiner to order ankle or foot x-rays when certain criteria are met. When the rules are followed, unnecessary x-rays are significantly reduced. The examiner should order x-rays when the patient has ankle or midfoot pain/bone tenderness, has bone tenderness at the base of the 5th metatarsal, or is unable to bear weight for four steps when examined.

22. ***a***
Early functional rehab (beginning the day of the injury) speeds time of recovery and allows resumption of activities much earlier than not. Early rehab includes range of motion exercises initially, with progression to muscle strengthening, proprioception, and activity-specific training (walking, speed walking, running).

23. ***b***
X-rays are not needed for a sprain. This question stem states the patient's injury. RICE is the acronym for rest, ice, compression, and elevation. Anti-inflammatory medications are recommended, but one NSAID has not been shown to be superior to another.

24. ***b***
The anterior cruciate ligament (ACL) is often injured in athletes. The typical injury occurs when the foot is planted and the knee is extended; or in collision injuries such as in football, basketball, or soccer. Pain is reported by the athlete immediately after the injury. To perform the anterior drawer test, the patient lies down on his back and his knee is flexed to 90 degrees. Once the foot is stabilized, the tibia is grasped and forcibly pulled toward the examiner. Abnormal movement (or laxity) is assessed by comparing the injured knee to the opposite knee.

25. ***d***
The origin of shoulder pain can be intrinsic or extrinsic. In evaluation of a patient with shoulder pain, this is the initial determination. The shoulder is a common joint where pain is extrinsic. In the cardiovascular system, pain can be due to myocardial ischemia or thoracic outlet syndrome. In the abdomen, hepatobiliary disease, ectopic pregnancy or splenic injury can produce shoulder pain. Infectious organisms in the joint (intrinsic pain) or pneumonia can produce shoulder pain. Gout has a propensity for distal joints, not the shoulder.

26. The drop arm test is used to assess patients with suspected:

a. **cervical injury.**
b. **rotator cuff injury.**
c. **impingement syndrome.**
d. **malingering.**

27. Which of the following is NOT true regarding cervical whiplash injury?

a. **This occurs after a traumatic event.**
b. **It may be accompanied by severe pain, spasm.**
c. **Is identifiable on MRI or CT, but not x-ray.**
d. **Occipital pain and headache can occur.**

26. *b*
Rotator cuff injury is one of the most common causes of shoulder pain. The rotator cuff is composed of 4 muscles. The one most susceptible to injury is the supraspinatus. Consequently, this is the one most commonly torn. To assess whether the supraspinatus muscle is intact, the drop arm test is performed. The patient is asked to abduct his affected arm laterally to 90 degrees. He is then asked to slowly lower it to his side. A positive test is noted when the arm "drops". This usually indicates that the supraspinatus is injured.

27. *c*
Whiplash injury commonly follows a car accident when a rear collision is involved. Loss of range of motion is common as is delayed pain sensation. Pain may not be perceived until the next day. There is usually no identifiable abnormality on x-ray, CT scan, or MRI. Sometimes muscle spasm can be identified with an imaging study, but, there is usually no abnormality found despite a complaint of pain by the patient.

Pregnancy

1. A female who is being counseled preconceptually is found to have a negative rubella titer. If she is immunized today, for how long should she avoid pregnancy?

   a. 1 month
   b. 3 months
   c. 6 months
   d. 12 months

2. What immunizations may be safely administered during the first trimester of pregnancy?

   a. MMR and Hepatitis B
   b. Tdap and inactive influenza
   c. Pneumococcal and varicella
   d. Hepatitis A and varicella

3. The NP suspects that a pregnant patient may have been physically abused by a domestic partner. The NP knows that:

   a. abuse often ends in homicide by the abuser.
   b. abuse can worsen during pregnancy.
   c. this is reportable in all 50 states.
   d. this will usually end when the pregnancy ends.

4. The classic symptoms of an ectopic pregnancy are:

   a. shoulder pain, bleeding, amenorrhea.
   b. abdominal pain, nausea, vaginal bleeding.
   c. amenorrhea, vaginal bleeding, abdominal pain.
   d. abdominal pain, vaginal discharge, fever.

5. Few pregnant patients actually deliver on their due dates. Why is a due date established?

   a. To evaluate fetal growth
   b. For evaluation of maternal uterine size
   c. For determination of adequate fetal nutrition
   d. To determine timing of maternal/fetal screenings

1. *a*
Women of childbearing age should be advised to avoid pregnancy for 28 days after immunization with MMR. However, CDC has collected data on women who have accidentally received the immunization while pregnant, and there has been no documented injury to offspring. The vaccine is safe for women who are breastfeeding even though the rubella virus is excreted in breast milk. It is safe for young children of pregnant mothers to be immunized with MMR because infection is not transmitted from immunized individuals.

2. *b*
Tdap and inactive influenza immunizations can be safely given during the first trimester if needed by the pregnant patient. Live and attenuated immunizations should not be given during pregnancy. Therefore, MMR and varicella should not be given during pregnancy. CDC recommends pneumococcal, hepatitis A, and hepatitis B vaccines during pregnancy only if there is some risk factor present; otherwise, these should be delayed until pregnancy has terminated. Influenza may be given, but it must be inactivated.

3. *b*
The incidence of abuse during pregnancy ranges between 7-20% and is higher when pregnancies are unplanned. This percentage is higher than gestational diabetes and pre-eclampsia. Screening is routinely performed for these 2 conditions. Domestic violence often begins during pregnancy and can accelerate when it has existed prior to pregnancy. Therefore, it is important to screen. Unfortunately, this is not reportable in all 50 states.

4. *c*
A majority of patients with ectopic pregnancy report these common symptoms: abdominal pain: 99%, amenorrhea: 74%, and vaginal bleeding: 56%. Classic symptoms of an ectopic pregnancy usually appear 6-8 weeks after the last menstrual period. The usual symptoms of pregnancy are also present. Shoulder pain can be present after the tube has ruptured because blood irritates the diaphragm producing referred pain. Abdominal pain, vaginal discharge and fever should cause the examiner to think of an infection, usually associated with sexually transmitted diseases.

5. *d*
Accurate dating is critical so that maternal and fetal screening tests may be done at the most appropriate time. If a screening test is supposed to take place at 20 weeks, and it is done too early, the opportunity to identify an abnormality may be missed. In the U.S., if a last menstrual period (LMP) cannot be established, or a woman becomes pregnant while taking contraceptives, an ultrasound should be performed.

6. In order to establish pregnancy, a pregnancy test of the urine or blood is routinely performed. This test assesses for:

  a. **presence of beta hCG.**
  b. **quantity of beta hCG.**
  c. **fetal immunoglobulins.**
  d. **pregnancy hormones.**

7. A patient who is found to be pregnant has asymptomatic bacteriuria. How should this be managed?

  a. **Force fluids only**
  b. **Prescribe trimethoprim-sulfamethoxazole**
  c. **Prescribe nitrofurantoin**
  d. **Prescribe amoxicillin**

8. A 17 year-old female is found to be pregnant. What is the most important part of her initial screening?

  a. **Toxoplasmosis**
  b. **Hepatitis A and B**
  c. **Iron deficiency anemia**
  d. **STDs and HIV**

9. A 24 year-old pregnant patient has a TSH performed. The most likely reason for this is because:

  a. **she has hypothyroidism.**
  b. **it is routinely done in pregnant women.**
  c. **she is losing weight.**
  d. **she has iron deficiency anemia.**

10. An ultrasound is commonly performed during early pregnancy because it:

  a. **predicts fetal outcomes.**
  b. **improves maternal outcomes.**
  c. **identifies fetal malformations.**
  d. **reduces need for later ultrasounds.**

6. ***a***

Whether performed on urine or blood, the presence of the beta subunit of human chorionic gonadotropin (hCG) indicates pregnancy. This can be found in detectable quantities in the first morning urine or at any time in a serum sample from a pregnant woman. Both tests are highly sensitive. However, if the pregnancy is very early and first morning urine is NOT used, the urine test could be negative in a pregnant patient. A serum specimen will indicate pregnancy at any time of day if it is present. Quantifying the beta hCG level is not necessarily used to diagnose pregnancy, but may be used to determine whether a pregnancy is progressing as expected since beta hCG levels are predictable during pregnancy.

7. ***c***

A pregnant patient with asymptomatic bacteriuria should be treated with an antibiotic because she is at increased risk of pyelonephritis. Trimethoprim-sulfamethoxazole is a sulfa drug and this class of medications should be avoided during pregnancy. Amoxicillin is safe to use during pregnancy but has poor coverage of the most likely pathogen, *E. coli.* Nitrofurantoin is safe for use during pregnancy and has very good coverage of the most common urinary tract pathogens.

8. ***d***

Routine prenatal screening is important for all pregnant women. As a sexually active adolescent, she is at high risk for STDs and should be screened. These screenings include the most common STDs as well as HIV, hepatitis B and C. Hepatitis A is not transmitted to the fetus. Iron deficiency anemia is very common but is easy to correct. Toxoplasmosis is contracted after exposure to feces of cats and undercooked meats.

9. ***a***

Routine screening for hypothyroidism is not performed during pregnancy. However, ACOG (American College of Obstetricians and Gynecologists) recommends screening when a patient has a personal history of hypothyroidism, a family history of hypothyroidism, or is symptomatic. ACOG also recommends screening if another disease is present which is associated with thyroid dysfunction, like gestational diabetes.

10. ***c***

Ultrasounds are excellent tools for identifying fetal malformations. They are helpful in detecting multiple fetuses, status of the placenta, and assessing gestational age. While it may be argued that ultrasound use improves outcomes in the fetus or mother, this is not why they are commonly performed during pregnancy. There is no evidence that performing an ultrasound early in pregnancy eliminates or reduces the need for ultrasounds later in pregnancy.

11. A pregnant patient asks if engaging in sexual activity will place her fetus at increased risk. The nurse practitioner responds:

- **a. there is absolutely no increased risk to the fetus.**
- **b. there is a slight cardiovascular risk to the fetus.**
- **c. this may stimulate labor and so should be avoided.**
- **d. this may increase the risk of pre-term labor.**

12. A pregnant patient is 30 weeks gestation. She wants to travel to a higher elevation in order to go on a hiking trip. She will fly in an airplane. The nurse practitioner knows:

- **a. travel on an airplane at this period during pregnancy is risky.**
- **b. travel to a city of high altitude can precipitate pre-term labor.**
- **c. this may precipitate a change in fetal heart rate.**
- **d. there is no risk associated with this particular trip.**

13. Routine screening for gestational diabetes:

- **a. takes place only if the mother is symptomatic.**
- **b. at about 16-20 weeks.**
- **c. at about 24-28 weeks.**
- **d. routinely in each trimester.**

14. A patient in her first trimester of pregnancy is found to be infected with chlamydia and gonorrhea. Which statement below is true?

- **a. She should be treated now and re-screened later in pregnancy.**
- **b. She should be treated in the second trimester.**
- **c. She should be screened for other STDs later in pregnancy.**
- **d. She should be treated now and re-screened if symptoms re-appear.**

15. When should folic acid be initiated in a female patient contemplating pregnancy?

- **a. Now**
- **b. At the diagnosis of pregnancy**
- **c. In the second trimester**
- **d. In the third trimester**

11. ***d***
Sexual activity during pregnancy could precipitate pre-term labor because the lower uterine segment may be physically stimulated. Additionally, oxytocin is released which may precipitate pre-term labor. However, in the absence of complications associated with the pregnancy, sexual activity is not contraindicated. If vaginal discharge or bleeding occurs; or rupture of membranes occurs, sexual intercourse should be avoided until assessed by the patient's provider.

12. ***b***
There is no risk for the pregnant patient (prior to 35-36 weeks) who is traveling in an airplane with a pressurized cabin. Travel to a city of moderate or high altitude may impose the risk of pre-term labor and bleeding complications. She may be allowed to hike at higher elevations but she should be apprised of the potential risks to her and the fetus. These include dehydration, shortness of breath, tachycardia, pre-term labor, and increased risk of bleeding complications. Practically speaking, serious trauma could occur if she falls. Her balance may be compromised at 30 weeks and falling might be likely. In any event, she should have adequate time to acclimate at this higher elevation before engaging in physical activities like hiking.

13. ***c***
The routine time for screening is at 24-28 weeks. This has been identified as the ideal time because she is more likely to exhibit elevations in glucose at 24-28 weeks due to placental hormones that increase insulin insensitivity. This is also a good time to initiate interventions that will decrease complications in the fetus associated with glucose elevations. If the pregnant patient has risk factors or symptoms of diabetes, she can be screened earlier in pregnancy, routinely at 24-28 weeks, and later if warranted.

14. ***a***
She should be treated for chlamydia and gonorrhea now. Since the percentage of patients who become re-infected with an STD later in pregnancy (even after being treated and educated) is great, this patient should be re-screened later in pregnancy regardless of whether symptoms emerge. Deleterious effects can occur if she is infected and left untreated.

15. ***a***
Folic acid has been found to significantly decrease the incidence of neural tube defects (NTD). It should be supplemented at a dosage of 0.4 mg daily in all women of child bearing age before becoming pregnant. Folate plays an essential role in synthesis of amino acids and DNA. Since these are critical in cell division and adequate amounts should be on board when cell division begins, folic acid should be taken preconceptually. NTDs are the second most common congenital anomaly.

16. All of the factors listed below increase the risk of ectopic pregnancy. Which one confers the lowest risk?

a. **Prior history of ectopic pregnancy**
b. **Intrauterine device use**
c. **History of pelvic inflammatory disease**
d. **Young age**

17. A pregnant patient with urinary frequency is found to have a UTI. What drug is safest to treat this?

a. **Doxycycline**
b. **Amoxicillin**
c. **Ciprofloxacin**
d. **Nitrofurantoin**

18. A pregnant patient complains of lower extremity edema and asks for a "fluid pill". The NP explains that:

a. **fluid pills will not be effective.**
b. **fluid pills are safe to use during pregnancy.**
c. **this could signify gestational hypertension.**
d. **this is best treated with rest and elevation of the legs.**

19. Persistent, intractable vomiting during pregnancy is:

a. **morning sickness.**
b. **hyperemesis gravidarum.**
c. **hydatiform mole.**
d. **probably multiple gestation.**

20. A patient has a positive pregnancy test that she performed using an over the counter kit. What are the chances that a serum pregnancy test will be negative?

a. **About 25%**
b. **About 10%**
c. **About 50%**
d. **Almost none**

16. ***d***
In an ectopic pregnancy, the developing embryo becomes implanted outside the uterus. A common site is the fallopian tube. Young age is not considered a risk factor for ectopic pregnancy. The other choices all confer high risk of ectopic pregnancy. Other high risk factors are previous tubal surgery or pathology, and tubal ligation.

17. ***d***
Medication safety during pregnancy is of utmost concern. Therefore, medications are rated according to safety for the developing fetus. In the current rating system, nitrofurantoin is the safest and most efficacious medication listed. Amoxicillin is as safe as nitrofurantoin but has a lower efficacy against typical urinary tract pathogens. Doxycycline is associated with fetal tooth discoloration and so it should be avoided. Ciprofloxacin is not recommended during pregnancy due to potential problems with bone and cartilage formation.

18. ***d***
It is very common during pregnancy to have lower extremity edema. While this should be monitored to make certain that other more serious conditions are not occurring (pre-eclampsia, heart failure, etc.), this is best treated with rest and elevation of the legs. Lower extremity edema is no longer considered a criterion for pre-eclampsia.

19. ***b***
Hyperemesis gravidarum (HEG) is a severe form of nausea and vomiting which occurs during pregnancy. In contrast, morning sickness is significantly milder. A common definition used to define HEG is persistent vomiting which produces a weight loss exceeding 5% of pre-pregnancy body weight. The etiology of morning sickness and HEG is unknown.

20. ***d***
The over the counter urine pregnancy kits have very high sensitivity and specificity. Consequently, their results can be trusted. A positive urine test will correlate with positive serum results. The tests identify hCG in the specimen.

Professional Issues

1. **Who certifies nurse practitioners?**

    a. The state where they practice
    b. State board of medicine or nursing
    c. A state board of nursing
    d. A nurse practitioner certifying body

2. **A nurse practitioner's scope of practice is influenced by a number of factors. Which one does not influence scope of practice?**

    a. Code of ethics
    b. State and federal laws governing practice
    c. Court of law
    d. Educational preparation

3. **Standards of practice are established to:**

    a. regulate and control nurse practitioner practice.
    b. limit liability of nurse practitioners.
    c. protect nurse practitioners from frivolous law suits.
    d. promote autonomous practice.

4. **Licensure is:**

    a. used to establish a designated level of professional competence.
    b. contingent on certification.
    c. intended to limit entry into the profession.
    d. necessary for reimbursement.

5. **Certification:**

    a. is required by all 50 states.
    b. validates competence.
    c. is recognized by all 50 states.
    d. provides for title protection.

1. *d*
The 2 certifying bodies for adult, adult-gero and family nurse practitioners in the United States are American Nurses Credentialing Center (ANCC) and American Association of Nurse Practitioners (AANP). State boards of nursing grant a *license* to nurse practitioners in the state where they practice. Most states require certification in order to become licensed.

2. *c*
The scope of practice for nurse practitioners is established legally, ethically, and by boards of nursing and professional organizations. Scope of practice sets the boundaries and indicates what is permitted legally, etc. Scope of practice is not influenced by court of law. Scope of practice is determined by state statutes, state nursing boards, common practice in a locale, educational preparation, and others. Scope of practice can vary from state to state.

3. *a*
Standards of practice for all professionals (nurses, physicians, dentists, etc.) are established to regulate and control practice. They are intended to provide accountability for professionals and to help protect the public from unethical behavior and unsafe practice.

4. *a*
Licensure is used by many states to protect the public and establish minimal level of professional competence. Licensure and competence are two distinct recognitions and are conveyed by different organizations/bodies. Licensure and reimbursement are not usually related; however, reimbursement and certification are commonly related.

5. *b*
Certification is a process used to validate competence of an individual in an area of specialty. For example, certification exams are available for nurse practitioner graduates in the areas of family, pediatrics, women's health, adult-gerontological. While Medicare requires certification in order for a nurse practitioner to independently bill, it is not required for reimbursement by all organizations. Certification is not required by all states to practice as a nurse practitioner. Title protection is provided by licensure, not certification.

6. A nurse practitioner has worked for a large hospital as an RN. As a new nurse practitioner, she has developed a nurse practitioner managed clinic for hospital employees and is employed by the hospital. This nurse practitioner is described as a(n):

- **a. intrapreneur.**
- **b. entrepreneur.**
- **c. risk taker.**
- **d. nurse specialist.**

7. Prescriptive authority:

- **a. is a right of every practicing nurse practitioner.**
- **b. varies from state to state.**
- **c. is not part of the consensus model.**
- **d. is dependent on certification.**

8. The legal authority to practice as a nurse practitioner in any state is determined by:

- **a. state boards of nursing.**
- **b. state legislatures.**
- **c. federal guidelines.**
- **d. certification boards.**

9. A nurse practitioner gives a patient 2 weeks of sample medications that will be taken once daily by the patient. The sample medications are packaged by the drug manufacturer. The nurse practitioner's actions are an example of:

- **a. prescriptive rights.**
- **b. prescriptive authority.**
- **c. dispensing.**
- **d. administering.**

10. The name given to subjects in a research study who do not have the disease or condition being studied, but who are included in the study for comparison are:

- **a. studied subjects.**
- **b. controls.**
- **c. case series.**
- **d. cross sectionals.**

6. ***a***
An intrapreneur is someone who is able to carve out a specialty role within an existing organization, healthcare setting, or business/industrial setting. An entrepreneur is someone who assumes the financial and personal risks of owning and operating a business.

7. ***b***
Prescriptive authority refers to the ability of a nurse practitioner to work within the legal scope of practice in all 50 states. Although nurse practitioners are allowed to prescribe in all 50 states, there is great variability in how this occurs. Some states allow broader prescriptive authority, other much narrower authority.

8. ***b***
The authority to practice as a nurse practitioner is determined by each state's legislature. Rules and regulations may be promulgated by state boards of nursing that reflect scope of practice of nurse practitioners specific to that state. Certification boards like ANCC and AANP "certify" that a nurse practitioner has met the requirements set by the certifying body.

9. ***c***
Although definitions vary from state to state, a reasonable definition of dispensing is the legal right to select (as from stock) and/or label a medication to be self-administered by a patient. Most states allow registered nurses to dispense medications provided they are pre-packaged. A registered nurse is not allowed to prescribe the medication being dispensed. Administering usually refers to the act of giving a single dose of a medication to a patient. Medication administration may be performed by nurses in all states.

10. ***b***
Studied subjects are those members of a study who have a specific disease or condition of interest or who are receiving a specific treatment. Case series may refer to an observational study where a group of patients with interesting characteristics are studied. Cross sectional is a type of observational study where a particular characteristic is studied at one time rather than over time. Controls are commonly employed in many types of research studies.

11. The nurse practitioner decides to study a group of patients who are trying to quit smoking. They all will be taking the same type of medication for 42 days to help them stop smoking. The patients have agreed to return to the clinic once weekly for the study's duration. This type of study design is termed:

a. **experimental study.**
b. **cohort study.**
c. **case control study.**
d. **controlled trial.**

12. A nurse practitioner knows that she is HIV positive. She is employed in a private clinic and performs wellness exams on ambulatory adults. The nurse practitioner:

a. **is obligated to inform her employer of her HIV status.**
b. **is obligated to inform her patients of her HIV status.**
c. **is under no obligation to inform anyone.**
d. **is under obligation to inform the patient if she performs invasive procedures.**

13. A nurse practitioner is working in a minor care area of an emergency department. An illegal immigrant has a puncture wound caused by an unknown sharp object in a trash container. A dirty needle is suspected. The nurse practitioner:

a. **should administer a tetanus injection only since the patient has no medical insurance.**
b. **should prescribe appropriate medications for HIV exposure even though the nurse practitioner knows the patient can't afford them.**
c. **should not mention the possibility of HIV exposure from a dirty needle to the patient.**
d. **can offer to buy the HIV medications for $50 with the professional discount at the pharmacy next door.**

14. The nurse practitioner is examining an elderly patient with dementia. She is noted to have bruises on her arms and on her posterior thoracic area. The nurse practitioner suspects elder abuse, but cannot be certain. The daughter of this elderly patient is her caregiver. The daughter is a patient of the nurse practitioner. What should the nurse practitioner do?

a. **Do not report the abuse until the NP is certain of it.**
b. **Rule out elder abuse since her daughter is the caregiver.**
c. **Report it to the appropriate authorities.**
d. **Ask the daughter if she is abusing her mother.**

11. ***b***
A cohort study describes an observational study that is prospective in nature, such as the case with this group of smokers. Cohort studies usually ask the question, "what will happen?" A case control study looks backward in time (retrospective). Case control studies usually ask the question, "what happened?" A controlled trial is an experimental study, not observational.

12. ***c***
The nurse practitioner's health information is protected health information. She is not obligated to inform her employer, patient, or state board of nursing as long as the performance of her job does not impose unnecessary risk to anyone.

13. ***b***
The standard of care followed by the nurse practitioner should not depend on whether the patient has insurance or not. It is unethical to not properly inform the patient of risks he may have been exposed to from the puncture wound. Offering to buy the medications for the patient is very noble but is not a sustainable practice. The nurse practitioner should prescribe the medications as for anyone with possible HIV exposure and refer to social services or a community referral agency that can help this patient acquire the appropriate medications.

14. ***c***
Actual or suspected elder abuse is reportable in all 50 states and healthcare providers are all mandatory reporters. Most elders are abused by their caregivers; particularly when the elder is demented. If the nurse practitioner asks the patient's daughter if she is abusing her mother it will likely result in a negative response by the daughter. Additionally, the daughter is not likely to seek this nurse practitioner's help in the future because of fear of retribution.

15. A nurse practitioner examined a patient who had been injured by a cat. There was a 4 centimeter gaping laceration on the patient's forearm. The nurse practitioner sutured the laceration. The patient subsequently became infected, needed hospital admission, and required IV antibiotics with incision and drainage. How can this situation be characterized?

- **a. This is a clinical judgment with an unexpected complication.**
- **b. The nurse practitioner's actions followed standard of care.**
- **c. The act of suturing this type of wound represents malpractice.**
- **d. This is poor judgment, but not malpractice.**

16. A nurse practitioner examined a patient who had been bitten by her husband during an assault. There were numerous bite marks and lacerations on the patient's forearms. The nurse practitioner sutured the lacerations, though this was contraindicated because of the highly infectious nature of human bites. The patient suffered no ill effects after suturing. How can this be described?

- **a. This is negligence.**
- **b. This was a fortunate situation for the patient.**
- **c. This is malpractice.**
- **d. This is poor judgment and malpractice.**

17. A nurse practitioner (NP) works in an HIV exclusive practice. In talking with a patient, the NP learns that the patient's sister lives next door to the NP. When the NP sees her neighbor (the patient's sister), the NP states that she met her sister in the clinic today. The neighbor replies, "Don't you work in an HIV clinic?" How can this situation be characterized?

- **a. This is negligence.**
- **b. This is a breach of confidentiality.**
- **c. This is not a breach of confidentiality.**
- **d. The NP has no liability.**

The next two questions relate to each other.

18. Anne and Laura work as nurse practitioner (NP) partners in an NP practice. Anne learns that Laura frequently changes patient's narcotic prescriptions to a different dosage, and then requests that the patient give her the remaining narcotic medications. Some patients have called Anne aside to tell her of this. How can Laura's actions best be characterized?

- **a. Laura is committing theft.**
- **b. Laura's behavior is not illegal but is unethical.**
- **c. Requesting the patient's medication is within Laura's scope of practice.**
- **d. This appears to be diversion of medications by Laura.**

15. ***c***
This is malpractice. Cat bites, known to be dirty bites with high probability of infection, should not be sutured. Malpractice is usually described as having multiple elements which all must be satisfied for malpractice to occur. There must be a duty, a breach of the duty, and subsequent injury due to the breach. Comparison of performance is based on the standard of care delivered by nurse practitioners.

16. ***a***
This is not malpractice. This is negligence. Negligence occurs when one fails to exercise the care that a reasonable person would exercise. Injury does not have to occur for negligence to occur. Human bites, known to be dirty bites with high probability of infection should not be sutured. Malpractice is usually described as having multiple elements that all must be satisfied for malpractice to occur. There must be a duty, a breach of the duty, and a subsequent injury due to the breach. Comparison of performance is based on the standard of care delivered by nurse practitioners.

17. ***b***
This is a breach of the patient's confidentiality. The neighbor's sister is the NP's patient. The NP is bound to confidentiality regarding protected health information for any of her patients. Even though the NP did not acknowledge that her sister was a patient, she breached patient confidentiality by telling the patient's sister that she had met her in the clinic. This is different than telling her sister she met her at the grocery store.

18. ***d***
Diversion of medications occurs when medications intended for one person, end up in the hands of another person. This is particularly serious when the medication involved is a narcotic. The question stem does not state what Laura is doing with the medications, but because of the nature of the action and the fact that it involves narcotics, Laura should not be engaging in this behavior because of the look of impropriety.

19. Laura admits to Anne that she keeps the medications and takes them occasionally. She states that sometimes she gives them to patients who can't afford these medications. What is Anne's first professional responsibility?

a. Report this to the police.
b. Report Laura's actions to the state board of nursing.
c. Report Laura's actions to the state board of pharmacy.
d. Anne has no professional responsibility for Laura's practice.

20. A liability policy that pays claims only during the period that the policy is active is termed:

a. claims made policy.
b. tail coverage.
c. liability protection.
d. bobtail coverage.

19. ***b***

Anne has a responsibility to report unsafe practice to the state board of nursing. This should be done first. She also has a responsibility to report a potentially impaired healthcare provider, especially if she observes this. Since there is no specific evidence to indicate what Laura has done with the medications she took from patients, theft will be hard to establish. State Board of Pharmacy will probably become involved in the investigation but their role varies from state to state.

20. ***a***

Liability insurance that covers the holder only during the time of the active policy is known as a "claims made" policy. This kind of policy is usually less expensive than other policies that will protect the policyholder against claims not known about at the end of the policy period.

Psychosocial Disorders

1. A 29 year-old postpartum female reports that she is having difficulty with concentration, sleep, and has feelings of guilt. She states that she feels sad most of the time. These symptoms have been present since the birth of her baby about one month ago. She can be diagnosed with:

- **a. dysthymia.**
- **b. minor depressive disorder.**
- **c. postpartum depression.**
- **d. hypothyroidism.**

2. The most common co-morbidity associated with depression is:

- **a. anxiety.**
- **b. panic disorder.**
- **c. obsessive-compulsive disorder.**
- **d. somatic disorder.**

3. Which patient is most likely to exhibit depression related to his illness? A patient with:

- **a. femur fracture.**
- **b. Parkinson's disease.**
- **c. diabetes.**
- **d. loss of a finger.**

4. A 69 year-old female patient reports feelings of anhedonia for the last month. What should be part of the nurse practitioner's assessment?

- **a. Libido**
- **b. Suicidal ideations**
- **c. Mania**
- **d. Depression**

5. Which depressed patient below has characteristics that are risk factors for suicide?

- **a. 34 year-old female recently married**
- **b. 46 year-old Hispanic male who is jobless**
- **c. 78 year-old male recently widowed**
- **d. 60 year-old dentist nearing retirement**

1. *c*

This patient is correctly diagnosed with postpartum depression. Postpartum depression is diagnosed when depression begins within the first month after delivery. There are 9 symptoms that characterize depression (in non-pregnant patients) and these are used in postpartum patients as well. When a patient exhibits fewer than 5 symptoms, but at least 2 of these symptoms every day for most of the day for at least 2 weeks, s/he may be diagnosed with minor depressive disorder. Depressed mood must be one of these symptoms. If s/he exhibits 5 or more, s/he may be diagnosed with major depressive disorder. In dysthymia, similar symptoms are evaluated, and they must be present at least 2 years. Hypothyroidism can account for feelings of low energy, but hypothyroidism does not produce feelings of guilt or other symptoms associated with depression.

2. *a*

Anxiety is the most common co-morbidity associated with depression; especially panic disorder, obsessive-compulsive disorder, and post-traumatic stress disorder. All of the other choices listed are co-morbidities associated with depression, but do not occur with the same frequency. When these co-morbidities occur in conjunction with depression and are not treated, they worsen the prognosis.

3. *b*

Diseases associated with the central nervous system are associated with high rates of depression. These include stroke, Parkinson's disease, multiple sclerosis, and dementia. Other illnesses associated with high rates of depression are cancer and cardiovascular illnesses like myocardial infarction. Depression worsens the outcome of any physical illness.

4. *d*

Anhedonia is the loss of pleasure or interest in things that have always brought pleasure or interest. If this is the case, this patient should be screened for depression. Anhedonia is a red flag for depression.

5. *c*

Demographic risk factors for suicide are male gender, older age, having been recently widowed, and living alone. Dentists and other health care workers are at risk for successful suicide because of their knowledge of and access to medications that could be used to commit suicide.

6. **A 38 year-old patient diagnosed with bipolar disease has taken lithium for many months. His mood has stabilized. He was told to report frequent urination while taking lithium. What might be the underlying cause of his frequent urination?**

    a. **Blood sugar elevations**
    b. **Diabetes insipidus**
    c. **Urinary tract infection**
    d. **Elevated lithium level**

7. **A 79 year-old female lost her husband of 55 years four days ago. She presents today with her daughter because she believes that she is "going crazy". She reports that she often hears his voice though she realizes that he has died. She has not slept well since his death and hasn't eaten very much. She has taken her usual medications for hypertension, osteoporosis, osteoarthritis, and hypothyroidism. She has no history of psychiatric illness. How should the nurse practitioner manage this?**

    a. **Prescribe a benzodiazepine for relief of anxiety.**
    b. **Tell her that this is a normal response and that it will resolve.**
    c. **Encourage her daughter to consider assisted living placement.**
    d. **Prescribe an antidepressant and follow up in 1-2 weeks.**

8. **The major advantage of the CAGE questionnaire is:**

    a. **brevity of questions.**
    b. **its sensitivity and specificity.**
    c. **identifies at risk drinkers.**
    d. **ease of interpretation.**

9. **Which findings suggest that a patient may be abusing alcohol?**

    a. **Macrocytosis, tremulousness, hypertension**
    b. **Rhinophyma, hypotension, peripheral neuropathy**
    c. **Telangiectasias, flat affect, thyroid dysfunction**
    d. **Hepatosplenomegaly, murmur, osteoarthritis**

10. **A nurse practitioner suspects that a patient is abusing ethanol. What laboratory values would support this suspicion?**

    a. **Elevated alkaline phosphatase**
    b. **Decreased TSH, macrocytosis**
    c. **Elevated ALT, AST, and GGT**
    d. **Elevated AST, alkaline phosphatase**

6. *b*

The most common side effect of lithium therapy is nephrogenic diabetes insipidus (NDI). Polyuria and polydipsia secondary to NDI occur in about 20% of patients who take lithium. Lithium accumulates in the collecting tubule cells and causes damage. This leads to changes in antidiuretic hormone (ADH) production, sodium levels, and hypercalcemia. Other changes can occur in the renal system such as mild renal insufficiency. Patients on lithium therapy should be monitored closely for side effects and to ensure that lithium levels are maintained within therapeutic range because lithium has a narrow therapeutic index.

7. *b*

This imagined hearing or seeing of a deceased person is referred to as "searching behavior" and is not indicative of psychiatric illness. It is a common response after the death of a loved one, especially after 55 years of marriage. This patient and her daughter should be educated regarding the stages of grief and the variable length of each of the stages. Usually by 6 months, grief has begun to resolve, but this is a variable process. She should be encouraged to maintain her usual sleep, nutrition, and activity patterns as much as possible.

8. *a*

The CAGE questionnaire is a screen for alcohol abuse. It consists of 4 questions that can be quickly and easily incorporated when eliciting a patient's history. The "C" is to remind the questioner to ask the patient whether he's ever felt the need to "C"ut down on drinking; "A"nnoyed by criticism about his drinking; "G"uilty about his drinking; in need of an "E"ye opener. These 4 questions are very easy to ask and can be answered with a simple yes/no response. The majority of patients with alcoholism respond yes to at least 2 of these questions. Patients without alcohol problems virtually never respond "yes" to 2 or more. The questionnaire is known to have high sensitivity and specificity, but other screens for alcohol abuse do too.

9. *a*

Findings that should trigger an examiner to suspect alcohol abuse in a patient are tremors, hypertension, rhinophyma, peripheral neuropathy, telangiectasias, and hepatosplenomegaly. A patient does not usually exhibit all of these characteristics. In fact, he may not exhibit any of these symptoms and still abuse alcohol. The symptoms listed in the other choices are not specifically associated with alcoholism. Macrocytosis is common in alcoholics because there is a high rate of B12 deficiency and folate deficiency; both produce macrocytic anemias.

10. *c*

Liver enzymes rise in response to acute injury to the liver. ALT and AST are frequently elevated when alcohol abuse occurs. Specifically, the AST is usually the higher of the two enzymes and can signify alcohol abuse when it is more than 2 times greater than the ALT. In patients who abuse alcohol daily, the ALT and AST may be normal. GGT, gamma-glutamyl transferase, is often elevated even when ALT and AST are normal. It can help identify damage to the liver as a result of alcohol abuse.

11. An adolescent female patient with anorexia nervosa must exhibit 4 criteria for diagnosis. Which criterion listed below is NOT part of the diagnostic criteria?

a. **Intense fear of weight gain**
b. **Weight below 90% of ideal body weight**
c. **Severe body image disturbance**
d. **Absence of menstrual cycle**

12. Which of the following characterizes bulimia nervosa?

a. **Binge eating**
b. **Purging**
c. **Food restriction**
d. **Concern over body weight**

13. A patient with an eating disorder may concomitantly exhibit:

a. **thyroid disease.**
b. **sleep disorders.**
c. **anxiety disorders.**
d. **liver disease.**

14. A 19 year-old college student with anorexia is being treated as an outpatient. Today she is bradycardic and occasionally has orthostatic hypotension. What might accompany today's findings?

a. **Insomnia**
b. **Sleep apnea**
c. **Amenorrhea**
d. **Intermittent tachycardia**

15. In patients who exhibit depression, selective serotonin reuptake inhibitors (SSRIs) are commonly chosen as a medication for treatment. SSRIs are often chosen because they:

a. **are more efficacious than other drug classes.**
b. **are safer than other medications for depression.**
c. **require fewer laboratory tests for follow-up.**
d. **help patients reach normal states more quickly.**

11. *b*
Weight below 85% of ideal body weight is the correct criterion. This involves refusal to gain or maintain weight within normal range. Occasionally weight below ideal body range does not involve losing weight, but instead involves refusal to gain weight during a growth spurt. This is commonly observed during pubertal growth spurts and is more common in adolescent females than males. The other three criteria are correct as listed.

12. *a*
Recurrent episodes of binge eating characterize bulimia. Loss of control is always present, especially when eating. This results in eating quantities of food far beyond what would normally be consumed. Binge eating is always followed by a compensatory activity. This may take the feature of purging or nonpurging. Nonpurging involves excessive exercise or post-binge fasting. Binges and the compensatory activity occur a minimum of twice weekly for at least 3 months for diagnosis of bulimia nervosa.

13. *c*
Affective disorders, anxiety disorders, and substance abuse issues are common in patients who have eating disorders. Obsessive-compulsive disorder is also commonly observed. Patients with eating disorders are more likely to have a first or second degree relative with an eating disorder, affective disorder, or alcohol abuse. There is no evidence that patients with eating disorders exhibit a higher incidence of sleep disorders or liver disease. Thyroid disease should always be assessed in patients with eating disorders, but this does not represent the reason for weight loss when eating disorder is present.

14. *c*
This patient has anorexia nervosa. She is far below ideal body weight and exhibits evidence of poor nutrition and health. More than 90% of patients with anorexia are amenorrheic. These patients have low levels of luteinizing hormone and follicle stimulating hormone. Because of prolonged hypoestrogenic states, they are highly susceptible to osteopenia and osteoporosis. It is not known why, but many patients with anorexia also exhibit mitral valve prolapse, not mitral regurgitation. Because she is bradycardic, an EKG should be performed. QT prolongation is common in these patients, especially when bradycardia is present. Hypotension is more common than hypertension in anorexic patients.

15. *b*
SSRIs are commonly chosen over tricyclic antidepressants (TCAs) and other medication classes for depression because they have fewer side effects and are thus better tolerated by patients; and because they are safer if overdose occurs. The SSRIs have never been shown to be more efficacious than the TCAs, though publication bias may demonstrate this. Generally, levels of antidepressant medications are not monitored and so laboratory testing is not an issue.

16. A patient is taking a generic version of a selective serotonin reuptake inhibitor (SSRI). She reports intermittent nausea and mild headache daily since she started this medication 5 days ago. How should the nurse practitioner respond?

a. **Brand name medication may help the side effects resolve.**
b. **These are typical complaints of patients who take SSRIs.**
c. **This sounds like a viral syndrome. Continue the SSRI.**
d. **These symptoms are common in patients with depression.**

17. A common side effect of trazodone may be alleviated by:

a. **taking this medication with food.**
b. **taking this medication at bedtime.**
c. **drinking a big glass of water with each dose.**
d. **eating increased fiber while taking this medication.**

18. Within 6 months of treatment, patients who are treated for depression with selective serotonin reuptake inhibitors often exhibit:

a. **insomnia.**
b. **weight gain.**
c. **increased libido.**
d. **hyperglycemia.**

19. Elderly patients who are treated for depression with tricyclic antidepressants (TCAs) often exhibit:

a. **increased libido.**
b. **hypoglycemia.**
c. **arrhythmias.**
d. **cognitive changes.**

20. A common strategy used to minimize the incidence of side effects when giving an elderly patient a selective serotonin reuptake inhibitor (SSRI) is:

a. **take the medications at bedtime.**
b. **stand slowly to minimize dizziness.**
c. **prescribe a low dose initially.**
d. **take the medication with food.**

21. Which patient is at highest risk of suicide?

a. **86 year-old male with chronic pain**
b. **75 year-old female with history of depression**
c. **45 year-old female with a terminal illness**
d. **51 year-old male who abuses alcohol**

16. *b*
Typical symptoms of SSRIs include mild headache, nausea, insomnia, restlessness, and agitation. The emergence of these symptoms is typically dose related and will resolve within 2 weeks. The patient should be encouraged to eat small bites when she feels like she is becoming nauseated and may take acetaminophen or a similar product if the headaches are bothersome. Changing drug classes is also a possibility if the symptoms become too distracting or bothersome.

17. *b*
Trazodone is a tricyclic antidepressant that can produce profound drowsiness. It is often taken at bedtime to induce sleep. This medication should always be taken at bedtime. Trazodone is often given to treat insomnia related to depression or to alleviate the jitteriness and restlessness sometimes associated with SSRI and SNRI use.

18. *b*
Weight gain is common among men and women who take SSRIs and tricyclic antidepressants (TCAs) because they stimulate appetite. Decreased libido may occur several weeks after starting SSRIs, but this can also be a symptom of depression. The tricyclic and heterocyclic compounds are often associated with blood sugar elevations. Elevations almost never occur within 6 months of starting use. Jitteriness and restlessness are commonly associated with SSRI use. These side effects generally subside after a month or less of therapy.

19. *c*
The TCAs have pronounced anticholinergic activity and thus, produce bothersome side effects like dry mouth, constipation, urinary retention, confusion, and even delirium. The TCAs block H1 receptors that may be responsible for sleepiness and weight gain. Hypotension may also result, especially in the elderly. This may be due to an alpha-1 receptor blockade. These medications must be used very cautiously in the elderly because they can produce bradycardia and prolongation of the QT interval. Therefore, a resting EKG is necessary prior to starting any TCA.

20. *c*
A principle that is employed when prescribing medications for elderly patients is to "start low and go slow". This should be employed when prescribing SSRIs too. The lowest dose should be a starting point; or a prescriber may order an even lower dose initially. The dose may be slowly increased until therapeutic effects are observed.

21. *a*
Elderly patients and males are more successful when they attempt suicide. Those at highest risk are white males 85 years or older. Symptoms in the elderly that should be of particular concern to healthcare providers, because they are associated with increased risk of suicide, are hopelessness, insomnia, unremitting pain, alcohol abuse, restlessness, and impaired concentration.

22. A male patient has a family history of bipolar disorder in two first degree relatives. Bipolar disorder:

- a. often affects multiple family members.
- b. affects only siblings.
- c. is not associated with suicide.
- d. is considerably more common in males.

23. What is the usual age of onset of symptoms for patients with bipolar disorder?

- a. Childhood
- b. Third decade
- c. Between 15 and 30 years
- d. Adolescence

24. A 34 year-old bipolar patient has been placed on a fluoxetine and valproate for manic depressive symptoms. He has had great improvement in his symptoms and has returned to work. The psychiatrist has released him to your care. What must be monitored in this patient?

- a. Renal function, platelet count, BUN, Cr
- b. Valproate levels, hemoglobin, BUN, Cr
- c. Liver function studies, renal studies
- d. Valproate levels, platelet count, liver function studies

25. Carbamazepine is used in patients with bipolar disorder for mood stabilization. Prescribers who have patients taking carbamazepine should be alert to:

- a. alcohol abuse.
- b. electrolyte abnormalities.
- c. renal failure.
- d. drug-drug interactions.

26. A newly diagnosed pregnant teenager has suspected depression. Before a diagnosis is made, she should have a CBC, TSH, renal and liver function tests and:

- a. sedimentation rate.
- b. quantitative beta hCG level.
- c. hemoglobin A1C.
- d. urine toxicology screen.

22. *a*
There is strong familial component to bipolar disorder. Patients with bipolar disorder have shortened life expectancies. Up to 50% of patients with this disorder will attempt suicide at least once. Approximately 15% will be successful. Risk factors for suicidal behavior in patients with bipolar disorder include family history of suicide attempts, substance abuse, presence of impulsivity or aggression, and frequent depressive episodes.

23. *c*
The usual age of onset of symptoms is between 15 and 30 years. Onset of symptoms almost never occurs in patients older than age 65 years or younger than 15 years.

24. *d*
Valproate has been associated with liver toxicity and failure, and thrombocytopenia. Liver function studies and platelet counts should be monitored prior to therapy and then regularly as indicated by the drug manufacturer. Valproate levels should be measured to insure target blood level between 50-125 micrograms/mL. Common side effects of valproate are nausea, vomiting, easy bruising, and tremors.

25. *d*
Carbamazepine is an enzyme inducer in the cytochrome P450 system. Consequently, there are a number of drug-drug interactions that can take place as a result. Any time a new medication is prescribed, pharmacist oversight or a drug interaction checker should be employed. Additionally, any time new symptoms develop, medication use and compliance should be assessed.

26. *d*
There is a high correlation between psychiatric disorders and drug/alcohol use. This should be ascertained as soon as possible since these can have serious implications on the fetus/mother's health. None of the other tests listed have an impact on diagnosis of depression in a pregnant patient. CBC, TSH, and renal/hepatic function tests are used to screen depression "look a likes" (anemia, hypothyroidism, renal or hepatic dysfunction). Hemoglobin A1C is a good idea but is not as urgent as the urine toxicology screen unless there are diabetes risk factors present.

27. The nurse practitioner (NP) is treating a 22 year-old for depression with high dose fluoxetine. After several months of dosage changes, she is finally doing well and comes today for a follow up visit. She is happy and states that she might be pregnant. A urine test indicates pregnancy. The NP has referred the patient to an obstetrician who will see the patient in 4 weeks. How should the fluoxetine be handled today?

- **a. Discontinue it immediately.**
- **b. Let the obstetrician and patient make a decision about continuing fluoxetine.**
- **c. Let the patient make a decision about discontinuing the medication.**
- **d. Wean it off as she waits to see the obstetrician.**

27. *b*

Fluoxetine is one of the best studied selective serotonin reuptake inhibitors in pregnancy and lactation. There has been no reported evidence of teratogenicity. While the healthcare provider would rather this patient not take a medication while she is pregnant, consideration must be given to the severity of her depression and her response to treatment. The discussion the NP and obstetrician will have with the patient should include risks and benefits of treatment, and potential risks of stopping fluoxetine. The risk of exposure to medication must always be weighed against the risk of not treating this patient. All psychotropic medications cross the placenta and so developing fetuses are exposed to these medications. Fluoxetine is a category C medication.

Respiratory Disorders

1. **Which drug may be associated with cough?**

    a. **Dextromethorphan**
    b. **Guaifenesin**
    c. **Albuterol**
    d. **Ramipril**

2. **Which of the following is NOT part of the differential for a patient who complains of cough?**

    a. **Heart failure**
    b. **Reflux disease**
    c. **Asthma**
    d. **Obesity**

3. ***M. pneumoniae* and *C. pneumoniae* are respiratory pathogens that:**

    a. **are spread via direct contact.**
    b. **associated with immunosuppression.**
    c. **cause atypical pneumonia.**
    d. **transmitted via direct contact.**

4. **What does a peak flow meter measure?**

    a. **Exercise capacity**
    b. **Oxygen saturation**
    c. **Peak flow capacity**
    d. **Expiratory flow**

5. **Which patient might be expected to have the *worst* FEV1?**

    a. **An asthma patient in the green zone**
    b. **A 65 year-old with emphysema**
    c **A 60 year-old with pneumonia**
    d. **A patient with bronchiolitis**

1. ***d***
Ramipril is an ACE inhibitor. Though estimates vary, 5 - 20% of patients who receive ACE inhibitors develop a cough. Angiotensin converting enzyme is believed to be responsible for metabolism of bradykinin and tachykinin. Bradykinin is thought to be responsible for the cough because it induces production of arachidonic acid metabolites and nitric oxide. These substances may promote cough. The cough associated with ACE inhibitors appears to be a class effect.

2. ***d***
All of the other conditions listed, heart failure, GERD, and asthma are associated with cough. Obesity does not produce cough and is not associated with cough.

3. ***c***
These two organisms are common causes of pneumonia. Specifically, they are called atypical pathogens because they produce atypical pneumonia. They are transmitted via respiratory droplets from the nose and throat of infected people. Prolonged close contact is probably needed for transmission to occur. Patients are usually contagious for 10 days or so. Most commonly these infections occur in younger patients, but all ages may be affected. Generally, the atypical pathogens are eradicated with macrolide antibiotics or tetracyclines.

4. ***d***
A peak flow meter measures peak expiratory flow; that is, air flow out of a patient's lungs. Peak flow is very sensitive to changes in the respiratory tubules and so, reflects narrowing of the airways. The utility of a peak flow meter is especially important for patients with asthma because of the rapid changes that occur prior to the onset of an asthma exacerbation. There is minimal to no benefit of measuring these airway changes in patients with COPD and pneumonia.

5. ***b***
FEV 1 stands for "forced expiratory volume in one second". This is the volume of air that is forcefully exhaled in the first second of exhalation after a deep breath. Patients with emphysema are not able to do this very efficiently because their alveoli are stretched and mostly contain trapped air. FEV 1 is used to assess airway obstruction. An asthma patient in the green zone would be expected to have a normal (compared to himself) FEV1. An FEV1 measurement or pulmonary function tests would not be performed on a patient with pneumonia or bronchiectasis because he would be expected to have diminished respiratory capacity related to his infection.

6. Which drug class is never used to treat chronic obstructive pulmonary disease (COPD)?

- **a. Long-acting bronchodilator**
- **b. Long-acting anti-cholinergic**
- **c. Leukotriene blockers**
- **d. Systemic steroids**

7. A patient is diagnosed with asthma. Which question is most important to ask when deciding on medication management?

- **a. Do you smoke?**
- **b. How severe are your symptoms?**
- **c. How often do your symptoms occur?**
- **d. Do you ever wheeze?**

8. Mr. Smith has smoked for 45 years. He has a history of hypertension, gout, and benign prostatic hyperplasia. Which of the following medications may worsen one of his diseases?

- **a. Amlodipine**
- **b. Multivitamin with iron**
- **c. Vitamin B 12**
- **d. Propanolol**

9. Which medication below would be contraindicated in a patient with COPD?

- **a. Cough suppressant with codeine**
- **b. Dextromethorphan**
- **c. Mucolytics**
- **d. Decongestant with guaifenesin**

10. The most common cause of atypical pneumonia in adults is:

- **a. *Streptococcus pneumoniae.***
- **b. *Mycoplasma pneumoniae.***
- **c. *Chlamydophila pneumoniae.***
- **d. *Staphylococcus aureus.***

11. The most common cause of pneumonia in people of all ages is:

- **a. *S. pneumoniae.***
- **b. Group A *Strept.***
- **c. *S. aureus.***
- **d. *Mycoplasma* sp.**

6. ***c***
There is no data to suggest efficacy in treating COPD patients with leukotriene blockers like zafirlukast or montelukast. Long-acting bronchodilators (used twice daily) like salmeterol and formoterol are commonly used. The long-acting anticholinergic medication, tiotropium can be used once daily. Systemic steroids may be used for exacerbations of COPD or daily in patients with severe disease.

7. ***c***
Diagnosis of asthma, as well as pharmacologic management of asthma, is based on frequency of occurrence of symptoms (wheezing, shortness of breath, cough, etc.). Bronchodilators, both short and long-acting, and inhaled steroids, represent the cornerstone of management of most patients who have asthma. Not all patients with asthma wheeze, therefore, asking that question might not be of great help. Severity of symptoms is subjective. Smoking cessation is important, but not a determinant in selecting medications for asthma management.

8. ***c***
After smoking for 45 years, Mr. Smith can be assumed to have COPD. Propanolol, a beta-blocker, can block the beta receptors (theoretically) in the lungs and produce respiratory difficulty in this patient. Propanolol is a non-selective beta-blocker and might be potentially more harmful in a COPDer than a cardioselective beta-blocker. In any event, beta-blocker use should be avoided or used with caution in this patient. Gout, HTN and BPH will not be adversely affected by any of the medications above.

9. ***a***
Codeine would be contraindicated (or used with extreme caution) because the sedative effect of codeine or any narcotic can potentially worsen respiratory depression and worsen hypercapnia.

10. ***b***
In patients who have atypical pneumonia, Mycoplasma is the most common pathogen. ***M. pneumoniae*** **is so named because of its "atypical" appearance on chest x-ray. This organism causes "walking pneumonia" that is very prevalent in a young adult population. This accounts for about 15% of pneumonia. It is transmitted via respiratory droplet.**

11. ***a***
Streptococcus pneumoniae **(*S. pneumo*) is the most common pathogen in community acquired pneumonia (CAP) world-wide. It is more common in age extremes (the very young and very old) and during winter months. Group A** ***Strept*** **can cause a fulminant pneumonia even in patients who are immunocompetent.** ***Mycoplasma*** **is the most common atypical pathogen that causes pneumonia.** ***Staphylococcus*** **pneumonia is more common post-influenza in the very young and very old.**

12. A patient has cough, pharyngitis, nasal discharge, and fever. Which symptom is most common in a patient with acute bronchitis?

a. **Cough**
b. **Pharyngitis**
c. **Nasal discharge**
d. **Fever**

13. A patient with acute bronchitis and cough for 5 days calls to report that his cough is productive of discolored sputum. He has no other new symptoms. How should the nurse practitioner manage this?

a. **Consider pneumonia; prescribe a macrolide antibiotic.**
b. **Continue the original plan of care.**
c. **Encourage the patient to return to the clinic for a recheck.**
d. **Order a chest x-ray and treat accordingly.**

14. A patient with acute bronchitis was diagnosed at an urgent care center 10 days ago. He reports that he was given an anti-tussive for nighttime cough, a steroid injection and oral steroids, an antibiotic, and a nasal decongestant. Which of these interventions was actually indicated for acute bronchitis?

a. **Steroid injection and oral steroids**
b. **Antibiotic**
c. **Decongestant and antitussive**
d. **Antibiotic and steroids**

15. "Good control" of asthma is measured by the number of times weekly a patient uses a rescue inhaler. What choice below indicates "good control"?

a. **Six times monthly at nighttime**
b. **Once weekly**
c. **Not more than three times weekly**
d. **Not more than once daily and once nightly**

16. A patient with asthma uses one puff twice daily of an inhaled steroid and has an albuterol inhaler for PRN use. He requests a refill on his albuterol inhaler. His last prescription was filled 5 weeks ago. What action by the NP is appropriate?

a. **Refill the albuterol only**
b. **Prescribe a longer acting bronchodilator, continue the steroid**
c. **Increase the dose of the inhaled steroid, refill the albuterol**
d. **Prescribe a long acting bronchodilator and increase the steroid**

12. *a*
Cough is the most common symptom associated with acute bronchitis. In the first few days of acute bronchitis, upper respiratory symptoms predominate. In fact, it may be impossible to distinguish upper respiratory infection from acute bronchitis. Pharyngitis and nasal discharge/congestion are common. Acute bronchitis is suggested when cough lasts longer than 5 days. Fever is a relatively uncommon symptom of acute bronchitis. When fever appears along with cough, pneumonia should be strongly considered.

13. *b*
This is the typical course of acute bronchitis. Acute bronchitis is characterized by cough lasting greater than 5 days, but usually less than 20 days. More than 50% of patients report discolored sputum. Since the overwhelming majority of cases of acute bronchitis are secondary to viral causes, antibiotics are not indicated. Discolored sputum is related to sloughing of epithelial cells and is the reason for the discoloration. Discolored sputum does not indicate bacterial infection. CDC recommends treating acute bronchitis with antibiotics ONLY when the etiology is pertussis. In all other cases, the patient should be treated with supportive and symptomatic management only.

14. *c*
Acute bronchitis is almost always due to a viral infection. The antibiotic had no effect in symptom resolution. Unfortunately, antibiotics are commonly given for acute bronchitis. There is no evidence to support use of steroids as they do not result in quicker resolution of symptoms than placebo. In fact, multiple studies have failed to demonstrate benefit. Only the decongestant and antitussive may be beneficial for symptom relief.

15. *b*
Good asthma management is characterized by using short-acting bronchodilators (rescue medication) no more than twice weekly during daytime or twice monthly at nighttime. Using short-acting inhaled bronchodilators this frequently necessitates better use of prophylactic medications such as inhaled steroids and possible use of long-acting bronchodilators in conjunction with inhaled steroids.

16. *c*
The patient is using his short acting bronchodilator excessively if he needs a refill of his inhaler in only 5 weeks. Inhalers typically contain 200 puffs. They should be used 2 or fewer times per week. His inhaled steroid dose should be increased and his albuterol inhaler should be refilled. In fact, he should not be without a prescription for the albuterol. Consideration could be given to choice *d*, but this is not the best choice because this does not include a refill of the albuterol and this patient cannot be without access to a rescue inhaler.

17. Which of the following medications should be avoided in a patient who has asthma?

a. **Timolol ophthalmic drops**
b. **Naproxen**
c. **Lisinopril**
d. **Amlodipine**

18. An adult has upper respiratory symptoms and cough for the past 14 days. What should be considered?

a. ***H. influenza***
b. ***S. pneumoniae***
c. **Viral agents**
d. **Pertussis**

19. Which of the following may be used to diagnose COPD?

a. **Chest radiograph**
b. **CT scan of the chest**
c. **Pulmonary function tests**
d. **Arterial blood gases**

20. A 60 year-old patient reports chronic cough and sputum production. He has a long history of exposure to second hand cigarette smoke from his wife. What diagnosis is most likely?

a. **Lung cancer**
b. **Emphysema**
c. **COPD**
d. **Allergic cough**

21. Ipratropium is very widely used in the treatment of COPD. Which of the following statements about ipratropium is correct?

a. **It slows the progression of COPD.**
b. **It decreases parasympathetic tone and produces bronchodilation.**
c. **It has anti-inflammatory actions and reduces bronchoconstriction.**
d. **It is more effective than a beta agonist in producing bronchodilation.**

17. *a*
Timolol is a beta-blocker. This class of medications can precipitate an asthma exacerbation in patients. Even though timolol is being administered in the eye, it is absorbed through mucous membranes and can exert systemic effects. Beta-blockers should be avoided in patients with asthma and used very cautiously in patients with COPD. The other medications listed have no specific contraindications for patients with asthma.

18. *d*
Pertussis should always be considered in adults who present with acute cough of greater than 5 days duration. The incubation period is about 7-10 days. Patients present with URI symptoms for 1-2 weeks. The classic paroxysmal cough usually begins in the second week of the illness. The duration of symptoms and cough are about 3 months. This is highly infectious and is a reportable disease.

19. *c*
Pulmonary function tests (PFTs) are essential to diagnose COPD. The most important measures are the FEV1 (forced expiratory volume in one second) and FVC (forced vital capacity). Chest radiograph has a poor sensitivity in diagnosing COPD. Only about half of patients with moderately severe COPD can be diagnosed using chest radiography alone. CT scan is able to identify emphysema, but not chronic bronchitis. Arterial blood gases demonstrate hypoxia, but a specific cause is not able to be determined from this test alone.

20. *c*
This patient's exposure to second hand cigarette smoke from his wife represents a risk factor for COPD even though this patient does not smoke. COPD must be considered in anyone with a history of chronic cough and sputum production, dyspnea at rest or exertion, and history of exposure to tobacco smoke.

21. *b*
Ipratropium is the most widely studied anticholinergic medication used to treat patients with COPD. It produces its helpful effects by reducing cholinergic tone in the lungs. It should be avoided in combination with a beta agonist unless shortness of breath is present because beta agonists increase the likelihood of side effects like tachycardia and tremor and do not improve efficacy.

22. Which of the following characteristics is always present in a patient with COPD?

a. **Productive cough**
b. **Obstructed airways**
c. **Shortness of breath**
d. **Hypercapnia**

23. A patient with pneumonia reports that he has rust colored sputum. What pathogen should the nurse practitioner suspect?

a. ***Mycoplasma pneumoniae***
b. ***Chlamydophila pneumoniae***
c. ***Staphylococcus aureus***
d. ***Streptococcus pneumoniae***

24. The major laboratory abnormality noted in patients with pneumonia is:

a. **eosinophilia.**
b. **leukocytosis.**
c. **leukoplakia.**
d. **leukopenia.**

25. A patient with cough and fever is found to have infiltrates on chest x-ray. What is his likely diagnosis?

a. **Pneumonia**
b. **Heart failure**
c. **Tuberculosis**
d. **Pneumonitis**

26. Mycoplasma pneumonia is:

a. **a diagnosis of exclusion.**
b. **a typical respiratory pathogen.**
c. **only identifiable on chest x-ray.**
d. **a disease with extrapulmonary manifestations.**

22. *b*
COPD, chronic obstructive pulmonary disease, is characterized by obstructed airways. The obstruction is NOT completely reversible. Asthma is completely reversible. This is the reason many learned authorities do not consider asthma to be part of the COPD umbrella. Productive cough is not always present in patients with emphysema. Shortness of breath does not have to be present (or perceived in patients with COPD). Hypercapnia is more prevalent in patients with emphysema since air trapping occurs.

23. *d*
Clinical descriptions of mucus do not really help in clinical decision-making regarding pneumonia, but certain clinical characteristics are associated with specific types of pneumonia. Strept pneumonia, also known as pneumococcal pneumonia, is associated with rust colored sputum. Scant or watery sputum is associated with atypical pathogens like *Mycoplasma* and *Chlamydophila* pneumonia. Thick, discolored sputum may be associated with bacterial pneumonia.

24. *b*
An increased white count is typical in patients with pneumonia. This is more commonly seen in bacterial pneumonia. Eosinophils can be increased in patients who develop pneumonia secondary to exposure to a very irritating substance like a toxic gas. Gram stain can demonstrate gram positive or negative pathogens. Leukopenia is an ominous finding in a patient with pneumonia. This indicates a poor prognosis because it means that the immune system is not responding to a potentially fatal pathogen.

25. *a*
The finding of infiltrates on chest x-ray, in conjunction with clinical findings of fever and cough, should direct the examiner to consider pneumonia as the diagnosis. Other common clinical findings with pneumonia include chest pain, dyspnea, and sputum production. Though not common, some patients with pneumonia exhibit gastrointestinal symptoms like nausea, vomiting, and diarrhea.

26. *d*
Mycoplasma is an atypical pathogen and produces an atypical pneumonia. It can be difficult to diagnose because symptoms can be varied and involve multiple body systems (extrapulmonary manifestations). Infection with *Mycoplasma* may present with a normal white blood cell count, maculopapular rash, GI symptoms, tender joints and aches, and rarely, cardiac rhythm disturbances. Respiratory symptoms may not be pronounced. On chest x-ray there are some unique findings (peribronchial pattern) with Mycoplasma. These include thickened bronchial shadow, streaks of interstitial infiltration, and atelectasis. These are more likely to occur in the lower lobes.

27. A 24 year-old college student who does not smoke is diagnosed with pneumonia. He is otherwise healthy and does not need hospitalization at this time. What antibiotic represents the best choice for treatment for him?

a. **Erythromycin**
b. **Levofloxacin**
c. **Clarithromycin**
d. **Amoxicillin**

27. *c*

A macrolide (like azithromycin or clarithromycin) or a tetracycline (like doxycycline) is used for initial treatment of uncomplicated pneumonia in outpatients who are otherwise healthy and have not had recent antibiotic exposure. These agents are chosen because they cover atypical pathogens (the organism most likely to have infected him) and provide coverage against non-drug resistant forms of Streptococcus. Fluoroquinolones are commonly used first line in these patients. However, guidelines strongly recommend using fluoroquinolones for patients with co-morbidities and/or those who have suspected macrolide resistant strains of *Streptococcus*. Inappropriate use of fluoroquinolones will promote development of fluoroquinolone resistant pathogens.

Urology / STDs

1. **Which of the following symptoms is usual in a male patient with trichomonas?**

   a. No clinical symptoms
   b. Urethritis
   c. Burning with urination
   d. Testicular pain

2. **Chancroid is considered a co-factor for transmission of:**

   a. HIV.
   b. Gonorrhea.
   c. Chlamydia.
   d. Trichomoniasis.

3. **A 21 year-old female presents with three 0.5 cm human papilloma virus (HPV) lesions on her vulva. An appropriate treatment option for this patient would be:**

   a. acetic acid.
   b. colposcopy.
   c. podophyllin.
   d. acyclovir.

4. **A patient has been diagnosed with HIV. The patient's viral load was ordered. What other test may be ordered to assess the status of the patient's immune system?**

   a. CBC
   b. CD4 cell count
   c. Western blot
   d. Westergren test

5. **A patient has been treated for HIV infection with anti-retroviral therapy. He is stable. How often should CD4 counts be repeated?**

   a. Every 1-2 weeks
   b. Every 1-2 months
   c. Every 3-6 months
   d. Annually

1. ***a***
Trichomonas produces classic symptoms in females of itching and discharge. In males, there are usually no symptoms. Less than 10% of time, men present with symptoms. However, when symptoms occur in males, they include urethritis with clear or mucopurulent urethral discharge and dysuria. Metronidazole can be used to treat this in symptomatic and asymptomatic patients. Prostadynia, also known as prostatitis, is an inflammation of the prostate gland. Sometimes males with trichomonas infections present with prostadynia, but this is not the usual presentation.

2. ***a***
Chancroid is an STD caused by *Haemophilus ducreyi* and is spread by sexual contact or by contacting pus from an infected lesion. This is common in tropical countries but is seen in the US. The ulcer is usually very painful in men, but not usually painful in women. The ulcer begins as a papule, fills with pus, and becomes an open, eroded area. Chancroid is a co-factor in the transmission of HIV. In patients with HIV, the chancroid heals much more slowly than in patients who are immunocompetent.

3. ***c***
This patient has HPV. This is a viral infection that increases a woman's risk of cervical cancer. In males there is an increased risk of cancer of the anus and penis. The warts that are produced are painless and usually appear within weeks of infection. There are several topical treatments for HPV, imiquimod, podophyllin, and trichloroacetic acid (TCA). One of these agents may be applied to the warts. Treatments are generally well tolerated. TCA may cause burning. The warts will slough off after one or more treatments. There are no oral antiviral agents indicated for treatment of HPV.

4. ***b***
The CD4 and HIV RNA ("viral load") tests are usually ordered when a patient is diagnosed with HIV. These tests are part of the initial laboratory baseline to assess the status of the patient's immune system. The normal CD4 count in adults ranges from 500 - 1,500 cells/ml. As the disease progresses, CD4 count declines. Once the CD4 count is under 200 cells/ml, the patient is diagnosed with AIDS.

5. ***c***
Once stable and on therapy, a prudent clinician would monitor counts every 3-6 months unless the patient's condition or status changed. Generally, CD4 counts don't change very quickly. The counts are usually measured every 2-8 weeks after starting or changing therapy. In an asymptomatic patient with HIV, CD4 counts can be measured annually unless the patient has a change in his condition. Though, this is not without shortcomings. Some patients feel well with falling counts and some patients may feel ill with normal CD4 counts. Consequently, CD4 counts are often checked in stable patients every 3-6 months since symptoms do not always reflect CD4 counts.

6. A female patient and her male partner are diagnosed with trichomonas. She has complaints of vulval itching and discharge. He is asymptomatic. How should they be treated?

- **a. She should receive metronidazole. He does not need treatment.**
- **b. They both should receive metronidazole.**
- **c. She should be treated with ceftriaxone; he should receive ciprofloxacin.**
- **d. They both should be treated with azithromycin and doxycycline.**

7. Which risk factor has the greatest impact on HIV transmission?

- **a. Viral load**
- **b. Type of sexual activity**
- **c. Presence of other STDs**
- **d. Patient gender**

8. A healthcare provider was exposed to the blood of a patient through a needle stick. When do the majority of patients seroconvert if they are going to do so?

- **a. One week**
- **b. Within 4 weeks**
- **c. Within 4-6 weeks**
- **d. Within 3 months**

9. A patient requests testing for HIV after a sexual exposure. What are CDC's recommendations for screening for this patient?

- **a. There are no recommendations for further testing.**
- **b. She should be tested today, with repeat testing at 6, 12, and 24 weeks.**
- **c. She should be re-tested in 6-12 months.**
- **d. She only requires retesting if she develops symptoms of HIV.**

10. A patient presents with generalized lymphadenopathy. He has no other symptoms. Based on the most likely etiology, what test should be performed?

- **a. HIV test**
- **b. CBC**
- **c. Lymph node biopsy**
- **d. Sedimentation rate**

6. ***b***
Metronidazole is considered the drug of choice to treat males and non-pregnant females. Even though he is asymptomatic, he needs treatment too. Neither partner should resume sexual intercourse until both have been treated. Tinidazole can also be used for treatment. 2 grams of either agent may be given as a single dose treatment.

7. ***a***
Viral load at the time of infection is the greatest risk factor in contracting HIV. It also is the greatest predictor of prognosis. High levels of viremia correspond to higher rates of infection. There are equal rates of transmission in sexual intercourse between same and opposite sex couples. The presence of STDs at the time of infection does increase risk of transmission, but not to as great an extent as viral load.

8. ***d***
The majority of patients who are going to seroconvert after HIV exposure will do so within the first 3 months. By 6 months, nearly 100% have seroconverted. Since there have been rare documented conversions between 6 and 12 months after exposure, some learned authorities advocate testing at 1 year after exposure.

9. ***b***
She does require further testing because a negative initial result does not insure that she is not infected. This signifies that she has not seroconverted at this time. The period within 3 months after exposure is termed the "window period" and a negative test must be confirmed. If the test is negative 6 months after the last exposure, she is considered to be negative. If the patient had an exposure and HIV was suspected, a HIV RNA should be performed as well as the rapid HIV. Rapid testing results are usually available in about 20-40 minutes. HIV testing should be performed in any patient who develops symptoms consistent with HIV after an exposure.

10. ***a***
During asymptomatic infection, patients often have persistent generalized lymphadenopathy (PGL). PGL is defined as enlarged lymph nodes involving at least 2 noncontiguous sites other than inguinal nodes. The lymphatic tissue serves as a primary reservoir for HIV. Studies of lymph nodes in patients at the asymptomatic phase demonstrate high concentrations of HIV.

11. The clinical syndrome resulting from replacement of normal vaginal flora with anaerobic bacteria is:

a. candidal vaginitis.
b. bacterial vaginosis.
c. pelvic inflammatory disease.
d. herpes simplex.

12. A male patient presents with dysuria. He states that his female partner has an STD, but he is not sure which one. Which of these should be part of the differential?

a. Bacterial vaginosis and trichomonas
b. Chlamydia and gonorrhea
c. HIV and herpes
d. Syphilis and chlamydia

13. A patient with newly diagnosed genital herpes would appropriately receive a prescription for:

a. cryotherapy.
b. ceftriaxone.
c. imiquimod.
d. famciclovir.

14. How should a patient with suspected syphilis be screened?

a. Ask about symptoms in the patient
b. Ask about symptoms of sexual partners
c. A urethral swab for culture
d. A serum assessment

15. A 72 year-old male patient has early renal insufficiency. What laboratory test best assesses his kidney function?

a. Serum creatinine
b. Presence of proteinuria
c. Glomerular filtration rate
d. Quantity of urine produced in 24 hours

16. A 70 year-old male patient is diagnosed with renal disease. What activity will help preserve kidney function?

a. Exercise 20 minutes daily
b. Increase water consumption daily
c. Weigh daily
d. Avoid red meat

11. *b*
Bacterial vaginosis (BV), results when normal vaginal flora such as Lactobacillus sp. are replaced with anaerobic bacteria like *Prevotella*, *Mobiluncus* and *Gardnerella*. This is usually, but not always associated with sexual activity. Women who have never been sexually active are less affected.

12. *b*
Bacterial vaginosis does not produce a discharge in male patients. Herpes produces lesions that are painful. HIV is not specifically associated with dysuria. Syphilis produces a painless lesion. Chlamydia and gonorrhea are usually associated with dysuria and discharge. Trichomonas can produce dysuria.

13. *d*
Genital herpes is a viral infection affecting the mucus membranes. Some learned authorities consider this to be the most common STD in the United States. Herpes is treated with an oral antiviral agent like valacyclovir, acyclovir, or famciclovir. It is initially prescribed for 7-14 days. Shorter dosing periods may be given after the initial infection has been treated. Suppressive therapy is initiated when patients have multiple outbreaks. The oral antiviral agents are dosed daily for suppressive therapy and given for at least one year.

14. *d*
Patients can be screened for syphilis in three ways. The nontreponemal tests are VDRL (venereal disease research laboratory), RPR (rapid plasma regain) or TRUST (toluidine red unheated serum test) tests. The main use of the treponemal tests is to confirm positive nontreponemal tests. These results are reported as reactive or non-reactive and are quantitative in nature, which is why they are used as confirmatory tests.

15. *c*
A patient with early chronic renal insufficiency typically has no physical symptoms but has a glomerular filtration rate (GFR) that will begin to change. GFR best reflects the function of the kidney and so is helpful for trending kidney function. Because the nephrons can adapt to declining function, the serum creatinine concentration may be normal in the presence of impaired kidney function. The urinalysis may demonstrate proteinuria. This represents damage to the kidney. The quantity of urine produced is not helpful when measuring kidney function.

16. *b*
Volume depletion decreases renal perfusion. Decreased renal perfusion secondary to volume depletion is potentially correctable by increasing fluids. As glomerular filtration rates improve, renal function improves. Water is critical to proper function of the kidneys.

17. A physically independent 75 year-old is living in an assisted living facility. She walks one mile daily on most days. She is beginning to have some memory issues but is otherwise healthy and takes only her "hormone". She is found to have asymptomatic bacteriuria. How should she be managed?

a. **Repeat the urinalysis in 7 days.**
b. **Treat her today with a one-day dose of an antibiotic.**
c. **Monitor her for symptoms of a urinary tract infection.**
d. **Repeat the urinalysis in 4 weeks.**

18. A 44 year-old female patient is diagnosed with a urinary tract infection (UTI). Which bacteria count collected via "midstream, clean catch" supports a diagnosis of UTI?

a. **> 10,000 bacteria**
b. **> 25,000 bacteria**
c. **> 50,000 bacteria**
d. **> 100,000 bacteria**

19. Ciprofloxacin given to treat a urinary tract infection would be contraindicated in a:

a. **pregnant patient.**
b. **19-year-old female.**
c. **patient with hypertension.**
d. **patient with pyelonephritis.**

20. A patient has been diagnosed with pyelonephritis. He probably will have:

a. **costovertebral angle tenderness.**
b. **a positive Murphy's sign.**
c. **burning with urination.**
d. **pain which waxes and wanes.**

21. A patient with urolithiasis is more likely to:

a. **have frequent urinary tract infections.**
b. **be of male gender.**
c. **have chills and fever.**
d. **demonstrate RBC casts.**

17. ***c***
Approximately 30-50% of elderly women living in institutions have asymptomatic bacteriuria. There is no data that supports treatment of patients to prevent future problems or complications. In fact, asymptomatic bacteriuria is not usually treated unless a patient is pregnant, has diabetes or other chronic immunosuppressive state, is undergoing a urinary procedure, or has polycystic renal disease.

18. ***d***
Urine should be devoid of bacteria unless there is an infection or when asymptomatic bacteriuria is present. When bacteria are present in a urine specimen, consideration must be given to how the specimen was collected. When the specimen is collected via midstream, clean catch, the tolerance for organisms is less than 100,000. It is expected that the urine collected in this way will include bacteria from external genitalia as urine exits the body. If the number of bacteria are greater than 100,000, a urinary tract infection is correctly diagnosed.

19. ***a***
Ciprofloxacin is a quinolone antibiotic and is contraindicated in patients who are pregnant or younger than 18 years old because of potential problems with bone and cartilage formation. There is no contraindication in a patient with hypertension. A quinolone might be a good choice in a patient with pyelonephritis and would not be contraindicated.

20. ***a***
CVA (costovertebral angle) tenderness is a classic finding in patients with pyelonephritis, an infection of the upper renal tract. A positive Murphy's sign (inspiratory arrest with deep palpation of the upper right quadrant) is demonstrated in a patient with cholecystitis. Pain that waxes and wanes usually describes a patient with a kidney stone. Burning with urination is often seen in patient with urinary tract infection.

21. ***b***
Males are more likely (4:1) than females to have urolithiasis. The overall incidence is about 2-5% in a lifetime. There is no increased incidence of stone formation among patients with frequent UTIs. Patients with urolithiasis may exhibit fever and chills if infection is associated with a very large stone, but this is not the usual case. RBC casts are mucoprotein complexes formed in the renal tubules. This generally indicates glomerular injury, not urolithiasis.

22. A patient reports that her urine has a light green hue. She feels well otherwise. The most likely reason for this is:

a. **something she has consumed.**
b. **a urinary tract infection.**
c. **a stone in the upper urinary tract.**
d. **a psychiatric illness.**

23. A patient with urinary burning, frequency, and urgency is found to have positive leukocytes and negative nitrites. A likely explanation is that the patient:

a. **has a kidney stone.**
b. **could be pregnant.**
c. **has a sexually transmitted disease.**
d. **is taking an antibiotic.**

24. Which patient is most likely to develop a urinary tract infection?

a. **20 year old sexually active female**
b. **60 year old sexually active male**
c. **Anyone who consumes multiple carbonated beverages daily**
d. **70 year old nursing home resident**

25. A 24 year-old female patient has been diagnosed with an uncomplicated UTI. Which assessment below is least important at this time?

a. **Body temperature**
b. **Abdominal exam**
c. **Assessment of CVA tenderness**
d. **Vaginal exam**

26. How long should a female patient with an uncomplicated UTI be treated with an oral antibiotic?

a. **One day**
b. **Three days**
c. **Five days**
d. **Seven days**

27. A 22 year-old male patient has symptoms of burning with urination. Which assessment below is least important at this time?

a. **Body temperature**
b. **Full genital exam and rectal exam**
c. **Abdominal exam**
d. **Assessment of CVA tenderness**

22. *a*
An unusual color imparted to the urine is nearly always due to something the patient has had to eat or drink in the last 24 hours. A urine specimen should be obtained for analysis to rule out blood, but blood in the urine is usually bright red or brown in color. A green hue should compel the examiner to consider a food dye.

23. *c*
The patient's symptoms are classic for a urinary tract infection. This is a possibility in this scenario but not a choice. In the alternative, the provider should consider an STD. This is not the usual presentation of a kidney stone. If the patient were pregnant, she might have frequency and urgency, but should not have burning. Taking an antibiotic would more likely diminish the presence of leukocytes than nitrites.

24. *a*
Young sexually active women are at much higher risk (some studies indicate 2.6 times higher risk) of UTI than non-sexually active females. Presumably, this occurs because the vaginal introitus becomes colonized with bacteria. UTI in males is unusual compared to females. *E. coli* is the most common urinary tract pathogen causing disease.

25. *d*
A vaginal exam would not be indicated in a patient with an uncomplicated UTI. History should be elicited regarding vaginal discharge and symptoms of STDs. A gynecological exam should take place if there is a doubt about the diagnosis, there is a urethral or vaginal discharge, or there is evidence or history of herpetic ulcerations.

26. *b*
Three days treatment with an appropriate antibiotic is as efficacious as 7-10 days of treatment. Three day treatment was associated with fewer side effects, better compliance, and fewer adverse reactions.

27. *c*
In female patients, an abdominal assessment is part of a routine exam for patients who present with symptoms of UTI. In males, urinary tract infections are far less likely than in females. Consequently, the differential diagnosis in males who complain of dysuria or LUTS (lower urinary tract symptoms) should include UTI, urethritis, epididymitis, prostatitis, or STDs. The physical exam should include inspection and palpation of the testicles and penis. The genital region should be assessed for ulcerations and lesions. The urethral meatus should be assessed for crusting, discharge, erythema, and a specimen should be collected if appropriate.

Practice Exams

Adult Exam #1 Questions

1. **Which finding below is considered "within normal limits"?**

    a. **A diastolic murmur in an 18 year-old**
    b. **An INR of 2.0 in a patient taking warfarin**
    c. **Cholesterol level of 205 in a 15 year-old**
    d. **Blood pressure of 160/70 in a 75 year-old**

2. **The most common place for indirect inguinal hernias to develop is:**

    a. **the internal inguinal ring.**
    b. **the external inguinal ring.**
    c. **Hesselbach's triangle.**
    d. **femoral ring.**

3. **The most appropriate time to begin screening for renal nephropathy in a patient with Type 1 diabetes is:**

    a. **at diagnosis.**
    b. **once annually after diagnosis.**
    c. **2-3 years after diagnosis.**
    d. **5 years after diagnosis.**

4. **A 43 year-old patient who has been diagnosed with hepatitis B has the following laboratory values. How should they be interpreted based on these values?**

    HCV IgG (-), RIBA (radio immuno blot assay) (-)

    a. **The patient has hepatitis B and hepatitis C.**
    b. **The patient does not have hepatitis C.**
    c. **The patient could have hepatitis C.**
    d. **The results are indeterminate.**

5. **What are the most common signs and symptoms associated with mononucleosis?**

    a. **Fatigue and lymphadenopathy**
    b. **Cough and pharyngitis**
    c. **Splenomegaly and fever**
    d. **Rash and pharyngitis**

6. A 40 year-old patient has the following laboratory values. How should they be interpreted?

HBsAg (-), HBsAb (+), HBcAb (-)

a. **The patient had hepatitis.**
b. **The patient has hepatitis.**
c. **The patient should consider immunization.**
d. **The patient has been immunized.**

7. Drugs that target the renin-angiotensin-aldosterone system are particularly beneficial in patients with:

a. **hypertension.**
b. **chronic heart failure.**
c. **kidney stones.**
d. **diabetic nephropathy.**

8. A 25 year-old male patient with subacute bacterial epididymitis should be treated initially with:

a. **an oral quinolone.**
b. **doxycycline.**
c. **anti-inflammatories and analgesics.**
d. **ice and scrotal support.**

9. An older adult has suspected Vitamin B12 deficiency. Which of the following lab indices is more indicative of a Vitamin B12 deficiency?

a. **Microcytosis**
b. **Macrocytosis**
c. **Leukocytosis**
d. **Thrombocytosis**

10. A patient who is at high risk for skin cancer should:

a. **examine his skin monthly for changes.**
b. **be examined by a dermatologist quarterly.**
c. **use emollients regularly.**
d. **eat foods high in vitamin C.**

11. A female patient has the following characteristics. Which one represents the greatest risk factor for development of Type II diabetes?

a. **BMI 26**
b. **Lack of exercise**
c. **Mediterranean decent**
d. **Lack of regular healthcare**

12. The major difference between varicose veins and arteriosclerosis is the:

a. **limbs affected.**
b. **gender affected.**
c. **vessels affected.**
d. **degree of pain.**

13. Which of the following symptoms is typical of GERD?

a. **Chest pain**
b. **Cough**
c. **Sore throat**
d. **Pyrosis**

14. An African American male complains of pain in his back and trunk. He is diagnosed with multiple myeloma. He is probably:

a. **about 21 years old.**
b. **about mid thirties.**
c. **younger than 50 years.**
d. **about 65 years old.**

15. A patient with testicular torsion will have a:

a. **positive cremasteric reflex on the affected side.**
b. **negative cremasteric reflex on the affected side.**
c. **a positive cremasteric reflex bilaterally.**
d. **negative cremasteric reflex bilaterally.**

16. A patient with a positive history of a tick bite about 2 weeks ago and erythema migrans has a positive ELISA for Borrelia. The Western blot is positive. How should he be managed?

a. **He should receive doxycycline for Lyme disease.**
b. **He should receive penicillin for Rocky Mountain spotted fever (RMSF).**
c. **He does not have Lyme disease or RMSF.**
d. **He needs additional testing to confirm Lyme disease.**

17. An elderly adult with an appendicitis is *unlikely* to exhibit:

a. generalized abdominal pain.
b. initial WBC elevation.
c. UTI symptoms.
d. low grade fever.

18. A patient has 2 non-fasting glucose values of 111 mg/dL and 124 mg/dL that were measured on 2 separate days in the same week. This patient:

a. has normal blood glucose values.
b. has impaired fasting glucose.
c. should have further glucose testing done for diagnosis.
d. should have a Hgb A1C performed.

19. Which medication listed below could potentially exacerbate CHF in a susceptible individual?

a. Naproxen
b. HCTZ
c. Lovastatin
d. Loratadine

20. A patient has the following laboratory values. What does this mean?
Hepatitis A: (-) IgM (-) IgG

a. He has hepatitis A.
b. He has immunity to hepatitis A.
c. He has no immunity to hepatitis A.
d. More data is needed.

21. Which group of medications should not be used to treat a patient with CHF?

a. Ramipril, aspirin, metoprolol
b. Digoxin, furosemide, aspirin
c. Fosinopril, HCTZ, verapamil
d. Furosemide, enalapril, aspirin

22. A male patient has epididymitis. His most likely complaint will be:

a. burning with urination.
b. testicular pain.
c. scrotal pain.
d. penile discharge.

23. A patient with diarrhea has a stool specimen positive for WBCs. What does this indicate?

a. A viral infection
b. A malignancy
c. Parasitic infection
d. Occult blood

24. A 35 year-old patient has the following laboratory values. How should they be interpreted?

HBsAg (-), HBsAb (-), HBcAb (-)

a. The patient had hepatitis B.
b. The patient has hepatitis B.
c. The patient should consider Hepatitis B immunization.
d. The patient has had Hepatitis B immunization.

25. An overweight 76 year-old female with a recent onset of diabetes has longstanding hypertension and hyperlipidemia. She has developed atrial fibrillation. The nurse practitioner knows that now she will be at risk for:

a. an S3 gallop.
b. CHF.
c. peripheral edema.
d. hypothyroidism.

26. A microscopic examination of the sample taken from a skin lesion indicates hyphae. What type infection might this indicate?

a. Bacterial
b. Viral
c. Parasitic
d. Fungal

27. Which medication listed below can exacerbate the symptoms of GERD?

a. Verapamil
b. Metformin
c. Ferrous sulfate
d. Ceftriaxone

28. Which patient would be expected to have the highest systolic blood pressure?

a. A 21 year-old male
b. A 50 year-old perimenopausal female
c. A 35 year-old patient with Type 2 diabetes
d. A 75 year-old male

29. A patient is in the clinic with a 36 hour history of diarrhea and moderate dehydration. Interventions should include:

a. oral rehydration with tea, cola, or Gatorade.
b. IV rehydration.
c. oral rehydration with an electrolyte replenishment solution.
d. resumption of usual fluid intake and solid food intake.

30. The nurse practitioner performs a fundoscopic exam on a patient who has recently been diagnosed with hypertension. What is the significance of AV nicking?

a. This is an incidental finding.
b. This is indicative of long standing hypertension.
c. The patient should be screened for diabetes.
d. The patient should be referred to ophthalmology.

31. A patient with gout has hypertension. Which drug class should be avoided in him if possible?

a. ACE inhibitors
b. Beta blockers
c. Calcium channel blockers
d. Thiazide diuretics

32. The most common risk factor for developing hepatitis B is:

a. homosexual activity.
b. injecting drug use.
c. heterosexual activity.
d. body piercings.

33. Benazepril should be discontinued immediately if:

a. dry cough develops.
b. pregnancy occurs.
c. potassium levels decrease.
d. gout develops.

34. Which of the following medications does not warrant monitoring of potassium levels?

a. **Fosinopril**
b. **Candesartan**
c. **Hydrochlorothiazide**
d. **Amlodipine**

35. A liability policy which pays claims even after the policy is no longer active is termed:

a. **claims made policy.**
b. **tail coverage.**
c. **liability protection.**
d. **"all-protect".**

36. A 50 year-old male patient reports that he has a sensation of scrotal heaviness. He reports that the sensation is worse at the end of the day. He denies pain. What is the likely etiology of these symptoms?

a. **Strangulated hernia**
b. **Inguinal hernia**
c. **Epididymitis**
d. **Hydrocele**

37. MMSE helps to identify patients with symptoms of:

a. **dementia.**
b. **depression.**
c. **behavioral changes.**
d. **delirium.**

38. A patient with acute anxiety will experience the fastest relief of symptoms when he is treated with:

a. **an SSRI.**
b. **a TCA**
c. **a benzodiazepine.**
d. **beta-blocker.**

39. A patient has been diagnosed with scabies. What is the medication of choice to treat this?

- a. **Permethrin**
- b. **Coal tar**
- c. **Ketoconazole**
- d. **Mupirocin**

40. An inguinal hernia is palpated on a male patient by an examiner. Which word below best describes what the hernia feels like when touched by the examiner?

- a. **Nodular**
- b. **Silky**
- c. **Firm**
- d. **Bumpy**

41. How should the nurse practitioner approach a patient who consumes excessive amounts of alcohol but denies that he has a problem?

- a. **Order liver function studies to show the patient that his liver has damage.**
- b. **Order a blood alcohol content and discuss results with patient.**
- c. **Tell him to find another healthcare provider.**
- d. **Tell him that you are concerned about his health.**

42. Which statement about bulimia nervosa is accurate?

- a. **High dose SSRIs are used to treat this.**
- b. **This is more common in men than women.**
- c. **Loss of control is not a characteristic of this illness.**
- d. **Bupropion is a good choice for treatment of these patients.**

43. An uncommon symptom associated with acute bronchitis is:

- a. **fever.**
- b. **cough.**
- c. **pharyngitis.**
- d. **purulent sputum.**

44. A healthcare provider ("the HCP") was stuck with a needle from a patient suspected to be infected with HIV ("the patient"). A rapid HIV test was performed and was found to be positive. This means that the:

- a. **healthcare provider has been infected with HIV.**
- b. **the patient is infected with HIV.**
- c. **the HIV status of the patient requires further testing.**
- d. **the HIV status of the healthcare provider requires further testing.**

45. Athletic amenorrhea increases the risk of:

a. osteoporosis.
b. an eating disorder.
c. covert hypothyroidism.
d. breast cancer.

46. In collection of a specimen for a PAP smear, how is the endocervical specimen collected?

a. After the ectocervical specimen with a broom
b. After the ectocervical specimen with a brush
c. Before the ectocervical specimen with a broom
d. Before the ectocervical specimen with a brush

47. The frequency for cervical screening depends on the patient and her age. What is the longest recommended time interval between cervical screens for patients who are 21-65 years of age?

a. 1 year
b. 2 years
c. 3 years
d. 5 years

48. A patient with anorexia nervosa (AN) had symptoms that began about 6 months ago. She presents today and is diagnosed with AN. She has a laboratory evaluation. What might be expected?

a. Elevated potassium
b. Decreased potassium, decreased glucose
c. Elevated BUN, Cr
d. Normal lab values

49. A woman who is 65 years old presents to your clinic with a breast lump. She has had only normal annual mammograms and her last one was 6 months ago. What is true about this lump?

a. It is probably breast cancer.
b. It may not be a lump at all.
c. It is likely a fibroadenoma.
d. It is probably a benign lesion.

50. A 15 year-old is about 10% below her ideal body weight. She complains of dizziness when she stands up. Laboratory studies were performed. Besides malnutrition, what else could account for her dizziness?

a. **BUN is mildly elevated**
b. **Glucose = 80 mg/dL**
c. **Hemoglobin = 9.6 mg/dL**
d. **Potassium is 3.5 meq/L**

51. A nurse practitioner is working in a minor care clinic. She realizes that a patient with a minor laceration does not have insurance and is using his brother's insurance information today so that his visit will be covered. How should she proceed?

a. **She should let him know that she knows what he is doing.**
b. **She should ignore this and proceed to suture his wound.**
c. **She should let the clinic's business office know what is happening.**
d. **She should not suture his wound and ask him to leave.**

52. An example of primary prevention is:

a. **using a condom to prevent infection with an STD.**
b. **diagnosis of chlamydia prior to symptom development.**
c. **treatment of chlamydia concurrently with gonorrhea.**
d. **early treatment of sexual partners.**

53. Classic symptoms of a deep vein thrombosis include:

a. **swelling, pain, redness.**
b. **calf complaints, pain with walking, history of exercise.**
c. **swelling, pain, and discoloration in lower extremity.**
d. **warmth, edema, and relief of pain with walking.**

54. A patient was exposed to HIV through sexual intercourse. He should be followed with screening tests to identify seroconversion for:

a. **4-6 weeks.**
b. **3-4 months.**
c. **about 6 months.**
d. **one year.**

55. A key component of the approach to a patient who has atopic dermatitis is hydration. Which agent should be avoided?

a. Lotions
b. Creams
c. Thick creams
d. Ointments

56. Topical 5-fluorouracil (5-FU) is used to treat:

a. atopic dermatitis.
b. hepatitis.
c. thalassemia.
d. basal cell carcinoma.

57. A 32 year-old patient is a newly diagnosed diabetic. She has developed a sinus infection. Her symptoms have persisted for 10 days. Six weeks ago she was treated with amoxicillin for an upper respiratory infection. It cleared without incident. What should be recommended today?

a. Prescribe amoxicillin again.
b. Prescribe amoxicillin-clavulanate today.
c. Do not prescribe an antibiotic; a decongestant is indicated only.
d. Prescribe a decongestant and antihistamine.

58. The single most effective maintenance therapy for allergic rhinitis is:

a. an antihistamine.
b. a decongestant.
c. a topical nasal steroid.
d. a topical antihistamine.

59. A patient has been diagnosed with Grave's disease. He is likely to have:

a. an elevated alkaline phosphatase.
b. an elevated T3 or T4.
c. an elevated TSH.
d. elevated liver function studies.

60. A patient has suspected peptic ulcer disease. Her symptoms occur a few hours after eating. She likely has a:

a. gastric ulcer.
b. duodenal ulcer.
c. gastric or duodenal ulcer.
d. infection with H. pylori.

61. A 74 year-old male patient has sustained a laceration to his foot. His last tetanus shot was more than 10 years ago. He has completed the primary series. What should be recommended?

- **a. Tetanus toxoid only**
- **b. Tetanus and diphtheria only**
- **c. His primary series will protect him.**
- **d. Tetanus, diphtheria, and acellular pertussis (Tdap)**

62. A patient has been prescribed metronidazole for treatment of C. difficile. What should be avoided in this patient?

- **a. Excess fluids**
- **b. Vitamin B12**
- **c. Grapefruit juice**
- **d. Alcohol**

63. A 66 year-old African American female has multiple risk factors for osteoporosis. Which choice listed below is NOT a risk factor for osteoporosis?

- **a. Her age**
- **b. Her race**
- **c. Glucocorticoid intake**
- **d. Excessive alcohol intake**

64. A patient with diarrhea is tested for *C. difficile*. How soon should the enzyme immunoassay (EIA) yield results?

- **a. Within 20 minutes**
- **b. About 24 hours**
- **c. About 3 days**
- **d. Less than one week**

65. The main difference between cellulitis and erysipelas is the:

- **a. infecting organism.**
- **b. length of time that infection lasts.**
- **c. treatment.**
- **d. layer of skin involvement.**

66. A patient has a lower leg wound that appears infected. It is red, warm to touch and edematous. He had an acute onset of pain, symptoms, and low grade fever. What is this?

- **a. Cellulitis**
- **b. Erysipelas**
- **c. Impetigo**
- **d. An allergic reaction**

67. The carotid arteries are auscultated for bruits because:

- **a. a bruit is indicative of an impending stroke.**
- **b. a bruit is indicative of significant carotid stenosis.**
- **c. this is indicative of generalized atherosclerosis.**
- **d. this is reflective of stroke risk.**

68. A 39 year-old has a sudden onset of a right red eye. He reports sensitivity to light and the sensation of a foreign body, though his history for a foreign body is negative. He does not wear contact lenses. How should the NP manage this?

- **a. Refer to ophthalmology**
- **b. Treat for viral conjunctivitis**
- **c. Treat for bacterial conjunctivitis**
- **d. Observe for 24 hours if visual acuity is normal**

69. A 51 year-old female patient presents with a 2 cm palpable breast mass. How should this be evaluated to determine whether it is solid or cystic in nature?

- **a. Mammogram**
- **b. Ultrasound**
- **c. MRI**
- **d. Clinical breast exam**

70. Which test below is most cost-effective to screen for abdominal aortic aneurysm?

- **a. CT of the abdomen**
- **b. MRI of the abdomen**
- **c. Abdominal ultrasound**
- **d. Two hand palpation test**

71. What class of medications can be used to treat benign prostatic hyperplasia and provide immediate relief?

a. **Alpha-1 blockers**
b. **5-alpha reductase inhibitors**
c. **Diuretics**
d. **Analgesics**

72. An elderly male patient is taking finasteride, a 5-alpha-reductase inhibitor. What affect might this have on his PSA level?

a. **It will increase.**
b. **It will decrease.**
c. **There is no predictable change.**
d. **There will be no change.**

73. The classic description of transient ischemic attack is " a sudden onset of focal neurological symptoms that lasts less than":

a. **one minute.**
b. **five minutes.**
c. **one hour.**
d. **24 hours.**

74. A male patient takes HCTZ daily for hypertension. He developed severe pain in his great toe yesterday. He was diagnosed with gout today and started on a medication. Which medication listed below would be contraindicated at this time?

a. **Allopurinol**
b. **Prednisone**
c. **Colchicine**
d. **Indomethacin**

75. A high purine diet can contribute to gouty arthritis. Which food listed below contributes most to a high purine diet?

a. **Coffee**
b. **Eggs**
c. **Beef**
d. **Bread**

76. A patient who is 60 years old complains of low back pain for the last 5-6 weeks. She states that the severity is about 4/10 and that she gets no relief from sitting, standing, or lying. The NP should consider:

a. sciatica.
b. ankylosing spondylitis.
c. disc disease.
d. systemic illness.

77. A nurse practitioner has agreed to participate in the Medicare health insurance program. Medicare paid 80% of the charges billed for a clinic visit. What can be done about the other 20% that is owed?

a. The NP can bill the patient for a percentage of the remainder.
b. The NP is prohibited from billing the patient.
c. The NP can collect 100% if billed incident to the MD.
d. The NP can resubmit the bill for additional payment.

78. Which medication below is contraindicated for lone use in treating asthma?

a. Short-acting bronchodilator
b. Long-acting bronchodilator
c. Inhaled steroid
d. Oral steroid

79. A short-acting anticholinergic medication can be used alone or in combination with a short-acting beta agonist to manage symptoms of which disease?

a. COPD
b. Asthma
c. Glaucoma
d. Tachyarrhythmias

80. A healthy 32 year-old female has fever, left flank pain, and nausea. What is the most likely diagnosis?

a. Urinary tract infection
b. Renal stone
c. Cholecystitis
d. Pyelonephritis

81. A patient with dysuria has a urine specimen that reveals < 10,000 bacteria and numerous trichomonads. How should this patient be managed?

- a. **Increased fluids and a urinary tract analgesic**
- b. **Ciprofloxacin for 3 days**
- c. **Metronidazole for 7 days**
- d. **Ciprofloxacin and metronidazole**

82. A homeless patient presents to the free clinic. She should be screened for diseases and conditions most prevalent in this population. She should be screened for:

- a. **TB, HIV, and hepatitis.**
- b. **pregnancy, headaches, and STDs.**
- c. **urinary tract infection and STDs.**
- d. **diabetes, HIV, and neuropathy.**

83. A patient presents to your clinic numerous times with vague complaints. She seems to respond poorly to medical treatment that is given to her. What should be considered when obtaining a history from her?

- a. **Physical abuse or depression**
- b. **Depression or HIV**
- c. **Hepatitis or HIV**
- d. **Anemia or Depression**

84. How should a 20 year-old college age student who presents with cough, night sweats, and weight loss be screened for TB?

- a. **A chest x-ray**
- b. **A TB skin test**
- c. **A sputum specimen**
- d. **Questionnaire about symptoms**

85. An ACE inhibitor is specifically indicated in patients who have:

- a. **hypertension, diabetes with proteinuria, heart failure.**
- b. **diabetes, hypertension, hyperlipidemia.**
- c. **asthma, hypertension, diabetes.**
- d. **renal nephropathy, heart failure, hyperlipidemia.**

86. A female vegetarian presents to your clinic with iron deficiency anemia. What can the NP suggest she eat to help with resolution of iron deficiency anemia?

a. **Dark green leafy vegetables and dried peas and beans**
b. **Mushrooms, oatmeal, and whole grain breads**
c. **Beets, broccoli, and beef**
d. **Baked potatoes, beets, and broccoli**

87. Thalassemia minor can be recognized by:

a. **microcytic, normochromic red cells.**
b. **normocytic, normochromic red cells.**
c. **microcytic, hypochromic red cells.**
d. **normocytic, hyperchromic red cells.**

88. Which symptom below is true of cluster headaches but not migraine headaches?

a. **It is more common in females.**
b. **The length of the headache duration is about 30-90 minutes.**
c. **The most common characteristic is familial history.**
d. **Sunlight is a common trigger.**

89. Which criterion below is a criterion for Alzheimer's Disease?

a. **Focal neurologic signs**
b. **Laboratory evidence of dementia**
c. **Radiologic evidence of dementia**
d. **Impairment of executive function**

90. How would you create a therapeutic relationship with a patient?

a. **Tell the patient that he can trust you.**
b. **At the end of the visit, tell the patient you enjoyed taking care of him.**
c. **Ask open-ended questions.**
d. **Touch the patient during the interview.**

91. The risk of HIV transmission is increased:

a. **when other STDs are present.**
b. **in females.**
c. **when patients are aware of their HIV status.**
d. **in patients with diabetes.**

92. A 65 year-old patient presents to your clinic with evidence of hyperthyroidism. In assessing her cardiovascular status, what should the NP assess immediately?

a. **Cardiac enzymes**
b. **Electrocardiogram**
c. **Electrolytes**
d. **Auscultation of systolic murmurs**

93. Which symptom listed below is typical of depression?

a. **Difficulty falling asleep**
b. **Snoring**
c. **Early morning wakening**
d. **Keeping late night hours reading**

94. A patient who frequently has episodes of gout should avoid which groups of food?

a. **Beans, rice, and tea**
b. **Scrambled eggs, milk, and toast**
c. **Roast beef with gravy, rice**
d. **Fish and steamed vegetables**

95. A common side effect of thiazide diuretics is:

a. **prostatitis.**
b. **erectile dysfunction.**
c. **fatigue.**
d. **hyperkalemia.**

96. A mammogram in a healthy 50 year-old female patient is considered to be an example of:

a. **primary prevention.**
b. **secondary prevention.**
c. **tertiary prevention.**
d. **quaternary prevention.**

97. An elderly patient has been diagnosed with shingles on the right lateral aspect of her trunk. It appeared initially yesterday. It is very painful. How should she be managed?

a. **Treatment with a topical lidocaine patch only.**
b. **An oral antiviral agent and NSAIDs.**
c. **An oral antiviral agent and pain medication.**
d. **An oral antiviral agent, pain medication, and oral steroids.**

98. The most common pathogen associated with pyelonephritis is:

a. ***E. coli.***
b. ***H. influenzae.***
c. ***Streptococcus sp.***
d. ***Staphylococcus sp.***

99. A patient with a primary case of scabies was probably infected:

a. **1-3 days ago.**
b. **1 week ago.**
c. **2 weeks ago.**
d. **3-4 weeks ago.**

100. A patient calls your office. He states that he just came in from the woods and discovered a tick on his upper arm. He states that he has removed the tick and the area is slightly red. What should he be advised?

a. **No treatment is needed.**
b. **He should be prescribed doxycycline.**
c. **He needs a topical scrub to prevent Lyme Disease.**
d. **He should come to the office for a ceftriaxone injection.**

101. What temperature should be set on a water heater in the home of an elderly patient to prevent burn injury?

a. **Less than 110 degrees**
b. **Less than 120 degrees**
c. **Less than 130 degrees**
d. **Less than 140 degrees**

102. A patient cannot stick his tongue out of his mouth and move his tongue from side to side. What cranial nerve is responsible for this movement?

a. **Cranial Nerve III**
b. **Cranial Nerve VII**
c. **Cranial Nerve X**
d. **Cranial Nerve XII**

103. AV nicking may be identified in a patient with what disease?

a. **Glaucoma**
b. **Cataracts**
c. **Diabetes**
d. **Hypertension**

104. A 40 year-old female patient presents to the clinic with multiple, painful reddened nodules on the anterior surface of both legs. She is concerned. These are probably associated with her history of:

a. **deep vein thrombosis.**
b. **phlebitis.**
c. **ulcerative colitis.**
d. **alcoholism.**

105. Which class of medications is NOT used for migraine prophylaxis?

a. **Beta blockers**
b. **Calcium channel blockers**
c. **Triptans**
d. **Tricyclic antidepressants**

106. A patient has 2 palpable, tender, left pre-auricular nodes that are about 0.5 cm in diameter. What might also be found in this patient?

a. **Sore throat**
b. **Ulceration on the tongue**
c. **Conjunctivitis**
d. **Ear infection**

107. A patient presents to your clinic with a painless red eye. Her vision is normal, but her sclera has a blood red area. What is this termed?

a. **Conjunctivitis**
b. **Acute iritis**
c. **Glaucoma**
d. **Subconjunctival hemorrhage**

108. A 24 year-old patient presents to your clinic. She states that she has vomited for the last 5 mornings and until early afternoon. She feels better in the evenings. She denies fever. What lab tests should be monitored?

a. **CBC and urine for ketones**
b. **Electrolytes and serum pregnancy**
c. **Electrolytes and hepatitis panel**
d. **Metabolic panel and potassium level**

109. What laboratory test could help differentiate acute bronchitis from pneumonia in a patient with a productive cough?

a. **CBC**
b. **Chest x-ray**
c. **Sputum specimen**
d. **Pulmonary function tests**

110. A patient who has been treated for hypothyroidism presents for her annual exam. Her TSH is 4.1 (normal = 0.4- 3.8). She feels well. How should she be managed?

a. **Continue her current dosage of thyroid replacement.**
b. **Increase her replacement.**
c. **Decrease her replacement.**
d. **Repeat the TSH in 2-3 weeks.**

111. A 26 year-old male patient has been diagnosed with gonorrhea. How should he be managed?

a. **Ceftriaxone only**
b. **Ceftriaxone and azithromycin**
c. **Cefixime and azithromycin**
d. **Penicillin G**

112. A 70 year-old male patient has an elevated MCV with an anemia. His triglycerides are 420. What should be suspected?

a. **Pernicious anemia**
b. **Folate deficiency**
c. **Alcohol abuse**
d. **Hypertriglyceridemia**

113. A young female adult presents with vaginal discharge and itching. Besides trichomoniasis and yeast, what else should be included in the differential?

a. **Bacterial vaginosis**
b. **Chlamydia**
c. **Herpes genitalis**
d. **Syphilis**

114. A 45 year-old male who is in good health presents with complaints of pain in his left heel. He states that the first few steps out of bed in the morning are extremely painful. He has no history of trauma. What is the likely etiology of his pain?

a. **Achilles tendinitis**
b. **Plantar fasciitis**
c. **Calcaneal spur**
d. **Arthritis of the foot**

115. An elderly hypertensive patient has osteoporosis. Which antihypertensive agent would have the secondary effect of improving her osteoporosis?

a. **A thiazide diuretic**
b. **A calcium channel blocker**
c. **An ACE inhibitor**
d. **A beta blocker**

116. The most common polyneuropathy in the elderly is:

a. **Charcot-Marie-Tooth disease.**
b. **diabetes mellitus.**
c. **urinary incontinence.**
d. **Guillain-Barre syndrome.**

117. A patient reports that he has been taking saw palmetto. Why is this used?

a. **It prevents blood clots.**
b. **It improves urine flow.**
c. **It decreases environmental allergies.**
d. **It decreases risk of colon cancer.**

118. A patient who is 52 years old presents to your clinic for an exam. You notice a yellowish plaque on her upper eyelid. It is painless. What should the NP assess?

a. **Vision in the affected eye**
b. **Sedimentation rate**
c. **Lipid levels**
d. **Liver function studies**

119. The greatest risk of transmitting HIV is during:

a. **the acute phase.**
b. **the time that detectable antibody is present.**
c. **high viral load periods.**
d. **late infection phase.**

120. A 70 year-old is diagnosed with multiple cherry angiomas. The nurse practitioner knows that:

- a. **this is a mature capillary proliferation more common in young adults.**
- b. **an angioma occurs as a single lesion.**
- c. **these may bleed profusely if ruptured.**
- d. **these are precursors of skin malignancies.**

121. A 78 year-old has been diagnosed with diabetes about 10 years ago. An older adult with a hypoglycemic episode is more likely to exhibit:

- a. **tremors.**
- b. **sweating.**
- c. **dizziness and weakness.**
- d. **symptoms of hyperglycemia.**

122. Metformin is a good choice for many older adults with type 2 diabetes. What should be monitored carefully?

- a. **Hypoglycemia**
- b. **Fluid retention**
- c. **Lactic alkalosis**
- d. **Renal dysfunction**

123. An 83 year-old patient is diagnosed with diverticulitis. The most common complaint is:

- a. **rectal bleeding.**
- b. **bloating and crampiness.**
- c. **left lower quadrant pain.**
- d. **frequent belching and flatulence.**

124. A 70 year-old male presents to your clinic with a lump in his breast. How should this be evaluated?

- a. **Palpation and ultrasound**
- b. **Mammogram and ultrasound**
- c. **Ultrasound only**
- d. **Mammogram only**

125. A 70 year-old African American male complains of pain in his back and trunk. Cardiovascular disease is ruled out. He has a normocytic normochromic anemia with hypercalcemia. A likely diagnosis is:

- **a. multiple myeloma.**
- **b. lymphoma.**
- **c. leukemia.**
- **d. prostate cancer.**

126. A 75 year-old is diagnosed with essential tremor. What is the most commonly used medication to treat this?

- **a. Carbidopa**
- **b. Long acting propanolol**
- **c. Phenobarbital**
- **d. Gabapentin**

127. An elderly patient reports that he is dizzy. Which symptom listed below likely indicates that dizziness is of a central etiology?

- **a. Tinnitus**
- **b. Hearing loss**
- **c. Carotid bruit**
- **d. Hyperventilation**

128. Which elderly patient is at highest risk of suicide?

- **a. 86 year-old male with chronic pain and depression**
- **b. 75 year-old female with history of depression**
- **c. 65 year-old female with a terminal illness**
- **d. 81 year-old male with active alcohol abuse**

129. Besides inadequate intake of Vitamin D in elder adults, what other factor contributes to deficiencies?

- **a. Impaired synthesis of previtamin D**
- **b. Decreased physical activity**
- **c. Diminished hepatic function**
- **d. Decreased body mass**

130. The "get up and go" test in an elderly patient is used to evaluate:

- **a. risk for falls.**
- **b. lower extremity strength.**
- **c. mental acuity.**
- **d. driving safety.**

131. A 49 year-old patient has osteoarthritis in the lumbar spine and hip. His hip x-ray demonstrates bone on bone. What can be done to resolve his complaints of pain in his hip?

a. **Acetaminophen only**
b. **An NSAID only**
c. **Acetaminophen and physical therapy**
d. **Acetaminophen and a referral to orthopedics**

132. A 75 year-old female who is otherwise healthy has osteoarthritis in her right knee. She complains of pain not relieved by acetaminophen 2000 mg daily. What should be done?

a. **Increase her acetaminophen to 4 grams daily**
b. **Consider an NSAID**
c. **Continue acetaminophen and order physical therapy**
d. **Continue acetaminophen and refer to orthopedics**

133. Which recommendation below reflects CDC's recommendation for administration of the zoster vaccine?

a. **It should be given to immunocompetent adults age 60 and older.**
b. **It should be given to immunocompetent adults age 65 and older.**
c. **It can be given regardless of immune status at age 50.**
d. **It can be given regardless of immune status at age 60.**

134. In elderly females, which screening test has demonstrated greatest reduction in mortality from cancer?

a. **Breast**
b. **Cervical**
c. **Ovarian**
d. **Lung**

135. Older adults have a unique blood pressure pattern. Which blood pressure reading below reflects this pattern?

a. **100/50**
b. **140/100**
c. **160/60**
d. **160/100**

136. A 76 year-old patient who is very active has elevated cholesterol and LDLs. He had been treated for hypertension for > 10 years with near normal blood pressures. What is the current recommendation for managing his lipids?

a. **No treatment should take place since his age exceeds 75 years.**
b. **He should be treated with an aspirin only.**
c. **He should be treated with a statin.**
d. **The benefits of treating this patient do not exceed the risk of using a statin or aspirin.**

137. The incidence of osteoporosis in the elderly is high. Which characteristics below would increase the risk of osteoporosis in an elderly male patient?

a. **Low body weight, age 60 years**
b. **Smoker, age 65 years**
c. **Chronic glucocorticoid therapy, age 70 years**
d. **Family history of hypothyroidism, age 65 years**

138. Screening for abdominal aortic aneurysm should take place:

a. **once for all males aged 65-75 who have ever smoked.**
b. **once for all men and women who have hypertension.**
c. **annually after age 75 years for males and females.**
d. **only if the patient has smoked and has hypertension.**

139. In older adults, the three most common ailments are:

a. **hearing loss, vision loss, hypertension.**
b. **hearing loss, hypertension, arthritis.**
c. **depression, vision loss, hypertension.**
d. **arthritis, hearing loss, depression.**

140. A 72 year-old patient presents an immunization record that reflects having received the pneumococcal immunization when she was 65 years old. Which statement below reflects the current standard of practice recommended by ACIP and CDC for this patient?

a. **She should be revaccinated today.**
b. **She should receive the immunization every 5 years.**
c. **She can elect to receive it today if she has COPD.**
d. **She does not need the immunization.**

141. A 67 year-old patient with COPD presents an immunization record that reflects having last received the pneumococcal immunization when he was 60 years old. Which statement below reflects the current standard of practice recommended by ACIP and CDC for this patient?

- a. He should be revaccinated today.
- b. He should receive the immunization every 5 years.
- c. He may elect to receive it today because he has COPD.
- d. He does not need the immunization.

142. Mr. Smith is a 72 year-old patient who takes warfarin for chronic atrial fibrillation. Today his INR is 4.0. His CBC is normal and there is no evidence of bleeding. The nurse practitioner should:

- a. stop the warfarin for the next four days and repeat the INR on day 5.
- b. admit to the hospital immediately.
- c. administer Vitamin K and repeat INR in two hours.
- d. stop the warfarin today and repeat the INR tomorrow.

143. A 91 year-old female with longstanding history of chronic heart failure has renal and liver studies that have slowly worsened over the past year. This probably indicates:

- a. final stage of heart failure.
- b. target organ damage secondary to heart failure.
- c. poor nutrition intake and need for nutrition assessment.
- d. new disease processes involving the liver and kidneys.

144. An 84 year-old female patient is a resident in an assisted living facility. She has early dementia. She walks daily and has had urinary incontinence for years. Her urinary incontinence is likely to be:

- a. urge.
- b. stress.
- c. mixed.
- d. unable to be determined.

145. Mrs. Johnson is an 89 year-old resident at a long-term care facility. Her state of health has declined rapidly over the past 2 months, and she can no longer make her own decisions. Her daughter requests a family conference with the nurse practitioner. Some important principles that need discussion at this time, if not previously documented, are:

- a. **bereavement support for the family, quality of life for the resident, and living will.**
- b. **health care proxy, living will, and hospice referral.**
- c. **withdrawing therapy, hospice referral, and managing symptoms.**
- d. **end of life decisions, quality of life, and advance directives.**

146. A 61 year-old male presents with a 12-hour history of an extremely painful left red eye. The patient complains of blurred vision, haloes around lights, and vomiting. It began yesterday evening. On examination, the eye is red, tender and inflamed. The cornea is hazy and pupil reacts poorly to light. The most likely diagnosis in this patient is:

- a. **acute angle glaucoma.**
- b. **increased intracranial pressure.**
- c. **macular degeneration.**
- d. **detached retina.**

147. A 70 year-old female states that she sees objects better by looking at them with her peripheral vision. She is examined and found to have a loss of central vision, normal peripheral vision, and a normal lens. This best characterizes:

- a. **glaucoma.**
- b. **cataracts.**
- c. **macular degeneration.**
- d. **detached retina.**

148. Arcus senilis is described as:

- a. **normal in people over 50 years of age.**
- b. **copper deposits in the cornea.**
- c. **loss of central vision.**
- d. **degeneration of the arcus and obstruction of tear ducts.**

149. Which of the following skin lesions in the elderly is a premalignant condition?

- a. **Xanthelasma**
- b. **Chalazion**
- c. **Hordeolum**
- d. **Actinic keratosis**

150. The correlation between blood pressure and age greater than 60 years is:

- **a. as age increases, diastolic blood pressure increases.**
- **b. as age increases, systolic blood pressure decreases.**
- **c. as age increases, blood pressure remains about the same.**
- **d. as age increases, diastolic blood pressure decreases.**

Adult Exam #1 Answers

1. *b*

An INR (International Normalized Ratio) is considered the best measure of clotting status in outpatients. Depending on the reason for anticoagulation, a common target is 2.0 – 3.0. Diastolic murmurs are always considered abnormal regardless of age. Cholesterol levels in adolescents should be less than 170 mg/dL (according to National Heart, Lung and Blood institute, NHLBI). Blood pressure of 160/75 constitutes isolated systolic hypertension, and, so this is abnormal.

2. *a*

The internal inguinal ring is the most common site for development of an indirect inguinal hernia. These can occur in men and women. Though most are probably congenital, symptoms may not be obvious until later in life. Indirect hernias are more common on the right side. Direct inguinal hernias occur through Hesselbach's triangle.

3. *d*

Patients with type 1 diabetes should be screened for renal nephropathy 5 years after diagnosis. Since nephropathy takes several years to develop, it is highly improbable that a newly diagnosed patient will have nephropathy secondary to diabetes. Nephropathy develops in about 30% of patients with diabetes. Diabetic nephropathy is defined as the presence of diabetes and more than 300 mg/d of albuminuria on at least 2 occasions separated by 3-6 months.

4. *b*

This patient does not have hepatitis C. This patient has a negative hepatitis C IgG. Currently, this is the screen. The RIBA was not necessary to perform, but, it confirms that this patient has a true negative screen for hepatitis C. If the HCV IgG had been positive, the RIBA would have been necessary to perform. There is no laboratory information that helps conclude that this patient has hepatitis B, except the history in the stem of the question.

5. *a*

The most common symptoms associated with mononucleosis (mono) are adenopathy (100%) and fatigue (90-100%). Pharyngitis occurs in 65-85% of patients. Cough occurs less than 50%; splenomegaly occurs 50-60%; fever 80-95%. The least common symptom of mono is rash. It occurs in only 3-6% of patients.

6. *d*

This patient has a negative hepatitis B surface antigen (HBsAg). Therefore, he does not have hepatitis B. The patient has a negative hepatitis B core antibody (HBcAb). Therefore, he has never had hepatitis B. The patient has a positive hepatitis B surface antibody (HBsAb). Therefore, he is considered immune. The patient is immune from

immunization because his hepatitis B core antibody is negative. If the core antibody had been positive, he would be considered immune from the disease. The correct answer is choice D.

7. ***d***
Examples of drugs that target the renin-angiotensin-aldosterone system are angiotensin converting enzyme (ACE) inhibitors and angiotensin receptor blockers (ARBs). These drugs are particularly beneficial to patients with diabetic nephropathy because they both prevent and treat diabetic nephropathy. Additionally, these agents also lower blood pressure which has been shown to be renoprotective. Management of glucose levels and hypertension is especially important in preventing diabetic nephropathy, but so is aggressive management of hyperlipidemia.

8. ***b***
In a 25 year-old male with subacute bacterial epididymitis, the most likely organism is Chlamydia. Therefore, until cultures are back, he should be treated empirically with doxycycline 100 mg BID for 10-14 days or longer. Quinolones should specifically be avoided if the suspected agent is gonorrhea because of rising resistance. Anti-inflammatory agents, ice, and scrotal support will help the patient's symptoms but not treat the underlying cause.

9. ***b***
A Vitamin B12 deficiency can produce an anemia called pernicious anemia. This is most commonly found in older adults and is characterized by macrocytosis. In other words, the red cells are larger than expected. Microcytosis may be seen in iron deficiency anemia or thalassemia. Leukocytosis refers to large numbers of white cells in the blood stream. Thrombocytosis refers to an increased number of platelets in the blood stream.

10. ***a***
Patients should be examined periodically for evidence of skin cancer by a professional examiner (NP, MD or PA). The frequency and type of examiner depends on the risk level, and personal and family history of the patient. However, a patient should examine his own skin regularly for changes. Once he has begun to examine his skin, research demonstrates that he will identify early changes and can make his provider aware of them.

11. ***a***
A BMI of 26 or higher imparts an increased risk of Type II diabetes. Mediterranean decent does not impart a specific risk factor for Type II diabetes, but African-American, Asian-American, and Hispanic races have an increased risk.

12. ***c***
Varicose veins and arteriosclerosis are very different disease processes. While differences can be found in the gender affected, the major difference between the two diseases is the vessel affected; arteriosclerosis affects the arteries, varicose veins affect the veins. While there is a predilection for the lower extremities in varicose veins,

peripheral artery disease (PAD) is most common in the lower extremities too. Varicose veins are especially common in women 2:1; PAD is more common in men 2:1 after age 70 years. Pain is a subjective measure.

13. ***d***
Typical symptoms of GERD include pyrosis (heartburn). The other symptoms listed are considered atypical symptoms of GERD. Patients who present with atypical symptoms of GERD, especially if older than 50 years, should be considered for endoscopy.

14. ***d***
Multiple myeloma is a neoplastic proliferation in the bone marrow which results in skeletal destruction. It is more common in older patients; the average age of diagnosis is 66 years. Common clinical findings are pain in the long bones, especially those of the trunk and back. Accompanying findings are anemia, usually normocytic / normochromic, hypercalcemia, and renal insufficiency.

15. ***b***
A patient with testicular torsion will have a negative cremasteric reflex and a high riding testis. There can also be profound testicular swelling and an acute onset of scrotal pain.

16. ***a***
The first serologic test for Lyme disease is the ELISA. If this is positive, it should be confirmed. In this case, it was confirmed by a Western blot and it is positive. This patient can be diagnosed with Lyme disease. The appropriate treatment for treatment of erythema migrans is doxycycline, amoxicillin, or cefuroxime for 21 days. All three medications were found to be of equal efficacy.

17. ***b***
Very young children and elderly adults are not likely to have initial WBC elevations. Consequently, appendicitis can be easily missed in these populations. Generalized abdominal pain is typical initially. UTI symptoms in older adults can manifest as lower abdominal pain and is a common presentation in this age group. Low grade fever is common too.

18. ***a***
This patient has normal non-fasting glucose. There is no need for further testing. At this time, this patient does not meet the criteria for diabetes and does not need further testing to arrive at a diagnosis.

19. ***a***
Naproxen is an NSAID. NSAIDs cause sodium retention and thus, water retention. A single dose of naproxen is unlikely to produce CHF symptoms, but, repeated subsequent doses are very likely to produce water retention sufficient to cause edema and possible shortness of breath in susceptible individuals. The other medications listed are unlikely to have any direct effect on cardiac output in a patient with CHF.

20. *c*
This patient does not have immunity to hepatitis A, as evidenced by the negative IgG. He is not currently infected, as evidenced by the negative IgM. This patient should be referred for immunization. The immunization consists of two immunizations given 6-12 months apart. They can be given to infants or adults.

21. *c*
The medications usually used in managing patients with CHF are ACE inhibitors, beta blockers, diuretics, aspirin, digoxin; specifically, some combination of these. Verapamil is a calcium channel blocker and is contraindicated in patients with CHF because these depress myocardial contractility.

22. *c*
The most common complaint is scrotal pain. It usually develops over a period of days. Occasionally, it develops acutely and will be accompanied by fever, chills, and a very ill-appearing patient. Burning with urination is possible if the underlying cause is a urinary tract infection, but, this is not usual. This presentation is seen more commonly in older males. Testicular pain is not a common complaint with epididymitis. Penile discharge would not indicate an infection in the epididymis since the epididymis is a tightly coiled tubular structure located on the testis.

23. *a*
When WBCs are found in stool specimens, it is indicative of infection or inflammation. In the case of a patient with symptoms suggestive of an infectious etiology, bacterial or viral infections should be considered. When considering a differential diagnosis and no infectious etiology is likely, Crohn's disease or ulcerative colitis could be considered.

24. *c*
This patient has a negative hepatitis B surface antigen (HBsAg). Therefore, he does not have hepatitis B. The patient has a negative hepatitis B core antibody (HBcAb). Therefore, he has never had hepatitis B. The patient has a negative hepatitis B surface antibody (HBsAb). Therefore, he is not considered immune, and immunization should be considered. There is a remote possibility that this patient has been immunized but did not produce hepatitis B surface antibodies. If this were the case, he should consider immunization once again. The correct answer is choice C.

25. *b*
This patient has longstanding hypertension that will increase her risk of CHF. Once she develops atrial fibrillation (a-fib) she will lose about 30% of her cardiac output, the amount contributed by her atria when she is not in a-fib. Shortness of breath, peripheral edema or an S3 gallop may develop but are secondary to a consequence of CHF or an embolism for which she is also at risk. Hypothyroidism can increase her risk of CHF but the risk of hypothyroidism does not increase once a-fib develops. The most obvious risk of a-fib is stroke but this was not a choice.

26. *a*
Under microscopic exam, hyphae are long, thin and branching and indicate dermatophytic infections. Hyphae are typical in tinea pedis, tinea cruris, and tinea corporis.

27. *a*
Verapamil is a calcium channel blocker. Calcium is needed for muscle contraction. Since the lower esophageal sphincter is opened and closed by muscles, the contraction of these muscles will be less forceful. GERD can be exacerbated in this case. Calcium channel blockers should be avoided in patients with severe GERD or in patients in whom calcium channel blockers exacerbate GERD symptoms.

28. *d*
Nearly 25% of the US population has hypertension. The greatest incidence is in elderly patients because of changes in the intima of vessels as aging and calcium deposition occur. Males of any age are more likely to be hypertensive than females of the same age. African American adults have the highest incidence in the general population. Among adolescents, African Americans and Hispanics have the highest rates. Hypertension affects about 5-10% of pregnancies.

29. *c*
The goal in managing a patient who presents with dehydration is rehydration. This is typically done with a commercially prepared electrolyte solution. Infamously, these are poor tasting. Patients usually prefer to rehydrate with fluids like tea, cola or a sports drink. However, these usually contain too much carbohydrate, too little potassium, and too much sodium for ideal fluid replenishment. Consequently, these are avoided when rehydration is needed. These are preferred by patients because of their good taste. The oral tract is always preferred for rehydration when it can be used. Resumption of the usual fluid and solid food intake should occur AFTER rehydration has occurred.

30. *b*
Normally, veins are larger than arteries in the eyes. The vessels in the eyes are particularly susceptible to increased blood pressure. AV (arterio-venous) nicking can be observed as arteries cross veins when the arteries have narrowed secondary to hypertension. Generally, AV nicking takes time to develop and would be expected in patients with long standing hypertension; especially when it is poorly controlled. Cotton wool exudates should prompt the examiner to screen for diabetes. An ophthalmology referral is not required at this point for AV nicking. In severe hypertension, the retina can become detached.

31. *d*
Gout is characterized by hyperuricemia. Uric acid levels are increased when a patient consumes any medication that results in less circulating fluid volume; specifically, any diuretic. Diuretics will produce hyperuricemia, and thus, increase the risk of gout in susceptible patients. Diuretics should be avoided when possible in patients with history of gout.

32. ***c***
Hepatitis B can be contracted by any of the choices listed. However, the one with the highest likelihood of disease transmission, and the one that is most common, is heterosexual activity.

33. ***b***
Benazepril is an ACE inhibitor and this class of drugs is contraindicated during pregnancy because of the teratogenic effects to the renal system of the developing fetus. Dry cough is an aggravating side effect that occurs in some patients who take ACE inhibitors, but, discontinuation is elective. ACE inhibitor use is associated with increased potassium levels, not decreased levels. Gout is not exacerbated by ACE inhibitor use.

34. ***d***
Amlodipine is a calcium channel blocker and its use does not warrant monitoring potassium levels. Fosinopril is an ACE inhibitor and candesartan is an ARB. Both warrant monitoring potassium levels because both have the potential to produce hyperkalemia, especially in patients who have renal impairment or CHF. Hydrochlorothiazide has the potential to produce hypokalemia, so, it too warrants monitoring of potassium levels.

35. ***b***
This is termed tail coverage because it extends beyond the time that the policy is active. This type insurance is important for protection against claims that may come in after the healthcare provider has left the practice or retired. These are generally more expensive than claims made policies.

36. ***b***
Inguinal hernias are very common in males. A typical symptom reported by men with an inguinal hernia is scrotal heaviness, especially at the end of the day. These symptoms are often experienced with heavy lifting, prolonged standing, or straining to have a bowel movement. If pain is present (which is unusual), it can usually be relieved by lying down or ceasing the activity that produced the symptoms. If this does not relieve the pain, or if the pain is severe, the hernia may have become strangulated. This requires immediate referral. Epididymitis can produce scrotal pain, not usually "heaviness". Hydrocele results in fluid in the scrotum.

37. ***a***
The mini mental status exam (MMSE) is a very common and easily administered cognitive evaluation for dementia. It tests orientation, recall, attention, calculation, language manipulation, and constructional praxis. It is not sensitive for mild dementia and may be influenced by educational level and age. Even with these limitations, the MMSE is the most widely used cognitive test for dementia in the US.

38. ***c***
The most rapid relief of anxiety symptoms will occur with a benzodiazepine. The relief occurs with each dose and tapers as the dose is metabolized. The other agents listed will take multiple doses, or days to weeks before relief is experienced. With daily and continued use of benzodiazepines, the anti-anxiety effect may become diminished.

39. ***a***
Scabies is eradicated by using permethrin and good hygiene. All household and personal contacts must be treated simultaneously, and meticulous care must be exercised to prevent transmission by cross contamination. All clothing, stuffed animals, linens, mattresses, and cloth furniture must be treated to prevent further transmission.

40. ***b***
Patients should be in the standing position when examined for a hernia. They are asked to strain, cough, or bear down after the examiner has inserted his fingertip within the external ring. The word used to describe the impulse of the hernia bumping into the finger is "silky". Nodular might be the word used to describe a prostate gland. Bumpy implies an irregular surface on some object. This is not the case with a hernia.

41. ***d***
The first step in being able to receive help for a problem is to be able to acknowledge that a problem exists. Since this patient is not willing to acknowledge a problem, but he needs help, one tack is to let him know that you are concerned about his health. If LFTs are ordered, they may not demonstrate elevation; especially if he consumes alcohol every day. Ordering a blood alcohol content, even if positive will be little or no help in having this patient realize that he consumes excessive amounts of alcohol. The provider could tell him to find another health care provider, but, this will do little to get this patient help.

42. ***a***
The medications of choice to treat bulimia nervosa are the SSRIs. Generally, high doses are required. Wellbutrin is not an SSRI and should not be given to patients with eating disorders because of great fluctuations in drug levels related to purging. Generally, this is more common in women than men. Loss of control IS a characteristic of this illness.

43. ***a***
Fever is an unusual symptom associated with acute bronchitis. Cough is the most common symptom associated with acute bronchitis. Purulent sputum is identified in more than 50% of patients with acute bronchitis. The color imparted to the sputum is usually due to sloughing of epithelial cells, not bacterial infection. Concurrent upper respiratory symptoms are typical of acute bronchitis. Pharyngitis is very common.

44. ***c***
The rapid HIV is always performed on the source patient ("the patient"). It is known as an ELISA (enzyme linked immunosorbent assay). In the patient suspected of being HIV positive, it is performed to establish whether or not he was positive at the time of the

needle stick. In this case, it was found to be positive, but, this is a screening test, and false positives can occur. Therefore, a confirmatory test, the western blot, is routinely performed on the patient's specimen to confirm the findings of the ELISA. The healthcare provider will usually be tested with a rapid HIV but it is done to establish HIV status at the time of the needlestick. It is not used to establish infection in the healthcare provider. The results of a rapid test can be reported in 20-40 minutes.

45. ***a***
Athletic amenorrhea creates states of prolonged hypoestrogenemia. This results in an increased risk of osteoporosis.

46. ***b***
Ectocervical specimens are collected first to minimize any bleeding that can occur from endocervix when it is sampled. The brush is considered a superior tool for collection of endocervical specimens because it produces the highest yield of endocervical cells, and thus, is a good reflection of the health of the cervix. Alternatively, a cervical broom can be used to collect cells. It collects endocervical cells and ectocervical cells simultaneously. It is rotated for 5 turns before the samples are placed on the slide. This may be used in pregnant women.

47. ***d***
Women ages 21-65 who have a cervix should be screened for cervical cancer. Screening intervals every 3 years should take place for women of average risk who are aged 21-29 years. Women aged 30-65 of average risk should take place every 3 years if only cytology is performed; or every 5 years if cytology plus HPV screening takes place. Women who are at increased risk of cervical cancer should be screened more frequently. Increased risk includes females who have had cervical cancer, those who are immunocompromised, or have infection with HIV.

48. ***d***
Most lab values remain normal until late stages of the illness in patients who are anorectic. The initial lab assessment should include a CBC, glucose, electrolytes, BUN, Cr, and a pregnancy test in females who are amenorrheic.

49. ***d***
The vast majority of breast lumps, even in older women are benign. However, because of the risk of breast cancer in any female patient, especially an older patient, she must be evaluated for breast cancer. Fibroadenomas are common in younger women. Cysts are common throughout the lifespan. Sometimes women identify a lump, but, instead it is the lumpiness of the breast tissue and not a distinct lump.

50. ***c***
This patient does not meet the strict criteria for an eating disorder, but it should be suspected. The other laboratory values are not the cause of her dizziness with standing. This is likely due to a low hemoglobin. She needs treatment for a probable iron deficiency anemia and elicitation of history to help identify the cause of her low

hemoglobin.

51. c

The nurse practitioner cannot ignore the fact that this patient is attempting to defraud the clinic and insurance company in order to receive free care. If she does not let the business office know, she is a party to the fraud. She should let the business office know what is happening and have the patient present documents verifying that he is who he states that he is. If he cannot, he can still receive care if he is willing to pay for it. An alternative site to receive care should be offered to him.

52. *a*

Primary prevention refers to preventing an event prior to its occurrence. Using a condom to prevent infection from an STD is primary prevention. Early diagnosis refers to secondary prevention. Tertiary prevention refers to an intervention that has the potential to prevent worsening of the disease.

53. *c*

Swelling, pain, and discoloration from impaired blood flow are the classic symptoms. Choice A could describe infection, like cellulitis, and is not classic for DVT. A history of exercise actually decreases the risk of DVT. Pain secondary to DVT is not relieved by walking. The lower extremities are the most likely location of DVT, but symptoms don't always correlate with location of the thrombosis. Patients must be asked about history, family history of DVT, and precipitating conditions.

54. *d*

Greater than 95% of patients who are exposed to HIV will seroconvert within 6 months. The majority of patients convert within 4-10 weeks after exposure. CDC recommends follow up for one year.

55. *a*

In contrast to creams and ointments, lotions have a high water content and a low oil content. These can worsen xerosis (dry skin) due to evaporation of water on the skin. Creams have a lower water content. Ointments have no water and are excellent agents to use on dry skin as well as to prevent dry skin.

56. *d*

5-FU is a topical agent that can be used to treat basal cell carcinoma (BCC). It is most effective on rapidly proliferating cells. This treatment should only be used on superficial BCCs. If it is used on more invasive BCC, the cure rate is significantly lower. Therefore, 5-FU should be used only on superficial BCCs in non-critical locations. It is used as a 5% formulation twice daily for 3-6 weeks.

57. *b*

Amoxicillin is no longer indicated for initial treatment in adults who have acute bacterial sinusitis. A bacterial cause can be assumed since she's had symptoms for 10 days. A viral infection likely would have run its course by now. After 10 days of

persistent symptoms, treatment is reasonable with an antibiotic; especially since this patient is diabetic. She may be having blood sugar elevations that facilitate growth of the causative organism of the sinus infection. A decongestant could be added depending on her blood pressure and personal history of using decongestants.

58. ***c***
Many studies have shown that topical nasal steroids like budesonide, fluticasone, and mometasone provide superior relief of nasal stuffiness, nasal discharge, sneezing, and postnasal drip than antihistamines. Decongestants treat symptoms associated with nasal stuffiness. Currently, topical nasal steroids are the treatment of choice for relief of symptoms associated with allergic rhinitis (AR). Antihistamines and decongestants can be added to the regimen of a patient with AR.

59. ***b***
Grave's disease is the most common form of hyperthyroidism. There will be elevated levels of thyroid hormones like T3 and/or T4. Patients become symptomatic with palpitations, elevated blood pressure, inability to sleep, restlessness, and heat intolerance. An elevated TSH can be found in patients with hypothyroidism. Choices A and D do not relate to Grave's disease.

60. ***b***
Symptoms have a poor correlation with disease found during endoscopy. However, duodenal symptoms tend to occur within 2-5 hours of eating. These patients derive relief from eating or taking antacids. This is in contrast to a patient with a gastric ulcer who has symptoms within minutes of eating. He tends to derive less relief from antacids.

61. ***d***
More than 10 years has elapsed since this patient's last tetanus shot. He needs another one. Tdap is specifically indicated for adolescents, older adults, healthcare providers, and pregnant patients who have completed a primary series. Tetanus toxoid is indicated in the rare adult or child who is allergic to the aluminum adjuvant in the Td immunization.

62. ***d***
Patients should always be cautioned against alcohol ingestion (in any form) if they take metronidazole. Alcohol can (and usually does) produce a disulfiram reaction. This is characterized by abdominal cramps, nausea, vomiting, headache, and elevated body temperature. Precautions should remain until 72 hours after the last dose of metronidazole.

63. ***b***
Risk factors for osteoporosis (in addition to those listed) include low body weight, cigarette smoking, rheumatoid arthritis, previous fracture, and parental history of hip fracture. African American race is not a risk factor but Caucasian and Asian races are.

64. ***b***
The enzyme immunoassay allows detection of Clostridium difficile toxin, not the organism. It is the most commonly used assay in the US because it is easy to perform, yields results in less than 24 hours. The assay has good specificity, but moderate sensitivity. More sensitive tests can be performed but they are more expensive and take longer to yield results.

65. ***d***
Erysipelas and cellulitis both cause skin erythema, edema, warmth. However, erysipelas involves the upper dermis and superficial lymphatics; cellulitis involves the deeper dermis and subcutaneous fat. Erysipelas is usually caused by *Streptococcus*; cellulitis may be caused by *Staphylococcus* and less commonly by *Streptococcus.*

66. ***b***
Erysipelas is characterized by an acute onset of symptoms as described in this scenario. Fever and chills are common. Patients with cellulitis tend to have a more gradual course with development of symptoms over several days. The erythema noted in erysipelas is well demarcated and raised above the level of the skin. This elevation reflects that the more superficial dermis is involved.

67. ***c***
Asymptomatic bruits in the carotid area are more indicative of atherosclerotic disease than increased stroke risk. A symptomatic bruit requires attention immediately. Patients with carotid artery disease are more likely to die of cardiovascular disease than cerebrovascular disease. The Framingham Heart Study found that patients with an asymptomatic carotid bruit were at increased risk of stroke, but, the majority of strokes occurred in an area away from the carotid artery. The overall risk of stroke was insignificant when an asymptomatic carotid bruit was identified.

68. ***a***
While no clear diagnosis can be made from this scenario, there are several red flags. Collectively, the red flags necessitate referral to ophthalmology. First, the eye is red. He is photophobic and has the sensation of a foreign body. There is no mention of eye discharge but, eye discharge with this scenario would cause the examiner to consider bacterial conjunctivitis or keratitis. The symptoms of photophobia and foreign body sensation are symptoms of an active corneal process. Glaucoma should also be considered in the differential. He should be referred to ophthalmology.

69. ***b***
The diagnostic test of choice to differentiate a solid from a fluid filled breast mass is ultrasound. More than 90% of breast masses in women in the 20s to early 50s are benign. However, they must be evaluated. Clinical breast exam is unable to differentiate fluid filled from solid masses. MRI is not used unless a history of breast cancer is present. Mammography has the potential to evaluate the presence of a mass, but is of inadequate benefit in assessing whether it is fluid filled or not.

70. ***c***
While an abdominal aortic aneurysm (AAA) might be detected by multiple modalities, including a plain film of the abdomen, it is most cost effectively and efficiently identified using ultrasound (US). The sensitivity and specificity for AAA identification with US is nearly 100%. Both CT and MRI are very accurate in identifying AAA, but, they are both more expensive than US.

71. ***a***
Alpha blockers (alpha-adrenergic antagonists) provide immediate relief of symptoms. The alpha-1 receptors are abundant in the prostate gland and base of the bladder. The body of the bladder has very few alpha-1 receptors. Those alpha blockers most commonly used are terazosin, doxazosin, tamsulosin, and alfuzosin. Prazosin is a short-acting and so has less utility than the other agents mentioned.

72. ***b***
The 5-alpha-reductase inhibitors will reduce PSA levels by 50% or greater within the first 3 months and will sustain this reduction as long as the medication is taken. This class of medication interferes with the prostatic intracellular androgen response mechanism.

73. ***d***
Most learned authorities agree on the above definition but realize that it is inadequate. Infarction usually begins once an area has been ischemic for an hour. Therefore, a TIA is not benign and even brief ischemia can produce irreversible brain damage.

74. ***a***
Allopurinol has no role in treatment of acute gout because it plays no role in inflammation. Therefore, it should not be initiated during an acute attack for relief of symptoms. Most learned authorities agree that if a patient takes an antihyperuricemic agent like allopurinol, and has an attack, the therapy should be continued.

75. ***c***
Meat and fish contribute significantly to the risk of developing gout, especially in susceptible individuals. Dietary products and coffee were associated with lower risks of developing gout. Tea does contribute to development of gout. Alcohol, of course, contributes to development of gout.

76. ***d***
Systemic illness, like cancer or infection is a serious consideration when patients report no relief of pain with lying down. Additionally, this patient is female, older, and has pain more than 4 weeks. These are three risk factors for systemic cause of low back pain. Sciatica presents with pain down the leg. Ankylosing spondylitis is typical in males in their 40s. Disk disease is a consideration, but, an absence of relief with lying down is unusual.

77. ***a***
The NP is a "participating" provider because he agreed to accept assignments. An assignment is an agreement between Medicare and the NP to accept the Medicare Approved Amount (MAA) as payment in full and not charge Medicare recipients a higher rate. The NP can bill the patient for a percentage of the remaining bill that was not paid by Medicare. The NP may opt out of participating.

78. ***b***
A long-acting bronchodilator can be used to treat asthma when it is used in combination with an inhaled steroid. Otherwise, using a long-acting bronchodilator like formoterol or salmeterol is absolutely contraindicated. There is an increased risk of sudden death with asthma exacerbations when this class is used solo to treat asthma. The other choices above can be used to treat asthma. Choices vary depending on the patient.

79. ***a***
First line treatment for patients with COPD who have intermittent symptoms of shortness of breath is an anticholinergic alone or in combination with a beta agonist. Both medications improve lung function. Asthma patients do not use anticholinergic medications as sole agents to manage symptoms. The underlying basis of asthma is inflammation and so inhaled steroids are used except for intermittent asthma.

80. ***d***
The most common presentation of acute uncomplicated pyelonephritis includes fever, flank pain, and nausea and vomiting. Sometimes patients present like they have pelvic inflammatory disease (PID). In this presentation, abdominal pain is common too. Fever is so strongly correlated with acute pyelonephritis, that it is very unusual not to have fever. Renal stone patients may have this presentation, but, fever is usually NOT present. It is unlikely that cholecystitis would present with left sided flank pain. The gall bladder is on the right side of the body.

81. ***c***
This patient has trichomoniasis. This is the likely cause of her dysuria. She could be treated with metronidazole initially. This should eradicate the infection. Her partner will need treatment too. She has an inconsequential number of bacteria in her urine. She does not need treatment for the bacteria in her urine.

82. ***a***
The most common diseases in the homeless population are not seen in the same proportion in the general population. These include hepatitis, HIV, STDs, pregnancy in females, TB, skin and foot problems, and late immunizations, especially tetanus. When given the opportunity, screenings should take place and treatment when appropriate.

83. ***a***
Violence is very common in the United States. While men and women are both victims, women are more commonly victims. Patients who have been victims of violence are

more likely to utilize healthcare and to have poor response to treatment. If the patient is suspected to have been a victim of violence, they should also be screened for anxiety, depression, and post-traumatic stress disorder.

84. *b*
Screening for TB in this patient should take place with a skin test known as the Mantoux. A chest x-ray is typically performed after a positive skin test. A sputum specimen is used for diagnosis, not screening. A questionnaire is used for screening patients who have had a history of a positive TB skin test. If symptoms are acknowledged on the questionnaire, generally, a chest x-ray is performed. The questionnaire is used to prevent too frequent exposure to radiation in patients in whom regular screening is required, like healthcare providers.

85. *a*
ACE inhibitors have numerous indications. Three are indicated in the first choice. ACE inhibitors are also indicated in patients who have renal insufficiency. However, ACE inhibitors can worsen renal insufficiency, so the patients must be monitored closely with lab tests for BUN, Cr, and potassium. Diabetes without proteinuria is not a specific indication for ACE inhibitors though, they are used by some healthcare providers in this way. This is an off-label use.

86. *a*
This patient likely has iron deficiency anemia because she consumes limited quantities of iron in her diet. In addition to an iron supplement, she should be encouraged to eat liberal amounts of iron rich foods like dark green leafy vegetables (spinach is a good example), peas and beans such as lentils, black beans, red beans, and white beans. Coupling these foods with foods rich in vitamin C will enhance absorption of iron.

87. *c*
Thalassemia, like iron deficiency anemia can be recognized or suspected by the finding of small, pale red cells on the peripheral smear of a CBC. The definitive diagnosis of thalassemia can be made by hemoglobin electrophoresis.

88. *b*
The typical cluster headache lasts less than 3 hours; usually less than 90 minutes. Migraine headaches are usually 4-72 hours, more common in females. Cluster headaches are more common in males and are triggered by alcohol or nicotine intake. Migraines may be triggered by diet, skipping meals, sunlight, red wine, aged cheeses, or menses. Family history is the most common finding in patients who have migraine headaches.

89. *d*
The diagnostic criteria for Alzheimer's disease (AD) was established by DSM V and other organizations. The criteria are similar. Criteria include a gradual onset of cognitive decline. A rapid onset usually indicates another etiology, perhaps, delirium. Other criteria include impairment of recent memory, difficulty with language or

finding words, the inability to execute skilled motor activities, disturbances of visual processing or disturbances in executive function that includes abstract reasoning and concentration. Focal neurologic signs are consistent with a vascular dementia. Radiologic evidence is not a criterion for diagnosis, though it may support the diagnosis of AD. There is no laboratory evidence of AD.

90. ***c***
A therapeutic relationship with a patient can be established in many different ways. One way is to ask open-ended questions. This allows the patient to discuss what is most important to him; personal concerns may be vocalized by the patient. Telling the patient that he can trust you probably does little to establish trust. Actions that establish trust are more therapeutic than this statement. Touching the patient during the interview may be perceived as inappropriate by many patients. In contrast, touching the patient during the exam is different. Finally, telling the patient that you enjoyed taking care of him (if this was true) does little to establish trust.

91. ***a***
There are several risk factors for HIV transmission. Viral load is likely the greatest risk factor. The presence of STDs increases the risk of HIV transmission. Specifically, the presence of chlamydia increases the risk of acquiring HIV by 5 times. Lack of circumcision increases the risk of transmission..

92. ***b***
An urgent threat to this patient is the possibility of stroke from atrial fibrillation. A common presentation in older patients who have hyperthyroidism is atrial fibrillation. Unless she is anti-coagulated, she is at very high risk for stroke, especially as her hyperthyroidism is treated and she returns to a normal sinus rhythm. She probably will exhibit a systolic murmur, but this poses little threat to her. She should also be monitored for angina and heart failure. These are commonly found when patients present urgently to a clinic or emergency department.

93. ***c***
Sleep difficulty is a common complaint among patients with depression. Patients with difficulty falling asleep are often anxious. Frequent waking and early morning wakening are often complaints by patients with depression. There is no agreed on physiologic explanation, but, this is a common symptom.

94. ***c***
Patients who have gout exacerbations should avoid foods high in purines. A low purine diet can significantly reduce risk of gout. Uric acid is a byproduct of purine metabolism. Purines can be found in high concentrations in beef, pork, bacon, lamb, seafood, beer, bread, gravy, and most alcoholic beverages. Foods considered low in purines are fruits and fruit juices, green veggies, nuts, dairy products, chocolate.

95. ***b***
Several studies have demonstrated that erectile dysfunction (ED) was associated with

use of thiazide diuretics, specifically chlorthalidone. When ED was evaluated in patients taking chlorthalidone, acebutolol, amlodipine, enalapril, and doxazosin (the major antihypertensive drug classes), the thiazide diuretic, chlorthalidone had the greatest incidence of ED. The other drugs in the study were no more likely to cause ED than a placebo. However, a common complaint of men on antihypertensive medications is ED. This should always be evaluated as a side effect of antihypertensive treatment.

96. *b*
This is an example of secondary prevention. Secondary prevention is represented by screenings intended to identify early course of a disease. In this example, a mammogram is intended to identify early breast cancer.

97. c
The primary goal of antiviral therapy in a patient diagnosed with shingles is to reduce the risk of, or severity of post-herpetic neuralgia. Since she has been identified within 72 hours of onset of lesions, she can be treated with most benefit with an oral antiviral agent. Studies do not demonstrate that patients have reduction of pain or resolution of symptoms faster if oral steroids are given. They should be avoided in older patients because there is no identified benefit. Shingles can be very painful and so treatment for pain should be priority.

98. *a*
The most common pathogen associated with pyelonephritis is E. coli. This is a gram negative pathogen which commonly inhabits the lower genitourinary (GU) tract. It also is the most common pathogen associated with urinary tract infections (UTI). Untreated or undertreated UTIs are the most common reason for pyelonephritis. Hence, it is reasonable for the pathogen to be similar. The other organisms listed are not common inhabitants in the lower GU tract.

99. *d*
The incubation period for scabies is about 3-4 weeks after primary infection. Patients with subsequent infections with scabies will develop symptoms in 1-3 days. The classic symptom is itching that is worse at night coupled with a rash that appears in new areas over time.

100. *a*
Many factors must be present for a patient to develop Lyme Disease from a tick bite. First, the tick must belong to Ixodes species. The tick must have been attached for at least 48-72 hours before disease can be spread. Time of year, stage of organism's development, and others all affect transmission. There is no need for prophylactic treatment in this case because the tick has not been present long enough, though, many patients will feel antibiotics are necessary.

101. *b*
Hot water heaters are common sources of burns in homes of elderly patients and very young patients. Many safety organizations in the United States believe that burns can

be prevented if hot water heaters are set to less than 120 degrees.

102. ***d***
Cranial nerve (CN) XII enables a patient to stick his tongue out and to move it from side to side in his mouth. CN III is partly responsible for eye movement. CN VII is responsible for the ability to close eyes tightly, wrinkle the forehead, and smile. CN X is partly responsible for speaking and tongue movement.

103. ***d***
Arteriovenous nicking (AV nicking), or nipping, is commonly seen in patients who have hypertension. It represents retinal microvascular changes. These are typically early changes and usually reflective of current and past blood pressures. More severe damage can be seen when flame hemorrhages or cotton wool spots are identified. These often represent current blood pressure elevations since these tend to be more acute evidence of elevated blood pressure.

104. ***c***
These nodules describe erythema nodosum. These are most common in women aged 15-40 years old. They are typically found in pretibial locations and can be associated with infectious agents, drugs, or systemic inflammatory disease like ulcerative colitis. They probably occur as a result of a delayed hypersensitivity reaction to antigens. It is not unusual to find polyarthralgia, fever, and or malaise that precede or accompany the skin nodules.

105. ***c***
The class of medications known as triptans, which includes sumatriptan, is used as abortive agents, not for prophylaxis. The other classes mentioned can be used for prophylaxis. Some of these medications are used off-label for migraine prophylaxis. Other prophylactic agents include lithium, SSRIs, anticonvulsants, ACEs and ARBs.

106. ***c***
The eyes are drained partly by the pre-auricular lymph nodes. They are palpated near the ear and can swell in response to eye infections, allergies, or foreign bodies in the eye.

107. ***d***
This represents leakage of blood out of the ophthalmic vasculature. It is usually painless and can be the result of coughing, sneezing, hypertension, or trauma. This will resolve without treatment, but, aspirin or other agents that can produce bleeding should be discontinued until the etiology is determined.

108. ***b***
There are a number of possible etiologies for her vomiting. Without knowing her last menstrual period (and even if she reported one), pregnancy must be ruled in or out. The other concern is her electrolyte status, especially her potassium.

109. ***b***
Nearly all cases of pneumonia can be identified on chest x-ray by the presence of infiltrates. Patients with bronchitis have a normal chest x-ray unless there are other underlying pathologies. CBCs distinguish bacterial from viral infections. Sputum specimens are indicated when there is a need to identify organisms in the sputum. Pulmonary function tests are indicated in chronic lung diseases like COPD or asthma.

110. ***d***
When an abnormal TSH is received, especially when a patient is not symptomatic, it should be repeated. Sometimes there are periods of transient hypothyroidism, lab error, and missed doses that can cause changes in TSH levels.

111. ***b***
In 2010, CDC released its most recent guidelines for management of STDs. There was a major update for management of gonorrhea in Fall, 2012. Cefixime is no longer recommended as a cephalosporin for treatment of gonorrhea because of cephalosporin resistant strains of gonorrhea. 250 mg ceftriaxone should be given IM in conjunction with either azithromycin or doxycycline by mouth when gonorrhea is diagnosed. Treatment failure should be reported to CDC.

112. ***c***
This patient has an elevated mean corpuscular volume. This indicates a macrocytic anemia. Common macrocytic anemias are B12 deficiency and folate deficiency. These are common in older patients, especially if they consume large quantities of alcohol. This patient also has elevated triglycerides. Triglycerides are commonly elevated when patients are exposed to alcohol and carbohydrates. This patient's history indicates two elements that indicate alcohol abuse. He should be questioned regarding alcohol abuse.

113. ***a***
The most common cause of vaginal discharge in women of child-bearing age is bacterial vaginosis. The most common presentation is a complaint of vaginal discharge with a fishy odor, most noticeable after sexual intercourse. The vaginal discharge is cream colored and thin. Chlamydia produces a discharge but it is not reported as pruritic. Herpes does not produce a discharge. Syphilis produces a lesion.

114. ***b***
Plantar fasciitis is an inflammation of the ligaments in the plantar fascia. The fascia is a thick white tissue that begins at the heel and extends under the foot to the toes. It supports the foot during walking. Patients who are at increased risk are long-distance runners, dancers, people who are on their feet for long periods of time. This can be treated with rest, ice, NSAIDs short-term, stretching exercises, orthotics, and steroid injections.

115. ***a***
Thiazide diuretics have the secondary effect of increasing serum calcium by decreasing fluid. This makes more calcium available for absorption. This would not be used to

treat a patient with osteoporosis, but, this mechanism of action could be helpful as an adjunct for patients who are receiving other forms of treatment for osteoporosis. The other agents listed would have no effect on osteoporosis. Calcium channel blockers impede movement of calcium into cells. This has no effect on available serum calcium.

116. ***b***
A polyneuropathy is a term that refers to a process that affects multiple nerves, usually peripheral. The distal nerves are more commonly affected. Symptoms described by patients are burning, weakness, or loss of sensation. Charcot-Marie-Tooth disease is a rare, hereditary primary motor sensory neuropathy. Guillain-Barre is an acute autoimmune neuropathy that is primarily demyelinating. Urinary incontinence does not represent a common polyneuropathy in the elderly.

117. ***b***
Saw palmetto is an extract of fruit of the American dwarf tree. It is commonly used to treat benign prostatic hypertrophy (BPH) but there is no objective data supporting its use. It is available over the counter and is purchased by men for BPH. It has an unknown mechanism of action but men with BPH report a subjective increase in urine flow rate when taking saw palmetto.

118. ***c***
The description in the question describes a xanthelasma. It is slightly raised and is a well-circumscribed plaque on the upper eyelid usually. One or both lids may be affected. These are often associated with lipid disorders but may occur independent of any systemic or local disease. These plaques do not affect vision.

119. ***c***
The period of time that risk of transmission is greatest is when the viral load is high. Many times this is before a patient has been diagnosed and so he is capable of transmitting this disease without knowledge that he is doing so. The highest viral load may occur during the earliest stages of HIV and before there is detectable antibody.

120. ***c***
Cherry angiomas are mature capillary proliferations that are more common in middle and older adults. They blanch with pressure and are usually 0.1-0.4 cm in diameter. They are commonly found on the trunk as multiple lesions. Because they are a proliferation of capillaries, they will bleed significantly if they rupture. The bleed is not life threatening, but, in older adults who take aspirin, the bleeding will be worse. Pressure should be held over the ruptured area until bleeding stops. These are not precursors of skin malignancies.

121. ***c***
Hypoglycemia in older adults, like this 78 year-old, is more likely to have deleterious consequences than in younger adults because of the risk of falls and increased association with cardiac events. The symptoms associated with hypoglycemia in older adults tend to be neurological (dizziness and weakness) as compared to younger adults

who are more likely to exhibit adrenergic (tremors and sweating) symptoms. In fact, in older adults, hypoglycemic episodes may be misinterpreted as cardiovascular or neurological events.

122. ***d***
Metformin is a good agent to use in older diabetics because it does not produce hypoglycemia. However, renal function typically declines in older patients, lactic acidosis becomes more likely (though not common) when metformin is prescribed. Therefore, renal function should be monitored in all patients, but, especially older patients who have declining renal function due to any acute event (stroke, MI, infection).

123. ***c***
Diverticular disease is more common in older adults. About 70% of patients diagnosed with diverticulitis have left lower quadrant pain. Rectal bleeding may have varied etiologies like rectal carcinoma or hemorrhoids. Bloating and cramping are often found in patients with diverticular disease (diverticulosis) but not specifically diverticulitis. Belching and flatulence are not specifically associated with diverticulosis.

124. ***b***
This patient has a lump identified in the breast. Since males can develop breast cancer, it must be evaluated in the same means that a female breast lump would be evaluated. He should have a clinical breast exam to identify the position of the lump, and any other abnormal findings such as nodes or other lumps. Then, he should have mammogram and ultrasound to help evaluate the lump. If the findings were suspicious for a malignancy, the patient would be referred to a surgeon.

125. ***a***
Multiple myeloma is a neoplastic proliferation in the bone marrow which results in skeletal destruction. It is more common in older patients; the average age of diagnosis is 66 years. Common clinical findings are pain in the long bones, especially those of the trunk and back. Accompanying findings are anemia, usually normocytic/ normochromic, hypercalcemia, and renal insufficiency.

126. ***b***
Tremor is the most common of all movement disorders and essential tremor is the most common cause of all tremors. It is characterized by rhythmic movement of a body part, commonly the hands or head. Beta blockers are the most commonly used medication class to treat essential tremor. Propanolol is most commonly used medication, but other beta blocking agents are used as well. Both gabapentin and phenobarbital are used, but, not nearly as often. Carbidopa is used in patients with Parkinson's Disease.

127. ***c***
Dizziness in the elderly is a common complaint and can be due to multiple etiologies. In the elderly, the etiology is more likely from multiple characteristics: taking 5 or more medications, impaired balance from another disease, orthostatic hypotension, impaired

hearing, depression, and anxiety. Tinnitus (ringing in the ears) and hearing loss typically indicate a peripheral etiology. Hyperventilation can produce dizziness. An audible carotid bruit would steer the healthcare provider to explore carotid stenosis and underlying cardiovascular disease.

128. ***a***
Elderly patients are more successful than younger patients when they attempt suicide. Those at highest risk are white males 85 years or older with depression. Symptoms in the elderly which should be of particular concern to healthcare providers are hopelessness, insomnia, unremitting pain, alcohol abuse, restlessness, and impaired concentration.

129. ***a***
Elderly adults are at increased risk of Vitamin D deficiency related to several factors. In addition to those mentioned, lack of sun exposure decreases synthesis of Vitamin D. As renal status declines in older patients, hydroxylation diminishes which diminishes available Vitamin D. Patients with dark skin are also at increased risk of Vitamin D deficiencies.

130. ***a***
The "get up and go" test is used to evaluate musculoskeletal function. The patient is asked to rise from a seated position in an armchair, walk across the room, turn around, and return to the chair. This test evaluates the patient's gait, balance, leg strength, and vestibular function. It should be assessed in patients who report a fall or who present after a fall but who appear without injury.

131. ***d***
This patient has severe osteoarthritis if the x-ray reveals "bone on bone". He should be given something to help manage his pain (acetaminophen initially). He needs referral to an orthopedic doctor for evaluation if this is consistent with his desire. Medications alone will likely not resolve his pain. Additionally, he is 49 years old with no mention of other diseases and would likely be a good candidate because of his young age.

132. ***c***
Acetaminophen should be restricted to 3,250 mg acetaminophen daily. Daily doses of 4 grams daily are more likely to result in hepatotoxicity. Because osteoarthritis is a chronic disease, medications will be taken daily and NSAIDs would be better avoided if possible. NSAID use can be tried if acetaminophen does not provide relief. Consider physical therapy (PT) for pain relief. Strengthening of muscles may result in some relief. If cost is an issue, low does NSAID could be tried, but is a riskier option than PT.

133. ***a***
The zoster vaccine, to prevent shingles and postherpetic neuralgia from shingles is currently FDA approved for use in immunocompetent adults age 50 or older. CDC's recommendation is for immunocompetent adults aged 60 years and older. The difference in age recommendation is due to the anticipated shortage of vaccine if it were

given to ages 50 years and older. It should never be used to treat shingles.

134. ***a***
There are no recommendations for screening for ovarian or lung cancer in elderly women. Cervical cancer is primarily a disease found in younger women, though, when it is identified in elderly patients, there is usually a higher mortality rate than in younger women. However, the incidence of cervical cancer is much lower in the elderly. Screening for breast cancer has demonstrated the highest reduction in mortality and it is recommended that women who have a life expectancy of >4 years have screening for breast cancer with mammography. Mammography should be performed every 1-2 years according to the American Geriatrics Society.

135. ***c***
Nearly 2/3 of all older adults who are hypertensive have isolated systolic hypertension, i.e., the systolic blood pressure is elevated, the diastolic is normal. This probably occurs because vessels stiffen as people age and a higher systolic is required to move blood through stiffened vessels. Elevated systolic blood pressure is an important risk factor for cardiovascular disease and stroke in the elderly.

136. ***c***
Numerous studies (PROSPER, 2006) and learned authorities (including the USPSTF) have found that lipid lowering drug therapy decreases the incidence of coronary heart disease and vascular events in middle aged and older adults. The current recommendation is to screen and treat lipid abnormalities in patients who are at risk for a cardiac event. It is unclear whether treatment of middle aged and older adults at low risk for cardiac events is beneficial.

137. ***c***
Women should be screened for osteoporosis starting at age 65 years; sooner if risk factors are present. Males greater than age 65 years should be screened with DEXA scanning if they exhibit risk factors. Those with the greatest impact on bone density include primary hyperparathyroidism, chronic glucocorticoid therapy and hypogonadism.

138. ***a***
The prevalence of abdominal aortic aneurysm (AAA) is greater in men than women. American Heart Association and USPSTF recommend screening males once between ages 65-75 years if they have ever smoked. Smoking increases the risk of AAA. The USPSTF does not recommend routinely screening for AAA in women and do not recommend screening for AAA in men who have never smoked. Screening may be considered in men aged 65-75 years if they have a first-degree relative who required repair of AAA.

139. ***b***
Hypertension and arthritis are the two most common ailments that are seen in older adults. Hearing loss occurs in half to almost 2/3 of older adults. The most common

form is known as presbycusis. There is no consensus for the frequency of screening for hearing loss, but minimally, it should be grossly evaluated at each visit and screened more thoroughly if deficits are observed. Blood pressure should be screened annually, but is usually screened at each visit. Arthritis is not routinely screened.

140. ***d***
The recommendations by ACIP and CDC recommend pneumococcal immunization once at age 65 years. Routine revaccination is not recommended for this patient because she received an immunization at age 65 years. It should not be routinely given every 5 years.

141. ***a***
The recommendations by ACIP and CDC are pneumococcal immunization once at age 65 years regardless of other diseases present. However, if the initial immunization was given prior to age 65 years and 5 years has elapsed since the initial one, he should be revaccinated today.

142. ***d***
An INR of 4.0 is elevated and this patient could suffer a devastating bleed anywhere in the body. A patient with an INR < 5 without bleeding may have warfarin stopped temporarily and decrease the maintenance dose when it is safe to resume warfarin, i.e. when the INR is closer to the patient's therapeutic range. If the patient was at high risk for bleeding, was bleeding, or if the INR was higher, Vitamin K could be administered. A good history should be completed to find out the reason for the increase in INR. A high risk client with an elevated INR would be admitted to the hospital and closely monitored, but a client with no co-morbidities (no bleeding history or thrombocytopenia) and considered low risk, may be monitored as an outpatient. Five days is too long to stop warfarin without an INR check.

143. ***b***
This patient is experiencing secondary effects from long term chronic heart failure. The major organ systems in the body take an eventual toll from poor perfusion. The renal and hepatic systems demonstrate slow demise when the heart is unable to meet the tissue's perfusion needs. This is a severe complication of long-term CHF.

144. ***c***
The most common type of urinary incontinence in women is mixed incontinence. This refers to at least two simultaneous mechanisms. Usually detrusor overactivity and impaired urethral sphincter function are present, giving mixed incontinence characteristics of urge and stress (exertional) incontinence. Stress incontinence is characterized by leakage of urine following sneezing, coughing, or laughing. Urge incontinence is characterized by the sudden urge to urinate that cannot be delayed.

145. ***a***
American Geriatrics Society stresses not only care of the patient, but care of the family as well. Choice A includes meeting the current and future needs of the patient, family

needs, and end of life issues with the living will. The living will is recognized as a valid advanced directive. Choice A includes developmental landmarks for the patient and family.

146. ***a***
The clinical presentation of a patient with acute angle glaucoma is as this patient has presented, with a hard eyeball, eye pain, along with blurred vision. Nausea and vomiting are common. Pain is usually present when the intraocular pressure rises rapidly. This produces conjunctival redness. Symptoms are more common in the evening when light levels diminish and mydriasis occurs. In chronic angle closure, pressures rise slowly and pain is usually absent. Both can produce blindness.

147. ***c***
Macular degeneration presents most commonly with a loss of central vision. The macula is the central part of the retina. As it degenerates, central vision is lost. Questions should be asked about the rate of loss of vision. Reports of rapid vision loss require urgent ophthalmologic evaluation. Known risk factors are age greater than 50 years with the greatest prevalence over age 65, smoking, family history, and history of stroke, MI, or angina.

148. ***a***
Arcus senilis describes an arc or circle around the cornea that is common in older adults. The circle is due to deposition of lipids in the cornea but is not necessarily due to hypercholesterolemia. However, when this is seen in young adults, it is termed arcus juvenilis, and is often associated with lipid abnormalities.

149. ***d***
Actinic keratosis is a premalignant condition of the skin and is considered an evolving carcinoma in situ. It is a precursor of squamous cell carcinoma. The lesions are usually multiple in occurrence and sit on an erythematous base. They appear dry, scaly, and flat and are usually secondary to sun damaged skin so can be found on sun exposed areas. The most common sites are the face, ears, lateral forearms, and tops of hands.

150. ***d***
As age (beyond 60 years) increases, systolic blood pressure tends to increase, but diastolic blood pressure tends to decrease. This is evidence by the observation of isolated systolic hypertension, seen almost exclusively in the elderly population. This results in a widening pulse pressure, a predictor of cardiovascular events in the elderly. The pulse pressure is calculated by subtracting the diastolic blood pressure from the systolic blood pressure. Measurements greater than 60-70 points indicate "stiffening" of the vessels. Stiffening commonly occurs as aging occurs.

Adult Exam #2 Questions

1. **A female patient who takes oral contraceptives has just completed her morning exercise routine. She complains of pain in her right calf. Her blood pressure and heart rate are normal. She is not short of breath. Her calf is red and warm to touch. What is NOT part of the differential diagnosis?**

    a. **Deep vein thrombosis**
    b. **Cellulitis**
    c. **Calf muscle strain**
    d. **Trochanteric bursitis**

2. **A 70 year-old presents to the nurse practitioner's office for a well exam today. What medication probably has no affect on screening for occult blood in the stool?**

    a. **Aspirin**
    b. **Clopidogrel**
    c. **Acetaminophen**
    d. **Ibuprofen**

3. **A patient with eczema asks for a recommendation for a skin preparation to help with xerosis. What should the NP respond?**

    a. **Use a petroleum based product**
    b. **Use a hypoallergenic lotion**
    c. **Use any hypoallergenic product**
    d. **No particular product is better than another**

4. **Which patient below should be screened for osteoporosis?**

    a. **60 year-old male with rheumatoid arthritis**
    b. **50 year-old Caucasian female**
    c. **A 65 year-old male who is otherwise healthy**
    d. **A 62 year-old post menopausal female**

5. **A 77 year-old patient has had an increase in blood pressure since the last exam. The blood pressure has risen to 150/88 with 2 readings. The last exam's reading was 144/90. If medication is to be started on this patient, what would be a good first choice?**

    a. **ACE inhibitor**
    b. **Beta blocker**
    c. **Calcium channel blocker**
    d. **Thiazide diuretic**

6. **Which set of symptoms is most likely in a patient infected with *C. difficile*?**

    a. **Headache, diarrhea, body aches**
    b. **Body aches, fever, abdominal cramps**
    c. **Fever, headache, diarrhea**
    d. **Diarrhea, abdominal pain, nausea or vomiting**

7. **A patient who presents with a complaint of sudden decreased visual acuity has a pupil that is about 4 mm, fixed. The affected eye is red. What might be the etiology?**

    a. **Stroke**
    b. **Brain tumor**
    c. **Glaucoma**
    d. **Cataract**

8. **An 80 year-old patient with long standing hypertension takes Monopril and HCTZ for hypertension. His blood pressure is 148-156/92-98 on several blood pressure checks. What should be done about his blood pressure?**

    a. **Add an angiotensin receptor blocker (ARB)**
    b. **Add another diuretic**
    c. **Add a calcium channel blocker**
    d. **Stop the HCTZ and add a beta blocker**

9. **Which of the following results in a clinically insignificant increase in the prostate specific antigen (PSA)?**

    a. **Digital rectal exam**
    b. **Ejaculation**
    c. **Prostatitis**
    d. **Prostate biopsy**

10. An elderly patient with hypertension and angina takes multiple medications. Which one of the following decreases the likelihood of his having angina?

a. **ACE inhibitor**
b. **Beta-blocker**
c. **Diuretic**
d. **Angiotensin receptor blocker**

11. An example of a premalignant lesion that develops on sun-damaged skin is:

a. **actinic keratosis.**
b. **basal cell carcinoid.**
c. **squamous cell carcinoma.**
d. **molluscum contagiosum.**

12. A patient with COPD has been using albuterol with good relief for shortness of breath. He is using it 3-4 times daily over the past 4 weeks. How should the NP manage this?

a. **Encourage its use.**
b. **Add a long acting anticholinergic.**
c. **Tell him to use it only once daily.**
d. **Add an oral steroid.**

13. A typical description of sciatica is:

a. **deep and aching.**
b. **worse at nighttime.**
c. **burning and sharp.**
d. **worse with coughing.**

14. An example of a short-acting beta agonist is:

a. **levalbuterol.**
b. **salmeterol.**
c. **mometasone.**
d. **beclomethasone.**

15. A 30 year-old female presents with lower abdominal pain. The nurse practitioner immediately considers an ectopic pregnancy as the cause. Which factor listed below does NOT increase her risk of an ectopic pregnancy?

a. **Prior history of ectopic pregnancy**
b. **IUD use**
c. **History of PID**
d. **Age**

16. A 40 year-old patient has the following laboratory values. How should they be interpreted?

HBsAg (-), HBsAb (+), HBcAb (+)

- **a. The patient had hepatitis.**
- **b. The patient has never had hepatitis.**
- **c. The patient should consider immunization.**
- **d. The patient has been immunized.**

17. A patient that you are caring for in your clinic has Medicare Part B. What does this mean?

- **a. The federal government will pay for his visit to your clinic today.**
- **b. His medicare benefit covers outpatient services.**
- **c. He will have a co-pay for his visit today.**
- **d. His prescriptions will be partly paid for today.**

18. A patient presents with costovertebral angle (CVA) tenderness, fever of 101 degrees. She is anorexic. What is her likely diagnosis?

- **a. Diverticulosis**
- **b. Renal stone**
- **c. Pyelonephritis**
- **d. Urinary tract infection**

19. A 76 year-old patient has fasting glucose values of 151 mg/dL and 138 mg/dL on different days. This patient:

- **a. can be diagnosed with Type 2 diabetes.**
- **b. has impaired fasting glucose.**
- **c. should have a Hgb A1C performed for diagnosis.**
- **d. has normal glucose values.**

20. Ipratropium is very widely used in the treatment of COPD. Which of the following statements about ipratropium is correct?

- **a. It slows the progression of COPD.**
- **b. It decreases parasympathetic tone and produces bronchodilation.**
- **c. It has anti-inflammatory actions and reduces bronchoconstriction.**
- **d. It is less effective than a beta agonist in producing bronchoconstriction.**

21. A patient being treated for trichomoniasis is given a prescription for metronidazole. What instructions should she be given?

- a. **Take this medication with food.**
- b. **Do not take this medication if you are pregnant.**
- c. **Take this medication on an empty stomach.**
- d. **This medication should not be taken with alcohol.**

22. An 80 year-old patient who is overweight and sedentary has developed elevated, fasting glucose levels (142, 153, and 147 mg/dL). She was diagnosed with diabetes today. Considering her age, how should the nurse practitioner proceed?

- a. **Treat with dietary interventions only**
- b. **Initiate insulin**
- c. **Start metformin**
- d. **Start a sulfonylurea**

23. A 35 year-old patient who is HIV positive is diagnosed with thrush. A microscopic exam of this patient's saliva demonstrates:

- a. **epithelial cells.**
- b. **yeast.**
- c. **spores.**
- d. **red blood cells.**

24. You are volunteering at a clinic that cares for homeless patients. What's the most important aspect of a patient's first visit?

- a. **A complete head to toe exam**
- b. **Establish trust**
- c. **Take an excellent history**
- d. **Ask about problems with alcohol**

25. Which of the following medications may have an unfavorable effect on a hypertensive patient's blood pressure?

- a. **Lovastatin**
- b. **Ibuprofen**
- c. **Fluticasone**
- d. **Amoxicillin**

26. The agent commonly used to treat patients with scabies is permethrin. How often is it applied to eradicate scabies?

a. **Once**
b. **Once daily for 3 days**
c. **Twice daily for 3 days**
d. **Once daily for one week**

27. What is the proper technique to safely remove a tick from a human?

a. **Pull it off with tweezers**
b. **Use petroleum jelly**
c. **Use isopropyl alcohol**
d. **Use a hot match**

28. A patient has developed rapid loss of hearing over the past several weeks. What cranial nerve should be assessed?

a. **Cranial Nerve III**
b. **Cranial Nerve V**
c. **Cranial Nerve VIII**
d. **Cranial Nerve X**

29. A patient who has been treated for hypothyroidism presents for her annual exam. Her TSH is 14.1 (normal = 0.4- 3.8). She complains of weight gain and fatigue. How should the NP proceed?

a. **Ask what time of day she is taking her medication**
b. **Ask if she is taking her medication**
c. **Increase her dose of thyroid supplement**
d. **Repeat the TSH in 2-3 months**

30. If plantar fasciitis is suspected in a patient, how is this diagnosed?

a. **X-ray of the foot**
b. **CT scan**
c. **Physical exam**
d. **Bone scan**

31. Which mitral disorder results from redundancy of the mitral valve's leaflets?

a. **Acute mitral regurgitation**
b. **Chronic mitral regurgitation**
c. **Mitral valve prolapse**
d. **Mitral stenosis**

32. What is the AM fasting glucose goal for a 75 year-old patient who has diabetes?

a. 80-100 mg/dL
b. 100-120 mg/dL
c. 80-120 mg/dL
d. 120-140 mg/dL

33. All of the following characteristics may be found in an older adult with dementia. Which one is common in a patient with Alzheimer's disease, but uncommon in a patient with another type of dementia?

a. Visual hallucinations
b. Personality change
c. Abrupt onset
d. Indifference

34. A patient reports that she takes kava kava regularly for anxiety with good results. What should the NP evaluate?

a. Liver function studies
b. Risk of bleeding
c. Thyroid function
d. Colon polyps

35. When examining the vessels of the eye:

a. the veins are smaller than the arteries.
b. the arteries are smaller than the veins.
c. the arteries are dark red.
d. the arteries pulsate.

36. A 70 year-old male has a yellowish, triangular nodule on the side of the iris. This is probably:

a. a stye.
b. a chalazion.
c. a pinguecula.
d. subconjunctival hemorrhage.

37. A good first choice of antidepressants in an older adult is:

a. a tricyclic antidepressant (TCA).
b. an SSRI.
c. an MAO inhibitor.
d. any agent is a good first choice.

38. An older adult has a cold. She calls your office to ask for advice for an agent to help her runny nose and congestion. She has hypertension, COPD, and glaucoma. What agent is safe to use?

- **a. Pseudoephedrine**
- **b. Oxymetazoline nasal spray**
- **c. Guafenesin**
- **d. Diphenhydramine**

39. A 28 year-old female presents with a slightly tender 1.5 cm lump in her right breast. She noticed it two days ago. She has no associated lymphadenopathy and there is no nipple discharge. How should she be managed?

- **a. Mammogram**
- **b. Ultrasound and mammogram**
- **c. Re-examination after her next menses**
- **d. Clinical exam only**

40. A common, early finding in patients with chronic aortic regurgitation (AR) is:

- **a. an hypertrophied left ventricle.**
- **b. atrial fibrillation.**
- **c. pulmonary congestion.**
- **d. low systolic blood pressure.**

41. Besides inadequate intake of Vitamin D in elder adults, what other factor contributes to deficiencies?

- **a. Impaired synthesis of previtamin D**
- **b. Decreased physical activity**
- **c. Diminished hepatic function**
- **d. Decreased body mass**

42. The usual clinical course of mitral valve prolapse:

- **a. is benign.**
- **b. results in sudden cardiac death.**
- **c. results in congestive heart failure.**
- **d. is associated with multiple episodes of emboli.**

43. What should be avoided in a patient being treated with metronidazole for trichomonas?

- a. **Direct sunlight**
- b. **Alcohol**
- c. **Tea**
- d. **Penicillin**

44. You have been asked to manage thyroid disease in a pregnant patient. A pregnant patient took L-thyroxin prior to becoming pregnant. What should be done about the L-thyroxin now that she is pregnant?

- a. **It should be discontinued during pregnancy.**
- b. **She should continue it and have monthly TSH levels.**
- c. **She should be switched to a supplement with a category B rating.**
- d. **She can continue it during pregnancy without concern.**

45. The most common place for basal cell carcinoma to be found is the:

- a. **scalp.**
- b. **face.**
- c. **anterior shin.**
- d. **upper posterior back.**

46. Where would the murmur associated with mitral regurgitation best be auscultated?

- a. **Aortic listening point**
- b. **Mitral listening point**
- c. **Pulmonic listening point**
- d. **Tricuspid listening point**

47. A 74 year-old is diagnosed with shingles. The NP is deciding how to best manage her care. What should be prescribed?

- a. **An oral antiviral agent**
- b. **An oral antiviral agent plus an oral steroid**
- c. **An oral antiviral agent plus a topical steroid**
- d. **A topical steroid only**

48. An 80 year-old with COPD is likely to have concurrent:

- a. **anxiety or depression.**
- b. **thyroid disease.**
- c. **diabetes.**
- d. **obesity.**

49. The diagnosis of mitral valve prolapse can be confirmed by:

a. physical examination.
b. electrocardiography.
c. echocardiography.
d. chest x-ray.

50. The incidence of pyelonephritis is:

a. least common in young adults.
b. less common than urinary tract infections.
c. always associated with urinary tract infections.
d. more likely in elderly males.

51. A patient complains of "first step in the morning" pain in his heel. He states that it has progressed to "end of the day" heel pain. What probably has contributed to this most?

a. Driving a vehicle long distances
b. Walking in new tennis shoes
c. Riding a bicycle
d. Pes planus

52. A patient who has diabetes presents with pain when he walks and pain resolution with rest. When specifically asked about the pain in his lower leg, he likely will report pain:

a. in and around the ankle joint.
b. in the calf muscle.
c. radiating down his leg from the thigh.
d. pain in his lower leg which waxes and wanes.

53. The two tests which can indicate with certainty that a patient has hepatitis B at present are:

a. hepatitis B surface antigen and antibody.
b. hepatitis B surface antigen and IgM.
c. hepatitis B surface antibody and core antibody.
d. positive IgG and positive core antibody.

54. Bone mineral density screening in women over age 65 years is an example of:

a. primary prevention.
b. secondary prevention.
c. tertiary prevention.
d. quaternary prevention.

55. A patient has non-fasting glucose values of 110 mg/dL and 116 mg/dL. This patient:

- **a. can be diagnosed with Type 2 diabetes.**
- **b. has impaired fasting glucose.**
- **c. should have a Hgb A1C performed.**
- **d. has normal glucose values.**

56. Which of the following characteristics is always present in a patient with COPD?

- **a. Productive cough**
- **b. Obstructed airways**
- **c. Shortness of breath**
- **d. Hypercapnia**

57. An older adult has renal insufficiency, hypertension, osteoarthritis, hypothyroidism, and varicose veins. Which medication should be avoided?

- **a. Acetaminophen**
- **b. Beta blockers**
- **c. NSAIDs**
- **d. Low dose aspirin**

58. In a patient with mononucleosis, which laboratory abnormality is most common?

- **a. Lymphocytosis and atypical lymphocytes**
- **b. Elevated monocytes**
- **c. A decreased total white count**
- **d. Elevated liver enzymes**

59. A 65 year-old male is diagnosed with an initial episode of gout. It is likely that he:

- **a. will have elevated uric acid levels.**
- **b. is consuming too much meat.**
- **c. will have involvement in a joint like the hip or shoulder.**
- **d. will have severe inflammation in a single joint.**

60. A 24 year-old female presents with abdominal pain. On exam, she is found to have cervical motion tenderness. What finding supports a diagnosis of pelvic inflammatory disease (PID)?

- **a. A positive pregnancy test**
- **b. Vaginal discharge**
- **c. Positive RPR**
- **d. Oral temperature 102F**

61. A male patient who injured his back lifting a heavy object reports that he has low back pain. He is diagnosed with a lumbar strain. He is afraid to continue activities of daily living and especially walking because he has pain with these activities. What statement below is true?

a. **Stop doing any activities that produce pain in your lower back.**
b. **Continue your activities of daily living, but stop walking, except to go to the bathroom.**
c. **Bedrest will help your back pain.**
d. **Continue your activities of daily living and walking.**

62. An elderly male has benign prostatic hyperplasia (BPH). What drug should be avoided in him?

a. **Acetaminophen**
b. **NSAIDs**
c. **Cortisone**
d. **Hydrochlorothiazide (HCTZ)**

63. A 63 year-old male has been your patient for several years. He is a former smoker who takes simvastatin, ramipril, and an aspirin daily. His blood pressure and lipids are well controlled. He presents to your clinic with complaints of fatigue and "just not feeling well" for the last few days. His vital signs and exam are normal. What should be done next?

a. **Order a CBC and consider waiting a few days if normal.**
b. **Inquire about feelings of depression and hopelessness.**
c. **Order a CBC, metabolic panel, TSH, and urine analysis.**
d. **Order a B12 level, TSH, CBC, and chest x-ray.**

64. A patient has cut himself on a fence post while working outside. He has not had a tetanus shot in more than 10 years. How long can he wait before getting the immunization and still prevent tetanus?

a. **24 hours**
b. **48 hours**
c. **72 hours**
d. **5 days**

65. A male patient is found to have positive leukocytes and positive nitrites in his urine. What medication should be given and for how many days?

a. **Doxycycline for 3 days**
b. **Trimethoprim-sulfamethoxazole (TMPS) for 7- 10 days**
c. **Ciprofloxacin for 3 days**
d. **Nitrofurantoin for 14 days**

66. A 25 year-old female presents with lower abdominal pain. Which finding below would likely indicate the etiology as pelvic inflammatory disease?

a. **Presence of hyphae**
b. **Hematuria**
c. **Temperature > 101F**
d. **Normal sedimentation rate**

67. A patient has had an anaphylactic reaction to eggs. She should avoid immunization with:

a. **varicella.**
b. **hepatitis B.**
c. **IPV.**
d. **influenza.**

68. A 70 year-old male who is diabetic presents with gait difficulty, cognitive disturbance, and urinary incontinence. What is part of the nurse practitioner's differential diagnosis?

a. **Diabetic neuropathy**
b. **Normal pressure hydrocephalus**
c. **Parkinson's Disease**
d. **Multiple sclerosis**

69. A 5 year-old has been diagnosed with pinworms. He lives with his mother. There are no other members of the household. How should his mother be managed?

a. **Reassure the mother that if she develops symptoms, she will need to be treated.**
b. **Visually assess the mother's rectum for redness or presence of worms.**
c. **Have the mother collect a stool specimen and send it to the laboratory.**
d. **Perform the "scotch tape" test and look at the collection under the microscope.**

70. The lipid particle with the greatest atherogenic effect is:

a. **total cholesterol.**
b. **HDL.**
c. **LDL.**
d. **triglycerides.**

71. The gold standard for diagnosing pneumonia on chest x-ray is the presence of:

- a. infiltrates.
- b. interstitial fluid.
- c. cavitation.
- d. "pooling".

72. An elderly patient had a total knee replacement (TKR) 10 months ago. He is doing well. What information should he be given regarding the knee replacement?

- a. He should take an aspirin daily for the first year.
- b. He should receive an antibiotic prior to dental procedures.
- c. He should take the flu shot annually.
- d. There are no recommendations 6 months after his surgery.

73. A 74 year-old patient has a pill-rolling tremor. With what disease is this often associated?

- a. Psychosomatic disorder
- b. Multiple sclerosis
- c. Parkinson's disease
- d. Benign essential tremor

74. Pharmacologic treatment for very elderly adults with hypertension should be initiated:

- a. only if there is a life expectancy of 10 years or more.
- b. for any type of hypertension.
- c. without regard to lifestyle modifications.
- d. only for those who are symptomatic.

75. Which statement below is true regarding NSAIDs for low back pain?

- a. They are as equally efficacious as acetaminophen for pain.
- b. They are associated with more side effects than acetaminophen.
- c. They provide superior relief of symptoms at one week post injury.
- d. They should not be used to treat acute low back pain.

76. A 60 year-old patient newly diagnosed with COPD presents to your office. He would like to get the influenza immunization. He has no evidence of having had the pneumococcal immunization. What statement is correct?

a. **He should receive pneumonia immunization after age 65 years.**
b. **He should receive both today.**
c. **He should receive the flu immunization annually until age 65 years.**
d. **He should not receive both on the same day.**

77. A patient received the pneumonia immunization at age 60 years. He is 65 years-old and presents to your clinic today. What recommendation should be made about the pneumococcal immunization?

a. **He should receive another one today.**
b. **He does not need another one today.**
c. **He needs to get one annually starting at age 65 years.**
d. **He should get it every 5 years.**

78. *Mycoplasma pneumoniae* is:

a. **a diagnosis of exclusion.**
b. **a typical respiratory pathogen.**
c. **only identifiable on chest x-ray.**
d. **a disease with extrapulmonary manifestations.**

79. The most common cause of diarrhea in adults is:

a. ***E. coli.***
b. ***salmonella.***
c. ***C. difficile.***
d. **viral gastroenteritis.**

80. A 55 year-old male is obese, does not exercise, and has hyperlipidemia. He is diagnosed with Stage 1 hypertension today. How should he be managed?

a. **He should be given low dose thiazide diuretic.**
b. **An ACE inhibitor is appropriate.**
c. **Lifestyle modifications are appropriate.**
d. **He should receive an ACE inhibitor and thiazide diuretic.**

81. A patient recently received an antibiotic for 10 days for pneumonia. His respiratory symptoms have resolved but today he calls the office. He reports having severe watery diarrhea, abdominal cramping, and low-grade fever. What should be done?

- **a. Give an anti-diarrheal agent**
- **b. Encourage the patient to force fluids**
- **c. Order a stool specimen**
- **d. Wait 24 hours for resolution of symptoms**

82. The three most common causes of bacterial diarrhea in the US are Salmonella, Campylobacter, and:

- **a. *E. coli.***
- **b. *Enterovirus.***
- **c. *Yersinia.***
- **d. *Shigella.***

83. A patient has been diagnosed today with Type II diabetes. A criterion for diagnosis is:

- **a. an abnormal random blood glucose.**
- **b. proteinuria.**
- **c. a fasting glucose $\geq$ 126 and confirmed on a previous day.**
- **d. an abnormal post-prandial glucose.**

84. A medication considered first line for a patient with allergic rhinitis is a:

- **a. decongestant.**
- **b. non-sedating antihistamine.**
- **c. leukotriene blocker.**
- **d. topical nasal steroid.**

85. A female patient reports fatigue. She is found to have an iron deficiency anemia. An iron supplement is best taken:

- **a. in the morning.**
- **b. with food.**
- **c. with a food rich in Vitamin D.**
- **d. on an empty stomach.**

86. Testicular torsion can produce:

a. penile erythema.
b. scrotal edema.
c. scrotal erythema.
d. penile edema.

87. A 20 year-old male reports nocturnal headaches of recent onset. What is NOT part of the differential diagnosis in this patient?

a. Migraine headache
b. Brain tumor
c. Hydrocephalus
d. Cluster headache

88. An elderly adult has constipation. A supplement known to cause constipation is:

a. Vitamin A.
b. calcium.
c. magnesium.
d. Vitamin B-12.

89. Serotonin is thought to play a role in the etiology of:

a. depression.
b. multiple myeloma.
c. multiple sclerosis.
d. ulcerative colitis.

90. Mild persistent asthma is characterized by:

a. limitation in activity due to bronchoconstriction.
b. symptoms occurring more than twice weekly.
c. wheezing and coughing during exacerbations.
d. shortness of breath with exercise.

91. A 37 year-old overweight male is diagnosed today with Type II diabetes. His fasting glucose is 159 mg/dL. He is hyperlipidemic (LDL = 210 mg/dL) and hypertensive (146/102). What medications should be initiated today?

a. Metformin, ASA, and pravastatin
b. Metformin, niacin, Monopril
c. Glimepiride, ASA, fosinopril
d. Metformin, atorvastatin, ramipril, ASA

92. A patient with allergic rhinitis developed a sinus infection 10 days ago. He takes fexofenadine daily. What should be done with the fexofenadine?

- a. Stop the fexofenadine.
- b. Stop the fexofenadine and add a nasal steroid.
- c. Continue the fexofenadine and prescribe an antibiotic.
- d. Continue the fexofenadine and add a decongestant.

93. An 18 year-old female patient has iron deficiency anemia. If this anemia has occurred in the past 3-4 months, what might be expected?

- a. An increased RDW
- b. A decreased RDW
- c. An elevated serum ferritin
- d. A decreased total iron binding capacity

94. A 17 year-old presents with complaints of dysmenorrhea. What finding below suggests that this is secondary dysmenorrhea?

- a. Normal pelvic exam
- b. Dysmenorrhea is not limited to menses
- c. Unpredictable menses
- d. Nausea with menses

95. A medication belonging to the class of triptans could be used to treat a patient with migraine headaches and:

- a. tension headaches.
- b. cluster headaches.
- c. serotonin abnormalities.
- d. depression.

96. A nurse practitioner is taking care of a patient with health insurance and allergic complaints. The NP is aware that the patient is not using the prescribed allergy medication for her. Instead, the patient is giving the medication to her husband because he does not have insurance. What should the NP do?

- a. Continue to prescribe the medication
- b. Stop prescribing the medication for the patient
- c. Only prescribe the medication if the patient promises to use it
- d. Prescribe the medication only once more

97. Which study listed below is considered an experimental study?

- a. Case series
- b. Cross-sectional study
- c. Cohort study
- d. Meta-analysis

98. The preferred medication class to treat patients with an initial episode of depression is:

- a. tricyclic antidepressants.
- b. monoamine oxidase inhibitors.
- c. selective serotonin reuptake inhibitors.
- d. any class. There is no preferred class.

99. A female patient has been diagnosed with chlamydia. How should this be managed?

- a. Treat with azithromycin
- b. Treat with ceftriaxone by injection
- c. Treat with doxycycline
- d. Treat for gonorrhea also

100. A B-12 deficiency can produce:

- a. a microcytic anemia.
- b. pernicious anemia.
- c. sideroblastic anemia.
- d. insomnia.

101. Serotonin syndrome may result from taking an SSRI and:

- a. dextromethorphan.
- b. loratadine.
- c. pravastatin.
- d. niacin.

102. What would be the study of choice to determine the cause of a cluster of adult leukemia cases found in an isolated area of a rural state?

- a. Randomized clinical trial
- b. Cohort study
- c. Case series
- d. Case control

103. An elderly male diagnosed with a microcytic, hypochromic anemia:

- a. should be worked up for a malignancy.
- b. might be consuming excessive amounts of alcohol.
- c. will have a increased RBC count.
- d. may have a GI bleed.

104. The early signs and symptoms of appendicitis in an adult:

- a. are subtle.
- b. produce marked pain in the lower right abdominal quadrant.
- c. produce symptoms in the periumbilical region only.
- d. include fever, nausea and vomiting.

105. An 80 year-old female who is otherwise well, has a blood pressure of 176/80. How should she be managed pharmacologically?

- a. Thiazide diuretic
- b. ACE inhibitor
- c. Calcium channel blocker
- d. Angiotensin receptor blocker

106. A patient with diabetes has a right lower leg that has recently become edematous, erythematous, and tender to touch over the anterior shin. There is no evidence of pus, but the leg is warm to touch. What is the most likely diagnosis to consider?

- a. Deep vein thrombosis (DVT)
- b. Buerger's disease
- c. Cellulitis
- d. Venous disease

107. Which medication used to treat diabetes is associated with diarrhea and flatulence?

- a. Pioglitazone
- b. Insulin
- c. Metformin
- d. Glimepiride

108. A patient has a penicillin allergy. He describes an anaphylactic reaction. Which medication class should be specifically avoided in him?

- a. Quinolones
- b. Macrolides
- c. Cephalosporins
- d. Tetracyclines

109. A serum ferritin level:

- a. could indicate thalassemia in a patient.
- b. demonstrates the amount of iron in storage.
- c. indicates when a patient has iron deficiency anemia.
- d. confirms a low hemoglobin and hematocrit.

110. Which imaging study of the abdomen would be LEAST helpful in diagnosing an acute appendicitis?

- a. Ultrasound
- b. CT scan
- c. MRI
- d. X-ray

111. An elderly adult has chronic constipation. How should this be managed initially?

- a. Avoid all constipating medications/foods when possible
- b. Add dietary fiber and increase fluids
- c. Add sorbitol solution daily
- d. Use an oil retention enema

112. A sexually active male patient presents with epididymitis. What finding is likely?

- a. Abnormal urinalysis
- b. Dysuria
- c. Recent history of heavy physical exercise
- d. Scrotal edema

113. A depressed patient is started on an SSRI. When should another antidepressant be tried if there is no response?

- a. 3-7 days
- b. 2-3 weeks
- c. 4-6 weeks
- d. 8-12 weeks

114. A 42 year-old hypertensive patient was given a thiazide diuretic 4 weeks ago. On his return visit today, he reports feeling weak and tired. What should the NP consider to evaluate the weakness and fatigue?

- a. Blood pressure
- b. Potassium level
- c. CBC
- d. Cr/BUN

115. A 28 year-old has thick, demarcated plaques on her elbows. Which features are suggestive of psoriasis?

- **a. Scaly lesions on the scalp**
- **b. Pruritis around the lesions**
- **c. A scaly border around the plaques**
- **d. Silvery scales that are not pruritic**

116. A 52 year-old presents with symptoms of diabetes today. His glucose is 302 mg/dL. How should this be managed today?

- **a. Have him return tomorrow to recheck his blood glucose**
- **b. Start metformin**
- **c. Start insulin**
- **d. Start metformin plus pioglitazone**

117. Swimmer's ear is diagnosed in a patient with tragal tenderness. What other symptom might he have?

- **a. Otitis media**
- **b. Hearing loss**
- **c. Otic itching**
- **d. Fever**

118. A patient has heavy menses. Which lab value below reflects an iron deficiency anemia?

- **a. Increased TIBC**
- **b. Decreased TIBC**
- **c. Normal serum iron**
- **d. Decreased RDW**

119. A man fell off a 3-foot stepladder while working at home. He presents to your office with complaints of foot pain. He has point tenderness over the lateral malleolus, swelling, but he is able to ambulate. How should this be managed?

- **a. ACE wrap and rest**
- **b. Rest, ice, compression, and elevation**
- **c. X-ray of the foot and ankle**
- **d. Non-weight bearing for 3-7 days**

120. An initial pharmacologic approach to a patient who is diagnosed with primary dysmenorrhea could be:

- a. acetaminophen.
- b. NSAIDs at the time symptoms begin or onset of menses.
- c. NSAIDs prior to the onset of menses.
- d. combination acetaminophen and NSAIDs.

121. A patient complains of right leg numbness and tingling following a back injury. He has a diminished right patellar reflex and his symptoms are progressing to both legs. What test should be performed?

- a. Lumbar x-rays
- b. Lumbar CT scan
- c. Lumbar MRI
- d. Lumbar MRI with contrast

122. A patient may derive benefit from a tricyclic antidepressant (TCA) if he experiences depression and:

- a. chronic pain.
- b. constipation.
- c. bipolar disease.
- d. hyperlipidemia.

123. A 73 year-old patient is thought to have benign prostatic hyperplasia. What would be part of the initial workup?

- a. Digital rectal exam (DRE) only
- b. DRE, urinalysis, PSA
- c. PSA only
- d. PSA, DRE, BUN, Cr

124. The cranial nerve responsible for vision is Cranial Nerve:

- a. I.
- b. II.
- c. III.
- d. IV.

125. The research design that provides the strongest evidence for concluding causation is:

a. randomized controlled trials.
b. cohort studies.
c. case control studies.
d. prospective studies.

126. The clinical difference between minor depression and major depression is:

a. the length of time symptoms have lasted.
b. the number of symptoms present.
c. the severity of the symptoms.
d. presence of suicidal ideations.

127. A characteristic of an ACE inhibitor induced cough is that it:

a. is mildly productive.
b. is worse at nighttime.
c. usually begins within a week of starting therapy.
d. is more common in men.

128. Which description is more typical of a patient with acute cholecystitis?

a. The patient rolls from side to side on the exam table.
b. The patient is ill appearing and febrile.
c. An elderly patient is more likely to exhibit Murphy's sign.
d. Most are asymptomatic until a stone blocks the bile duct.

129. A nurse practitioner has decided to initiate insulin in a patient who takes oral diabetic medications. How much long acting insulin should be initiated in a patient who weighs 100 kg?

a. About 5 units
b. 10 units
c. 15 units
d. 20 units

130. The throat swab done to identify Streptococcal infection was negative in a 12 year-old female with tonsillar exudate, fever, and sore throat. What statement is true regarding this?

a. A second swab should be done to repeat the test.
b. The patient does not have Strept throat.
c. The patient probably has mononucleosis.
d. A second swab should be collected and sent to microbiology.

131. A patient demonstrates leukocytosis. This means:

- a. he has a bacterial infection.
- b. he has a viral infection.
- c. he has an infection of unknown origin.
- d. he does not have an infection.

132. An adolescent has suspected varicocele. He has dull scrotal pain that is relieved by:

- a. standing.
- b. recumbency.
- c. having a bowel movement.
- d. elevation of the testicle.

133. A female with complaint of dysuria has a urine specimen that is positive for leukocytes and nitrites. There is blood in the specimen. An appropriate diagnosis is:

- a. urinary tract infection.
- b. asymptomatic bacteriuria.
- c. UTI with hematuria.
- d. UTI or chlamydia.

134. A patient is found to have eosinophilia. An expected finding is:

- a. asthma exacerbation.
- b. bronchitis.
- c. hepatitis.
- d. osteoporosis.

135. A 93 year-old demented adult has been recently treated for an upper respiratory infection (URI) but drainage from the right nostril persists. What should the NP suspect?

- a. Allergic rhinitis
- b. Presence of a foreign body
- c. Unresolved URI
- d. Dental caries

136. A 24 year-old presents with fever, rhinorrhea, and paroxysmal, high-pitched whooping cough. This is:

a. bronchiolitis.
b. croup.
c. pertussis.
d. epiglottitis.

137. A nurse practitioner is volunteering in a homeless clinic to gain clinical experience. Which statement is true about this?

a. Malpractice insurance is not needed because this is volunteer work.
b. Volunteerism negates susceptibility to lawsuits.
c. Malpractice insurance is needed by the nurse practitioner.
d. Coverage will be provided by the state where the clinic is located.

138. The most common symptoms associated with gastroesophageal reflux disease (GERD) are heartburn and:

a. cough.
b. regurgitation and dysphagia.
c. cough and hoarseness.
d. belching and sore throat.

139. Niacin is known to:

a. increase fasting glucose levels.
b. produce hypertension.
c. decrease triglycerides.
d. decrease HDLs.

140. An example of a first generation cephalosporin used to treat a skin infection is:

a. cephalexin.
b. cefuroxime.
c. cefdinir.
d. ceflamore.

141. A patient has been prescribed pioglitazone. The nurse practitioner must remember to:

a. check a hemoglobin A1C in 3 months.
b. order liver function studies in about 2-3 months.
c. screen for microalbuminuria.
d. wean off metformin.

142. A patient has been diagnosed with mononucleosis. Which statement is correct?

a. **He is likely an adolescent male.**
b. **Splenomegaly is more likely than not.**
c. **He cannot be co-infected with Strept.**
d. **Cervical lymphadenopathy may be prominent.**

143. Which statement is true about Vitamin B-12?

a. **It is easily absorbed through the gastrointestinal tract.**
b. **Deficiencies are seen in elderly patients only.**
c. **Low levels can result in elevated lipid levels.**
d. **Inadequate amounts can produce cognitive changes.**

144. A patient who has hyperlipidemia should have:

a. **a statin daily.**
b. **a thyroid stimulating hormone (TSH) level.**
c. **a second measurement to confirm diagnosis.**
d. **a stress test done.**

145. An adolescent athlete has sprained his ankle. What instruction should be given to him regarding activity?

a. **He can resume regular activities in about one week.**
b. **He should be able to walk pain-free before he starts to run.**
c. **His ankle should be taped prior to competition.**
d. **He can resume activity when the edema has resolved.**

146. An adolescent female has had normal menses for almost 2 years. She has not had menses in 3 months. She is diagnosed with polycystic ovarian syndrome (PCOS). What else is a common finding?

a. **Obesity**
b. **Elevated insulin levels**
c. **Positive pregnancy test**
d. **Elevated blood pressure**

147. Clue cells are found in patients with:

a. **leukemia.**
b. **bacterial vaginosis.**
c. **epidermal fungal infections.**
d. **pneumonia.**

148. A 26 year-old female presents with flank pain that waxes and wanes. Her urine specimen indicates the presence of:

- **a. blood.**
- **b. nitrites.**
- **c. leukocytes.**
- **d. calcium.**

149. A positive Tinel's test can be used to assess carpal tunnel syndrome. What other test can be used to assess for this?

- **a. Patrick's test**
- **b. Finkelstein's test**
- **c. Phalen's test**
- **d. Allen's test**

150. A patient with bipolar disease has purchased a $10,000 baby grand piano. He does not play the piano. This behavior is typical during:

- **a. depression.**
- **b. mania.**
- **c. hypomania.**
- **d. psychosis.**

Adult Exam #2 Answers

1. ***d***
Trochanteric bursitis does not produce pain in the calf. Pain is concentrated in the affected hip. While it is not likely that someone who exercises regularly would have a DVT, this patient does take oral contraceptives. Therefore, DVT should always be part of the differential given the potential risks associated with untreated DVT (pulmonary embolism).

2. ***c***
The exam for occult blood is a screen for colorectal cancer. Aspirin, clopidogrel, NSAIDs, warfarin all decrease the positive predictive value of the test because they all can exacerbate bleeding if it is occuring in the colon secondary to a polyp or tumor. Ideally, the medications mentioned (except acetaminophen) would be stopped prior to the exam to increase the likelihood of test sensitivity, but this is not always possible.

3. ***a***
Xerosis is dry skin. It is common in patients who have eczema. Using thick creams or ointments can prevent xerosis. Lotions should be avoided because they have high water content that promotes evaporation of water from the skin. Hypoallergenic refers to the allergenicity of a product. This is not related to the water content of products.

4. ***a***
Routine screening for osteoporosis is not recommended in males unless risk factors are present, like rheumatoid arthritis. Screening in women is recommended starting at age 65. If risk factors are present in a female, screening is recommended at an earlier age. Screening is usually performed by bone mineral density using a dual energy x-ray absorptiometry (DXA) scan.

5. ***d***
This patient is 77 years old and should have his blood pressure lowered. He has consistently demonstrated Stage 1 hypertension. A thiazide diuretic is considered a good first choice in elderly patients. A long acting calcium channel blocker is appropriate for patients with isolated systolic hypertension. Beta-blockers are no longer recommended first line for uncomplicated hypertension. ACE inhibitors are very effective in patients who are high renin producers. Elderly patients tend to produce lower amounts of renin.

6. ***d***
The classic symptoms that patients with C. difficile experience are described in choice D. This patient should be treated because symptoms are present. If no symptoms or mild symptoms are present, treatment can be delayed until symptoms develop or worsen. All patients who are infected do not exhibit symptoms. They do not need

treatment.

7. ***c***
This patient needs urgent referral to ophthalmology. While this is a relatively unusual patient in primary care, the primary care clinician must be able to recognize this patient and the need for urgent referral. In a patient with acute angle closure glaucoma, the patient is usually ill appearing, may have nausea and vomiting. This scenario should prompt urgent referral.

8. ***c***
This patient takes medications from 2 different classes of antihypertensives. If these are at maximum doses, consideration should be given to adding a medication from a different class. Adding an ARB may result in a precipitous decrease in his blood pressure because he takes an ACE inhibitor and both of these medications work in the renin-angiotensin-aldosterone system. Adding another diuretic will likely produce hypokalemia with a small decrease in blood pressure. The calcium channel blocker is a good choice because it will have an additive effect with the other medications he is taking. A beta blocker will slow the heart rate, not a preferred outcome in an elderly patient unless he has underlying angina or a heart rate problem.

9. ***a***
Digital rectal exam (DRE) leads to a clinically insignificant increase of 0.26-0.4 ng/ml for about 48-72 hours afterwards. Prostate biopsy increases the PSA about 8 ng/ml for up to 4 weeks following biopsy. Prostate infection and ejaculation both can increase the PSA levels.

10. ***b***
The beta-blocker slows down heart rate, depresses myocardial contractility, and decreases sympathetic stimulation. These decrease myocardial oxygen demand and improve angina symptoms. It is an excellent drug class to use to prevent symptoms of angina in patients with underlying coronary artery disease. Calcium channel blockers are another class of medications that could be used to improve symptoms of angina.

11. ***a***
Actinic keratoses (AK) are a result of solar damage to the skin. They are most common on the face, bald scalp, and forearms. Patients who present with AK usually have multiple of them. A characteristic that helps identification of AK is an area of erythema that surrounds the lesion. AK is better felt than seen.

12. ***b***
The patient is using albuterol too frequently. It should be used only a few times weekly because if it is used too frequently, it will lose its effectiveness over time. This medication should be used as a rescue medication only, but you cannot tell a patient to use it only once daily. This patient's medication regimen needs adjusting. The best choice is to consider adding a long acting anticholinergic and have him use albuterol as a rescue medication. Another consideration is a short-acting anticholinergic in

combination with his albuterol for symptom management.

13. *c*
Sciatica represents irritation of the nerve root. Patients usually complain of sharp, burning pain that can be accompanied by numbness, tingling and radiating pain down the posterior aspect of one leg. Disc herniation, which could cause sciatica, produces increased pain with coughing, sneezing, or the Valsalva maneuver.

14. *a*
An example of a short-acting beta agonist is albuterol, levalbuterol, pirbuterol, or bitolterol. These provide rapid dilation of the bronchioles and can give immediate relief; hence the term for this class of medications: rescue medications. Salmeterol is a long-acting beta agonist. These should never be used without an inhaled steroid to treat a patient with asthma. Mometasone and beclomethasone are steroids commonly used to treat patients with asthma.

15. *d*
In an ectopic pregnancy, the developing embryo becomes implanted outside the uterus. A common site is the fallopian tube. Young age is a low risk factor for ectopic pregnancy. The other choices all confer high risk of ectopic pregnancy. Other high risk factors are previous tubal surgery or pathology, tubal ligation, and in utero DES exposure.

16. *a*
This patient has a negative hepatitis B surface antigen (HBsAg). Therefore, he does not have hepatitis B. The patient has a positive hepatitis B surface antibody (HBsAb). Therefore, he is considered immune. The patient also has a positive hepatitis B core antibody (HBcAb). Therefore, he is immune because he has had hepatitis B. The correct answer is choice A.

17. *b*
Part B pays the examiner (NP, PA, MD, etc.). Part B of Medicare pays for outpatient care, ambulatory surgery services, x-rays, durable medical equipment, laboratory, and home health. Part B is an option that Medicare recipients can pay for with a monthly option. This charge is based on income. Since there is an initial co-pay, the federal government's insurance plan may NOT pay for his visit to your clinic today.

18. *c*
CVA tenderness is typical of patients who have pyelonephritis. Additionally, the most common symptom associated with pyelonephritis is fever. A patient who presents with this scenario has to be considered to have pyelonephritis until proven otherwise.

19. a
Glucose values that equal or exceed 126 mg/dL on different days constitute a diagnosis of diabetes. Therefore, an A1C is not needed for diagnosis but may be ordered to establish a baseline for this patient. Impaired fasting glucose can be diagnosed when

two glucose values are between 100 mg/dL and 125 mg/dL on different days.

20. ***b***

Ipratropium is the most widely studied anticholinergic medication used to treat patients with COPD. It produces its helpful effects by reducing cholinergic tone in the lungs. It should not be used with a beta agonist unless shortness of breath is present because beta agonists increase side effects like tachycardia and tremor and do not improve efficacy.

21. ***d***

Metronidazole may be associated with a disulfiram reaction when mixed with alcohol. Advice that should be given to all patients who take metronidazole is to avoid alcohol entirely while this medication is being taken. Additionally, alcohol should be avoided for 72 hours after the last dose of medication. The disulfiram reaction is characterized by fever, abdominal pain, nausea, vomiting, and headache. This reaction is called the "Antabuse" reaction.

22. ***c***

This patient should be treated with medication and lifestyle interventions. Metformin would be a good medication to initiate treatment with because it is generally well tolerated and should not produce hypoglycemia if given alone. It should be initiated at 500 mg daily and the dose increased as tolerated.

23. ***b***

The visualization of yeast in saliva usually indicates Candida species. Yeast are commonly seen in patients who have thrush, vaginitis secondary to yeast, or intertrigo. While thrush is uncommon in adults, it is not uncommon in patients who are immunocompromised, such as a patient with HIV.

24. ***b***

The most important aspect of the initial visit is to establish trust. Many patients will not be willing to disclose a complete history to the examiner; especially one regarding alcohol or illegal drugs. A complete head to toe exam might be important, but most homeless patients are driven to care based on episodic illness. They will be interested in care for the problem that brought them in on the day of the exam. Additionally, resources may be limited which would not allow for a complete head to toe exam on each patient, but instead, a focused visit.

25. ***b***

Ibuprofen is an NSAID. NSAIDs produce sodium retention and hence, water retention. This produces many systemic effects such as an increase in blood pressure, lower extremity edema, increased workload of the heart, and inhibition of prostaglandin synthesis. Patients with hypertension and chronic heart failure should use NSAIDs cautiously. Neither lovastatin nor fluticasone would be expected to increase or decrease blood pressure. Amoxicillin is an antibiotic. These do not increase blood pressure.

26. ***a***
A single whole body application of permethrin is usually successful in eradicating infection with scabies. It is applied over the entire body from the neck down. The lotion is left on and then showered off 8-12 hours later. All contacts must be treated at the same time and all potential fomites (bed linen, mattresses, cloth furniture, etc.) must be treated as well. Permethrin can be sprayed on cloth fomites or they can be bagged for several days, washed and dried in washing machine and dryer. Ironing clothes after washing them is acceptable.

27. ***a***
If tweezers are not available, protected fingers should be used. The person removing the tick should take care NOT to crush the tick because it may contain infectious organisms. After the tick is removed, the skin should be washed well with soap and water. If mouth parts remain after the tick has been removed, they should NOT be removed. The area should be monitored for 30 days for erythema migrans.

28. ***c***
Cranial Nerve (CN) VIII is the CN responsible for hearing. When assessing CN VIII, each ear should be assessed individually. The Weber and Rinne are usually used to distinguish conductive and sensorineural hearing loss. An audiogram gives more reproducible results than the Weber and Rinne tests.

29. ***b***
Her TSH is elevated. This is usually caused by insufficient supplementation in a patient with hypothyroidism. If the TSH was within normal range following her last annual exam, something has changed. The first point that must be established is whether the patient is still taking her medication. If she is still taking her medication, determining when she is taking it is very important. It should be taken on an empty stomach for absorption. These two important facts must be established BEFORE increasing her current dose. The TSH is usually repeated when an abnormal value is measured, but this patient has symptoms of an abnormal TSH.

30. ***c***
The easiest way to diagnose plantar fasciitis is to dorsiflex the patient's toes and palpate with the thumb along the fascia starting at the heel progressing toward the forefoot. The patient will experience pain with palpation. In fact, the pain is reproducible as the "exact same" pain that is experienced when the patient steps out of bed or performs another activity that recreates the pain.

31. ***c***
Mitral valve prolapse (MVP) is the most common adult murmur. It is a result of redundancy of the mitral valve leaflets and subsequent degeneration of the mitral tissue. The posterior leaflet is more commonly affected than the anterior leaflet. The valve's annulus becomes enlarged in conjunction with elongation of the chordae tendineae.

32. *c*
Considering this patient's age and the risk of hypoglycemia, a reasonable goal is 80-120 mg/dL pre-prandial. A value less than 130 mg/dL is desirable, but not less than 80 mg/dL. The goal bedtime glucose goal is 100-140 mg/dL. Hypoglycemia during sleep can result in stroke or seizures in this age group.

33. *d*
The most common characteristics in a patient with Alzheimer's Disease (AD) are memory impairment, visual-spatial disturbances, indifference, delusions occasionally, and agitation. Personality change can be seen in patients with fronto-temporal dementia. Abrupt onset can be seen in patients with delirium and vascular dementia. Visual hallucinations can be seen in patients with Lewy-body dementia.

34. *a*
Kava kava is an herb from the South Pacific that is used to treat anxiety, fibromyalgia, and hyperactivity, attention deficit disorder. Hepatotoxicity has been reported with kava kava use, especially when consumed as tea. Liver toxicity should be reviewed in this patient. If she is not willing to use another agent for treatment of her anxiety, liver function studies should be monitored periodically.

35. *b*
The arteries are 2/3 to 4/5 the diameter of the veins. The arteries appear as light red in color; veins are darker red. Interestingly, the veins in the eyes pulsate; the arteries do not. Loss of venous pulsations can be identified in patients with head trauma, meningitis, or elevated intracranial pressure.

36. *c*
Pinguecula are common as patients age. They usually appear on the nasal side first and then on the temporal side. This is a completely benign finding. A stye is also called a hordeolum. It is a tender, painful infection of a gland at the eyelid margin. These are self-limiting. A chalazion is a non-tender enlargement of a meibomian gland. A subconjunctival hemorrhage is a blood red looking area on the sclera that does not affect vision. It occurs and resolves spontaneously.

37. *b*
An SSRI is a good choice of an antidepressant in an older adult because of the decreased side effects seen when compared with the other agents listed, but especially a TCA. These can produce conduction defects in older adults, sedation, and potent anticholinergic side effects.

38. *c*
Pseudoephedrine will increase her blood pressure. Oxymetazoline can be absorbed across mucus membranes and elevate blood pressure too. Diphenhydramine is a sedating antihistamine with anti-cholinergic properties. This would be contraindicated with glaucoma. Guafenesin would be the safest agent to use.

39. *c*
Women who are less than age 35 years, who have no associated suspicious findings of breast cancer should delay imaging studies until re-examination 3-10 days after the last menstrual period to determine whether the lump changes in size or becomes non-palpable. If there are associated suspicious findings on exam like palpable nodes, a large lump (>2.0 cm), or nipple discharge, then diagnostic evaluation should not be delayed. If management involved a return visit for re-examination after menses, and the lump is unchanged, ultrasound is certainly advised. Mammogram may not yield good information in a 28 year-old because of the density of the breast tissue. Baseline mammogram may be advised. Direction from a radiologist or breast surgeon should be sought.

40. *a*
The left ventricle enlarges as blood regurgitates from the aorta. Atrial fibrillation is not typical or usual in aortic regurgitation (AR) since neither atrium is affected. Pulmonary congestion is seen later in the pathogenesis of AR. The blood pressure in patients with AR is characterized by an elevated systolic and decreased diastolic pressure. This is termed a wide pulse pressure.

41. *a*
Elderly adults are at increased risk of Vitamin D deficiency related to several factors. In addition to those mentioned, lack of sun exposure decreases synthesis of Vitamin D. As renal status declines in older patients, hydroxylation diminishes which diminishes available Vitamin D. Patient with dark skin are also at increased risk of Vitamin D deficiencies.

42. *a*
The usual course of mitral valve prolapse (MVP) is benign and most patients who have MVP are asymptomatic. In a minority of patients, symptoms of heart failure or sudden death may occur. When congestive heart failure results, it is usually a result of mitral regurgitation. Embolization may occur, but, this is not common or usual in the majority of patients.

43. *b*
A disulfiram reaction can take place in a patient who combines alcohol and metronidazole. The disulfiram reaction is described as elevation in body temperature, abdominal cramps, diarrhea, headache, and nausea/vomiting.

44. *b*
L-thyroxin is thyroid supplement used to treat patients with hypothyroidism. It is safe to use during pregnancy and should be continued. However, during pregnancy, thyroid hormone needs increase and so she will need frequent monitoring because if levels drop to a hypothyroid state, growth of the fetus can be severely affected.

45. *b*
The most common presentation of basal cell carcinoma (BCC) is on the face. This is

probably because BCC occurs secondary to sun damage. The most common sun exposure occurs on the face. In fact, 70% of BCC occurs on the face, 15% is found on the trunk.

46. *b*
The mitral listening point is where the murmur associated with mitral regurgitation (MR) can be heard loudest. Murmurs tend to be loudest at the point where they originate. In this case, that is the mitral listening point. As the left ventricle enlarges secondary to MR, the apical impulse becomes displaced left and laterally and becomes diffuse.

47. *a*
An oral antiviral agent such as acyclovir, famciclovir, valacyclovir should be prescribed, especially if it can be initiated within 72 hours after the onset of symptoms. The addition of oral corticosteroids to oral antiviral therapy demonstrates only modest benefit. Adverse events to therapy are more commonly reported in patients receiving oral corticosteroids. There is no evidence that corticosteroid therapy decreased the incidence or duration of post-herpetic neuralgia or improved quality of life. Corticosteroids should be limited to use in patients with acute neuritis who have not derived benefit from opioid analgesics.

48. *a*
About 40% of elderly patients with COPD have concomitant anxiety and/or depression. It should be treated because it affects the overall management of COPD. COPD is characterized by airflow limitation and dyspnea. This may contribute to feelings of chronic anxiety. Additionally, many chronic diseases are associated with depression. This is the case with COPD.

49. *c*
The best means to identify mitral valve prolapse (MVP) is with 2D echocardiography. It will identify bulging of either, or both, of the leaflets (anterior or posterior) into the left atrium. Approximately 1-2% of the US population is identified to have MVP. A chest x-ray will not enable visualization of the mitral leaflets. Electrocardiography identifies the heart's rhythm. A physical exam may provide great clues to MVP, but in the absence of definitive mid to late systolic clicks, a diagnosis cannot be confirmed.

50. *b*
The incidence of pyelonephritis in the US is much less common than urinary tract infections (UTIs). It is less likely in males, but is most common in females aged 15-29 years. Factors associated with pyelonephritis are frequent sexual intercourse, UTI within the last year, presence of diabetes, and presence of stress incontinence within the previous 30 days.

51. *d*
This patient's symptoms are descriptive of plantar fasciitis. Pain usually begins as only pain in the morning with resolution after several steps and the passage of time. As

plantar fasciitis worsens, patients complain of heel pain during the day, after sitting for a while, and at the end of the day. The most important contributor to this is pes planus, "flat feet". Approximately 70% of patients with plantar fasciitis have pes planus.

52. *b*
This patient's symptoms are typical of arteriosclerosis. The term for this symptom is intermittent claudication. When there is compromised arterial blood flow in the lower legs, a common complaint is reproducible pain in a specific group of muscles. The pain occurs because there is an incongruence between blood supply and demand. This produces pain that causes a patient to stop exercising in order to obtain relief of pain.

53. *b*
The earliest serologic marker that indicates acute hepatitis B infection is the hepatitis B surface antigen. It becomes positive about 2-6 weeks after infection, but before symptom onset. A positive IgM indicates acute infection at this time. The finding of a positive hepatitis B core antibody identifies with certainty, hepatitis B infection (either at present or in the past). It does not indicate timing of infection.

54. *b*
Secondary prevention is evidenced by early detection of disease in a patient. Bone mineral density screening is intended to identify women (or men) who may have decreased bone density but who are asymptomatic. Primary prevention is an example of an action intended to prevent a disease or condition before it starts. Tertiary prevention is an example of preventing worsening of a disease after it has already been discovered.

55. *d*
Non-fasting glucose values less than 125 mg/dL are considered normal values.

56. *b*
COPD, chronic obstructive pulmonary disease, is characterized by obstructed airways. The obstruction is NOT completely reversible. Asthma is completely reversible. This is the reason many learned authorities do not consider asthma to be part of the COPD umbrella. Productive cough is likely present in patients with acute bronchitis. Shortness of breath does not have to be present (or perceived in patients with COPD). Hypercapnia is more prevalent in patients with emphysema since air trapping occurs.

57. *c*
NSAIDs are contraindicated in patients with renal insufficiency. They may produce a transient decrease in renal function and likely produce sodium retention and thus, water retention. For the same reason, this may worsen hypertension. Acetaminophen, mild narcotics, and/or topical agents could be used to treat her osteoarthritis. NSAIDs will have no effect on her varicose veins or hypothyroidism.

58. a
Lymphocytosis, a predominance of lymphocytes, is the most common laboratory

abnormality seen with infectious mononucleosis (mono). Atypical lymphocytes are a common finding too. An elevation in monocytes is often found, but, does not occur with as high frequency as lymphocytosis. The total white count often is increased and may lie between 12,000-18,000/microL. Elevated liver enzymes, ALT and AST, are noted in the majority of patients but is a benign finding. These usually return to baseline within several weeks of onset of acute symptoms.

59. ***d***
Patients with gout do not always have elevated uric acid levels. In fact, during an acute attack, uric acid levels can be normal. Meat contains purines that are known to contribute to attacks of gout, but it is not likely that this patient is consuming too much meat. It is more likely due to multiple factors in his diet. The initial episode of gout usually involves a lower extremity. The great toe is the most common joint affected. Joints like the hip or shoulder are rarely affected initially and usually are never affected because they are close to the trunk and are at higher body temperature than the toes and fingers.

60. ***d***
PID is sometimes a difficult diagnosis to make. A high index of suspicion should exist in adolescents and young women who present with the symptoms indicated above. CDC recommends empiric treatment for PID in women who present with abdominal pain and one of these: cervical motion tenderness, fever > 101F, a shift to the left, abnormal vaginal discharge, presence of white cells in the vaginal secretions, and an elevated sed rate or C reactive protein.

61. ***d***
Pain associated with a lumbar strain does produce pain with activity and walking. This patient should be educated that pain is some pain is expected and that it will not produce permanent injury. He should be encouraged to engage in activities of daily living and normal walking. Generally, this will speed his return to normal activities. Bedrest is no longer recommended. Patients feel better sooner and have fewer complications if bed rest is avoided.

62. ***d***
Men with BPH should reduce their exposure to mild diuretics. This not only includes medication like HCTZ, but includes caffeine and alcohol since these can produce diuresis too. Avoiding fluids before bedtime and double voiding (to attempt to empty the bladder) may help with nighttime symptoms too.

63. ***c***
Fatigue is a difficult complaint to assess and diagnose. This patient's exam and vital signs are normal. There is no reason to think that he is infected or is bleeding, so a lone CBC, offers little diagnostic help. However, in addition to a CBC, adding a metabolic panel, TSH, and urine (to screen for blood in this former smoker) is a more thorough laboratory assessment of his fatigue.

64. *c*
A patient has 72 hours after an injury to receive the tetanus immunization and be protected from tetanus. In an elderly adult who has completed the initial tetanus series, a Tdap is recommended. This will provide immunization against both tetanus, diphtheria, and acellular pertussis. He should receive another immunization in 10 years if he has not had another "dirty" injury. In the case of a "dirty" injury, immunization is recommended after 5 years.

65. *b*
TMPS is usually an appropriate medication to treat urinary tract infections (UTIs) in most patients. In the case of community resistance to TMPS > 20%, another medication should be substituted. In men, the appropriate length of time is 7-10 days. Women may be treated for 3 days for uncomplicated UTIs.

66. *c*
Symptoms of pelvic inflammatory disorder (PID) include oral temperature > 101 F (38.8C), abnormal cervical or vaginal mucopurulent discharge, presence of abundant WBCs on microscopy or vaginal secretions, elevated sedimentation rate or C-reactive protein. CDC has indicated empiric treatment for PID if lower abdominal pain or pelvic pain is present concurrently with cervical motion tenderness or uterine/adnexal tenderness.

67. *d*
Influenza is contraindicated for persons who have had anaphylactic reactions to eggs. The immunization is made from eggs and thus, the contraindication. There is an adult influenza immunization approved by the FDA in 2013 that is made without eggs.

68. *b*
The classic triad of normal pressure hydrocephalus (NPH) is described above. Diabetic neuropathy would not be typical because this involves three different areas of complaint. Parkinson's Disease presents with tremor, gait disturbance, and bradykinesia. Multiple sclerosis almost never presents beyond the age of 50 years and would be unlikely in an elderly male. The incidence of NPH varies from 2-20 million people per year. It is more common in elderly patients and affects both genders equally. This is diagnosed demonstrated by the presence of enlarged ventricles on CT scan.

69. *d*
The diagnosis of pinworms (Enterobiasis) is made by using a piece of scotch tape on a tongue depressor. It is touched against the patient's rectum. The greatest yield of eggs will occur during the nighttime or early AM. Eggs will be found here if they are present. Worms and eggs are rarely found in stool specimens, so this is not a good plan. When the scotch tape is examined under a low power microscope, the eggs will be easily visualized since they are large and bean shaped. The finding of an adult worm would confirm the diagnosis. These are large enough to be seen with the naked eye. If the mother is symptomatic, she should be treated with or without a rectal exam. It is very likely she is infected.

70 ***c***

LDL cholesterol promotes atherosclerosis via several different mechanisms. Consequently, LDL cholesterol tends to be the primary target when patients are treated pharmacologically for elevated lipid levels. Low HDL levels and elevated triglyceride levels have also shown to accelerate atherogenesis.

71. ***a***

The finding of infiltrates on chest x-ray, in conjunction with clinical findings of fever, chest pain, dyspnea, and sputum production on clinical exam should direct the examiner to consider pneumonia as the diagnosis. Though not common, some patients with pneumonia exhibit gastrointestinal symptoms like nausea, vomiting, and diarrhea.

72. ***b***

American Dental Association and American Academy of Orthopedic Surgeons recommend dental prophylaxis for 2 years after any joint replacement. Up to two years after replacement, prophylaxis should be given about one hour before any dental procedures. Two grams of amoxicillin can be given. In penicillin allergic patients, clindamycin can be given.

73. ***c***

The three cardinal symptoms of Parkinson's disease are tremor, bradykinesia, and rigidity. The tremor is often described as a "pill-rolling" tremor. This is most noticeable when the body is at rest. Usually, the tremor disappears at night during sleep and may disappear with deliberate physical activities.

74. ***b***

Hypertension management has been found to be beneficial in preventing stroke and cardiac events in all ages. Treatment should begin without regard to age. Elderly patients are more likely to exhibit isolated systolic hypertension. This has been found to be a strong predictor of cardiac and cerebral events if not managed appropriately.

75. ***b***

Which statement below is true regarding NSAIDs for low back pain?

76. ***b***

This patient has COPD. He should receive the pneumonia immunization today. He belongs to a group of patients with chronic illness who are between the ages of 19 and 64 years and so, should be immunized for pneumonia. The flu immunization should be given to him annually.

77. ***a***

This patient should receive another one today because he is 65 years old and at least 5 years has elapsed since his last one. CDC does not recommend immunizing this patient every 5 years.

78. ***d***
Mycoplasma is an atypical pathogen and produces atypical pneumonia. It can be difficult to diagnose because symptoms can be varied and involve multiple body systems (extrapulmonary manifestations). Infection with Mycoplasma may present with a normal white blood cell count, maculopapular rash, GI symptoms, tender joints and aches, and though rare, cardiac rhythm disturbances. Respiratory symptoms may not be pronounced. On chest x-ray there are some unique findings (peribronchial pattern) with Mycoplasma. These include thickened bronchial shadow, streaks of interstitial infiltration, and atelectasis. These are more likely to occur in the lower lobes.

79. ***d***
Most cases of acute gastroenteritis are viral in origin. Severe diarrhea is usually caused by bacteria. This typically lasts longer than 3 days.

80. ***c***
According to JNC VII, a patient who is diagnosed with Stage I hypertension should have lifestyle modifications initiated for 3 months. If his blood pressure is not within normal range (< 140/90) after 3 months, a low dose diuretic is appropriate unless there is a compelling indication to give a different medication. Two medications should not be initiated for a patient with Stage I hypertension according to JNC VII.

81. ***c***
This history of recent antibiotic exposure suggests *C. difficile*. A stool specimen should be ordered to assess for *C. difficile*. Some clinicians will initiate treatment for *C. difficile* based on this history, especially if the patient's symptoms are severe or the patient is elderly.

82. ***d***
Shigella will be shed continuously in the stool and should be easily identified on stool culture. When bacterial gastroenteritis is suspected, a stool specimen could be ordered for confirmation. Generally, these three pathogens are easily identified if they are present.

83. ***c***
Type II diabetes is diagnosed after a random fasting glucose ≥ 126 mg/dL and confirmed on a subsequent day. Other diagnostic criteria include a random blood glucose ≥ 200 mg/dL with polyuria, polydypsia, or polyphagia; or an A1C ≥ 6.5% (and confirmed on a subsequent day). A glucose tolerance test may also be used for diagnosis but this is usually reserved for pregnant women.

84. ***d***
Allergy and asthma guidelines in the US recommend topical nasal steroids first line for management of symptoms of allergic rhinitis. A non-sedating antihistamine can be added to manage unresolved symptoms after a nasal steroid has been initiated. Antihistamines work well when the predominant symptoms are thin, clear nasal discharge. These can be safely used in combination for management. Decongestants are

not recommended as lone agents because they have no effect on the underlying allergic mechanisms. They work well in combination with antihistamines and nasal steroids for congestion. Sedating antihistamines are usually avoided for allergic rhinitis because of safety concerns.

85. ***d***
Iron is best absorbed on an empty stomach. However, iron consumption on an empty stomach is usually not well tolerated and is often taken with a meal. Reduced absorption of the iron is expected if it is not taken on an empty stomach. Vitamin C enhances absorption of iron and so if iron is taken with food, a Vitamin C rich one should accompany it, not a Vitamin D rich food. An example of a vitamin C rich beverage is orange juice. Citrus fruits are typically rich in Vitamin C.

86. ***b***
Testicular torsion is an emergency because the testicle is deprived of normal blood supply. If blood supply is not resumed within 12 hours, irreversible damage is certain to occur. Ideally, ischemia is resolved within 4-6 hours. The penis is not affected during testicular torsion. Besides testicular torsion, epididymitis, trauma, and an inguinal hernia are other common causes of scrotal pain.

87. ***c***
Migraine headaches usually begin in the early morning and can awaken patients from sleep, but they may begin at any time, including nocturnally. Cluster headaches are very likely in this age and gender patient. A brain tumor must always be considered since intracranial pressure increases in a horizontal patient. Hydrocephalus produces headache, but it is not specific for nighttime.

88. ***b***
Calcium does produce constipation in many patients. If this is taken as a supplement for osteoporosis or osteopenia, the patient should be encouraged to increase fluids and fiber.

89. ***a***
Serotonin (5-HT) is a neurotransmitter released in the brain. It is part of the monoamine oxidase system. These neurotransmitters are responsible for many emotional and behavioral disorders. Agents that cause more serotonin to be available in the brain have an ameliorating effect on symptoms of depression, anxiety, and obsessive-compulsive behavior.

90. ***b***
Mild intermittent asthma is characterized by symptoms that occur more than twice weekly but not daily; or 3-4 nocturnal awakenings per month due to asthma. It is treated with a daily inhaled steroid and a bronchodilator PRN for exacerbations. If symptoms occur more than twice weekly, therapy should be stepped up. Generally, a long acting bronchodilator is added to the steroid.

91. ***d***
This patient needs several medications started today. American Diabetes Association recommends starting treatment with metformin. This should be initiated today. The drug class of choice for treatment of his LDL cholesterol is a statin. Dietary modifications are usually attempted for 3 months prior to initiation of a statin. However, considering this patient's LDLs of 210 mg/dL (goal of less than 100 mg/dL), strong consideration should be given to initiating therapy today with a statin. An ACE inhibitor is the preferred antihypertensive medication to treat blood pressure elevations in this patient. An aspirin should be initiated if there are no contraindications.

92. ***c***
This patient should continue his fexofenadine. This treats his allergies and although he has a sinus infection, he still needs treatment for his allergies. A topical nasal steroid can be added if poor control of allergies exists, otherwise, this probably just increases the cost of treatment of during this sinus infection. If his sinus infection has been present for 10 days, an antibiotic seems prudent at this point.

93. ***a***
RDW is the red blood cell distribution width. Another way to think of this is that the RDW is the variation in the size of the red blood cells. In a patient with recent onset iron deficiency anemia (the last 3-4 months), some red blood cells will be of normal size and some will be of decreased size (microcytosis). The variation in size of the red blood cells will be demonstrated by an increased RDW. Serum ferritin is a measure of the iron in storage. The total iron binding capacity is always increased in a patient with iron deficiency anemia.

94. ***b***
Primary dysmenorrhea has been attributed to prolonged uterine contractions that cause ischemia to the myometrium. Some females with secondary dysmenorrhea may have a normal pelvic exam, but they tend to have an enlarged irregularly shaped uterus or tender uterus on exam. Most secondary dysmenorrhea is due to endometriosis. On physical exam, patients with secondary dysmenorrhea can have displacement of the cervix, cervical stenosis, adnexal enlargement, or nodular and/or tender uterosacral ligaments.

95. ***b***
The triptans are a class of medications that are helpful for many patients with migraine headaches because they produce cerebral vasoconstriction. This class is also helpful for patients who experience cluster headaches. The triptans are not helpful for patients with tension headaches. Some patients with cluster headaches use nasal oxygen at the onset of the cluster headache. Relief is usually realized in about 10 minutes or less.

96. ***c***
If the NP knowingly prescribes a medication for a patient other than the intended patient, the NP incurs medical liability and is deliberately diverting medications. This is illegal and constitutes theft in most states. The NP cannot legally continue to prescribe

the medication if she knows that the intended patient is not the recipient of the medication.

97. ***d***

Observational studies are studies where subjects are observed. No intervention takes place with them. Examples of these are found in the first three choices. A meta-analysis takes published information from other studies and combines the information to arrive at a conclusion. Although a meta-analysis can use observational studies, these should be reported separately.

98. ***c***

The major classes of antidepressants used to treat depression are listed in this question. Multiple studies have concluded that there is no clear choice on selection of one class over another for efficacy. However, SSRIs are usually the first choice because they are associated with fewer side effects and there is less danger of suicide with an overdose. Monoamine oxidase inhibitors are involved with a number of drug-drug and drug-food interactions and so these are seldom chosen initially.

99. ***a***

Chlamydia is commonly treated with a single dose of azithromycin (one-gram). This patient should be screened for other STDs now, including hepatitis B, C and HIV. According to the 2010 STD guidelines, this patient should not be treated for gonorrhea unless this is diagnosed too. When a patient is diagnosed with gonorrhea, she should be treated for concomitant chlamydia unless this has been ruled out.

100. ***b***

Pernicious anemia is the most common side effect of Vitamin B-12 deficiency. Pernicious anemia is characterized by a macrocytic anemia, not microcytic. Sideroblastic anemia is not related to B-12 deficiency. Insomnia is not a specific finding with B-12 deficiency.

101. ***a***

Serotonin syndrome is a potentially life-threatening condition. The syndrome occurs when there is too much serotonergic activity in the central nervous system. It can occur with an interaction between two medications, like an SSRI and dextromethorphan, an SSRI and a triptan, an intentional overdose, or with high doses of an SSRI in a particularly sensitive patient. Symptoms of serotonin syndrome include hyperreflexia, clonus, rigidity in the lower extremities, tachycardia, hyperthermia, hypertension, vomiting, disorientation, agitated delirium, or tremor. None of the other medications listed can precipitate serotonin syndrome.

102. ***d***

A case control study would be ideal for discovering the cause of this situation. Case control looks at "what happened"? It would identify those subjects who have leukemia and would identify a control group of adults from the area who did not have leukemia. Both groups would be analyzed for characteristics or risk factors that were present in

the "case" group but not the "control" group. This is an observational study.

103. ***d***
A microcytic, hypochromic anemia is typical in a patient with iron deficiency anemia; less common in patients with chronic disease, and even less common in patients with a malignancy. Excessive consumption of alcohol would result in a patient with a macrocytic anemia, not microcytic. RBC counts would be expected to be decreased in this patient. In an adult male, the most common place for loss of blood is the GI tract. This should be investigated initially. It is certainly possible that he has a malignancy---possibly leukemia, but this is not as common as a GI bleed in an elderly adult.

104. ***a***
The most consistent findings in adults with early presentation of acute appendicitis are very subtle and difficult to identify. Symptoms may be as vague as indigestion, flatulence, a feeling of ill-being. Initially, pain can be in the general abdomen, then become periumbilical, and finally localize to the lower right quadrant. Early symptoms are difficult to identify, especially in older adults.

105. ***c***
This patient has isolated systolic hypertension (ISH). This is common in older adults and is associated with tragic cardiac and cerebrovascular events. The drug class of choice to treat these patients is a long-acting calcium channel blocker. The class of calcium channel blockers recommended for ISH has the suffix "pine" (amlodipine, felodipine, etc).

106. ***c***
This description is one of cellulitis. Cellulitis involves an infection of the subcutaneous layers of the skin. It must be treated with an oral antibiotic. This is particularly important to identify early, and aggressively treat in a diabetic because elevated blood sugar levels will make eradication more difficult. Buerger's disease involves inflammation of the medium sized arteries and does not present on the anterior shin only. DVT seldom presents on the anterior shin. Venous disease does not present acutely as in this situation.

107. ***c***
Metformin is associated with these symptoms---especially in the first two weeks of use. These symptoms can also be seen with increases in the dose of metformin. The other medications listed do not produce lower gastrointestinal symptoms. If the medication can be continued for a couple of weeks, generally, GI symptoms will resolve. Metformin is known to decrease morbidity and mortality associated with diabetes.

108. ***c***
This patient should never have a cephalosporin prescribed for him because of the risk of cross-reactivity between the penicillin and cephalosporin classes. This could potentially give rise to another anaphylactic reaction to the cephalosporin prescribed. A good rule to follow if a patient has had an anaphylactic reaction to a penicillin is to

NEVER prescribe a cephalosporin. Although the risk is small, it should not be taken.

109. ***b***
A serum ferritin level is helpful in evaluating a patient being treated for iron deficiency anemia. When these levels rise to normal levels and the anemia has been corrected, it is considered appropriate to stop iron supplementation, as it is no longer needed.

110. ***d***
X-rays are usually not helpful in diagnosing appendicitis, however, some findings on radiograph can be associated with appendicitis: ileus, free air, right lower quadrant appendicolith or soft tissue density, or a deformity of the cecal outline. A CT scan is considered more accurate than an ultrasound, but ultrasound and CT are the most commonly used tests. The sensitivity and specificity with CT scan are 94 and 95% respectively. With an ultrasound, the sensitivity and specificity are 86 and 81% respectively. MRI is generally not used because it is more expensive, takes more time to complete, and is not as readily available.

111. ***a***
Initially, all medications known to cause constipation should be stopped when possible. Symptoms should be re-assessed. It is always preferable to stop a medication to correct a condition BEFORE adding a medication to correct a condition. If symptoms persist, 6-25 grams of dietary fiber should be added along with increasing fluid intake. Physical activity should be increased as tolerated. Choice 3 and 4 would be initiated if other options mentioned were not helpful.

112. ***c***
The typical presentation of an adult male with epididymitis is gradual development of scrotal pain. There is no scrotal edema. This is more typical in hydrocele. Common precipitants are sexual activity, heavy physical exertion as described in the question, and bicycle or motorcycle riding. In sexually active males under age 35 years, a common cause is an STD.

113. ***d***
Most learned authorities agree that if there is no response by 8-12 weeks at a maximal therapeutic dose, a different antidepressant should be tried. The 8-12 week period is an appropriate time frame because it will take this long to increase the dose and attempt to reach maximal dose for therapeutic response. 4-6 weeks is nearing the appropriate time frame, but this may be too short a period of time to reach and evaluate therapeutic effect.

114. ***b***
This patient has classic symptoms of hypokalemia associated with potassium loss from the thiazide diuretic. A potassium level should be measured and he should be supplemented if it is low. Generally, muscle weakness occurs as potassium levels drop below 2.5 mEq/L. If his potassium is low, strong consideration should be given to a thiazide diuretic in combination with a potassium sparing diuretic. In fact, this should

be considered when the thiazide is initially prescribed.

115. ***d***
There are many different presentations of psoriasis. Plaque psoriasis, which is described in this question, is usually found in a symmetrical distribution on the scalp, elbows, knees, and/or back. The size of the lesions ranges from 1-10 cm in diameter. Usually the plaques are asymptomatic, but may be mildly pruritic. Scaly lesions found on the scalp are not specific to psoriasis and could be seborrheic dermatitis. A scaly border around the plaque could describe the lesions associated with pityriasis rosea.

116. ***c***
This patient can be diagnosed with diabetes today because his glucose exceeds 200 mg/dL and he is symptomatic. Most learned authorities would describe him as glucose toxic. Oral agents will have little effect on his glucose and it should be lowered. Insulin is the best agent to reduce the blood sugar so that oral agents can be given a chance. He should return tomorrow for a recheck of blood glucose and adjustment of his medication.

117. ***c***
Swimmer's ear is termed otitis externa. It represents an infection of the external canal. This is characterized by tragal tenderness with light touch of the tragus on the affected side. Fever does not occur because this is a superficial infection. It is treated with a topical agents: an antibiotic and steroid placed in the external canal.

118. ***a***
Iron deficiency anemia is characterized by a reduced RBC count and decreased hemoglobin and hematocrit. During an iron deficiency anemia the TIBC (total iron binding capacity) is increased. This finding demonstrates the low circulating levels of serum iron. The RDW would be expected to be increased. This demonstrates a > 15% variation in the size of the RBCs.

119. ***c***
This patient suffered trauma to his foot and/or ankle after a fall. A sprain is in the differential, but a fracture must be ruled out before this patient is allowed to continue to ambulate. An x-ray is needed now and he must be kept non-weight bearing until this is ruled out. A fracture should be suspected since the stem of the question indicates "point tenderness".

120. ***b***
Pain associated with dysmenorrhea is likely due to prostaglandins which can cause prolonged contraction of the uterus. This produces uterine ischemia, sometimes termed "uterine angina". NSAIDs (non-steroidal anti-inflammatory drugs) are prostaglandin synthesis inhibitors. These are usually started at the onset of menses or onset of symptoms and continued for 2-3 days depending on the symptom pattern of the patient. There is no demonstrated increase in efficacy when acetaminophen is added or given alone.

121. ***c***
This patient has symptoms that could indicate an urgent neurological situation. Acute radiculopathy could indicate the need for intervention by a neurosurgeon. An MRI is a superior study because it provides excellent information about the soft tissues, like the lumbar discs. Contrast might be used in this patient if he had a history of previous back surgery. Then, contrast would be helpful to distinguish scar tissue from discs.

122. ***a***
Amitriptyline and nortriptyline are commonly used in patients who exhibit depression and chronic pain syndromes. TCAs are known to produce mild peripheral vasodilator effects and subsequent relief of pain by an unknown mechanism.

123. ***b***
Many tests can be used to evaluate an elderly patient with suspected BPH. The value of DRE is to evaluate the size, consistency and assess for malignancy of the prostate gland. Urinalysis is done to detect blood or infection, but hematuria is common in patients with BPH. The PSA is done as a screening test for prostate cancer in men. A serum creatinine can be part of the initial screening. This would help identify bladder outlet obstruction, renal, or prerenal disease. A BUN is not necessary. Of course, the patient's history will dictate other exams for a complete evaluation.

124. ***b***
Cranial nerve II evaluates vision. Cranial nerve I evaluates the ability to smell. Cranial nerve III evaluates eye movements, pupillary constriction, and accommodation. Cranial nerve IV, the trochlear nerve is partly responsible for eye movement. Cranial nerves III, IV, and VI are responsible for eye movement.

125. ***a***
A randomized clinical trial (RCT) is the epitome of all research designs. Subjects are randomly assigned to treatment groups. This type study provides the best evidence that the results were due to the intervention and not something else. A RCT is an experimental design, not an observational one.

126. ***b***
Major depression is diagnosed when at least 5 symptoms out of nine symptoms (that characterize depression) are identified by the examiner. Minor depression is characterized by the presence of 2-4 of the nine symptoms. Symptoms must be present for at least 2 weeks and must be present most of the day nearly every day. One symptom that must be present is depressed mood. The 9 criteria are identified by the DSM V manual.

127. ***c***
The cough associated with use of an ACE inhibitor is typically dry and non-productive. It is more common in women than men and is thought to be due to the buildup of bradykinin. Bradykinin is partly degraded by ACE (angiotensin converting enzyme). When degradation is impaired, bradykinin can accumulate and cough can ensue.

128. ***b***
A patient with acute cholecystitis usually complains of abdominal pain in the upper right quadrant or epigastric area. Many patients complain of nausea. The patient lies very still on the exam table because cholecystitis is associated with peritoneal inflammation that is worse with movement. Elderly patients are more likely to NOT exhibit Murphy's sign and thus, are more likely to suffer from complications of acute cholecystitis. Patients who are asymptomatic have cholelithiasis, not acute cholecystitis.

129. ***d***
A patient who will be starting insulin can have his daily insulin needs calculated by multiplying his weight in kilograms by 0.2. In this patient, (100 x 0.2= 20 units) 20 units could be used for insulin initiation. Once insulin has been initiated, 3 days of AM fasting glucose measurements should be collected and the insulin dose adjusted so that the AM fasting glucose levels are about 100-120 mg/dL. Giving fewer than 20 units will probably be too little to meet this patient's needs.

130. ***d***
A second swab is collected, but it is not used to repeat the test. The second swab is sent to microbiology for culture. The sensitivity varies in office Strept tests. Some are as low as 50% and a second swab should be collected. If beta-hemolytic Strept organisms are grown out, then the patient can be diagnosed with Streptococcal infection.

131. ***c***
A patient with leukocytosis has a predominance of white cells in the blood. Leukocytes can elevate in response to viral or bacterial infections. Possible clarification of the type of infection could be determined by looking at the number of lymphocytes and neutrophils.

132. ***b***
Varicocele may be asymptomatic but more commonly is accompanied by scrotal pain described as a dull ache. It becomes more noticeable with standing and is relieved by lying down. This occurs because lying down relieves dilation of the spermatic veins. This is present in about 15-20% of post-pubertal males and may be referred to as "a bag of worms" because of the scrotum's appearance. Wearing a scrotal supporter may also provide relief.

133. ***c***
UTI is a common abbreviation for urinary tract infection. The presence of leukocytes and nitrites in the urine indicates a very likely infection in the bladder. The presence of blood is common when a patient has a urinary tract infection. This is termed hematuria. A diagnosis of chlamydia cannot be made based on symptoms or these urinalysis results. Asymptomatic bacteriuria is the diagnosis given to patients who are found to have bacteria in the urine and who are asymptomatic. This patient has complaints of dysuria.

134. ***a***
Eosinophilia can be found in patients who have a predominance of eosinophils in the blood. An increase in eosinophils may be found in patients with allergic reactions or parasitic infections. In this instance, an asthma exacerbation could be due to an allergic response and so, could elicit the increase in circulating eosinophils.

135. ***b***
Two clinical clues should make the examiner suspect a foreign body. First, the patient has continued drainage despite treatment. Second, the drainage is unilateral. Unilateral drainage from a nostril should prompt the examiner to visualize the turbinates. In this case, a foreign body could probably be visualized.

136. ***c***
Pertussis is also called "whooping cough". This is a highly communicable respiratory disease caused by Bordetella pertussis. There are three recognized stages of pertussis: the catarrhal phase, the paroxysmal phase, and convalescence. More adults have contracted pertussis in the last decade than children. Since the outbreak of pertussis in Iowa in 2005, diminished titers were recognized and adolescents are being given a booster with tetanus booster.

137. ***c***
Malpractice insurance is needed in any situation where patients are treated by a nurse practitioner. Some states have a "good Samaritan" law which protects professional volunteers from being sued. Unless this is specifically provided by state law, a nurse practitioner should have professional liability insurance in the event the NP is sued.

138. ***b***
The three most commonly associated symptoms of GERD are heartburn, especially post-prandial, regurgitation, and dysphagia, especially after long-standing heartburn. Other common symptoms are chest pain, nausea, and odynophagia (painful swallowing).

139. ***a***
Niacin can decrease glucose tolerance. It should be used cautiously in patients with impaired fasting glucose. In the United States, niacin is primarily used to increase HDL levels. However, niacin is poorly tolerated by many patients who take it. The most common side effects are flushing, hypotension, and occasionally gout flares. Niacin should be taken in the evening with an aspirin to minimize side effects. Tolerance improves over time.

140. ***a***
Two common first generation cephalosporins used to treat skin and skin structure infections are cephalexin and cefadroxil. These are taken 2-4 times daily and are generally well tolerated. These antibiotics provide coverage against *Staphylococcus* and *Streptococcus,* common skin pathogens.

141. ***b***

Pioglitazone belongs to a class of medications that can cause hepatotoxicity. Therefore, assessment of liver function studies, particularly AST and ALT, should be performed in 1-3 or 4 months after initiation of this medication. The manufacturer has not suggested an ideal schedule to check AST and ALT. Depending on patient history and concurrent medications, a check of the AST and ALT may be prudently done in 1-3 months.

142. ***d***

Mononucleosis is a common viral infection in adolescents and early twenty year olds. Splenomegaly occurs in about 50% of patients with mononucleosis. While it is not common, it is possible to be co-infected with *Streptococcus* in the throat. If this is the case, treatment with penicillin should be avoided because of the possibility of an "ampicillin" rash. The most prominent symptoms are fever, fatigue, pharyngitis, and lymphadenopathy.

143. ***d***

Vitamin B-12 is absorbed through the gastrointestinal (GI) tract from foods that are consumed daily. Deficiencies are usually seen in patients who have difficulty absorbing B-12. Consequently, supplementation through the GI tract is not an efficient means to correct deficiencies. The most efficient way to supplement with B-12 is via intramuscular injection. Injections are usually needed lifelong once deficiency is diagnosed. Deficiencies are often seen in elderly patients and in patients who consume alcohol in excess.

144. ***b***

If a patient's lipids are elevated, a TSH should be performed. If the TSH is elevated, it may be the secondary cause of the elevated lipids. It is considered safe practice to NOT treat elevated lipid levels until the TSH level has decreased to at least 10 mU/L. If the lipids are still elevated, they should be treated at that time.

145. ***b***

A sprained ankle is a common orthopedic injury in athletes. Resumption of regular activities can take place when he is able to walk pain-free. His ankle does not necessarily need taping prior to competition but it may need support with an orthotic device. The edema may take weeks to completely resolve. In fact, edema after resumption of athletic activities is common.

146. ***b***

PCOS is a systemic disease characterized by multiple cysts about the ovaries. Overweight states are common but not obesity. Normal weight is also seen in these patients. This patient will not have a positive pregnancy test unless she is pregnant. There is no indication from the information that this is the case. She likely has had not had menses because of anovulation. There is no associated blood pressure elevation, though this should be watched closely. Elevated insulin levels are usual findings in patients who have PCOS.

147. ***b***
The hallmark finding in a patient with bacterial vaginosis (BV) is clue cells on microscopic exam. Clue cells are epithelial cells with adherent bacteria. The most common clinical feature is an unpleasant, "fishy" smelling discharge that is more noticeable after sexual intercourse. BV can produce a cervicitis. It is a risk factor for HIV acquisition and transmission. Metronidazole is the most successful therapy. The usual oral regimen is 500 mg twice daily for 7 days. Alcohol should be avoided.

148. ***a***
These symptoms describe a patient who has a kidney stone, urolithiasis. The cause of the pain is urine obstruction. Blood is almost always expected in the urine specimen of these patients. Nitrites and leukocytes are indicative of a urinary tract infection (UTI). UTI can present at the same time as stone, but this is not usual. Calcium is usually not found in the urine, though it may be a component of the stone if recovered.

149. ***c***
The other test commonly used to assess a patient with suspected carpal tunnel syndrome is Phalen's test. This test is also called the "backward praying test". It asks the patient to put the back of his hands together with flexion of the wrists. This narrows the carpal tunnel and may reproduce symptoms in a patient with carpal tunnel syndrome. The symptoms likely to be reproduced are paresthesias in the affected hand.

150. ***b***
During a period of mania, common symptoms are inflated self-esteem and grandiosity (like a buying a baby grand piano), decreased need for sleep, hyper verbosity (excessive talking), racing thoughts and flight of ideas, distractibility, and excessive involvement in pleasurable activities that can be associated with very painful consequences later.

Adult Exam #3 Questions

1. **A patient with diarrhea has a positive enzyme immunoassay for *C. difficile*. He is on clindamycin for a tooth abscess. How should he be managed?**

    a. **Stop the clindamycin, treat the diarrhea**
    b. **Treat the diarrhea, give metronidazole**
    c. **Stop the clindamycin if possible, give metronidazole**
    d. **Give metronidazole**

2. **A patient presents to clinic with a complaint of a red eye. Which assessment below rules out the most worrisome diagnoses?**

    a. **Usual visual acuity**
    b. **Normal penlight exam**
    c. **Normal fundoscopic exam**
    d. **Negative photophobia**

3. **A young male patient with a herniated disc reports bilateral sciatica and leg weakness. If he calls the NP with complaints of urinary incontinence, what should be suspected?**

    a. **Opioid overuse**
    b. **Medial or lateral herniation**
    c. **Rupture of the disc**
    d. **Cauda equina syndrome**

4. **The Medicaid funded health program is:**

    a. **funded with premiums from participants.**
    b. **unlimited on the number of adult visits.**
    c. **funded by both state and federal governments.**
    d. **basically the same from state to state.**

5. A 16 year-old complains that his knees hurt. His mother states that he has complained of knee pain for the past 2 weeks. He has a prominent tibial tubercle. What should be part of the differential diagnosis?

a. **Osgood–Schlatter disease**
b. **Growing pains**
c. **Acute lymphocytic leukemia (ALL)**
d. **Psychogenic pain**

6. A topical treatment for basal cell carcinoma is:

a. **sulfacetamide lotion.**
b. **5-fluorouracil.**
c. **tetracycline lotion.**
d. **trichloroacetic acid.**

7. The first step in evaluating a breast lump is:

a. **history and physical exam.**
b. **mammogram.**
c. **ultrasound.**
d. **MRI.**

8. Which beverage below does not increase the risk of gout in a male who is prone to this condition?

a. **Vodka**
b. **Beer**
c. **Wine**
d. **Bourbon**

9. A 13 year-old male has exhibited the first sign that he is experiencing sexual maturation. He has:

a. **an increase in testicular size.**
b. **an enlargement of the scrotum.**
c. **an increase in length of the penis.**
d. **scrotal and penile changes.**

10. A patient has suspected plantar fasciitis. The plantar fascia is best examined:

a. **with the great toe dorsiflexed.**
b. **with the foot in neutral position.**
c. **while the patient stands.**
d. **with the ankle at a 90 degree angle.**

11. A 19 year-old female presents with lower abdominal pain that began about 12 hours ago. She is febrile. She denies vaginal discharge. Which choice below is the least likely cause of her symptoms?

a. **Appendicitis**
b. **Urinary tract infection**
c. **Renal stone**
d. **Ovarian cyst**

12. A 74 year-old patient has peripheral artery disease (PAD). Which item listed below is the most important risk factor for PAD?

a. **Cigarette smoking**
b. **Hyperlipidemia**
c. **Diabetes**
d. **Alcohol consumption**

13. A 60 year-old adult with an antalgic gait and complaints of hip pain is examined. He has trochanteric tenderness. What is the most common cause of this?

a. **Bone cancer**
b. **Trochanteric strain**
c. **Trochanteric bursitis**
d. **Osteoarthritis**

14. You have been asked to evaluate a heart murmur in a pregnant patient. Can a 3D echocardiogram be safely used to evaluate her?

a. **Yes, but this will not yield the best information.**
b. **Yes, this is perfectly safe.**
c. **No, this will emit radiation and is not safe.**
d. **Yes, but the mother will be exposed to radiation.**

15. The most common symptom associated with acute bronchitis is:

a. **fever.**
b. **cough.**
c. **pharyngitis.**
d. **purulent sputum.**

16. A young athlete is found to have a depression of the longitudinal arch of both feet. He complains of heel pain bilaterally. The rest of his foot is normal and he has continued with his activities. What could be recommended for his heel pain?

- **a. An x-ray of the foot is needed first.**
- **b. He needs some heel support in his shoes.**
- **c. NSAIDs should be used initially.**
- **d. Rigid orthotics could be ordered for his shoes.**

17. A patient who is 62 years old asks if she can get the shingles vaccine. She has never had shingles but states that she wants to make sure she doesn't get it. What should the nurse practitioner advise?

- **a. The immunization will protect you from acquiring shingles.**
- **b. You are not old enough to receive the immunization.**
- **c. The immunization is offered only to those who have had shingles.**
- **d. You are eligible to receive it but you still may get shingles.**

18. A 20 year old student has an MMR titer that demonstrates an unprotective titer for rubella. She is HIV positive. Which statement is true?

- **a. She should not receive the MMR immunization because she is low risk for the disease.**
- **b. MMR is safe to give but she does not need this.**
- **c. She is at risk for MMR but should not be immunized.**
- **d. She should receive this. The immunization is not alive.**

19. A 40 year-old patient who has aortic stenosis wants to know what symptoms indicate worsening of his stenosis. The nurse practitioner replies:

- **a. palpitations and weakness.**
- **b. ventricular arrhythmias.**
- **c. shortness of breath and syncope.**
- **d. fatigue and exercise intolerance.**

20. What medication may be used to treat GERD if a patient has tried over the counter ranitidine without benefit?

- **a. Calcium carbonate**
- **b. Prescription strength ranitidine**
- **c. Cimetidine**
- **d. Pantoprazole**

21. A patient with mononucleosis has pharyngitis, fever, and lymphadenopathy. His symptoms started 3 days ago.

- a. **He will have a positive "Monospot".**
- b. **He will have a normal CBC.**
- c. **He could have negative "Monospot".**
- d. **He could have a positive "Monospot" and a normal CBC.**

22. A patient has a positive hepatitis B surface antibody. His core antibody is negative. This indicates:

- a. **he has acute hepatitis B and needs immunization.**
- b. **he has chronic hepatitis B.**
- c. **he is immune to hepatitis B.**
- d. **he needs immunization to hepatitis B.**

23. A patient taking an ACE inhibitor should avoid:

- a. **strenuous exercise.**
- b. **potassium supplements.**
- c. **protein rich meals.**
- d. **grapefruit juice.**

24. A patient with mitral regurgitation (MR) has developed the most common arrhythmia associated with MR. The intervention most likely to prevent complications from this arrhythmia is:

- a. **immediate referral for a pacemaker.**
- b. **anticoagulation.**
- c. **beta-blocker administration.**
- d. **valve replacement.**

25. A patient who takes HCTZ 25 mg daily has complaints of muscle cramps. He probably has:

- a. **hypocalcemia.**
- b. **hypomagnesemia.**
- c. **hypokalemia.**
- d. **hypercalcemia.**

26. A 58 year-old patient has an annual exam. A fecal occult blood test was used to screen for colon cancer. Three were ordered on separate days. The first test was positive; the last two were negative. How should the nurse practitioner proceed?

- **a. Re-screen in one year.**
- **b. Perform a fourth exam.**
- **c. Refer him for a colonoscopy.**
- **d. Examine him for hemorrhoids.**

27. Which choice contains 3 medications that should have liver function tests measured prior to initiation of the medications?

- **a. Niacin, atorvastatin, simvastatin**
- **b. Naproxen, metformin, aspirin**
- **c. Cimetidine, pravastatin, and propanolol**
- **d. Ketoconazole, simvastatin, iron**

28. An 83 year-old healthy adult is diagnosed with pneumonia. He is febrile but in no distress. What is the preferred treatment for him?

- **a. Supportive measures, it is probably viral**
- **b. Levofloxacin**
- **c. Azithromycin**
- **d. Doxycycline**

29. A patient with mitral valve prolapse (MVP) reports chest pain and frequent arrhythmias. In the absence of other underlying cardiac anomalies, the drug of choice to treat her symptoms is a(n):

- **a. ACE inhibitor.**
- **b. beta blocker.**
- **c. calcium channel blocker.**
- **d. diuretic.**

30. A patient with pneumonia reports that he has rust colored sputum. What pathogen should the nurse practitioner suspect?

- **a. *Mycoplasma pneumoniae***
- **b. *Chlamydophila pneumoniae***
- **c. *Staphylococcus aureus***
- **d. *Streptococcus pneumoniae***

31. A 26 year-old being treated for community-acquired pneumonia (CAP) has been taking azithromycin in therapeutic doses for 72 hours. His temperature has gone from 102F to 101F. What should be done?

a. **Continue the same dose and monitor his status**
b. **Increase the dose to high dose azithromycin**
c. **Stop azithromycin and initiate a penicillin**
d. **This is probably viral, stop the antibiotic**

32. An older adult has osteopenia. Her healthcare provider has recommended calcium 500 mg three times daily. What is the most common side effect of calcium supplementation?

a. **Stomach upset**
b. **Diarrhea**
c. **Constipation**
d. **Mild nausea initially**

33. Niacin can:

a. **decrease total cholesterol and triglycerides.**
b. **decrease serum glucose and LDLs.**
c. **cause flushing and hypertension.**
d. **increase liver enzymes.**

34. A patient presents to the nurse practitioner's clinic and states that she feels sad and thinks she's depressed. What information is important to elicit in order to diagnose her with depression?

a. **How long have you felt like this?**
b. **Does anyone in your family have depression?**
c. **Are you thinking about harming yourself?**
d. **Do you have a plan for harming yourself?**

35. An elderly patient with urinary frequency is found to have a UTI. What medication could produce arrhythmias in her?

a. **Doxycycline**
b. **Amoxicillin**
c. **Ciprofloxacin**
d. **Macrodantin**

36. A 17 seven year-old has a complaint of ear pain. If he has otitis externa, which complaint is most likely?

a. **Tragal pain**
b. **Difficulty hearing the TV**
c. **Fever**
d. **Concurrent upper respiratory infection**

37. A 48 year-old patient has the following laboratory values. How should they be interpreted?

HCV IgG (+), RIBA (radio immuno blot assay) (+)

a. **The patient has hepatitis C.**
b. **The patient does not have hepatitis C.**
c. **The patient should consider immunization.**
d. **The results are indeterminate.**

38. The major laboratory abnormality noted in patients with pneumonia is:

a. **eosinophilia.**
b. **leukocytosis.**
c. **Gram stain positive.**
d. **leukopenia.**

39. Which patient is most likely to have mitral valve prolapse?

a. **An adolescent male with no cardiac history**
b. **A 25 year-old male with exercise intolerance**
c. **A 30 year-old female with no cardiac history**
d. **A 65 year-old male with shortness of breath**

40. A 14 year-old was diagnosed and treated for left acute otitis media 4 weeks ago. She presents today for a follow up visit. There is an effusion in the left ear. She denies complaints. How should this be managed?

a. **This should be monitored.**
b. **She should be given another antibiotic.**
c. **She should be evaluated with pneumatic otoscopy.**
d. **She needs a tympanogram.**

41. A 63 year-old male has been your patient for several years. He is a former smoker who takes simvastatin, ramipril, and an aspirin daily. His blood pressure and lipids are well controlled. He presents to your clinic with complaints of fatigue and "just not feeling well" for the last few days. His vital signs and exam are normal. His CBC, TSH, urine analysis are normal. His liver enzymes are six times the upper limits of normal. What should be done next?

- **a. Order a hepatitis panel and stop his medications**
- **b. Refer to gastroenterology**
- **c. Refer for a toxicology evaluation**
- **d. Order a hepatitis panel and stop his simvastatin and aspirin**

42. A patient has elevated liver enzymes. ALT = 642 U/L; AST= 150 U/L. What is the likely etiology of the elevation?

- **a. Acetaminophen toxicity**
- **b. Alcohol abuse**
- **c. Hepatitis**
- **d. Drug overdose**

43. Group A Strept pharyngitis:

- **a. is characterized by a single symptom.**
- **b. can be accompanied by abdominal pain.**
- **c. usually does not have exudative symptoms.**
- **d. is commonly accompanied by an inflamed uvula.**

44. The most common presentation of Parkinson's Disease is:

- **a. muscular rigidity.**
- **b. tremor.**
- **c. falling.**
- **d. bradykinesia.**

45. The most common indicator of end-organ damage in adolescents with hypertension is:

- **a. left ventricular hypertrophy.**
- **b. seizure.**
- **c. renal dysfunction.**
- **d. renal artery damage.**

46. A 44 year-old non-smoker is diagnosed with pneumonia. He is otherwise healthy and does not need hospitalization at this time. Which antibiotic can be used for empirical treatment according to the 2007 Infectious Diseases Society of America/American Thoracic Society?

a. **Erythromycin**
b. **Levofloxacin**
c. **Azithromycin**
d. **Amoxicillin**

47. A patient is diagnosed with thrush. What might be found on microscopic exam?

a. **Budding yeasts, pseudohypha**
b. **Cocci**
c. **Spores**
d. **Rods, spores, cocci**

48. The most common pathogen found in patients with pyelonephritis is:

a. ***Pseudomonas.***
b. ***Streptococcus.***
c. ***E. coli.***
d. ***Klebsiella.***

49. A 45 year-old patient has the following laboratory values. How should they be interpreted?

HBsAg (+), HBsAb (-), HBcAb (+)

a. **The patient has hepatitis.**
b. **The patient had hepatitis.**
c. **The patient should consider immunization.**
d. **The results are indeterminate.**

50. Tables are used for determination of maximum blood pressure values for adolescents. How are blood pressure values established for adolescents?

a. **Height percentile, body mass index, and gender**
b. **Gender and age**
c. **Height percentile, gender, and age**
d. **Body mass index and gender**

51. A 63 year-old male has been your patient for several years. He is a former smoker who takes simvastatin, ramipril, and an aspirin daily. His blood pressure and lipids are well controlled. He presents to your clinic with complaints of fatigue and "just not feeling well" for the last few days. His vital signs and exam are normal, but his lever enzymes are elevated. His hepatitis panel is negative for infectious hepatitis. What is the most likely cause of his elevated liver enzymes?

- **a. He has received a generic version of simvastatin**
- **b. He is an alcoholic in denial**
- **c. Daily grapefruit consumption for the past 10 days**
- **d. Rare liver toxicity from a usual dose of simvastatin**

52. Which patient has NO indication for further evaluation of his diarrhea? One with:

- **a. bloody diarrhea.**
- **b. temperature > 101.3F.**
- **c. duration of illness >48 hours.**
- **d. watery diarrhea and fever.**

53. A patient has suspected serotonin syndrome. How can this be diagnosed?

- **a. CT scan of the brain**
- **b. Elevated white count and C-reactive protein**
- **c. Elevated CK**
- **d. Clinical exam and index of suspicion**

54. The Framingham study of cardiovascular disease initiated in the early 1970s is an example of a:

- **a. randomized clinical trial.**
- **b. cohort study.**
- **c. case control study.**
- **d. sequential control study.**

55. A 20 year-old female patient presents with tenderness at McBurney's point. Appendicitis is considered. What laboratory test would be LEAST helpful to the nurse practitioner in excluding appendicitis as part of the differential?

- **a. CBC with elevated white count**
- **b. Urinalysis with leukocytes**
- **c. Positive serum pregnancy**
- **d. Positive pelvic cultures**

56. A 40 year-old complains of back pain after heavy lifting. This began 2 weeks ago. He has had little improvement in his pain. Which statement is true regarding plain x-rays in this patient?

a. **They should be gotten since 2 weeks have passed without improvement.**
b. **X-rays will be of benefit in diagnosis.**
c. **X-rays usually detect findings unrelated to symptoms.**
d. **X-rays can detect herniated discs.**

57. A patient has hepatitis B. He probably has a predominance of:

a. **leukocytes.**
b. **lymphocytes.**
c. **neutrophils.**
d. **eosinophils.**

58. Which of the following medications may have an unfavorable effect on a hypertensive patient's blood pressure?

a. **Lovastatin**
b. **Furosemide**
c. **Naproxen**
d. **Loratadine**

59. A patient with aortic stenosis has been asymptomatic for decades. On routine exam he states that he has had some dizziness associated with activity but no chest pain or shortness of breath. The best course of action for the nurse practitioner is to:

a. **monitor closely for worsening of his status.**
b. **refer to cardiology.**
c. **consider a non-cardiac etiology for dizziness.**
d. **assess his carotid arteries for bruits.**

60. Which choice below characterizes a patient with aortic regurgitation?

a. **Long asymptomatic period followed by exercise intolerance, then dyspnea at rest**
b. **An acute onset of shortness of breath in the fifth or sixth decade**
c. **Dyspnea on exertion for a long period of time before sudden cardiac death**
d. **A long asymptomatic period with sudden death usually during exercise**

61. A 16 year-old has been diagnosed with Lyme disease. Which drug should be used to treat him?

- a. Doxycycline
- b. Amoxicillin-clavulanate
- c. Trimethoprim-sulfamethoxazole
- d. Cephalexin

62. The most appropriate time to begin screening for renal nephropathy in a patient with Type II diabetes is:

- a. at diagnosis.
- b. once year after diagnosis.
- c. 2-3 years after diagnosis.
- d. 5 years after diagnosis.

63. An example of a drug that targets the renin-angiotensin-aldosterone system is:

- a. an ACE inhibitor.
- b. a beta blocker.
- c. a calcium channel blocker.
- d. a diuretic.

64. A patient taking candesartan should avoid:

- a. strenuous exercise.
- b. potassium supplements.
- c. protein rich meals.
- d. grapefruit juice.

65. A skin disorder has a hallmark finding of silvery scales. What word below describes this common condition?

- a. Chronic
- b. Infectious
- c. Contagious
- d. Acute

66. A patient has a urinary tract infection. What findings on urine dipstick best describe a typical urinary tract infection?

- a. Positive leukocytes
- b. Positive nitrates
- c. Positive leukocytes, positive nitrites
- d. Positive nitrates and hematuria

67. A patient with mononucleosis would most likely have:

a. lymphocytosis.
b. eosinophilia.
c. leukocytosis.
d. monocytosis.

68. A female patient has the following characteristics. Which one represents a risk factor for Type II diabetes?

a. Hyperlipidemia
b. History of gestational diabetes
c. Infrequent, regular exercise
d. Family history of Type I diabetes

69. A patient with iron deficiency anemia takes iron supplementation daily. What should he be advised to avoid within a couple of hours of taking iron?

a. An antacid
b. Heavy exercise
c. Potassium supplements
d. Grapefruit juice

70. A patient with anemia of chronic disease probably has a:

a. macrocytic anemia.
b. normocytic anemia.
c. hypochromic anemia.
d. hyperchromic anemia.

71. A patient has 2 non- fasting glucose values of 101 mg/dL and 114 mg/dL that were measured on 2 separate days in the same week. This patient:

a. has normal blood glucose values.
b. has impaired fasting glucose.
c. should have further glucose testing done for diagnosis.
d. should have a Hgb A1C performed.

72. A patient who takes oral contraceptive pills is at increased risk of:

a. gallbladder disease.
b. depression.
c. hypothyroidism.
d. varicose veins.

73. A patient has nasal septal erosion with minor, continuous bleeding. There is macerated tissue. What is a likely etiology?

a. **Improper use of a nasal steroid**
b. **Chronic sinusitis**
c. **Severe allergic rhinitis**
d. **Cocaine abuse**

74. Which form of birth control presents the highest risk to a female patient if she is exposed to a sexually transmitted disease (STD)?

a. **Intrauterine device**
b. **Progestin only pill**
c. **Diaphragm**
d. **Oral contraceptives**

75. Patients with asthma:

a. **all wheeze.**
b. **all cough.**
c. **can cough or wheeze.**
d. **have dyspnea.**

76. A patient is examined and found to have a positive Kernig's and Brudzinski's signs. What is the most likely diagnosis?

a. **Hepatitis**
b. **Encephalitis**
c. **Meningitis**
d. **Pneumonitis**

77. Most cases of atopic dermatitis exacerbation are treated with:

a. **emollients.**
b. **topical steroids.**
c. **antihistamines.**
d. **antibiotics.**

78. A patient presents with severe toothache. She reports sensitivity to heat and cold. There is visible pus around the painful area. What is this termed?

a. **Pulpitis**
b. **Caries**
c. **Gingivitis**
d. **Periodontitis**

79. A college age basketball player landed awkwardly on his foot and ankle after jumping during a game yesterday. He states that he sprained his ankle. He complains of ankle pain and foot pain but is able to limp into the exam room. How should he be managed?

a. **Rest, ice, compression, elevation**
b. **Non-weight bearing until fracture is ruled out**
c. **Short leg splint**
d. **NSAIDs and rest with partial non-weight bearing**

80. A patient is at increased risk of osteopenia if she uses which form of birth control?

a. **Injectable progestin**
b. **Intrauterine device**
c. **Oral contraceptives**
d. **Natural family planning**

81. A child and father live in an old house. They both are found to be lead toxic. What type anemia is typically observed in patients who are lead toxic?

a. **Pernicious anemia**
b. **Iron deficiency anemia**
c. **Lead anemia**
d. **Anemia of chronic disease**

82. A characteristic that is true of tension headaches but not of cluster headaches is:

a. **cluster headaches are always bilateral.**
b. **tension headaches are always bilateral.**
c. **cluster headaches always cause nausea.**
d. **tension headaches cause photosensitivity.**

83. In a private NP clinic, a patient presents with trichomonas. State law requires reporting of STDs to the public health department. The patient asks the NP not to report it because her husband works in the public health department. How should this be managed by the NP?

a. **Respect the patient's right to privacy and not report it.**
b. **Tell the patient that it won't be reported, but report it anyway.**
c. **Report it to public health as required by law.**
d. **Report it to public health but don't divulge all the details.**

84. A patient reports to the minor care area of the emergency department after being bitten by a dog. The patient states that the dog had a tag around his neck and had been seen roaming around the neighborhood. The dog did not exhibit any odd behavior. How should this be managed?

a. **If the bites are only minor, do not mention rabies prophylaxis to the patient.**
b. **Give the patient tetanus immunization only. Don't call animal control.**
c. **Clean the wounds, provide tetanus and rabies prophylaxis.**
d. **Report the bite to animal control and administer appropriate medical care.**

85. A neurologic disease that produces demyelination of the nerve cells in the brain and spinal cord is:

a. **Parkinson's disease.**
b. **late stage Lyme disease.**
c. **multiple sclerosis.**
d. **amyotrophic lateral sclerosis.**

86. Which of the following statements regarding HIV is correct?

a. **There are few conditions that cause depletion of CD4 cells other than HIV.**
b. **CD4 cell counts vary very little in individuals infected with HIV.**
c. **A normal CD4 count is $< 200/mm^3$.**
d. **CD4 counts are the first abnormality seen in patients with HIV.**

87. A patient has been diagnosed with MRSA. She is sulfa allergic. Which medication could be used to treat her?

a. **Augmentin**
b. **Trimethoprim-sulfamethoxazole (TMPS)**
c. **Ceftriaxone**
d. **Doxycycline**

88. Women who use diaphragms for contraception have an increased incidence of:

a. **sexually transmitted diseases.**
b. **pregnancy.**
c. **urinary tract infection.**
d. **pelvic inflammatory disease.**

89. What is the effect of digital rectal examination (DRE) on a male's PSA (prostate specific antigen) level if it is measured on the same day as DRE?

- a. The change is insignificant
- b. A decrease in the PSA will occur
- c. An increase in the PSA will occur
- d. There will be a change, but it is not predictable

90. Papilledema is noted in a patient with a headache. What is the importance of papilledema in this patient?

- a. It is not related to this patient's headache.
- b. It is an incidental finding in patients with migraines.
- c. It could be an important finding in this patient.
- d. This is a common finding in patients with headaches.

91. Syphilis may present as:

- a. a discharge.
- b. a rash.
- c. a painful lesion.
- d. dysuria.

92. Depression is diagnosed on clinical presentation. What time frame is important for distinguishing between depressed mood and clinical depression?

- a. 1 week
- b. 2 weeks
- c. 3 weeks
- d. 4 weeks

93. A patient with bipolar disease has purchased a $10,000 baby grand piano. He does not play the piano. Consistent with a manic episode in bipolar disease, this is an example of:

- a. grandiosity.
- b. poor judgment.
- c. racing thoughts.
- d. psychosis.

94. Patients with cough variant asthma:

- a. all exhibit wheezing.
- b. all exhibit cough.
- c. may exhibit cough or wheeze.
- d. have dyspnea.

95. An older patient presents with left lower quadrant pain. If diverticulitis is suspected, how should the NP proceed?

a. Order a chest and abdominal x-ray
b. CT scan with IV and oral contrast
c. Barium enema
d. Ultrasound of the abdomen

96. A patient has fatigue, weight loss, and a TSH of .05. What is his likely diagnosis?

a. Hypothyroidism
b. Hyperthyroidism
c. Subclinical hypothyroidism
d. More tests are needed to establish his diagnosis

97. A female should be told to take her OCP at bedtime if she experiences:

a. weight gain.
b. headaches.
c. nausea.
d. spotting.

98. The following PSA levels have been observed in a patient. What conclusion can be made following these annual readings?

Year 1: 3.2 ng/mL
Year 2: 3.8 ng/mL
Year 3: 4.2 ng/mL

a. They are all within normal range.
b. None are within normal range.
c. There is a steady increase that is worrisome.
d. There is a steady increase but not worrisome.

99. A patient asks the NP's advice about an herb to help with her hot flashes. The NP knows these:

a. are safe to use in all patients.
b. may be contraindicated in patients with history of breast cancer.
c. substances have a mild estrogenic effect and will halt hot flashes.
d. help prevent osteoporosis.

100. A 15 year-old female has never menstruated. She and her mother are concerned. What is most important for the NP to assess?

- **a. Stature**
- **b. Tanner stage**
- **c. Anemia**
- **d. Family history of amenorrhea**

101. A female patient has the following characteristics. Which one represents a risk factor for Type II diabetes?

- **a. BMI 31**
- **b. Osteopenia**
- **c. Mediterranean decent**
- **d. Hypothyroidism**

102. What finding characterizes shingles?

- **a. Pain, burning, and itching**
- **b. Unilateral dermatomal rash**
- **c. Grouped vesicles**
- **d. Resolution of rash and crusting**

103. A 45 year-old patient started taking paroxetine one week ago for depression. She calls to report intermittent headache and nausea. What is a likely etiology?

- **a. Gastroenteritis**
- **b. Viral infection**
- **c. Drug side effect**
- **d. Depression**

104. A male with gonorrhea might complain of:

- **a. dysuria.**
- **b. a penile lesion.**
- **c. abdominal pain.**
- **d. fatigue.**

105. What medication used to treat patients who have GERD provides the fastest relief of heartburn symptoms?

- **a. Calcium carbonate**
- **b. Ranitidine**
- **c. Amantadine**
- **d. Pantoprazole**

106. A patient exhibits petechiae on both lower legs but has no other complaints. How should the NP proceed?

a. **Refer to hematology**
b. **Order a CBC**
c. **Order blood cultures**
d. **Stop aspirin and re-assess in one week**

107. A vitamin B-12 deficiency might be suspected in an older patient with what complaints?

a. **Fatigue and restless legs**
b. **Memory issues and glossitis**
c. **Painful legs with exercise**
d. **Insomnia and anorexia**

108. Which drug listed below is NOT associated with weight gain?

a. **Insulin**
b. **Pioglitazone**
c. **Citalopram**
d. **Metoprolol**

109. The primary therapeutic intervention for patients who present with hives is:

a. **steroids.**
b. **anti-histamines.**
c. **calcium channel blockers.**
d. **topical steroid cream.**

110. Kegel exercises may be helpful for patients with what type of incontinence?

a. **Stress**
b. **Urge**
c. **Mixed**
d. **Overflow**

111. A 52 year-old patient presents with an acute drooping right eye and drooping right upper lip. The right side of her face is numb. She is otherwise healthy. Based on the most likely etiology, how should she be managed?

a. **Steroids plus an antiviral agent**
b. **Immediate referral to the emergency department**
c. **Antihistamines and steroids**
d. **Steroids only**

112. A patient presents to the NP clinic with a complaint of nocturnal paresthesias. What is the likely underlying etiology?

a. **De Quervain's tenosynovitis**
b. **Carpal tunnel syndrome**
c. **Ulnar radiculopathy**
d. **Medial epicondylitis**

113. What is the recommendation from American Cancer Society for assessment of the prostate gland in a man who is 45 years old and of average risk for development of prostate cancer? He should have:

a. **screening starting at 50 years of age.**
b. **prostate specific antigen (PSA) now.**
c. **PSA and digital rectal exam now.**
d. **digital rectal exam only.**

114. A 24 year-old female patient who is sexually active complains of vaginal itching. If she has bacterial vaginosis, she might complain of:

a. **a "fishy" vaginal odor after coitus.**
b. **a truncal rash.**
c. **copious vaginal discharge.**
d. **midcycle bleeding.**

115. A patient is diagnosed with mild chronic heart failure (CHF). What drug listed below would be a good choice for managing his symptoms and improving long-term outcomes?

a. **Verapamil**
b **Digoxin**
c. **Furosemide**
d. **Metoprolol**

116. A patient who has been in the sun for the past few weeks is very tanned. He has numerous 3-6 mm light colored flat lesions on his trunk. What is the likely etiology?

a. **Tinea corporis**
b. **Tinea unguium**
c. **Tinea versicolor**
d. **Human papilloma virus**

117. A patient has been diagnosed with anxiety. What sleep disturbance might she have?

a. **Early morning wakening**
b. **Difficulty remaining asleep**
c. **Difficulty falling asleep**
d. **Never feeling tired**

118. A female patient complains of dysuria with vaginal discharge. How should she be managed?

a. **Order a urinalysis**
b. **Order a urine culture**
c. **Perform a pelvic exam**
d. **Perform an abdominal exam, urinalysis, and pelvic exam**

119. Ankle inversion is a common complaint from a patient with a:

a. **medial ankle sprain.**
b. **lateral ankle sprain.**
c. **severely torn ligament.**
d. **fracture of the medial malleolus.**

120. A 60 year-old has been on NSAIDs for the past week for shoulder pain. He has complaints of blood on toilet tissue when wiping after a bowel movement. What should be suspected?

a. **He has a GI bleed from NSAIDs.**
b. **He could have hemorrhoids.**
c. **He does not have a GI bleed. The bleeding is from tissue friability from NSAIDs.**
d. **This is unrelated to the NSAIDs.**

121. A 65 year-old patient has a firm, non-tender, symmetrical enlarged prostate gland on examination. His PSA is 3.9 ng/mL. This probably indicates:

a. **prostate cancer.**
b. **benign prostatic hypertrophy (BPH).**
c. **prostate infection.**
d. **a perfectly normal prostate gland.**

122. A contact lens wearer presents with an erythematous conjunctiva. He denies blurred vision. There is scant drainage and crusting around the eye. He reports that there was crusting when he woke up this morning. How should the exam begin?

- a. **The patient should wash his hands.**
- b. **His visual acuity should be measured in each eye.**
- c. **Fluorescein staining should be assessed.**
- d. **Extraocular eye movements should be assessed.**

123. The hearing loss associated with aging involves:

- a. **8th cranial nerve.**
- b. **sensorineural hearing loss.**
- c. **conductive hearing loss.**
- d. **noise damage.**

124. In a research study, the difference between the smallest and largest observation is the:

- a. **standard deviation.**
- b. **first degree of freedom.**
- c. **range.**
- d. **absolute value.**

125. An older adult has suspected B12 deficiency. Which of the following lab indices is more indicative of a B12 deficiency?

- a. **Microcytosis**
- b. **Macrocytosis**
- c. **Leukocytosis**
- d. **Thrombocytosis**

126. A patient presents with symptoms of influenza during influenza season. What should be used to help diagnose influenza in him?

- a. **A nasal culture**
- b. **A nasal swab**
- c. **CBC**
- d. **Based on symptoms**

127. A patient who is taking long acting insulin basal insulin has elevated blood sugars. Which blood sugars are important to review in order to increase the dose of insulin?

a. AM fasting
b. 2 hour post prandial
c. Pre-prandial
d. Bedtime

128. A patient with sciatica is most likely to describe relief of symptoms with:

a. sitting.
b. standing.
c. side lying or standing.
d. walking.

129. A patient with asthma presents with chest tightness, wheezing, coughing, and fever. He is wheezing in the upper right lobe. His cough is non-productive, and he denies nasal symptoms. Which symptoms are not likely related to his asthma?

a. Fever
b. Coughing
c. Wheezing
d. Chest tightness

130. A 60 year-old female presents with history of low back pain of recent origin. Her gait is antalgic and she reports loss of bladder function since the onset of back pain this morning. What should be done?

a. Order physical therapy
b. Refer to the emergency department
c. Refer to a neurologist
d. Keep non-weight bearing until x-rays are completed

131. After a vaginal exam, a patient received a prescription for metronidazole. What was her likely diagnosis?

a. Syphilis
b. Trichomonas
c. Chlamydia
d. Gonorrhea

132. A patient presents with small vesicles on the lateral edges of his fingers and intense itching. On close inspection, there are small vesicles on the palmar surface of the hand. What is this called?

- a. **Seborrheic dermatitis**
- b. **Dyshidrotic dermatitis**
- c. **Herpes zoster**
- d. **Varicella zoster**

133. A patient has a "herald patch" and is diagnosed with pityriasis rosea. Where is the "herald patch" found?

- a. **On the affected limb**
- b. **On the chest**
- c. **Close to the scalp**
- d. **Behind one of the ears**

134. A patient with environmental allergies presents to your clinic. She takes an oral antihistamine every 24 hours. What is the most effective single maintenance medication for allergic rhinitis?

- a. **Antihistamine**
- b. **Decongestant**
- c. **Intranasal glucocorticoids**
- d. **Leukotriene blockers**

135. A patient presents with tragal pain. What is the most likely diagnosis?

- a. **Otitis media**
- b. **Otitis externa**
- c. **Presbycusis**
- d. **Mastoiditis**

136. A patient has been diagnosed with viral gastroenteritis. He has nausea, vomiting, and has started having lower abdominal cramps. What is the most effective intervention for him?

- a. **An anti-diarrheal**
- b. **An anti-emetic**
- c. **An anti-spasmodic**
- d. **Oral rehydration**

137. A characteristic of rheumatoid arthritis not typical in osteoarthritis is:

a. **weight loss.**
b. **morning stiffness.**
c. **symmetrical joint involvement.**
d. **the presence of Bouchard's nodes.**

138. A patient with migraine headaches and hypertension should receive which medication class with caution?

a. **Beta-blockers**
b. **Triptans**
c. **Pain medications**
d. **ACE inhibitors**

139. A female patient who is 45 years old states that she is having urinary frequency. She describes episodes of "having to go right now" and not being able to wait. Her urinalysis is normal. What is part of the differential?

a. **Diabetes**
b. **Lupus**
c. **Stress incontinence**
d. **Asymptomatic bacteriuria**

140. A 30 year-old male who is sexually active presents with pain during bowel movements. He is negative when checked for hemorrhoids, but has a tender prostate gland. What should be suspected?

a. **Acute bacterial prostatitis**
b. **Prostate cancer**
c. **Benign prostatic hyperplasia**
d. **Gonorrhea**

141. Which of the following can NOT be a microcytic anemia?

a. **Vitamin B12**
b. **Anemia of chronic disease**
c. **Iron deficiency anemia**
d. **Thalassemia**

142. A patient reports that her knee "locks" sometimes and feels like it will "give out". She denies injury. She has no complaint about her other knee. What is her likely problem?

a. **Torn anterior cruciate ligament**
b. **Knee effusion**
c. **Premature osteoarthritis**
d. **Meniscal tear**

143. A nurse practitioner has not increased the dosage of an antihypertensive medication even though the patient's blood pressure has remained 140/90. This might be described as:

a. **clinical inertia.**
b. **malpractice.**
c. **resistant hypertension.**
d. **lackadaisical attitude.**

144. Which choice below would be the best choice for an 80 year-old patient whose blood pressure is 172/72 mm Hg?

a. **Chlorthalidone**
b. **Amlodipine**
c. **Monopril**
d. **Acebutolol**

145. A patient who is diagnosed today with diabetes has microalbuminuria. What can be concluded about this finding?

a. **The patient has diabetic nephropathy.**
b. **There is renal damage.**
c. **The patient should have a repeat test in one month.**
d. **The patient might have been diabetic for a long time before diagnosis.**

146. A patient with bulimia nervosa probably has concurrent:

a. **hypothyroidism.**
b. **malnutrition.**
c. **anxiety.**
d. **hypoalbuminemia.**

147. What symptom listed below might be seen in a male patient with benign prostatic hyperplasia?

- a. **Dysuria**
- b. **Nocturia**
- c. **Low back pain**
- d. **Pain with bearing down**

148. A nurse practitioner performs a fundoscopic exam. He identifies small areas of dull, yellowish-white coloration in the retina. What might these be?

- a. **Cotton wool spots**
- b. **Microaneurysms**
- c. **Hemorrhages**
- d. **Exudates**

149. A patient with intermittent asthma is using his "rescue" medication once daily. How should this be managed? He must receive a prescription for:

- a. **a bronchodilator.**
- b. **an inhaled steroid.**
- c. **a long-acting beta agonist.**
- d. **a leukotriene blocker.**

150. Which medication should be avoided in a patient with a sulfa allergy?

- a. **Sulfonylurea**
- b. **Sulfamethoxazole**
- c. **Naproxen**
- d. **Cefazolin**

Adult Exam #3 Answers

1. *c*

The most important step in treating infection with C. difficile is stopping ingestion of the offending antibiotic. In this case, stopping the clindamycin, if possible, is the most important part of treatment. Metronidazole is recommended initially for non-severe infection. If the antibiotic cannot be stopped, treatment for C. difficile should be continued as long as the patient must take the offending antibiotic.

2. *a*

This is a test that should be done on every patient who presents with an eye complaint; especially if the eye is red. It is not necessary to determine exactly what the visual acuity is; it is necessary to establish that vision is usual. If this is the case, the most worrisome diagnoses can be ruled out: infectious keratitis, iritis, and angle closure glaucoma.

3. *d*

Cauda equina is a medical emergency. It is characterized by compression of the spinal cord. A common manifestation of this is bowel or bladder dysfunction. This patient needs immediate neuro or orthopedic referral.

4. *c*

Medicaid is state run and specific to each state. The state programs are funded by a combination of state and federal funds. Most states have limits on the number of adult visits. Some states have no limits on visits for children. Participants generally do not pay premiums like Medicare recipients pay.

5. *a*

Osgood-Schlatter is an osteochondritis of the tibial tubercle that can produce pain in the knees of adolescents. Pain gradually increases over time and can become extremely painful, especially if the knee sustains a direct hit or when the patient kneels. The diagnosis can be made on clinical presentation without the need for imaging studies. This is usually treated by rest, ice/heat, NSAIDs, and strengthening of the quadriceps muscle. Activity should not be stopped, but instead slowed down if symptoms become too painful.

6. *b*

Several treatments exist for basal and squamous cell carcinoma. The majority are simple procedures like cryotherapy, electrodessication, surgical excision, and a topical treatment like 5-fluorouracil (5-FU). The other agents listed are not used to treat basal or squamous cell carcinoma. 5-FU works by inhibiting DNA synthesis. It is effective if used for superficial basal cell carcinomas. It is available in cream and solution and is usually applied twice daily for 3-6 weeks.

7. *a*

Although most patients will need further work-up of a breast mass, historical information is critically important in directing the health care provider to the next step. Historical information that should be ascertained is the location of the lump, how and when it was first noticed, whether there is nipple discharge, and whether it changes in size related to menses. Other historical information is the patient's personal and family history of breast cancer and/or history of breast biopsies.

8. *c*

Alcohol is known to be a contributing factor in development of gouty arthritis. Males are more prone to gout than females, and alcohol consumption increases the likelihood of gout development. Of all alcohols, wine contributes least to the development of gout. Consumption of meat and fish increase the concentration of uric acid and thus, the risk of developing gout.

9. *a*

A male with Tanner Stage II development will have an increase in testicular volume from 1.5 ml or less, to up to 6 ml. The skin on the scrotum will begin to thin, redden, and enlarge. The penile length will remain the same. Males begin sexual maturity later than females. In the United States, males begin sexual maturation about 2 years later than females. Maturity begins in girls about 9-12 years.

10. *a*

When the great toe is dorsiflexed, the plantar fascia is easy to palpate because it tightens and can be easily palpated on the sole of the foot. Anterior heel pain is usually easily appreciated when the patient has plantar fasciitis.

11. *c*

A renal stone can produce lower abdominal pain, but is unlikely to produce fever. Fever can be associated with the presence of a stone if pyelonephritis also accompanies this. However, this is not nearly as likely as the other diagnoses listed. Another diagnosis that must be considered because of her age, is pelvic inflammatory disease. In this case, a pelvic exam should be performed.

12. *a*

Cigarette smoking is considered the most important risk factor for PAD. Stopping cigarette smoking reduces the progression of PAD and is associated with lower rates of amputation, and improves rest ischemia and pain in patients who experience this. The other major risk factors for PAD are presence of diabetes, hypertension, hyperlipidemia. Alcohol consumption actually reduces the risk of PAD but can increase the risk of many other diseases.

13. *c*

Tenderness over the trochanter is common in trochanteric bursitis. There are superficial and deep bursa that can be assessed. Other causes of trochanteric tenderness are fractures, stress fractures, and diseases where metastases have occurred, like

prostate cancer.

14. ***b***
An echocardiogram is the best test to evaluate a heart murmur whether the patient is pregnant or not. Echocardiography can be used safely in this patient because no radiation is emitted from 3D echo. The most common murmur in pregnant women is a venous hum murmur. It resolves within several weeks after delivery. It is harmless.

15. ***b***
Fever is an unusual symptom associated with acute bronchitis. Cough is the most common symptom associated with acute bronchitis. Purulent sputum is identified in more than 50% of patients with acute bronchitis. The color imparted to the sputum is usually due to sloughing of epithelial cells, not bacterial infection. Concurrent upper respiratory symptoms are typical of acute bronchitis. Pharyngitis is very common.

16. ***b***
A description of functional flat foot is described in this question. It is common among athletes. Although pain is not always present with this finding, it may accompany the finding but is usually not severe enough to inhibit activity. The treatment deemed to be best is a well-supported heel counter. The heel counter is the rigid part of the shoe that supports the heel. A radiograph is not needed unless the patient presents with other symptoms or fails to derive relief from the heel counter. NSAIDs may help symptoms of pain, but they will not correct the underlying problem. Orthotics may increase his pain. These are more helpful in patients with more severe pes planus.

17. ***d***
Patients must be at least 50 years old to receive the shingles immunization. It is generally well tolerated but provides protection from shingles in 50-64% of patients. The incidence of post-herpetic neuralgia is decreased up to 65% after immunization. The patient still may develop shingles after receiving the immunization. The vaccine may be offered regardless of whether the patient has history of shingles. However, since it is a live vaccine, it may be contraindicated because of steroid use or immune status.

18. ***c***
This patient is at risk for rubella because she does not have a sufficient titer. The MMR immunization is an attenuated virus. Though an attenuated immunization is weakened, it is still considered live and so is contraindicated in anyone who is immunocompromised. She should be advised not to get pregnant.

19. ***c***
The three most common symptoms associated with aortic stenosis are angina, syncope, and congestive heart failure evidenced by dyspnea. Syncope is usually exertional. Angina may be due to aortic stenosis, but, underlying coronary artery disease accounts for half of anginal symptoms in these patients. There is usually a prolonged asymptomatic phase, but the presence of symptoms usually indicates a need for valve replacement. Without replacement, there is a rapid decline in the patient's status and

death will ensue.

20. ***d***
If a patient has been diagnosed with GERD and he is symptomatic on an H2 blocker like ranitidine, a proton pump inhibitor (PPI) should be considered. An example of a proton pump inhibitor is pantoprazole. Relief of symptoms after using a PPI does not indicate a benign condition. This patient could have esophageal erosions, Barrett's esophagitis, or esophageal cancer. He should be screened for risk factors for these conditions and then a decision to refer this patient to gastroenterology can be made.

21. ***c***
The "Monospot" detects the presence of heterophile antibodies in mononucleosis (mono). If the "Monospot" is performed too early in the course of the illness, it will be negative even though the patient has mono. If the patient has persistent symptoms suspicious of mono, a "Monospot" should be repeated. It is likely that in several days after a negative result, a positive result will be obtained. Lymphocytosis characterizes mononucleosis; therefore, it is highly unlikely that a patient will not have a normal CBC if he has mono.

22. ***c***
This patient is immune to hepatitis B because he has a positive hepatitis B surface antibody. He does not need immunization. His immunity is due to immunization because he has a negative core antibody. The finding of a positive surface antibody and a negative core antibody in this patient indicates immunity from hepatitis B from immunization. If his immunity had been derived from infection, his core antibody would have been positive.

23. ***b***
An ACE inhibitor potentially can produce hyperkalemia because its mechanism of action is in the renin-angiotensin-aldosterone system where potassium is spared. If potassium is taken in the form of potassium supplements, the effect will be additive and the risk of hyperkalemia can be great.

24. ***b***
The most common arrhythmia associated with mitral regurgitation (MR) is atrial fibrillation. Anti-coagulation with warfarin will help prevent arterial embolism that can result in stroke or myocardial infarction. Atrial fibrillation occurs because the fibers in the atrium are stretched as the atrium dilates. The stretch results in conduction defects, notably, atrial fibrillation.

25. ***c***
HCTZ ia a thiazide diuretic that is potassium-wasting. Patients can become hypokalemic and experience side effects of this. A common one is muscle cramps.

26. ***c***
A fecal occult blood test is performed multiple times on different days because tumors

don't consistently excrete blood. The reason multiple are performed is to increase the likelihood of identifying blood. The patient needs to have a colonoscopy performed for examination of the colon. The standard of practice is to refer all positive colon cancer screens for colonoscopy.

27. ***a***
Patients who take niacin and the statins should have liver enzymes measured prior to initiation. The need for periodic monitoring of liver enzymes with the statins is no longer required. However, baseline values are prudently measured. There is no need to do this routinely with aspirin, cimetidine, propanolol, or iron in patients without risk factors. There are more than 600 commonly prescribed drugs that can produce liver enzyme elevations. Care with prescribing is always warranted.

28. ***b***
At age extremes, the most common pathogen is *Streptococcus pneumoniae.* Because of the age of the patient and the consequences of potential treatment failure, a respiratory quinolone should be considered. Quinolone antibiotics can produce QT prolongation and should be used cautiously in older adults. Azithromycin or doxycycline would be chosen if an atypical pathogen was suspected. This is unlikely in this patient because of his age.

29. ***b***
Beta blockers are recommended to alleviate atrial or ventricular arrhythmias associated with mitral valve prolapse. However, long-term effectiveness of beta-blockers is uncertain. Most patients with MVP who do not have symptoms of arrhythmias or ectopy at rest usually do not require further evaluation. However, they should be monitored at least annually for a change in their condition.

30. ***d***
Clinical descriptions of mucus do not really help in clinical decision-making regarding pneumonia, but certain clinical characteristics are associated with specific types of pneumonia. Strept pneumonia, also known as pneumococcal pneumonia, is associated with rust colored sputum. Scant or watery sputum is associated with atypical pathogens like *Mycoplasma* and *Chlamydophila* pneumonia. Thick, discolored sputum may be associated with bacterial pneumonia.

31. ***c***
A 26 year-old with CAP should show improvement in symptoms in 24-48 hours if he is on appropriate antibiotic therapy. Azithromycin treats atypical pathogens like *Mycoplasma* and *Chlamydophila*, but, has poor *Streptococcus* coverage. The most likely pathogen in this age group that causes pneumonia is an atypical pathogen, but at this point the most common typical pathogen, *Streptococcus pneumoniae*, must be considered. The best choice is to consider *Streptococcus pneumoniae* as the pathogen and treat with penicillin. Specifically, this patient should receive high dose penicillin because of the increased incidence of resistant *Streptococcus pneumoniae.*

32. ***c***
Constipation is the most common side effect of calcium supplementation. To improve tolerance, the nurse practitioner can suggest 500 mg daily for a week, then 500 mg twice daily for a week, then three times daily. The patient should be encouraged to increase the intake of fruits, vegetables, fluid, and fiber. Weight bearing exercise and Vitamin D should be encouraged to improve bone density.

33. ***d***
Niacin is used to decrease total cholesterol, LDLs, and increase HDLs. Liver function studies should be monitored prior to, with dosage increases, and periodically during consumption of niacin because elevations can occur. Glucose levels should be monitored as well because glucose levels can increase slightly in some patients who take niacin. Monitor for myalgias and rhabdomyolysis as with the statins. Niacin commonly causes flushing in patients, but, not hypertension. Hypotension is common in patients who take niacin.

34. ***a***
In order to diagnose a patient with depression, certain criteria must be met. DSM V has established specific criteria that must be present for a diagnosis of depression to be made. One essential criterion is the presence of depressed mood for at least 2 weeks. If the depressed mood has lasted less than this, a diagnosis is premature. Information about family history supports a diagnosis but is not a criterion. The last two questions assess for risk of suicide.

35. ***c***
Ciprofloxacin is a quinolone antibiotic. All quinolones have the potential to produce prolongation of the QT interval. It should be prescribed with caution in older adults.

36. ***a***
A patient with otitis externa has swimmer's ear, an infection of the external canal. The classic complaint is tragal pain or even pinnae pain. If there is such significant edema in the external canal, hearing may be impaired, but the most common complaint is tragal pain. Systemic complaints do not accompany swimmer's ear unless a second diagnosis is present simultaneously. Fever and upper respiratory infection are not likely.

37. ***a***
This patient has hepatitis C. He has a positive HCV IgG. This is a positive screen for hepatitis C. The confirmatory RIBA is positive. When both the HCV IgG and RIBA are positive, the patient can be diagnosed with hepatitis C. At this time, there is no immunization for hepatitis C.

38. ***b***
An increased white count is typical in patients with pneumonia. This is more commonly seen in bacterial pneumonia. Eosinophils can be increased in patients who develop pneumonia secondary to exposure to a very irritating substance like a toxic gas. Gram stain can demonstrate gram positive or negative pathogens. Leukopenia is an ominous

finding, especially in older patients. This indicates a poor prognosis because it means that the immune system is not responding to a potentially fatal pathogen.

39. ***c***
Mitral valve prolapse (MVP) is most common in women aged 14-30 years of age. However, it can be found in children (though not usually) or in older adults. The symptoms most commonly associated with MVP are arrhythmias, both atrial and ventricular, and chest pain. However, most patients with MVP are asymptomatic.

40. ***a***
About 40% of children have effusion at 4 weeks post acute otitis media. This should be monitored and not treated with another antibiotic. Effusion is a stage in the resolution of otitis media. Pneumatic otoscopy will identify the presence of fluid or pus behind the TM, but will not help in diagnosis or treatment once an effusion has been established. A tympanogram will establish that her hearing is diminished, a fact which should be assumed since there is fluid in the middle ear.

41. ***d***
This patient has very probable damage to his liver, as evidenced by his elevated liver enzymes. Elevations in liver enzymes can be a direct result of hepatic injury or something else. 2 important notes: first, these enzymes are not specific for the liver, although, the highest ALT content is in the liver. ALT and AST can be found in the heart, skeletal muscle, pancreas, kidney, brain, and in white and red blood cells. Second, normal ALT/AST levels can be found in the setting of hepatic injury. This is common in patients with chronic hepatitis C and in patients with cirrhosis because of the absence of continuing injury. Because the liver is responsible for making clotting factors, stopping the aspirin is prudent until the etiology of has been determined.

42. ***c***
These liver enzymes are elevated. In looking at the numbers, the ALT is grossly elevated compared to the AST. A diagnosis of hepatitis is far more common when the ALT is elevated. AST becomes the dominant liver enzyme when the patient has consumed a substance that causes the liver to be damaged. Examples of this are found in the choices suggesting acetaminophen, alcohol, and drug abuse.

43. ***b***
Group A Streptococcus is usually characterized by multiple symptoms with an abrupt onset. Sore throat is usually accompanied by fever, headache. GI symptoms are common too; nausea, vomiting and abdominal pain are usual. Even without treatment, symptoms usually resolve in 3-5 days.

44. ***b***
Approximately 70% of patients with Parkinson's Disease have tremor as the presenting symptom. The tremor typically involves the hand but can involve the legs, jaw, lips, tongue. It seldom involves the head.

45. *a*
The most common manifestation of end-organ damage in hypertensive adolescents is left ventricular hypertrophy (LVH). According to the "National high blood pressure education program working group on high blood pressure in children and adolescents", as many as 41% of children who have hypertension, have LVH identifiable on ECG.

46. *c*
The guidelines recommend macrolide use or doxycycline for initial treatment of uncomplicated pneumonia in outpatients who are otherwise healthy and have not had recent antibiotic exposure. The initial choices can be any of these: azithromycin, clarithromycin, or doxycycline. These agents are chosen because they cover atypical pathogens, the most likely pathogen in this population. Fluoroquinolones are commonly used first line in these patients; however, the guidelines strongly recommend using fluoroquinolones for patients with co-morbidities or those who have recent antibiotic exposure.

47. *b*
The visualization of yeasts and/or pseudohypha in saliva indicates a fungal infection, often Candida species. Budding is a process by which yeasts reproduce.

48. *c*
The most common pathogen in upper and lower urinary tract infections is E. coli. Approximately 70-95% of infection can be attributed to E. coli. As patients age, the incidence of E. coli declines (though it is still the most common pathogen), the incidence of Klebsiella increases.

49. *a*
This patient has a positive hepatitis B surface antigen (HBsAg). Therefore, he has hepatitis B. A positive HBcAb is found in patients who either have hepatitis now or who have had it. The surface antibody (HBsAb) would be expected to be negative in a patient with positive surface antigen (HBsAg) because these 2 markers will not be positive at the same time.

50. *c*
Body size is an important determinant in blood pressure in adolescents. Blood pressure tables are NOT based on body mass index. The tables include 50th, 90th, 95th, and 99th percentiles based on age, height, and gender. The age is up to 17 years. After this age, all blood pressures are based on adult values. At least 3 separate elevated blood pressure readings are required for diagnosis.

51. *c*
Grapefruit is a potent inhibitor of the cytochrome P450 enzyme system. Statins and calcium channel blockers are two infamous drug interactions that occur with grapefruit and grapefruit juice. Because they inhibit metabolism of the statin, the patient continues to have statin in circulation because he cannot significantly metabolize the medication. When the next day's dose is taken, its effect is coupled with the effect of the

previous day's dose. The effect is cumulative. Hepatoxicity can quickly develop. The simvastatin must be stopped immediately! The liver enzymes must be followed until they return to normal; which could take weeks, months or even longer.

52. ***d***
Diarrhea is extremely common. Evaluation of diarrhea should take place when specific criteria suggest severe illness. In addition to those listed, some conditions which indicate further work-up are: profuse watery diarrhea with signs of hypovolemia, passage of >6 unformed stools per 24 hours or a duration of illness > 48 hours, recent antibiotic use or recent hospitalization, and diarrhea in a patient ≥ 70 years old.

53. ***d***
Serotonin syndrome is a clinical diagnosis characterized by too much serotonergic activity in the central nervous system. There is no way to measure serotonin levels at this time. Therefore, no clinical laboratory or imaging study can identify this syndrome. However, these studies may rule out other conditions.

54. ***b***
The Framingham study was initiated in Framingham, Massachusetts in the early 1970s. The participants agreed to follow-up study (interviews and physical exam) every 2 years in a long-term study. This cohort study has examined what happens to disease over time. These are termed prospective studies because the events of interest occur after the study has begun.

55. ***a***
CBC with an elevated white count simply indicates that an infection is likely. It is not specific for the location of the infection. Urinalysis should be performed to rule out a UTI. Symptoms can mimic an appendicitis. Serum pregnancy test must be performed since this patient could have an ectopic pregnancy. Positive pelvic cultures could indicate pelvic inflammatory disease as the cause of the pain.

56. ***c***
X-rays are of little benefit in patients with back pain unless the underlying etiology is infection, fracture, malignancy, disc space narrowing, degenerative changes, or spondylolisthesis. They do not detect herniated discs and are generally of little benefit. If they are obtained, it is usually done after back pain of 4 weeks duration.

57. ***b***
Lymphocytes tend to be the predominant white cell present during viral infections. Hepatitis B is a viral infection. The total white count will likely be decreased. This happens very often in the presence of viral infections. A bacterial infection is frequently evidenced by an elevated leukocyte count, a increased neutrophil count, and a decreased lymphocyte count.

58. ***c***
Naproxen is an NSAID. NSAIDs produce sodium retention and hence, water retention.

This produces many systemic effects such as an increase in blood pressure, lower extremity edema, increased workload of the heart, and inhibition of prostaglandin synthesis. Patients with hypertension and chronic heart failure should use NSAIDs cautiously. Furosemide would be expected to have a favorable effect on a hypertensive patient's blood pressure. Lovastatin would not be expected to increase or decrease blood pressure. Loratadine is an antihistamine. These do not increase blood pressure; decongestants predictably increase blood pressure.

59. ***b***
In a patient with known aortic stenosis (AS) who has been asymptomatic for decades, one should be alert for symptoms that will precede angina, CHF, and syncope. Dizziness precedes syncope in these patients and so this is an early indication that the patient is becoming symptomatic from his AS. Once symptoms develop, there is a rapid downhill course. Therefore, being alert for dizziness, chest discomfort, or exercise intolerance are very important symptoms to assess in previously asymptomatic patients who have aortic stenosis.

60. ***a***
The natural course of aortic regurgitation (AR) is that the patient has a long asymptomatic period with slowing of activities but remains essentially asymptomatic. Then, shortness of breath develops with activity and finally, shortness of breath at rest. The left ventricle eventually fails unless the aorta is replaced.

61. ***a***
Doxycycline is frequently chosen first line to treat Lyme Disease. However, numerous studies have demonstrated that amoxicillin and cefuroxime have equal efficacy as doxycycline in treatment of early Lyme Disease. These drugs are recommended in patients who exhibit erythema migrans. Doxycycline is not recommended in children less than 9 years of age.

62. ***a***
Patients with Type II diabetes should be screened for renal nephropathy at diagnosis. Nephropathy takes several years to develop but develops in about 30% of patients with diabetes. Diabetic nephropathy is defined as the presence of diabetes and more than 300 mg/d of albuminuria on at least 2 occasions separated by 3-6 months. Screening should take place annually.

63. ***a***
Examples of drugs that target the renin-angiotensin-aldosterone system are angiotensin converting enzyme (ACE) inhibitors and angiotensin receptor blockers (ARBs). These drugs are particularly beneficial to patients with diabetic nephropathy because they both prevent and treat diabetic nephropathy. Additionally, these agents also lower blood pressure that has been shown to be renoprotective. Management of glucose levels and hypertension is especially important in preventing diabetic nephropathy, but so is aggressive management of hyperlipidemia.

64. ***b***
An ARB, like candesartan potentially can produce hyperkalemia because its mechanism of action is in the renin-angiotensin-aldosterone system and potassium is spared there. Potassium supplements will be additive and should be avoided because of the potential for hyperkalemia.

65. ***a***
"Silvery scales" describes the hallmark finding in psoriasis. This is a chronic condition. It is not infectious, contagious, or acute. There are several variants, but "silvery scales" is the most common form.

66. ***c***
Classic findings in a urinary tract infection (UTI) are positive leukocytes and nitrites. Leukocytes indicate the presence of white cells in the urine. Nitrates are a normal finding in a urine specimen. Nitrites are not normal in the urine. Positive nitrites indicate that an organism in the urine is consuming nitrates for nutrition. Hematuria indicates the presence of red blood cells in the urine. This is not unusual in the presence of a UTI.

67. ***a***
Mononucleosis (mono) is a viral infection. This is usually characterized by a predominance of lymphocytes. Eosinophilia is typical in parasitic infections and allergic reactions. Leukocytosis is a predominance of white cells but is not specific for mono. Monocytes can rise in mono, but their presence is not specific to mono.

68. ***b***
History of gestational diabetes conveys an 83% chance of developing Type II diabetes (within 17 years of delivery). Hyperlipidemia by itself is not a risk factor for diabetes, though it is commonly seen in conjunction with diabetes. Infrequent, regular exercise increases the risk of increased BMI, but by itself is not a risk factor for Type II diabetes. A family history of Type II diabetes increases the risk of developing it, but this is not true of Type I diabetes.

69. ***a***
Antacids should be avoided because they will inhibit absorption of iron. Other substances that should be avoided an hour before or 2 hours after iron supplementation are tetracyclines and dairy products. Foods that are rich in vitamin C, such as grapefruit juice should be encouraged because they enhance iron absorption. Potassium supplements have no known effect on iron absorption. Heavy exercise does not inhibit iron absorption.

70. ***b***
Anemia of chronic disease is usually a normocytic, normochromic anemia. In about 30% of cases, it is microcytic. The red blood cells that characterize anemia of chronic disease tend to be normal in size and hemoglobin content. Hence, the term for anemia of chronic disease, normocytic normochromic anemia.

correction: this patient has normal nonfasting glucose - no further testing necessary

71. ***b*** a

This patient has impaired fasting glucose. This is diagnosed when 2 fasting glucose values are between 100 mg/dL and 125 mg/dL. There is no need for further testing. At this time, this patient does not meet the criteria for diabetes and does not need further testing to arrive at a diagnosis.

72. ***a***

One of the major components of gallstones is estrogen. A patient with underlying gallbladder disease should not receive oral contraceptives (OC) since they will increase estrogen exposure and theoretically, formation of gallstones. Depression, hypothyroidism and varicose veins do not increase the risk of gallbladder disease.

73. ***d***

The nasal septum separates the right from left nostrils. It is made of thick cartilage and is covered with mucous membrane. It can be injured from foreign substances that contact it, like cocaine. A nasal septal erosion or perforation should always be assumed to have been from sniffing toxic substances in the nose, not nasal steroids.

74. ***a***

Exposure to an STD always increases the likelihood of contracting an STD. However, the patient is at very high risk of developing pelvic inflammatory disease when there is an implanted foreign body. An example of this is an intrauterine device (IUD). The risk is also increased with a diaphragm, but, because it is not implanted for long periods at a time, the risk is less than with an IUD.

75. ***c***

The second leading cause of cough in adults is asthma. Cough due to asthma is often accompanied by episodic wheezing or dyspnea, though some patients with asthma only cough. This is termed "cough variant asthma". The clinical presentation of asthma varies but hyper responsiveness of the airways is a typical finding.

76. ***c***

The findings of positive Kernig's and Brudzinski's signs are highly suggestive of meningitis. Kernig's sign is elicited by leg extension; then observing for neck pain and flexion. Brudzinski's sign is elicited by passively flexing the neck and observing for flexion of the legs.

77. ***b***

An exacerbation of atopic dermatitis is termed eczema. Under normal conditions, the skin should be kept well lubricated with emollients. These should be used liberally as often as needed to prevent skin from becoming dry. Dry skin is more prone to exacerbations. When an exacerbation occurs, topical steroids are very effective and are commonly used. The lowest potency steroid that resolves the exacerbation should be used.

78. ***a***
The predominant symptom of patients who exhibit pulpitis is pain especially elicited by thermal changes, cold and hot. The pain can become severe and patients are ill appearing. Pus may be seen around the gum area or may be restricted to the pulp cavity. Caries and gingivitis do not produce pus. Periodontitis is characterized by gingival inflammation and pain. Pus is not present in this disease. A periodontal abscess produces pain and pus, but the pus is usually only expressed after probing.

79. ***b***
The mechanism of injury suggests a possible ankle sprain or fracture. However, the foot pain is suspicious of a possible 5th metatarsal fracture, the most common fracture occurring with an ankle sprain. He should receive an x-ray of the foot and ankle and should be kept non-weight bearing until the fracture is ruled out.

80. ***a***
An injectable form of progestin, medroxyprogesterone acetate administered every 3 months by injection increases the risk of osteopenia and osteoporosis. Most learned authorities recommend calcium supplementation 500 mg T.I.D. while using this product.

81. ***b***
In patients with lead toxicity, many metabolic changes can occur. Some patients develop pica; many develop a sideroblastic anemia. This occurs because iron is unable to be incorporated into the heme molecule. An iron deficiency anemia results. This is treated by eliminating the patient's exposure to lead, increasing iron in the diet, and supplementing with iron.

82. ***b***
Cluster headaches are always unilateral. The affected side produces a red, teary eye with nasal congestion on the affected side. Tension headaches are always bilateral with no nausea or photosensitivity associated with them.

83. ***c***
If state law requires reporting of the STD, it should be reported. Patient names or other identifying data are not part of the reporting process and so, the NP's patient should not worry about being identified and associated with this finding. If the NP does not report it, she has violated state law. If she reports it but doesn't tell the patient, she is not being honest with the patient. Reporting data to public health with deliberate elimination of required illness details is inaccurate reporting and doesn't meet state law.

84. ***d***
All 50 states require reporting of animal bites to animal control or the state's appropriate authority for reporting animal bites. It sounds unlikely that the dog could be infected with rabies, but rabies prophylaxis must be considered after all history and information has been taken.

85. *c*
Multiple sclerosis is a disease of the central nervous system characterized by demyelination of the nerve cells. This produces varied neurological symptoms and deficits. This disease is typical in women between the ages of 16 and 40 years. It is rarely diagnosed after age 50 years.

86. *a*
HIV specifically attacks the number of circulating CD4 cells. There is very little variability in CD4 counts. There are a number of factors that will cause minor fluctuation in counts. These include things like seasonal and diurnal variations, infections, and steroid intake. The normal CD4 cell count ranges from 800-1050/mm^3. Every year after infection with HIV, the CD4 cell count decreases by about 50/ mm^3 per year. There is great variation in individual decreases. Some individuals experience very little decrease in counts, other patients experience great decreases in counts. Oral antiretroviral agents slow down the CD4 decreases.

87. *d*
MRSA is methicillin resistant Staph aureus. This is very common in the community and is typically treated with sulfa medications like TMPS (Bactrim DS and Septra DS). If the patient is sulfa allergic, this could not be used. A narrow spectrum antibiotic that can be used is doxycycline or minocycline. It is given twice daily and is generally well tolerated. MRSA is resistant to the antibiotics mentioned and so they should NOT be used to treat it.

88. *c*
The exact mechanism for increased urinary tract infections is unknown, but it is believed to be due to nonoxynol-9 induced changes in vaginal flora. Another consideration is the possible contamination that might accompany insertion before each episode of coitus. Care and cleaning of the diaphragm must take place, or that could be a contributor to increased bacteria.

89. *a*
There is an inconsequential rise in PSA levels within 72 hours after DRE. DRE should not prevent a patient from having a PSA level measured at any time.

90. *c*
Papilledema represents swelling of the optic nerve head and disc secondary to increased intracranial pressure (ICP). It is not a common finding in patients with headaches; only those with headache secondary to ICP. The pressure disrupts fluid flow within the nerve and swelling results. The cardinal symptom of ICP is a headache; papilledema is a secondary finding.

91. *b*
Secondary syphilis can present as a rash on the body, but more commonly as rash on the palms of the hands or soles of the feet. This can persist for up to 6 weeks. It will

resolve without treatment, however the patient will still be infected with syphilis. Primary syphilis is characterized by a chancre. This is a painless lesion that can persist for 1-5 weeks. It will resolve without treatment.

92. ***b***
Screening tests for depression include questions about depressed mood or other symptoms that have lasted at least two weeks. This is an important time frame. Typical screening questions ask: "in the past 2 weeks, have you felt little interest or pleasure in doing things" or "in the past 2 weeks, have you felt down, depressed, or hopeless"?

93. ***a***
During a period of mania, common symptoms are inflated self-esteem and grandiosity (like a buying a baby grand piano), decreased need for sleep, hyper verbosity (excessive talking), racing thoughts and flight of ideas, distractibility, and excessive involvement in pleasurable activities that can be associated with very painful consequences later.

94. ***b***
The second leading cause of cough in adults is asthma. Cough due to asthma is often accompanied by episodic wheezing or dyspnea, though some patients with asthma only cough. This is termed "cough variant asthma". The clinical presentation of asthma varies but hyper responsiveness of the airways is a typical finding.

95. ***b***
CT scan of the abdomen is the diagnostic test of choice for this patient with suspected diverticulitis. The CT scan is able to demonstrate inflammatory changes in the colonic wall, colonic diverticula, thickening of the bowel wall, fistula formation, peritonitis, and other complications associated with diverticulitis. A chest and abdominal x-rays are commonly ordered and can help exclude other causes of abdominal pain, but do not help diagnose diverticulitis. Barium enema would be contraindicated if there were a potential for perforation. Ultrasound is much less widely used than CT.

96. ***b***
This patient has hyperthyroidism. The symptoms of fatigue are present in patients with both hypo and hyperthyroidism. The very low TSH measurement in the presence of weight loss very likely indicates a patient who has hyperthyroidism. The TSH should be evaluated on a different day and a T4 should be measured too.

97. ***c***
A common side effect of oral contraceptives is nausea. This is probably related to increased hormone levels (estrogen and progesterone). An easy way to combat nausea is to take the pill before going to sleep at night. Most patients will sleep through the symptom of nausea.

98. ***c***
Generally, a PSA measurement less than 4 ng/mL is considered normal. However, the PSA velocity (the rate of PSA change over time), is concerning. A PSA velocity > .35

ng/mL per year is associated with high risk of death from prostate cancer. This patient should have prostate biopsy by a urologist.

99. ***b***
The herb that the patient is asking about is probably black cohosh, Actaea racemosa. It is a phytoestrogen. This means that it provides estrogen from a plant source. If estrogen is contraindicated in a patient, then it does not matter whether it comes from plants or is produced synthetically. There is a potential safety concern in using black cohosh in women with breast cancer or who are at high risk of breast cancer because of the estrogenic effects that are possible on the breasts.

100. ***b***
Tanner staging, or sexual maturity ratings are very predictable changes that occur with puberty. These should be assessed. In females, breasts and pubic hair signify specific pubertal changes that constitute maturation. These are not age specific, but at 15 years a Tanner Stage 3 or more would be characteristic of expected maturation. Menses should follow soon.

101. ***a***
A BMI of 26 or higher does increase the risk of developing Type II diabetes. Mediterranean decent does not impart a specific risk factor for development of Type II diabetes, but African-Americans and Asian-Americans are at increased the risk of developing Type II diabetes. Hypothyroidism may be found in some patients with diabetes, but this does not increase the risk.

102. ***b***
Shingles is herpes zoster. It characteristically affects a single dermatome. Grouped vesicles on an erythematous base can be seen in some patients with shingles, but this is not unique to shingles. In fact, it is typical in many viral infections. Crusting may be seen with shingles, chicken pox, or impetigo. Pain, burning, and itching describes the symptoms that some patients have with shingles, but not all patients report itching with shingles.

103. ***c***
Paroxetine is a selective serotonin reuptake inhibitor (SSRI). Nausea, headache, diarrhea are not unusual symptoms observed in patients who take SSRIs. The symptoms are more common with initiation of therapy and with dose increases. The symptoms tend to subside after a week or so.

104. ***a***
In males, gonorrhea can have a varied presentation. Gonorrhea produces a purulent inflammation of the mucous membranes, urethral discharge, and dysuria. It can be diagnosed with a urethral culture, a urine screen, or nucleic acid tests. Urine screens are not preferred, but are commonly used for people who are difficult to screen, like adolescents or pediatric patients.

105. *a*
Calcium carbonate is an antacid. It provides rapid changes in gastric pH. This provides relief that can be noticed immediately. The increase in pH lasts for about 30 minutes. Ranitidine is an H2 blocker. It provides relief in 1-2 hours. This usually lasts for about 6-12 hours. Amantadine is an antiviral not used to treat GERD. Pantoprazole is a proton pump inhibitor. This provides relief after several hours or days of daily consumption.

106. *b*
The presence of petechiae on the lower legs (or anywhere on the body) should prompt the NP to consider a problem that is platelet related. A CBC should be checked to assess the platelet count and any evidence of anemia from blood loss. If the platelet count is found to be low, referral to hematology should be done. Blood cultures are of no value in this patient who has no other complaints.

107. *b*
Vitamin B-12 deficiency is identified much earlier now because it is suspected earlier in older patients. However, patients do not always present with macrocytosis and anemia. Unexplained neurological symptoms like memory issues, weakness, paresthesias, should prompt suspicion and subsequent measurement of vitamin B-12 levels. Glossitis is an inflammation of the tongue that is associated with pernicious anemia. Glossitis as a lone finding should prompt measurement of B-12.

108. *d*
Metoprolol is a beta-blocker and is NOT associated with weight gain. Unfortunately, most drugs used to treat Type 2 diabetes are associated with weight gain. Most patients with Type 2 diabetes are overweight and so weight loss is difficult.

109. *b*
The primary cause of pruritis associated with hives is histamine. Histamine is released from mast cells with other substances of anaphylaxis. Anti-histamines are the primary therapeutic intervention. Since both H1 and H2 receptors participate in allergic inflammation, both H1 and H2 blockers are helpful in relieving symptoms in these patients. Topical steroid is not helpful. Calcium channel blockers (nifedipine) are used as a "last resort" for refractory cases of urticaria. Steroids do not inhibit mast cell degradation and so are less helpful than thought. Steroids can be used for persistent attacks of acute urticaria if antihistamines are not helpful.

110. *a*
Kegel exercises are exercises used to strengthen the pelvic muscles. The usual recommendation is 3 sets of 8-12 slow velocity contractions sustained for 6-8 seconds each. These should be performed 3-4 times weekly for about 3-4 months. Kegel exercises are now known to help patients who have mixed incontinence.

111. *a*
This patient probably has Bell's palsy that affects the facial nerve. This is an acute

event affecting only a single side of the face. Stroke must always be considered in the differential but is unlikely in a patient who is otherwise healthy. Early treatment with oral steroids like prednisone (60-80 mg/d and tapered over 7-14 days) should be started within 72 hours of the onset of symptoms. This has been found to decrease the risk of permanent facial paralysis. Oral antiviral agents may be of benefit because of the likely possibility of Bell's palsy having an herpetic etiology.

112. *b*
Nocturnal paresthesias are typical in patients who have carpal tunnel syndrome. A patient will complain of nighttime numbness, tingling, or "sleeping" hands and arms. This is a result of compression of the median nerve that traverses through the carpal tunnel. If the nerve is compressed, the symptoms (nocturnal paresthesias) usually result. With surgical decompression, symptoms usually abate.

113. *a*
At age 50 years, males of average prostate cancer risk should have PSA measurement with or without digital rectal exam (DRE). If they are deemed to be of high risk because of a family history (first degree relative with prostate cancer before age 65 years) or race (African American), screening discussions should take place at age 40-45 years. If initial PSA is $\geq$ 2.5 ng/mL; annual testing should take place. If the initial PSA is < 2.5 ng/mL; test every 2 years.

114. *a*
Bacterial vaginosis is a clinical syndrome where high concentrations of anaerobic bacteria replace normal vaginal flora. This produces many symptoms that cause complaints in women. The typical symptoms are a "fishy" odor emanating from the vagina, itching, and vulvovaginal pruritis and burning. A typical complaint is an unpleasant odor after coitus.

115. *d*
Metoprolol is a beta blocker. Beta blockers are known to reduce morbidity and mortality associated with CHF. Verapamil is a calcium channel blocker. These are contraindicated because they decrease contractility of the heart. Furosemide and digoxin will improve symptoms but not long-term outcomes. Their main benefit is in treating symptomatic patients.

116. *c*
Tinea versicolor is typically visualized during the spring and summer months when a patient has become tanned. The areas that are infected do not tan and so become very noticeable. The chest and back are common areas to observe tinea versicolor. There can be 100 or more in some infections. This can be treated with topical selenium sulfide or an oral antifungal agent.

117. *c*
Patients with anxiety complain of difficulty falling asleep. Patients with depression complain of early morning awakening and difficulty remaining asleep. A manic patient

may state that he never feels tired enough to sleep.

118. ***d***
A patient with dysuria and vaginal discharge should be assumed to have an STD until proven otherwise. She could have only an STD, or an STD and a UTI. She should have a vaginal exam with cultures and swab for trichomoniasis. The abdomen should be assessed because of the potential for pelvic inflammatory disease if STDs are present. A urinalysis can exclude a urinary tract infection.

119. ***b***
An ankle inversion causes the sole of the foot to roll into the body. This produces stretching of the lateral malleolar ligaments of the ankle and a lateral ankle sprain. Injury to the medial ligaments is a more serious injury and can produce a medial ankle sprain or an avulsion fracture. No information in the stem of the question suggests a fracture or tear of the ligament, though all sprains produce varying degrees of ligament tears.

120. ***b***
He could have hemorrhoids. It is unusual for a patient to have lower GI bleeding from one week's use of an NSAID. He is more likely to have upper GI symptoms (or bleeding) because of prostaglandin synthesis inhibition. This patient needs a colonoscopy to determine the etiology of the bleeding. The NSAID should be stopped.

121. ***b***
This probably indicates BPH. These findings of the prostate gland do not rule out prostate cancer. A prostate infection usually produces greater elevations in PSA as well as a tender gland. A PSA > 2.5 ng/mL in this instance may reflect PSA changes seen with BPH. An important historical note would be the value of his last PSA for comparison as well as to assess for PSA velocity.

122. ***b***
This patient's symptoms indicate that he could have conjunctivitis. Assessment of patients with eye complaints should always begin with assessment of vision in each eye. This should be documented.

123. ***b***
Hearing loss associated with aging is termed presbycusis and is a form of sensorineural hearing loss. This can be influenced by a number of factors including heredity. Conductive hearing loss involves the external canal and the middle ear. Sound cannot travel beyond the middle ear. The 8th cranial nerve and the inner ear are involved in sensorineural hearing loss. Noise damage can produce a sensorineural hearing loss. This usually occurs over time but is not necessarily associated with aging.

124. ***c***
The range is the difference between the smallest and the largest observation in a group of values.

125. *b*
A Vitamin B12 deficiency can produce an anemia called pernicious anemia. This is most commonly found in older adults and is characterized by macrocytosis. In other words, the red cells are larger than expected. Microcytosis may be seen in iron deficiency anemia or thalassemia. Leukocytosis refers to large numbers of white cells in the blood stream. Thrombocytosis refers to an increased number of platelets in the blood stream.

126. *b*
The flu is diagnosed based on the results of a flu swab and the patient's clinical presentation. A patient with influenza usually demonstrates Flu A (the most predominant strain during an outbreak) or Flu B (the strain identified occasionally during flu season but more often, throughout the rest of the year) if he is infected.

127. *a*
Long acting insulin mimics the amount of insulin the pancreas produces at a steady rate throughout the day and night. Adjustments in doses of long-acting insulin are typically based on the AM fasting glucose values. The other blood sugars reflect blood sugars in relation to meals.

128. *c*
Sciatica is caused by nerve root irritation. This produces a burning pain that usually radiates down the posterior aspect of the leg. The pain is often associated with numbness and tingling. Pain usually increases with coughing, sneezing, or straining. Relief of pain usually occurs in positions where nerve root irritation is minimized. These are commonly standing or side lying. It is usually worsened by sitting.

129. *a*
Wheezing is typical of asthma, but one must consider pneumonia in an asthma patient who presents with wheezing in only the upper right lobe. Fever is not typical of asthma or an exacerbation.

130. *b*
This patient has symptoms of cauda equina syndrome. This is a medical emergency. Urinary retention with overflow incontinence is typical. Other symptoms that can accompany this are saddle anesthesia, sciatica down both legs, and leg weakness, evidenced by the inability to support one's own weight on the affected side.

131. *b*
Trichomonas can be treated with metronidazole orally. This is usually effective and is generally well tolerated as long as the patient avoids alcohol. Alcohol in the presence of metronidazole can produce a disulfiram reaction. Another medication used to treat trichomonas is tinidazole. The exact mechanism of tinidazole is unknown, but is an antiprotozoal.

132. ***b***
This dermatitis is intensely pruritic and involves the palms and soles and lateral aspects of the fingers. Over a couple of weeks, the vesicles desquamate. Recurrences are common. Seborrheic dermatitis affects only hairy areas of the body. The vesicles might raise suspicion of a viral infection, but this is not the case.

133. ***b***
The herald patch associated with pityriasis rosea is typically found on the trunk. It precedes the generalized Christmas tree pattern rash that is easily noted on the rest of the body. Because it appears round and has a darkened center, it looks like a ringworm. In fact, it is commonly mistaken for ringworm until the Christmas tree pattern rash appears. It would be unusual to identify the herald patch on a body part other than the trunk, but there are case reports of this.

134. ***c***
These agents are particularly effective in the treatment of nasal congestion and would be a good choice for the patient in this scenario. Intranasal glucocorticoids are effective in relieving nasal congestion, discharge, itching, and sneezing. A trial of stopping the oral antihistamine could be tried in this patient. Symptoms would determine whether the antihistamine should be resumed.

135. ***b***
Otitis externa is "swimmer's ear". It is characterized by tragal tenderness. Otitis externa is an infection of the external canal. When the tragus is tender, it will be difficult to insert a speculum to examine the ear.

136. ***d***
Patients with viral gastroenteritis should be treated symptomatically. The goal of therapy is to prevent dehydration and replace electrolyte losses. Loperamide can decrease abdominal cramping and symptoms of diarrhea but should only be used in adults. Careful use or avoidance is suggested in older adults and children less than age 5 years.

137. ***c***
Rheumatoid arthritis is characterized by pain, symmetrical involvement of multiple joints, morning stiffness lasting longer than one hour. Patients with osteoarthritis have morning stiffness lasting less than one hour, usually less than 30 minutes. Weight loss is not typical in either of these diseases. Bouchard's nodes are typical in osteoarthritis and represent enlargement of the proximal interphalangeal joint.

138. ***b***
The class of medications called "triptans" work to eradicate migraine headaches by producing vasoconstriction. This can produce a potentially serious drug-disease interaction in patients with hypertension. An episode of severe hypertension can result. Triptans may be used in patients with well-controlled hypertension, but a hypertensive episode can always occur.

139. ***a***

Patients with diabetes can present with polyuria. An assessment of the patient's risk factors should be done with strong consideration given to checking glucose levels. If this is normal, other diagnoses to consider are urge incontinence and vaginitis. The patient's medications should be reviewed for medications producing urgency, like diuretics or herbal supplements.

140. ***a***

This patient probably has acute bacterial prostatitis. A common presenting symptom is prostate tenderness, especially with bowel movements. A common cause in a 30 year-old male who is sexually active is infection with chlamydia or trichomonas. He should be screened for sexually transmitted diseases. If these are negative, a urinary pathogen is the likely cause. Penile and urine cultures should be collected.

141. ***a***

Vitamin B 12 produces a macrocytic anemia. This is characterized by large red cells. Anemia of chronic disease usually produces a normocytic anemia, but about 30% of the time produces a microcytic one. Thalassemia and iron deficiency produce microcytic anemias.

142. ***d***

A report of a knee "locking" is a classic complaint of a patient who has a meniscal tear. Sometimes a knee effusion accompanies this but not always. Often loss of range of motion secondary to pain is observed. Recollection of an injury is not always part of history, but it occurred during some event in the past. A meniscal tear represents a disruption of the pads between the femoral condyles and the tibial plateaus. Clinical exam and MRI are usually used to make the diagnosis.

143. ***a***

Clinical inertia is an actual term used to describe healthcare providers who fail to intensify therapy despite patients not reaching goal. There are many reasons given as to why this takes place, but healthcare providers can potentially modify these.

144. ***b***

This patient has isolated systolic hypertension. According to JNC VII and other learned authorities, this is best treated with a long-acting calcium channel blocker, particularly the ones that end in "pine'. These belong to the class of calcium channel blockers termed dihydropyridines. Thiazide diuretics are not potent enough to decrease this patient's blood pressure into normal range and its effect is not additive when combined with calcium channel blockers.

145. ***d***

Microalbuminuria takes years to manifest after diabetes has developed. Microalbuminuria should never be diagnosed on a single reading because many factors can produce false microalbuminuria. Heavy exercise, elevated glucose levels, infection,

and others can produce false positive microalbuminuria. The ideal time for microalbuminuria to be repeated is 3-6 months after the first abnormal measurement. This gives some time for glucose values to improve and can help rule out false positive results.

146. ***c***
It is very common that other co-morbidities are present with eating disorders. Anorexia is commonly accompanied by anxiety, especially at mealtimes. Neurotransmitters are thought to play some role in the pathogenesis of anorexia nervosa. This is common in the United States in women especially between the ages of 15 and 30 years. It is relatively uncommon in males.

147. ***b***
Men with benign prostatic hypertrophy (BPH) have some classic symptoms that include: hesitancy, urgency, post-void dribbling, and frequency. They will seek help for these symptoms. Although these symptoms are typical of BPH, prostate cancer can also present in the same way.

148. ***a***
These are cotton wool spots. They are due to swelling of the surface layer of the retina. Swelling occurs because of impaired blood flow to the retina. The most common causes of cotton wool spots are diabetes and high blood pressure. A microaneurysm is the earliest manifestation of a diabetic retinopathy. These appear as small round dark red dots on the retinal surface. Exudates are an accumulation of lipid and protein. These are typically bright, reflective white or cream colored lesions seen on the retina.

149. ***b***
The patient is using his bronchodilator ("rescue" medication) more than twice weekly. This is a signal to the healthcare provider that the patient's asthma is not well controlled and another medication needs to be used. The next step for this patient is a trial of an inhaled steroid. This should relieve his symptoms and decrease the use of his rescue medication. If an inhaled bronchodilator is overused, it will not continue to produce bronchodilation over time.

150. ***b***
Sulfamethoxazole is the sulfa component in Bactrim DS. It is contraindicated in patients with a sulfa allergy. There is no allergic potential with the antihyperglycemic agents, sulfonylureas. Naproxen and cefazolin have no contraindications if a patient has a sulfa allergy. Some HIV protease inhibitors have the sulfonyl arylamine chemical group that is responsible for the allergic reaction.

Family Exam #1 Questions

1. **Which finding below is considered "within normal limits"?**

    a. **A diastolic murmur in an 18 year-old**
    b. **An INR of 2.0 in a patient taking warfarin**
    c. **Cholesterol level of 205 in a 15 year-old**
    d. **Blood pressure of 160/70 in a 75 year-old**

2. **A three year-old child presents with hematuria, petechiae, and a platelet count of 50,000 (Normal = 150,000-450,000/ml). The rest of his CBC is normal. He had an upper respiratory infection about 2 weeks ago. On exam today, he is found to have petechiae and bruises. The most likely diagnosis is:**

    a. **polycythemia vera.**
    b. **acute lymphocytic leukemia (ALL).**
    c. **von Willebrand's disease.**
    d. **idiopathic thrombocytopenia purpura (ITP).**

3. **The most common place for indirect inguinal hernias to develop is:**

    a. **the internal inguinal ring.**
    b. **the external inguinal ring.**
    c. **Hesselbach's triangle.**
    d. **femoral ring.**

4. **The rubella vaccine is contraindicated in pregnant women because:**

    a. **it can cause rubella in the mother.**
    b. **it can cause rubella in the infant.**
    c. **it does not cross the placenta.**
    d. **neurological toxicity may occur in the mother.**

5. **The most appropriate time to begin screening for renal nephropathy in a patient with Type 1 diabetes is:**

    a. **at diagnosis.**
    b. **once annually after diagnosis.**
    c. **2-3 years after diagnosis.**
    d. **5 years after diagnosis.**

6. **A two year-old with sickle cell anemia (SCA) should receive which immunizations?**

   a. **All routine childhood immunizations at an accelerated rate**
   b. **All routine childhood immunizations at a decelerated rate**
   c. **All routine childhood immunizations at the usual time**
   d. **Immunizations should be limited in this group**

7. **A 43 year-old patient who has been diagnosed with hepatitis B has the following laboratory values. How should they be interpreted based on these values?**

   HCV IgG (-), RIBA (radio immuno blot assay) (-)

   a. **The patient has hepatitis B and hepatitis C.**
   b. **The patient does not have hepatitis C.**
   c. **The patient could have hepatitis C.**
   d. **The results are indeterminate.**

8. **Immunizations are not routinely given during the first trimester of pregnancy. Which immunization(s) may be safely given during the first trimester of pregnancy?**

   a. **Varicella and MMR**
   b. **Influenza**
   c. **Pneumococcus**
   d. **Hepatitis A and B**

9. **What are the most common signs and symptoms associated with mononucleosis?**

   a. **Fatigue and lymphadenopathy**
   b. **Cough and pharyngitis**
   c. **Splenomegaly and fever**
   d. **Rash and pharyngitis**

10. **In a three year-old with fever, which finding might precipitate a febrile seizure?**

    a. **A sudden decrease in body temperature after high fever**
    b. **A worsening pneumonia**
    c. **Initiation of an antibiotic**
    d. **Returning to daycare prior to being fever free for 24 hours**

11. A 40 year-old patient has the following laboratory values. How should they be interpreted?
HBsAg (-), HBsAb (+), HBcAb (-)

a. **The patient had hepatitis.**
b. **The patient has hepatitis.**
c. **The patient should consider immunization.**
d. **The patient has been immunized.**

12. HIV testing during pregnancy:

a. **is recommended by many learned authorities.**
b. **is an "opt-in" approach.**
c. **is better performed in the third trimester.**
d. **produces many false positives.**

13. Drugs that target the renin-angiotensin-aldosterone system are particularly beneficial in patients with:

a. **hypertension.**
b. **chronic heart failure.**
c. **kidney stones.**
d. **diabetic nephropathy.**

14. Babies up to one year of age are called:

a. **newborns.**
b. **toddlers.**
c. **newbies.**
d. **infants.**

15. A 25 year-old male patient with subacute bacterial epididymitis should be treated initially with:

a. **an oral quinolone.**
b. **doxycycline.**
c. **anti-inflammatories and analgesics.**
d. **ice and scrotal support.**

16. In a viable pregnancy:

a. **fetal heart tones can be heard at 4-6 weeks.**
b. **heart rates can exceed 240 beats/minute.**
c. **fetal heart tones are audible at about 9-12 weeks.**
d. **the fetus begins to respire at 6-8 weeks.**

17. **Nagele's rule estimates:**

    a. **the age of the fetus.**
    b. **days past conception.**
    c. **timing of prenatal interventions.**
    d. **date of confinement (EDC).**

18. **A 7 year-old enters the nurse practitioner clinic. There is no evidence that he has received any immunizations. What should be administered today?**

    a. **Hepatitis B, Tdap, Hib, IPV, MMR**
    b. **Td, Hib, IPV, varicella**
    c. **Hepatitis B, Tdap, IPV, varicella, MMR**
    d. **Hepatitis B, IPV, varicella, MMR**

19. **A patient who is at high risk for skin cancer should:**

    a. **examine his skin monthly for changes.**
    b. **be examined by a dermatologist quarterly.**
    c. **use emollients regularly.**
    d. **eat foods high in vitamin C.**

20. **Naegele's rule is calculated by adding 7 days to the last menstrual period and:**

    a. **subtracting 3 months.**
    b. **adding 3 months.**
    c. **subtracting 4 weeks.**
    d. **adding 6 weeks.**

21. **A female patient has the following characteristics. Which one represents the greatest risk factor for development of Type II diabetes?**

    a. **BMI 28**
    b. **Lack of exercise**
    c. **Mediterranean decent**
    d. **Lack of regular healthcare**

22. **A 6-month old child comes into the clinic for immunizations. Which item below allows a delay in his getting immunizations today?**

    a. **Child is on antibiotics**
    b. **Child has otitis media with temperature of 103F**
    c. **Mom is pregnant**
    d. **Child has a family member on chemotherapy**

23. The major difference between varicose veins and arteriosclerosis is the:

a. limbs affected.
b. gender affected.
c. vessels affected.
d. degree of pain.

24. In order to establish pregnancy, a pregnancy test of the urine or blood is routinely performed. How early can this be done with reliable results?

a. Within 3 days after conception
b. Within 7 days after conception
c. 1-2 weeks after conception
d. 35 days after last menses

25. Which of the following symptoms is typical of GERD?

a. Chest pain
b. Cough
c. Sore throat
d. Pyrosis

26. A side effect of DTaP that should be reported is:

a. temperature of 103F.
b. vomiting.
c. non-stop crying (3h or more).
d. injection site soreness lasting greater than 2 days.

27. A 70 year-old African American male complains of pain in his back and trunk. Cardiovascular disease is ruled out. He has a normocytic normochromic anemia with hypercalcemia. A likely diagnosis is:

a. multiple myeloma.
b. lymphoma.
c. leukemia.
d. prostate cancer.

28. A patient who is found to be pregnant has asymptomatic bacteriuria. What is the likely pathogen?

a. *Klebsiella*
b. *E. coli*
c. *Staph saprophyticus*
d. No pathogen

29. A patient with testicular torsion will have a:

a. **positive cremasteric reflex on the affected side.**
b. **negative cremasteric reflex on the affected side.**
c. **positive cremasteric reflex bilaterally.**
d. **negative cremasteric reflex bilaterally.**

30. A contraindication to giving MMR is:

a. **family history of any adverse event after a dose.**
b. **fever of 104 F within 72 hours of immunization.**
c. **seizures within 7 days of immunization.**
d. **encephalopathy within 7 days after immunization.**

31. A patient with a positive history of a tick bite about 2 weeks ago and erythema migrans has a positive ELISA for Borrelia. The Western blot is positive. How should he be managed?

a. **He should receive doxycycline for Lyme disease.**
b. **He should receive penicillin for syphilis.**
c. **He does not have Lyme disease or syphilis.**
d. **He needs additional testing to confirm Lyme disease.**

32. A 17 year-old female is found to be pregnant. What is the LEAST likely risk to her fetus?

a. **Toxoplasmosis**
b. **Hepatitis B and C**
c. **Down Syndrome**
d. **Chlamydia**

33. An elderly adult with an appendicitis is *unlikely* to exhibit:

a. **generalized abdominal pain.**
b. **initial WBC elevation.**
c. **UTI symptoms.**
d. **low grade fever.**

34. What is the usual recommendation about administering MMR and varicella immunizations?

a. **They should not be given on the same day under any circumstances.**
b. **They should be given on the same day or at least one month apart.**
c. **They cannot be given with flu vaccine.**
d. **They can be given only with live viruses.**

35. A patient has 2 fasting glucose values of 101 mg/dL and 114 mg/dL that were measured on 2 separate days in the same week. This patient:

- a. can be diagnosed with Type 2 diabetes.
- b. has impaired fasting glucose.
- c. should have further glucose testing done for diagnosis.
- d. should have a Hgb A1C performed.

36. The need for thyroid replacement during pregnancy:

- a. increases.
- b. decreases.
- c. fluctuates unpredictably.
- d. stays about the same.

37. Which medication listed below could potentially exacerbate CHF in a susceptible individual?

- a. Naproxen
- b. HCTZ
- c. Lovastatin
- d. Loratadine

38. The pneumococcal immunization in infants has:

- a. decreased the episodes of acute otitis media due to *H. flu*.
- b. shifted the pathogenesis to fewer cases of *S. pneumoniae*.
- c. eradicated acute otitis media due to *S. pneumoniae*.
- d. improved the prognosis of acute otitis media.

39. A patient has the following laboratory values. What does this mean?
Hepatitis A: (-) IgM (-) IgG

- a. He has hepatitis A.
- b. He has immunity to hepatitis A.
- c. He has no immunity to hepatitis A.
- d. More data is needed.

40. Ultrasounds are commonly performed during the first trimester of pregnancy because they help estimate gestational age and:

- a. identify maternal risks.
- b. improve maternal outcomes.
- c. identify fetal malformations.
- d. reduce need for later ultrasounds.

41. Which group of medications should not be used to treat a patient with CHF?

a. **Ramipril, aspirin, metoprolol**
b. **Digoxin, furosemide, aspirin**
c. **Fosinopril, HCTZ, verapamil**
d. **Furosemide, enalapril, aspirin**

42. Which of the following increases the risk of cryptorchidism?

a. **Family history hearing problems**
b. **Premature birth**
c. **Maternal iron deficiency anemia**
d. **Constipation**

43. A male patient has epididymitis. His most likely complaint will be:

a. **burning with urination.**
b. **testicular pain.**
c. **scrotal pain.**
d. **penile discharge.**

44. A pregnant teenager asks if sexual activity is safe during pregnancy. The nurse practitioner responds:

a. **this can expose you to STDs.**
b. **there is a slight risk to cardiovascular system of the fetus.**
c. **this may stimulate labor and so should be avoided.**
d. **this does not increase the risk of pre-term labor.**

45. A patient with diarrhea has a stool specimen positive for WBCs. What does this indicate?

a. **A viral infection**
b. **A malignancy**
c. **Parasitic infection**
d. **Occult blood**

46. The term that describes the urethral opening on the ventral surface of the penis is:

a. **cryptorchidism.**
b. **hypospadias.**
c. **inguinal hernia.**
d. **hydrocele.**

47. A 35 year-old patient has the following laboratory values. How should they be interpreted?
HBsAg (-), HBsAb (-), HBcAb (-)

a. **The patient had hepatitis B.**
b. **The patient has hepatitis B.**
c. **The patient should consider Hepatitis B immunization.**
d. **The patient has had Hepatitis B immunization.**

48. A patient with an ectopic pregnancy:

a. **is not really pregnant.**
b. **will have a positive pregnancy test.**
c. **is at risk of pre-term labor.**
d. **will have a tubal rupture.**

49. An overweight 76 year-old female with a recent onset of diabetes has longstanding hypertension and hyperlipidemia. She has developed atrial fibrillation. The nurse practitioner knows that now she will be at risk for:

a. **an S3 gallop.**
b. **CHF.**
c. **peripheral edema.**
d. **hypothyroidism.**

50. Which of the following will decrease the risk of acute otitis media in a 6 month old?

a. **Cigarette smoke exposure**
b. **Breastfeeding**
c. **Sucking on pacifiers**
d. **Vitamin D supplementation**

51. A microscopic examination of the sample taken from a skin lesion indicates hyphae. What type infection might this indicate?

a. **Bacterial**
b. **Viral**
c. **Parasitic**
d. **Fungal**

52. A 30 year-old with Type I diabetes has become pregnant. The routine diabetic screening:

a. should occur earlier.
b. should occur at 24 weeks.
c. can be eliminated.
d. should be performed in the 3rd trimester.

53. Which medication listed below can exacerbate the symptoms of GERD?

a. Verapamil
b. Metformin
c. Ferrous sulfate
d. Ceftriaxone

54. An NP examines a screaming 2 year-old. A common finding is:

a. nasal discharge.
b. increased respiratory rate.
c. pink tympanic membranes.
d. coarse breath sounds.

55. Which patient would be expected to have the highest systolic blood pressure?

a. A 21 year-old male
b. A 50 year-old perimenopausal female
c. A 35 year-old patient with Type 2 diabetes
d. A 75 year-old male

56. A patient in her first trimester of pregnancy is found to have gonorrhea. Which statement below is true?

a. She should be treated now for gonorrhea and chlamydia.
b. She should be treated for gonorrhea only.
c. She should not be screened for other STDs later in pregnancy.
d. She should be treated now for gonorrhea and re-screened if symptoms re-appear.

57. A patient is in the clinic with a 36 hour history of diarrhea and moderate dehydration. Interventions should include:

a. oral rehydration with tea, cola, or Gatorade.
b. IV rehydration.
c. oral rehydration with an electrolyte replenishment solution.
d. resumption of usual fluid intake and solid food intake.

58. In a patient who is diagnosed with mastoiditis, which of the following is most likely?

- **a. Recent history of pharyngitis**
- **b. Fever, cough**
- **c. Displaced pinna**
- **d. Nuchal rigidity**

59. The nurse practitioner performs a fundoscopic exam on a patient who has recently been diagnosed with hypertension. What is the significance of AV nicking?

- **a. This is an incidental finding.**
- **b. This is indicative of long standing hypertension.**
- **c. The patient should be screened for diabetes.**
- **d. The patient should be referred to ophthalmology.**

60. The most effective way to decrease the incidence of neural tube defects in pregnant patients is to:

- **a. increase iron.**
- **b. decrease exposure to alcohol.**
- **c. eliminate exposure to cigarette smoke.**
- **d. increase folic acid.**

61. A patient with gout has hypertension. Which drug class should be avoided in him if possible?

- **a. ACE inhibitors**
- **b. Beta blockers**
- **c. Calcium channel blockers**
- **d. Thiazide diuretics**

62. The most common risk factor for developing hepatitis B is:

- **a. homosexual activity.**
- **b. injecting drug use.**
- **c. heterosexual activity.**
- **d. body piercings.**

63. Benazepril should be discontinued immediately if:

- **a. dry cough develops.**
- **b. pregnancy occurs.**
- **c. potassium levels decrease.**
- **d. gout develops.**

64. Which of the following medications does not warrant monitoring of potassium levels?

a. **Fosinopril**
b. **Candesartan**
c. **Hydrochlorothiazide**
d. **Amlodipine**

65. The most common place for direct inguinal hernias to develop is:

a. **the internal inguinal ring.**
b. **the external inguinal ring.**
c. **Hesselbach's triangle.**
d. **femoral ring.**

66. A 50 year-old male patient reports that he has a sensation of scrotal heaviness. He reports that the sensation is worse at the end of the day. He denies pain. What is the likely etiology of these symptoms?

a. **Strangulated hernia**
b. **Inguinal hernia**
c. **Epididymitis**
d. **Hydrocele**

67. MMSE helps to identify patients with symptoms of:

a. **dementia.**
b. **depression.**
c. **behavioral changes.**
d. **delirium.**

68. A patient who abuses alcohol will probably exhibit:

a. **elevated alkaline phosphatase.**
b. **decreased TSH.**
c. **elevated ALT, AST, and GGT.**
d. **elevated AST only.**

69. A patient with an eating disorder might exhibit evidence of:

a. **thyroid disease.**
b. **sleep disorders.**
c. **anxiety disorders.**
d. **sexual abuse.**

70. A 19 year-old college student is at least 15% below her ideal body weight. She reports doing well in classes but drinks alcohol nightly, and several cups of coffee throughout the day. She is bradycardic and gets dizzy when she stands. What may also be observed in this patient?

a. **Hypertension**
b. **Sleep apnea**
c. **Amenorrhea**
d. **Mitral regurgitation**

71. How should the nurse practitioner approach a patient who consumes excessive amounts of alcohol but denies that he has a problem?

a. **Order liver function studies to show the patient that his liver has damage.**
b. **Order a blood alcohol content and discuss results with patient.**
c. **Tell him to find another healthcare provider.**
d. **Tell him that you are concerned about his health.**

72. Which statement about bulimia nervosa is accurate?

a. **High dose SSRIs are used to treat this.**
b. **This is more common in men than women.**
c. **Loss of control is not a characteristic of this illness.**
d. **Bupropion is a good choice for treatment of these patients.**

73. An uncommon symptom associated with acute bronchitis is:

a. **fever.**
b. **cough.**
c. **pharyngitis.**
d. **purulent sputum.**

74. A healthcare provider ("the HCP") was stuck with a needle from a patient suspected to be infected with HIV ("the patient"). A rapid HIV test was performed and was found to be positive. This means that the:

a. **healthcare provider has been infected with HIV.**
b. **the patient is infected with HIV.**
c. **the HIV status of the patient requires further testing.**
d. **the HIV status of the healthcare provider requires further testing.**

75. Athletic amenorrhea increases the risk of:

a. osteoporosis.
b. an eating disorder.
c. covert hypothyroidism.
d. concussive syndromes.

76. In collection of a specimen for a PAP smear, how is the endocervical specimen collected?

a. After the ectocervical specimen with a broom
b. After the ectocervical specimen with a brush
c. Before the ectocervical specimen with a broom
d. Before the ectocervical specimen with a brush

77. The frequency for cervical screening depends on the patient and her age. What is the longest recommended time interval between cervical screens for patients who are 65 years-old or younger?

a. 1 year
b. 2 years
c. 3 years
d. 5 years

78. A woman who is 65 years-old presents to your clinic with a breast lump. She has had only normal annual mammograms and her last one was 6 months ago. What is true about this lump?

a. It is probably breast cancer.
b. It may not be a lump at all.
c. It is likely a fibroadenoma.
d. It is probably a benign lesion.

79. A nurse practitioner is working in a minor care area of an emergency department. A patient without insurance arrives with a puncture wound caused by an unknown sharp object in a trash container. A dirty needle is suspected. The nurse practitioner:

a. should administer a tetanus injection only since he has no insurance.
b. should prescribe appropriate medications for HIV exposure even though she knows he can't afford them.
c. should not mention the possibility of HIV from a dirty needle.
d. can offer to buy the HIV medications for $50 with her employee discount at the pharmacy next door.

80. A 15 year-old is about 10% below her ideal body weight. She complains of dizziness when she stands up. Laboratory studies were performed. Besides malnutrition, what else could account for her dizziness?

a. **BUN is mildly elevated**
b. **Glucose = 80 mg/dL**
c. **Hemoglobin = 9.6 mg/dL**
d. **Potassium is 3.5 meq/L**

81. An example of primary prevention is:

a. **using a condom to prevent infection with an STD.**
b. **diagnosis of chlamydia prior to symptom development.**
c. **treatment of chlamydia concurrently with gonorrhea.**
d. **early treatment of sexual partners.**

82. Classic symptoms of a deep vein thrombosis include:

a. **swelling, pain, redness.**
b. **calf complaints, pain with walking, history of exercise.**
c. **swelling, pain, and discoloration in lower extremity.**
d. **warmth, edema, and relief of pain with walking.**

83. A patient was exposed to HIV through sexual intercourse. He should be followed with screening tests to identify seroconversion for:

a. **4-6 weeks.**
b. **3-4 months.**
c. **about 6 months.**
d. **one year.**

84. A key component of the approach to a patient who has atopic dermatitis is hydration. Which agent should be avoided?

a. **Lotions**
b. **Creams**
c. **Thick creams**
d. **Ointments**

85. Topical 5-fluorouracil (5-FU) is used to treat:

a. **atopic dermatitis.**
b. **hepatitis.**
c. **thalassemia.**
d. **basal cell carcinoma.**

86. A 32 year-old patient is a newly diagnosed diabetic. She has developed a sinus infection. Her symptoms have persisted for 10 days. Six weeks ago she was treated with amoxicillin for an upper respiratory infection. It cleared without incident. What should be recommended today?

- **a. Prescribe amoxicillin again.**
- **b. Prescribe amoxicillin-clavulanate today.**
- **c. Do not prescribe an antibiotic; a decongestant is indicated only.**
- **d. Prescribe a decongestant and antihistamine.**

87. The single most effective maintenance therapy for allergic rhinitis is:

- **a. an antihistamine.**
- **b. a decongestant.**
- **c. a topical nasal steroid.**
- **d. a topical antihistamine.**

88. A patient has been diagnosed with Grave's disease. He is likely to have:

- **a. an elevated alkaline phosphatase.**
- **b. an elevated T3 or T4.**
- **c. an elevated TSH.**
- **d. elevated liver function studies.**

89. A patient has suspected peptic ulcer disease. Her symptoms occur a few hours after eating. She likely has a:

- **a. gastric ulcer.**
- **b. duodenal ulcer.**
- **c. gastric or duodenal ulcer.**
- **d. infection with *H. pylori.***

90. A 74 year-old male patient has sustained a laceration to his foot. His last tetanus shot was more than 10 years ago. He has completed the primary series. What should be recommended?

- **a. Tetanus toxoid only**
- **b. Tetanus and diphtheria only**
- **c. His primary series will protect him.**
- **d. Tetanus, diphtheria, and acellular pertussis (Tdap)**

91. A patient has been prescribed metronidazole for treatment of C. difficile. What should be avoided in this patient?

- a. **Excess fluids**
- b. **Vitamin B12**
- c. **Grapefruit juice**
- d. **Alcohol**

92. A 66 year-old African American female has multiple risk factors for osteoporosis. Which choice listed below is NOT a risk factor for osteoporosis?

- a. **Her age**
- b. **Her race**
- c. **Glucocorticoid intake**
- d. **Excessive alcohol intake**

93. A patient with diarrhea is tested for *C. difficile.* How soon should the enzyme immunoassay (EIA) yield results?

- a. **Within 20 minutes**
- b. **About 24 hours**
- c. **About 3 days**
- d. **Less than one week**

94. The main difference between cellulitis and erysipelas is the:

- a. **infecting organism.**
- b. **length of time that infection lasts.**
- c. **treatment.**
- d. **layer of skin involvement.**

95. A patient has a lower leg wound that appears infected. It is red, warm to touch and edematous. He had an acute onset of pain, symptoms, and low grade fever. What is this?

- a. **Cellulitis**
- b. **Erysipelas**
- c. **Impetigo**
- d. **An allergic reaction**

96. The carotid arteries are auscultated for bruits because:

- a. **a bruit is indicative of an impending stroke.**
- b. **a bruit is indicative of significant carotid stenosis.**
- c. **this is indicative of generalized atherosclerosis.**
- d. **this is reflective of stroke risk.**

97. A 39 year-old has a sudden onset of a right red eye. He reports sensitivity to light and the sensation of a foreign body, though his history for a foreign body is negative. He does not wear contact lenses. How should the NP manage this?

a. **Refer to ophthalmology**
b. **Treat for viral conjunctivitis**
c. **Treat for bacterial conjunctivitis**
d. **Observe for 24 hours if visual acuity is normal**

98. A 51 year-old female patient presents with a 2 cm palpable breast mass. How should this be evaluated to determine whether it is solid or cystic in nature?

a. **Mammogram**
b. **Ultrasound**
c. **MRI**
d. **Clinical breast exam**

99. Which test below is most cost-effective to screen for abdominal aortic aneurysm?

a. **CT of the abdomen**
b. **MRI of the abdomen**
c. **Abdominal ultrasound**
d. **Two hand palpation test**

100. What class of medications can be used to treat benign prostatic hyperplasia and provide immediate relief?

a. **Alpha-1 blockers**
b. **5-alpha reductase inhibitors**
c. **Diuretics**
d. **Analgesics**

101. An elderly male patient is taking finasteride, a 5-alpha-reductase inhibitor. What affect might this have on his PSA level?

a. **It will increase.**
b. **It will decrease.**
c. **There is no predictable change.**
d. **There will be no change.**

102. The classic description of transient ischemic attack is "a sudden onset of focal neurological symptoms that lasts less than":

- a. one minute.
- b. five minutes.
- c. one hour.
- d. 24 hours.

103. A male patient takes HCTZ daily for hypertension. He developed severe pain in his great toe yesterday. He was diagnosed with gout today and started on a medication. Which medication listed below would be contraindicated at this time?

- a. Allopurinol
- b. Prednisone
- c. Colchicine
- d. Indomethacin

104. A high purine diet can contribute to gouty arthritis. Which food listed below contributes most to a high purine diet?

- a. Coffee
- b. Eggs
- c. Beef
- d. Bread

105. A patient who is 60 years old complains of low back pain for the last 5-6 weeks. She states that the severity is about 4/10 and that she gets no relief from sitting, standing, or lying. The NP should consider:

- a. sciatica.
- b. ankylosing spondylitis.
- c. disc disease.
- d. systemic illness.

106. A nurse practitioner has agreed to participate in the Medicare health insurance program. Medicare paid 80% of the charges billed for a clinic visit. What can be done about the other 20% that is owed?

- a. The NP can bill the patient for a percentage of the remainder.
- b. The NP is prohibited from billing the patient.
- c. The NP can collect 100% if billed incident to the MD.
- d. The NP can resubmit the bill for additional payment.

107. Which medication below is contraindicated for lone use in treating asthma?

a. **Short-acting bronchodilator**
b. **Long-acting bronchodilator**
c. **Inhaled steroid**
d. **Oral steroid**

108. A short-acting anticholinergic medication can be used alone or in combination with a short-acting beta agonist to manage symptoms of which disease?

a. **COPD**
b. **Asthma**
c. **Glaucoma**
d. **Tachyarrhythmias**

109. A patient you are examining in the clinic states that he has Medicare Part A only. What does this mean?

a. **Your visit will be reimbursed by the federal government.**
b. **Your visit will be reimbursed if you bill incident to a physician.**
c. **Only hospital visits are covered.**
d. **He desires a cost-effective medication.**

110. A healthy 32 year-old female has fever, left flank pain, and nausea. What is the most likely diagnosis?

a. **Urinary tract infection**
b. **Renal stone**
c. **Cholecystitis**
d. **Pyelonephritis**

111. A patient with dysuria has a urine specimen that reveals < 10,000 bacteria and numerous trichomonads. How should this patient be managed?

a. **Increased fluids and a urinary tract analgesic**
b. **Ciprofloxacin for 3 days**
c. **Metronidazole for 7 days**
d. **Ciprofloxacin and metronidazole**

112. A homeless patient presents to the free clinic. She should be screened for diseases that are most prevalent in this population. These would be:

a. **TB, HIV, and hepatitis.**
b. **pregnancy and STDs.**
c. **urinary tract infection and STDs.**
d. **diabetes, HIV, and foot ulcers.**

113. A patient presents to your clinic numerous times with vague complaints. She seems to respond poorly to medical treatment that is given to her. What should be considered when obtaining a history from her?

a. **Physical abuse or depression**
b. **Depression or HIV**
c. **Hepatitis or HIV**
d. **Anemia or Depression**

114. How should a 20 year-old college age student presents with cough, night sweats, and weight loss. How should he be screened for TB?

a. **A chest x-ray**
b. **A TB skin test**
c. **A sputum specimen**
d. **Questionnaire about symptoms**

115. An ACE inhibitor is specifically indicated in patients who have:

a. **hypertension, diabetes with proteinuria, heart failure.**
b. **diabetes, hypertension, hyperlipidemia.**
c. **asthma, hypertension, diabetes.**
d. **renal nephropathy, heart failure, hyperlipidemia.**

116. A female vegetarian presents to your clinic with iron deficiency anemia. What can the NP suggest she eat to help with resolution of iron deficiency anemia?

a. **Dark green leafy vegetables and dried peas and beans**
b. **Mushrooms, oatmeal, and whole grain breads**
c. **Beets, broccoli, and beef**
d. **Baked potatoes, beets, and broccoli**

117. Thalassemia minor can be recognized by:

a. **microcytic, normochromic red cells.**
b. **normocytic, normochromic red cells.**
c. **microcytic, hypochromic red cells.**
d. **normocytic, hyperchromic red cells.**

118. Which symptom below is true of cluster headaches but not migraine headaches?

a. **It is more common in females.**
b. **The length of the headache duration is about 30-90 minutes.**
c. **The most common characteristic is familial history.**
d. **Sunlight is a common trigger.**

119. Which criterion below is a criterion for Alzheimer's Disease?

a. **Focal neurologic signs**
b. **Laboratory evidence of dementia**
c. **Radiologic evidence of dementia**
d. **Impairment of executive function**

120. How would you create a therapeutic relationship with a patient?

a. **Tell the patient that he can trust you.**
b. **At the end of the visit, tell the patient you enjoyed taking care of him.**
c. **Ask open-ended questions.**
d. **Touch the patient during the interview.**

121. The risk of HIV transmission is increased:

a. **when other STDs are present.**
b. **in females.**
c. **when patients are aware of their HIV status.**
d. **in patients with diabetes.**

122. A 65 year-old patient presents to your clinic with evidence of hyperthyroidism. In assessing her cardiovascular status, what should the NP assess immediately?

a. **Cardiac enzymes**
b. **Electrocardiogram**
c. **Electrolytes**
d. **Auscultation of systolic murmurs**

123. Which symptom listed below is typical of depression?

a. **Difficulty falling asleep**
b. **Snoring**
c. **Early morning wakening**
d. **Keeping late night hours reading**

124. A patient who frequently has episodes of gout should avoid which groups of food?

a. **Beans, rice, and tea**
b. **Scrambled eggs, milk, and toast**
c. **Roast beef with gravy, rice**
d. **Fish and steamed vegetables**

125. A common side effect of thiazide diuretics is:

a. prostatitis.
b. erectile dysfunction.
c. fatigue.
d. hyperkalemia.

126. A mammogram in a healthy 50 year-old female patient is considered to be an example of:

a. primary prevention.
b. secondary prevention.
c. tertiary prevention.
d. quaternary prevention.

127. An elderly patient has been diagnosed with shingles on the right lateral aspect of her trunk. It appeared initially yesterday. It is very painful. How should she be managed?

a. Treatment with a topical lidocaine patch only
b. An oral antiviral agent and NSAIDs
c. An oral antiviral agent and pain medication
d. An oral antiviral agent, pain medication, and oral steroids

128. The most common pathogen associated with pyelonephritis is:

a. *E. coli.*
b. *H. influenzae.*
c. *Streptococcus sp.*
d. *Staphylococcus sp.*

129. A patient with a primary case of scabies was probably infected:

a. 1-3 days ago.
b. 1 week ago.
c. 2 weeks ago.
d. 3-4 weeks ago.

130. A patient calls your office. He states that he just came in from the woods and discovered a tick on his upper arm. He states that he has removed the tick and the area is slightly red. What should he be advised?

a. No treatment is needed.
b. He should be prescribed doxycycline.
c. He needs a topical scrub to prevent Lyme Disease.
d. He should come to the office for a ceftriaxone injection.

131. What temperature should be set on a water heater in the home of an elderly patient to prevent burn injury?

a. **Less than 110 degrees**
b. **Less than 120 degrees**
c. **Less than 130 degrees**
d. **Less than 140 degrees**

132. A patient cannot stick his tongue out of his mouth and move it side to side. What cranial nerve is responsible for this movement?

a. **Cranial Nerve III**
b. **Cranial Nerve VII**
c. **Cranial Nerve X**
d. **Cranial Nerve XII**

133. AV nicking may be identified in a patient with what disease?

a. **Glaucoma**
b. **Cataracts**
c. **Diabetes**
d. **Hypertension**

134. A 40 year-old female patient presents to the clinic with multiple, painful reddened nodules on the anterior surface of both legs. She is concerned. These are probably associated with her history of:

a. **deep vein thrombosis.**
b. **phlebitis.**
c. **ulcerative colitis.**
d. **alcoholism.**

135. Which class of medications is NOT used for migraine prophylaxis?

a. **Beta blockers**
b. **Calcium channel blockers**
c. **Triptans**
d. **Tricyclic antidepressants**

136. A patient has 2 palpable, tender, left pre-auricular nodes that are about 0.5 cm in diameter. What might also be found in this patient?

a. Sore throat
b. Ulceration on the tongue
c. Conjunctivitis
d. Ear infection

137. A patient presents to your clinic with a painless red eye. Her vision is normal, but her sclera has a blood red area. What is this termed?

a. Conjunctivitis
b. Acute iritis
c. Glaucoma
d. Subconjunctival hemorrhage

138. A 24 year-old patient presents to your clinic. She states that she has vomited for the last 5 mornings and until early afternoon. She feels better in the evenings. She denies fever. What lab tests should be monitored?

a. CBC and urine for ketones
b. Electrolytes and serum pregnancy
c. Electrolytes and hepatitis panel
d. Metabolic panel and potassium level

139. What laboratory test could help differentiate acute bronchitis from pneumonia in a patient with a productive cough?

a. CBC
b. Chest x-ray
c. Sputum specimen
d. Pulmonary function tests

140. A patient who has been treated for hypothyroidism presents for her annual exam. Her TSH is 4.1 (normal = 0.4- 3.8). She feels well. How should she be managed?

a. Continue her current dosage of thyroid replacement
b. Increase her replacement
c. Decrease her replacement
d. Repeat the TSH in 2-3 weeks

141. A 26 year-old male patient has been diagnosed with gonorrhea. How should he be managed?

a. **Ceftriaxone only**
b. **Ceftriaxone and azithromycin**
c. **Cefixime and azithromycin**
d. **Penicillin G**

142. A 70 year-old male patient has an elevated MCV with an anemia. His triglycerides are 420. What should be suspected?

a. **Pernicious anemia**
b. **Folate deficiency**
c. **Alcohol abuse**
d. **Hypertriglyceridemia**

143. A young female adult presents with vaginal discharge and itching. Besides trichomoniasis and yeast, what else should be included in the differential?

a. **Bacterial vaginosis**
b. **Chlamydia**
c. **Herpes genitalis**
d. **Syphilis**

144. A 45 year-old male who is in good health presents with complaints of pain in his left heel. He states that the first few steps out of bed in the morning are extremely painful. He has no history of trauma. What is the likely etiology of his pain?

a. **Achilles tendinitis**
b. **Plantar fasciitis**
c. **Calcaneal spur**
d. **Arthritis of the foot**

145. An elderly hypertensive patient has osteoporosis. Which antihypertensive agent would have the secondary effect of improving her osteoporosis?

a. **A thiazide diuretic**
b. **A calcium channel blocker**
c. **An ACE inhibitor**
d. **A beta blocker**

146. The most common polyneuropathy in the elderly is:

a. **Charcot-Marie-Tooth disease.**
b. **diabetes mellitus.**
c. **urinary incontinence.**
d. **Guillain-Barre syndrome.**

147. A patient reports that he has been taking saw palmetto. Why is this used?

a. **It prevents blood clots.**
b. **It improves urine flow.**
c. **It decreases environmental allergies.**
d. **It decreases risk of colon cancer.**

148. A patient who is 52 years old presents to your clinic for an exam. You notice a yellowish plaque on her upper eyelid. It is painless. What should the NP assess?

a. **Vision in the affected eye**
b. **Sedimentation rate**
c. **Lipid levels**
d. **Liver function studies**

149. The greatest risk of transmitting HIV is during:

a. **the acute phase.**
b. **the time that detectable antibody is present.**
c. **high viral load periods.**
d. **late infection phase.**

150. A 14 year-old male client reports dull anterior knee pain, exacerbated by kneeling. What is the likely etiology?

a. **Patellar fasciitis**
b. **Osgood-Schlatter disease**
c. **Osteosarcoma of the tibia**
d. **Over developed quadriceps**

Family Exam #1 Answers

1. *b*

An INR (International Normalized Ratio) is considered the best measure of clotting status in outpatients. Depending on the reason for anticoagulation, a common target is 2.0 – 3.0. Diastolic murmurs are always considered abnormal regardless of age. Cholesterol levels in adolescents should be less than 170 mg/dL (according to National Heart, Lung and Blood institute, NHLBI). Blood pressure of 160/75 constitutes isolated systolic hypertension, and, so this is abnormal.

2. *d*

This child's platelet count is below normal. The term used to describe this is thrombocytopenia. ITP is the most common type found in children between the ages of 2-4 years. Nosebleeds and bleeding gums, especially with brushing of teeth, are common. Generally, children are monitored closely for decreasing platelet counts and bleeding after ITP is identified, but this usually resolves in several weeks without treatment. The underlying cause is unknown, hence the name idiopathic. A common historical finding is an upper respiratory infection within the previous 4 weeks of the onset of ITP.

3. *a*

The internal inguinal ring is the most common site for development of an indirect inguinal hernia. These can occur in men and women. Though most are probably congenital, symptoms may not be obvious until later in life. Indirect hernias are more common on the right side. Direct inguinal hernias occur through Hesselbach's triangle.

4. *b*

The rubella vaccine is contraindicated in pregnant patients because it crosses the placenta. Pregnant women should be advised to avoid pregnancy for 28 days after immunization with MMR. It should not be given during pregnancy. However, CDC has collected data on women who have accidentally received the immunization while pregnant and there has been no documented injury to the offspring. The vaccine is safe for women who are breastfeeding even though the rubella virus is excreted in breast milk.

5. *d*

Patients with type 1 diabetes should be screened for renal nephropathy 5 years after diagnosis. Since nephropathy takes several years to develop, it is highly improbable that a newly diagnosed patient will have nephropathy secondary to diabetes. Nephropathy develops in about 30% of patients with diabetes. Diabetic nephropathy is defined as the presence of diabetes and more than 300 mg/d of albuminuria on at least 2 occasions separated by 3-6 months.

6. *c*
Children with sickle cell anemia should receive all the routine childhood immunizations at the usual time for administration, including annual flu immunization. Sickle cell crises arise when children become ill. Unfortunately, children with SCA are more prone to sickle cell crises when illness occurs, so, decreasing the likelihood of illness by immunization decreases the likelihood of sickle cell crises.

7. *b*
This patient does not have hepatitis C. This patient has a negative hepatitis C IgG. Currently, this is the screen. The RIBA was not necessary to perform, but, it confirms that this patient has a true negative screen for hepatitis C. If the HCV IgG had been positive, the RIBA would have been necessary to perform. There is no laboratory information that helps conclude that this patient has hepatitis B, except the history in the stem of the question.

8. *b*
Influenza should be given during the first trimester to every pregnant patient. Live viruses should not be given during pregnancy. Therefore, MMR and varicella should never be given to a patient known to be pregnant. There are no specific risks associated with pneumococcus and it appears to be safe when given in the second and third trimesters. There is no pregnancy information for hepatitis A or B immunizations, but, the general recommendation is to avoid these during pregnancy unless the patient is particularly at risk for hepatitis.

9. *a*
The most common symptoms associated with mononucleosis (mono) are adenopathy (100%) and fatigue (90-100%). Pharyngitis occurs in 65-85% of patients. Cough occurs less than 50%; splenomegaly occurs 50-60%; fever 80-95%. The least common symptom of mono is rash. It occurs in only 3-6% of patients.

10. *a*
A sudden rise or fall in body temperature lowers the seizure threshold in children as well as adults. Therefore, gradually decreasing body temperature with antipyretics, consuming cool fluids, or removal of clothes is prudent when temperatures are > 101F. Fever is the most common precipitant of a febrile seizure. The most common diagnosis associated with febrile seizures is otitis media; pneumonia does not specifically increase the risk. Returning to daycare before being fever free for 24 hours increases the risk of transmission of most contagious illnesses, but, not seizure.

11. *d*
This patient has a negative hepatitis B surface antigen (HBsAg). Therefore, he does not have hepatitis B. The patient has a negative hepatitis B core antibody (HBcAb). Therefore, he has never had hepatitis B. The patient has a positive hepatitis B surface antibody (HBsAb). Therefore, he is considered immune. The patient is immune from immunization because his hepatitis B core antibody is negative. If the core antibody had been positive, he would be considered immune from the disease. Correct answer is D.

12. *a*
Centers for Disease Control (CDC) and American College of Obstetrics and Gynecology (ACOG), recommends an "opt-out" approach to HIV screening in pregnant patients. "Opt-out" means that HIV will be routinely performed unless the patient "opts-out." This practice has improved screening in pregnant patients and increased early intervention for HIV.

13. *d*
Examples of drugs that target the renin-angiotensin-aldosterone system are angiotensin converting enzyme (ACE) inhibitors and angiotensin receptor blockers (ARBs). These drugs are particularly beneficial to patients with diabetic nephropathy because they both prevent and treat diabetic nephropathy. Additionally, these agents also decrease blood pressure that has been shown to be renoprotective. Management of glucose levels and blood pressure are especially important in preventing diabetic nephropathy.

14. *d*
The appropriate term for babies up to one year of age is infants. Newborns are usually less than one month of age. Toddlers are two or three years of age.

15. *b*
In a 25 year-old male with subacute bacterial epididymitis, the most likely organism is Chlamydia. Therefore, until cultures are back, he should be treated empirically with doxycycline 100 mg BID for 10-14 days or longer. Quinolones should specifically be avoided if the suspected agent is gonorrhea because of rising resistance. Anti-inflammatory agents, ice, and scrotal support will help the patient's symptoms but not treat the underlying cause.

16. *c*
Fetal heart tones can be heard as early as 9-12 weeks if a Doppler is used. Transvaginal ultrasound can identify movement of the heart at 5-6 weeks.

17. *d*
Nagel's rule estimates a woman's due date based on the date of the last menstrual period. Three months are subtracted from the last menstrual period, 7 days and one year are added. This predicts her due date. This is based on a pregnancy lasting 281-282 days.

18. *c*
This child will be placed on CDC's catch-up schedule (a copy can be downloaded from CDC's website). Because of his age, he does not need a Hib immunization. He does need all of the immunizations listed in choice C.

19. *a*
Patients should be examined periodically for evidence of skin cancer by a professional examiner (NP, MD or PA). The frequency and type of examiner depends on the risk

level, and personal and family history of the patient. However, a patient should examine his own skin regularly for changes. Once he has begun to examine his skin, research demonstrates that he will identify early changes and can make his provider aware of them.

20. ***a***
Naegele's rule is an accepted means of predicting gestational age of the fetus. This is based on an average length of pregnancy of 280 days. If the maternal history is not reliable, ultrasound becomes the standard.

21. ***a***
A BMI of 26 or higher imparts an increased risk of Type II diabetes. Mediterranean decent does not impart a specific risk factor for Type II diabetes, but African-American, Asian-American, and Hispanic races increase the risk of diabetes.

22. ***b***
A 6 month old with acute otitis media and temperature of 103F is considered moderately ill. Persons with moderate or severe illnesses, with or without fever, can be vaccinated as soon as they are recovering and not considered acutely ill. Antibiotics would not be considered a contraindication for any routine immunizations today. Pregnancy in the mother would not contraindicate any immunizations today. Live vaccines would be contraindicated if a family member was on chemotherapy, however, a 6 month old will not be receiving any live viruses.

23. ***c***
Varicose veins and arteriosclerosis are very different disease processes. While differences can be found in the gender affected, the major difference between the two diseases is the vessel affected; arteriosclerosis affects the arteries, varicose veins affect the veins. While there is a predilection for the lower extremities in varicose veins, peripheral artery disease (PAD) is most common in the lower extremities too. Varicose veins are especially common in women 2:1; PAD is more common in men 2:1 after age 70 years. Pain is a subjective measure.

24. ***c***
Whether performed on urine or blood, the presence of the beta subunit of human chorionic gonadotropin (hCG) is evaluated to identify pregnancy. This can be found in great quantities in the first morning urine or at any time in a serum sample of a pregnant woman. Both tests are highly sensitive, however if the pregnancy is very early and a first morning urine is NOT used, the urine test may be negative in a pregnant woman. In this instance, the serum specimen will indicate pregnancy.

25. ***d***
Typical symptoms of GERD include pyrosis (heartburn). The other symptoms listed are considered atypical symptoms of GERD. Patients who present with atypical symptoms of GERD, especially if older than 50 years, should be considered for endoscopy.

26. ***a***
Non-stop crying for 3 hours or more (and) occurring within 48 hours of the immunization is not a specific contraindication, but careful consideration must be given to the benefits and risks of the vaccine under these circumstances. The temperature that should cause concern, but is not a contraindication to a subsequent dose of MMR is 105F within 48 hours of immunization. Vomiting and injection site soreness are not contraindications or concerns after MMR.

27. ***a***
Multiple myeloma is a neoplastic proliferation in the bone marrow which results in skeletal destruction. It is more common in older patients; the average age of diagnosis is 66 years. Common clinical findings are pain in the long bones, especially those of the trunk and back. Accompanying findings are anemia, usually normocytic/ normochromic, hypercalcemia, and renal insufficiency.

28. ***b***
A pregnant patient with asymptomatic bacteriuria should be treated with an antibiotic because she is at high risk of developing pyelonephritis. Nitrofurantoin is safe for use during pregnancy and has very good coverage of the most common urinary tract pathogens, including *E. coli.*

29. ***b***
A patient with testicular torsion will have a negative cremasteric reflex and a high riding testis. There can also be profound testicular swelling and an acute onset of scrotal pain.

30. ***d***
Encephalopathy within 7 days after MMR is an absolute contraindication. Fever of 105F or greater within 48 hours and seizures within 3 days after immunization are not a specific contraindication, but benefits should outweigh risks before giving a second dose. A family history of any adverse event after an MMR immunization does not contraindicate any immunization.

31. ***a***
The first serologic test for Lyme disease is the ELISA. If this is positive, it should be confirmed. In this case, it was confirmed by a Western blot and it is positive. This patient can be diagnosed with Lyme disease. The appropriate treatment for erythema migrans is doxycycline, amoxicillin, or cefuroxime for 21 days. All three medications were found to be of equal efficacy.

32. ***c***
Routine prenatal screening is important for all pregnant women. Based on her age and the likelihood of multiple partners, she should be screened for STDs to include HIV and hepatitis B and C and chlamydia. Down syndrome is more likely in older pregnant women. Toxoplasmosis is contracted after exposure to feces of cats and undercooked meats.

33. ***b***

Very young children and elderly adults are not likely to have initial WBC elevations. Consequently, appendicitis can be easily missed in these populations. Generalized abdominal pain is typical initially. UTI symptoms in older adults can manifest as lower abdominal pain and are a common presentation in this age group. Low grade fever is common too.

34. ***b***

MMR is an attenuated virus. Varicella is a live virus. They should be given on the same day or, at least one month must separate the two. The reason for this is that higher titers are achieved if they are given together as opposed to being given separately.

35. ***b***

This patient has impaired fasting glucose. This is diagnosed when 2 fasting glucose values are between 100 mg/dL and 125 mg/dL. There is no need for further testing. At this time, this patient does not meet the criteria for diabetes and does not need further testing to arrive at a diagnosis.

36. ***a***

Thyroid hormone needs in pregnant patients with a history of hypothyroidism increase during pregnancy. This occurs in nearly 80% of pregnant hypothyroid women. Since low circulating thyroid hormone can drastically affect growth, TSH levels should be monitored frequently. Needs can increase by up to 50%.

37. ***a***

Naproxen is an NSAID. NSAIDs cause sodium retention and thus, water retention. A single dose of naproxen is unlikely to produce CHF symptoms, but, repeated subsequent doses are very likely to produce water retention sufficient to cause edema and possible shortness of breath in susceptible individuals. The other medications listed are unlikely to have any direct effect on cardiac output in a patient with CHF.

38. ***b***

The heptavalent pneumococcal conjugate vaccine (PCV7), Prevnar®, protects children from the seven most common strains of *Streptococcus pneumoniae* (S. pneumo). It has reduced the incidence of ear infections caused by S. pneumo and has reduced the incidence of recurrent ear infections and tube placement by 10-20%. The pathogenesis of acute otitis media has shifted to more cases of *H. influenzae*, but, this organism is less likely to become resistant, as Strept pneumo has.

39. ***c***

This patient does not have immunity to hepatitis A, as evidenced by the negative IgG. He is not currently infected, as evidenced by the negative IgM. This patient should be referred for immunization. The immunization consists of two immunizations given 6-12 months apart. They can be given to infants or adults.

40. ***c***
Ultrasounds are excellent tools in the first trimester of pregnancy because they can help identify fetal malformations. They are helpful in detecting multiple fetuses, status of the placenta, and help assess gestational age. While it may be argued that ultrasound use improves outcomes in the fetus or mother, this is not why they are commonly performed during the first trimester. There is no evidence that performing an ultrasound early in pregnancy eliminates or reduces the need for ultrasounds later in pregnancy.

41. ***c***
The medications usually used in managing patients with CHF are ACE inhibitors, beta blockers, diuretics, aspirin, digoxin; specifically, some combination of these. Verapamil is a calcium channel blocker and is contraindicated in patients with CHF because these depress myocardial contractility.

42. ***b***
Cryptorchidism is the condition where one or both testicles have not descended into the scrotum by birth. This can be due to a short spermatic artery or poor blood supply. During normal prenatal development, the testicles develop in the abdominal cavity and descend through the groin tissue forming a scrotal sac. The incidence in premature birth is about 30% compared to full-term male infants where the rate is about 3%.

43. c
The most common complaint is scrotal pain. It usually develops over a period of days. Occasionally, it develops acutely and will be accompanied by fever, chills, and a very ill-appearing patient. Burning with urination is possible if the underlying cause is a urinary tract infection, but, this is not usual. This presentation is seen more commonly in older males. Testicular pain is not a common complaint with epididymitis. Penile discharge would not indicate an infection in the epididymis since the epididymis is a tightly coiled tubular structure located on the testis.

44. ***a***
Sexual activity during pregnancy could cause exposure to an STD; or precipitate pre-term labor because the lower uterine segment may be physically stimulated. Additionally, oxytocin is released which may precipitate pre-term labor. However, in the absence of complications associated with the pregnancy, sexual activity is not contraindicated. If vaginal discharge or bleeding occurs; or rupture of membranes occurs, sexual intercourse should be avoided until assessed by the patient's provider. STDs should be screened and treated.

45. ***a***
When WBCs are found in stool specimens, it is indicative of infection or inflammation. In the case of a patient with symptoms suggestive of an infectious etiology, bacterial or viral infections should be considered. When considering a differential diagnosis and no infectious etiology is likely, Crohn's disease or ulcerative colitis could be considered.

46. ***b***

Hypospadias describes a condition where the urethral opening is on the underside of the penis instead of at the tip. This happens once in every 300 male births, so, is very common. It is probably due to a defect in the hormone that influences the development of the urethra and foreskin. Hypospadias is more common in males born to in vitro fertilization, probably due to the mother's exposure to progesterone.

47. ***c***

This patient has a negative hepatitis B surface antigen (HBsAg). Therefore, he does not have hepatitis B. The patient has a negative hepatitis B core antibody (HBcAb). Therefore, he has never had hepatitis B. The patient has a negative hepatitis B surface antibody (HBsAb). Therefore, he is not considered immune, and immunization should be considered. There is a remote possibility that this patient has been immunized but did not produce hepatitis B surface antibodies. If this were the case, he should consider immunization once again. The correct answer is choice C.

48. ***b***

A patient with an ectopic pregnancy has a fertilized embryo that is developing outside the uterus. The fallopian tube is the most common location. If detected and managed early, a fallopian tube rupture does not have to occur. She will have a positive pregnancy test about 10 days after fertilization.

49. ***b***

This patient has longstanding hypertension that will increase her risk of CHF. Once she develops atrial fibrillation (a-fib) she will lose about 30% of her cardiac output, the amount contributed by her atria when she is not in a-fib. Shortness of breath, peripheral edema or an S3 gallop may develop but are secondary to a consequence of CHF or an embolism for which she is also at risk. Hypothyroidism can increase her risk of CHF but the risk of hypothyroidism does not increase once atrial fibrillation develops. The most obvious risk with a-fib is stroke but this was not listed as a choice.

50. ***b***

A patient with an ectopic pregnancy has a fertilized embryo that is developing outside the uterus. The fallopian tube is the most common location. If detected and managed early, a fallopian tube rupture does not have to occur. She will have a positive pregnancy test about 10 days after fertilization.

51. ***d***

Under microscopic exam, hyphae are long, thin and branching and indicate dermatophytic infections. Hyphae are typical in tinea pedis, tinea cruris, and tinea corporis.

52. ***c***

If a pregnant mother has been diagnosed with diabetes prior to pregnancy, there is no need to screen for gestational diabetes. In non-diabetic mothers, the routine time for screening for gestational diabetes is at 24-28 weeks. This has been identified as the ideal

time because she is more likely to exhibit elevations in glucose at 24-28 weeks due to placental hormones that increase insulin insensitivity. This is also a good time to initiate interventions that will decrease complications in the fetus associated with glucose elevations.

53. *a*

Verapamil is a calcium channel blocker. Calcium is needed for muscle contraction. Since the lower esophageal sphincter is opened and closed by muscles, the contraction of these muscles will be less forceful. GERD can be exacerbated in this case. Calcium channel blockers should be avoided in patients with severe GERD or in patients in whom calcium channel blockers exacerbate GERD symptoms.

54. *c*

The tympanic membrane normally becomes pink and can rarely become red when a child is screaming or crying. This is probably due to flushing and hyperemia of the face that occurs with crying. A distorted or erythematous tympanic membrane with decreased mobility is suggestive of otitis media.

55. *d*

Nearly 25% of the US population has hypertension. The greatest incidence is in elderly patients because of changes in the intima of vessels as aging and calcium deposition occur. Males of any age are more likely to be hypertensive than females of the same age. African American adults have the highest incidence in the general population. Among adolescents, African Americans and Hispanics have the highest rates. Hypertension affects about 5-10% of pregnancies.

56. *a*

She should be treated for chlamydia and gonorrhea now. Gonorrhea and chlamydia are found concurrently so often, that chlamydia is always treated when gonorrhea is identified. There is no danger with teratogenicity if standard treatment for these two STDs is employed. Since the percentage of patients who become re-infected with an STD later in pregnancy (even after being treated and educated) is very high, this patient should be re-screened later in pregnancy regardless of whether symptoms emerge. Deleterious effects can occur if she is left untreated.

57. *c*

The goal in managing a patient who presents with dehydration is rehydration. This is typically done with a commercially prepared electrolyte solution. Infamously, these are poor tasting. Patients usually prefer to rehydrate with fluids like tea, cola or a sports drink. However, these usually contain too much carbohydrate, too little potassium, and too much sodium for ideal fluid replenishment. Consequently, these are avoided when rehydration is needed. These are preferred by patients because of their good taste. The oral tract is always preferred for rehydration when it can be used. Resumption of the usual fluid and solid food intake should occur AFTER rehydration has occurred.

58. ***c***
Mastoiditis is an infection of the mastoid process. The mastoid process is a honeycomb-like structure with air pockets. These become infected with Streptococcus or H. flu most commonly. It is seen in patients (usually less than age 6 years) with chronic otitis media or less frequently in adults with chronic tooth abscesses. Patients may present with recent history of acute otitis media, history of abscess in the teeth and jaw, fever, and a displaced and erythematous pinna or post-auricular area. The tympanic membrane will usually be very red and the patient can become very sick very quickly. Nuchal rigidity is the term used to describe a stiff neck associated with meningitis.

59. ***b***
Normally, veins are larger than arteries in the eyes. The vessels in the eyes are particularly susceptible to increased blood pressure. AV (arterio-venous) nicking can be observed as arteries cross veins when the arteries have narrowed secondary to hypertension. Generally, AV nicking takes time to develop and would be expected in patients with long standing hypertension; especially when it is poorly controlled. Cotton wool exudates should prompt the examiner to screen for diabetes. An ophthalmology referral is not required at this point for AV nicking. In severe hypertension, the retina can become detached.

60. ***d***
Folic acid has been found to drastically decrease the incidence of neural tube defects (NTD). Folate plays an essential role in synthesis of amino acids and DNA. Since these are critical in cell division and adequate amounts should be on board when cell division begins, folic acid should be taken pre-conceptually. Since this is the second most common congenital anomaly, folic acid should be initiated pre-conceptually.

61. ***d***
Gout is characterized by hyperuricemia. Uric acid levels are increased when a patient consumes any medication that results in less circulating fluid volume; specifically, any diuretic. Diuretics will produce hyperuricemia, and thus, increase the risk of gout in susceptible patients. Diuretics should be avoided when possible in patients with history of gout.

62. ***c***
Hepatitis B can be contracted by any of the choices listed. However, the one with the highest likelihood of disease transmission, and the one that is most common, is heterosexual activity.

63. ***b***
Benazepril is an ACE inhibitor and this class of drugs is contraindicated during pregnancy because of the teratogenic effects to the renal system of the developing fetus. Dry cough is an aggravating side effect that occurs in some patients who take ACE inhibitors, but, discontinuation is elective. ACE inhibitor use is associated with increased potassium levels, not decreased levels. Gout is not exacerbated by ACE inhibitor use.

64. ***d***
Amlodipine is a calcium channel blocker and its use does not warrant monitoring potassium levels. Fosinopril is an ACE inhibitor and candesartan is an ARB. Both warrant monitoring potassium levels because both have the potential to produce hyperkalemia, especially in patients who have renal impairment or CHF. Hydrochlorothiazide has the potential to produce hypokalemia, so, it too warrants monitoring of potassium levels.

65. ***c***
Direct inguinal hernias occur through Hesselbach's triangle. These can be congenital or acquired. They result because of a weakness in the floor of the inguinal canal. The internal inguinal ring is the most common site for development of an indirect inguinal hernia. These can occur in men and women. Though most are probably congenital, symptoms may not be obvious until later in life. Indirect hernias are more common on the right side.

66. ***b***
Inguinal hernias are very common in males. A typical symptom reported by men with an inguinal hernia is scrotal heaviness, especially at the end of the day. These symptoms are often experienced with heavy lifting, prolonged standing, or straining to have a bowel movement. If pain is present (which is unusual), it can usually be relieved by lying down or ceasing the activity that produced the symptoms. If this does not relieve the pain, or if the pain is severe, the hernia may have become strangulated. This requires immediate referral. Epididymitis can produce scrotal pain, not usually "heaviness". Hydrocele results in fluid in the scrotum.

67. ***a***
The mini mental status exam (MMSE) is a very common and easily administered cognitive evaluation for dementia. It tests orientation, recall, attention, calculation, language manipulation, and constructional praxis. It is not sensitive for mild dementia and may be influenced by educational level and age. Even with these limitations, the MMSE is the most widely used cognitive test for dementia in the US.

68. ***c***
Liver enzymes rise in response to acute injury to the liver. ALT and AST are frequently elevated when alcohol abuse occurs. Specifically, the AST is usually the higher of the two enzymes and can signify alcohol abuse when it is more than 2 times greater than the ALT. In patients who abuse alcohol daily, the ALT and AST may be normal. GGT, gamma-glutamyl transferase, is often elevated even when ALT and AST are normal. It can help identify damage to the liver as a result of alcohol abuse.

69. ***c***
In patients with eating disorders, it is common to identify affective disorders, anxiety disorders, or substance abuse issues. Obsessive-compulsive disorder is also commonly observed. Patients with eating disorders are more likely to have a first or second degree

relative with an eating disorder, affective disorder, or alcohol abuse. There is no evidence that patients with eating disorders exhibit a higher incidence of sleep disorders, or have been sexually abused. Thyroid disease should always be assessed in patients with eating disorders, but this does not represent the reason for weight loss when eating disorder is present.

70. *c*
This patient has anorexia nervosa. She is far below ideal body weight and exhibits evidence of poor nutrition and health. More than 90% of patients with anorexia are amenorrheic. These patients have low levels of leutenizing hormone and follicle stimulating hormone. Because of prolonged hypoestrogenic states, they are highly susceptible to osteopenia and osteoporosis. It is not known why, but, many patients with anorexia also exhibit mitral valve prolapse, not mitral regurgitation. Because she is bradycardic, an EKG should be performed. QT prolongation is common in these patients, especially when bradycardia is present. Hypotension is more common than hypertension in anorexic patients.

71. *d*
The first step in being able to receive help for a problem is to be able to acknowledge that a problem exists. Since this patient is not willing to acknowledge a problem, but he needs help, one tack is to let him know that you are concerned about his health. If LFTs are ordered, they may not demonstrate elevation; especially if he consumes alcohol every day. Ordering a blood alcohol content, even if positive will be little or no help in having this patient realize that he consumes excessive amounts of alcohol. The provider could tell him to find another health care provider, but, this will do little to get this patient.

72. *a*
The medications of choice to treat bulimia nervosa are the SSRIs. Generally, high doses are required. Wellbutrin is not an SSRI and should not be given to patients with eating disorders because of great fluctuations in drug levels related to purging. Generally, this is more common in women than men. Loss of control IS a characteristic of this illness.

73. *a*
Fever is an unusual symptom associated with acute bronchitis. Cough is the most common symptom associated with acute bronchitis. Purulent sputum is identified in more than 50% of patients with acute bronchitis. The color imparted to the sputum is usually due to sloughing of epithelial cells, not bacterial infection. Concurrent upper respiratory symptoms are typical of acute bronchitis. Pharyngitis is very common.

74. *c*
The rapid HIV is always performed on the source patient ("the patient"). It is known as an ELISA (enzyme linked immunosorbent assay). In the patient suspected of being HIV positive, it is performed to establish whether or not he was positive at the time of the needle stick. In this case, it was found to be positive, but, this is a screening test, and false positives can occur. Therefore, a confirmatory test, the western blot, is routinely

performed on the patient's specimen to confirm the findings of the ELISA. The healthcare provider will usually be tested with a rapid HIV but it is done to establish HIV status at the time of the needlestick. It is not used to establish infection in the healthcare provider. The results of a rapid test can be reported in 20-40 minutes.

75. ***a***
Athletic amenorrhea creates states of prolonged hypoestrogenemia. This results in an increased risk of osteoporosis.

76. ***b***
Ectocervical specimens are collected first to minimize any bleeding that can occur from endocervix when it is sampled. The brush is considered a superior tool for collection of endocervical specimens because it produces the highest yield of endocervical cells, and thus, is a good reflection of the health of the cervix. Alternatively, a cervical broom can be used to collect cells. It collects endocervical cells and ectocervical cells simultaneously. It is rotated for 5 turns before the samples are placed on the slide. This may be used in pregnant women.

77. ***d***
Cervical screening for women aged 21-29 years should take place every 3 years with cytology only. Women aged > 30 years should be screened every 5 years with cytology and HPV. Generally, women who have been adequately screened do not need screening beyond age 65 years.

78. ***d***
The vast majority of breast lumps, even in older women are benign. However, because of the risk of breast cancer in any female patient, especially an older patient, she must be evaluated for breast cancer. Fibroadenomas are common in younger women. Cysts are common throughout the lifespan. Sometimes women identify a lump, but, instead it is the lumpiness of the breast tissue and not a distinct lump.

79. ***b***
The standard of care followed by the nurse practitioner should not depend on whether the patient has insurance or not. It is unethical to not properly inform the patient of risks he may have been exposed to from the puncture wound. Offering to buy the medications for the patient is very noble but is not a sustainable practice. The nurse practitioner should prescribe the medications as for anyone with possible HIV exposure and refer to social services or a community referral agency that can help this patient acquire the appropriate medications.

80. ***c***
This patient does not meet the strict criteria for an eating disorder, but it should be suspected. The other laboratory values are not the cause of her dizziness with standing. This is likely due to a low hemoglobin. She needs treatment for a probable iron deficiency anemia and elicitation of history to help identify the cause of her low hemoglobin.

81. ***a***

Primary prevention refers to preventing an event prior to its occurrence. Using a condom to prevent infection from an STD is primary prevention. Early diagnosis refers to secondary prevention. Tertiary prevention refers to an intervention with the potential to prevent worsening of the disease.

82. ***c***

Swelling, pain, and discoloration from impaired blood flow are the classic symptoms. Choice A could describe infection, like cellulitis, and is not classic for DVT. A history of exercise actually decreases the risk of DVT. Pain secondary to DVT is not relieved by walking. The lower extremities are the most likely location of DVT, but symptoms don't always correlate with location of the thrombosis. Patients must be asked about history, family history of DVT, and precipitating conditions.

83. ***d***

Greater than 95% of patients who are exposed to HIV will seroconvert within 6 months. The majority of patients convert within 4-10 weeks after exposure. CDC recommends follow up for one year.

84. ***a***

In contrast to creams and ointments, lotions have a high water content and a low oil content. These can worsen xerosis (dry skin) due to evaporation of water on the skin. Creams have a lower water content. Ointments have no water and are excellent agents to use on dry skin as well as to prevent dry skin.

85. ***d***

5-FU is a topical agent that can be used to treat basal cell carcinoma (BCC). It is most effective on rapidly proliferating cells. This treatment should only be used on superficial BCCs. If it is used on more invasive BCC, the cure rate is significantly lower. Therefore, 5-FU should be used only on superficial BCCs in non-critical locations. It is used as a 5% formulation twice daily for 3-6 weeks.

86. ***b***

Amoxicillin is no longer indicated for initial treatment in adults who have acute bacterial sinusitis. A bacterial cause can be assumed since she's had symptoms for 10 days. A viral infection likely would have run its course by now. After 10 days of persistent symptoms, treatment is reasonable with an antibiotic; especially since this patient is diabetic. She may be having blood sugar elevations that facilitate growth of the causative organism of the sinus infection. A decongestant could be added depending on her blood pressure and personal history of using decongestants.

87. ***c***

Many studies have shown that topical nasal steroids like budesonide, fluticasone, and mometasone provide superior relief of nasal stuffiness, nasal discharge, sneezing, and postnasal drip than antihistamines. Decongestants treat symptoms associated with nasal stuffiness. Currently, topical nasal steroids are the treatment of choice for relief of

symptoms associated with allergic rhinitis (AR). Antihistamines and decongestants can be added to the regimen of a patient with AR.

88. ***b***
Grave's disease is the most common form of hyperthyroidism. There will be elevated levels of thyroid hormones like T3 and/or T4. Patients become symptomatic with palpitations, elevated blood pressure, inability to sleep, restlessness, and heat intolerance. An elevated TSH can be found in patients with hypothyroidism. Choices A and D do not relate to Grave's disease.

89. ***b***
Symptoms have a poor correlation with disease found during endoscopy. However, duodenal symptoms tend to occur within 2-5 hours of eating. These patients derive relief from eating or taking antacids. This is in contrast to a patient with a gastric ulcer who has symptoms within minutes of eating. He tends to derive less relief from antacids.

90. ***d***
More than 10 years has elapsed since this patient's last tetanus shot. He needs another one. Tdap is specifically indicated for adolescents, older adults, healthcare providers, and pregnant patients who have completed a primary series. Tetanus toxoid is indicated in the rare adult or child who is allergic to the aluminum adjuvant in the Td immunization.

91. ***d***
Patients should always be cautioned against alcohol ingestion (in any form) if they take metronidazole. Alcohol can (and usually does) produce a disulfiram reaction. This is characterized by abdominal cramps, nausea, vomiting, headache, and elevated body temperature. Precautions should remain until 72 hours after the last dose of metronidazole.

92. ***b***
Risk factors for osteoporosis (in addition to those listed) include low body weight, cigarette smoking, rheumatoid arthritis, previous fracture, and parental history of hip fracture. African American race is not a risk factor but Caucasian and Asian races are.

93. ***b***
The enzyme immunoassay allows detection of Clostridium difficile toxin, not the organism. It is the most commonly used assay in the US because it is easy to perform, yields results in less than 24 hours. The assay has good specificity, but moderate sensitivity. More sensitive tests can be performed but they are more expensive and take longer to yield results.

94. ***d***
Erysipelas and cellulitis both cause skin erythema, edema, warmth. However, erysipelas involves the upper dermis and superficial lymphatics; cellulitis involves the deeper dermis and subcutaneous fat. Erysipelas is usually caused by *Streptococcus*; cellulitis

may be caused by *Staphylococcus* and less commonly by *Streptococcus*.

95. ***b***
Erysipelas is characterized by an acute onset of symptoms as described in this scenario. Fever and chills are common. Patients with cellulitis tend to have a more gradual course with development of symptoms over several days. The erythema noted in erysipelas is well demarcated and raised above the level of the skin. This elevation reflects that the more superficial dermis is involved.

96. ***c***
Asymptomatic bruits in the carotid area are more indicative of atherosclerotic disease than increased stroke risk. A symptomatic bruit requires attention immediately. Patients with carotid artery disease are more likely to die of cardiovascular disease than cerebrovascular disease. The Framingham Heart Study found that patients with an asymptomatic carotid bruit were at increased risk of stroke, but, the majority of strokes occurred in an area away from the carotid artery. The overall risk of stroke was insignificant when an asymptomatic carotid bruit was identified.

97. ***a***
While no clear diagnosis can be made from this scenario, there are several red flags. Collectively, the red flags necessitate referral to ophthalmology. First, the eye is red. He is photophobic and has the sensation of a foreign body. There is no mention of eye discharge but, eye discharge with this scenario would cause the examiner to consider bacterial conjunctivitis or keratitis. The symptoms of photophobia and foreign body sensation are symptoms of an active corneal process. Glaucoma should also be considered in the differential. He should be referred to ophthalmology.

98. ***b***
The diagnostic test of choice to differentiate a solid from a fluid filled breast mass is ultrasound. More than 90% of breast masses in women in the 20s to early 50s are benign. However, they must be evaluated. Clinical breast exam is unable to differentiate fluid filled from solid masses. MRI is not used unless a history of breast cancer is present. Mammography has the potential to evaluate the presence of a mass, but is of inadequate benefit in assessing whether it is fluid filled or not.

99. ***c***
While an abdominal aortic aneurysm (AAA) might be detected by multiple modalities, including a plain film of the abdomen, it is most cost effectively and efficiently identified using ultrasound (US). The sensitivity and specificity for AAA identification with US is nearly 100%. Both CT and MRI are very accurate in identifying AAA, but, they are both more expensive than US.

100. ***a***
Alpha blockers (alpha-adrenergic antagonists) provide immediate relief of symptoms. The alpha-1 receptors are abundant in the prostate gland and base of the bladder. The body of the bladder has very few alpha-1 receptors. Those alpha blockers most

commonly used are terazosin, doxazosin, tamsulosin, and alfuzosin. Prazosin is a short-acting and so has less utility than the other agents mentioned.

101. ***b***
The 5-alpha-reductase inhibitors will reduce PSA levels by 50% or greater within the first 3 months and will sustain this reduction as long as the medication is taken. This class of medication interferes with the prostatic intracellular androgen response mechanism.

102. ***d***
Most learned authorities agree on the above definition but realize that it is inadequate. Infarction usually begins once an area has been ischemic for an hour. Therefore, a TIA is not benign and even brief ischemia can produce irreversible brain damage.

103. ***a***
Allopurinol has no role in treatment of acute gout because it plays no role in inflammation. Therefore, it should not be initiated during an acute attack for relief of symptoms. Most learned authorities agree that if a patient takes an antihyperuricemic agent like allopurinol, and has an attack, the therapy should be continued.

104. ***c***
Meat and fish contribute significantly to the risk of developing gout, especially in susceptible individuals. Dietary products and coffee were associated with lower risks of developing gout. Tea does contribute to development of gout. Alcohol, of course, contributes to development of gout.

105. ***d***
Systemic illness, like cancer or infection is a serious consideration when patients report no relief of pain with lying down. Additionally, this patient is female, older, and has pain more than 4 weeks. These are three risk factors for systemic cause of low back pain. Sciatica presents with pain down the leg. Ankylosing spondylitis is typical in males in their 40s. Disk disease is a consideration, but, an absence of relief with lying down is unusual.

106. ***a***
The NP is a "participating" provider because he agreed to accept assignments. An assignment is an agreement between Medicare and the NP to accept the Medicare Approved Amount (MAA) as payment in full and not charge Medicare recipients a higher rate. The NP can bill the patient for a percentage of the remaining bill that was not paid by Medicare. The NP may opt out of participating.

107. ***b***
A long-acting bronchodilator can be used to treat asthma when it is used in combination with an inhaled steroid. Otherwise, using a long-acting bronchodilator like formoterol or salmeterol is absolutely contraindicated. There is an increased risk of sudden death with asthma exacerbations when this class is used solo to treat asthma.

The other choices above can be used to treat asthma. Choices vary depending on the patient.

108. ***a***
First line treatment for patients with COPD who have intermittent symptoms of shortness of breath is an anticholinergic alone or in combination with a beta agonist. Both medications improve lung function. Asthma patients do not use anticholinergic medications as sole agents to manage symptoms. The underlying basis of asthma is inflammation and so inhaled steroids are used except for intermittent asthma.

109. ***c***
Part A of Medicare refers to the hospital insurance program. There is no enrollment fee for most patients and they are charged a monthly premium based on the number of eligible quarters they or their spouse contributed. This benefit also covers some skilled nursing facilities.

110. ***d***
The most common presentation of acute uncomplicated pyelonephritis includes fever, flank pain, and nausea and vomiting. Sometimes patients present like they have pelvic inflammatory disease (PID). In this presentation, abdominal pain is common too. Fever is so strongly correlated with acute pyelonephritis, that it is very unusual not to have fever. Renal stone patients may have this presentation, but, fever is usually NOT present. It is unlikely that cholecystitis would present with left sided flank pain. The gall bladder is on the right side of the body.

111. ***c***
This patient has trichomoniasis. This is the likely cause of her dysuria. She could be treated with metronidazole initially. This should eradicate the infection. Her partner will need treatment too. She has an inconsequential number of bacteria in her urine. She does not need treatment for the bacteria in her urine.

112. ***a***
The most common diseases in the homeless population are not seen in the same proportion in the general population. These include hepatitis, HIV, STDs, pregnancy in females, TB, skin and foot problems, and late immunizations, especially tetanus. When given the opportunity, screenings should take place and treatment when appropriate.

113. ***a***
Violence is very common in the United States. While men and women are both victims, women are more commonly victims. Patients who have been victims of violence are more likely to utilize healthcare and to have poor response to treatment. If the patient is suspected to have been a victim of violence, they should also be screened for anxiety, depression, and post-traumatic stress disorder.

114. ***b***
Screening for TB in this patient should take place with a skin test known as the

Mantoux. A chest x-ray is typically performed after a positive skin test. A sputum specimen is used for diagnosis, not screening. A questionnaire is used for screening patients who have had a history of a positive TB skin test. If symptoms are acknowledged on the questionnaire, generally, a chest x-ray is performed. The questionnaire is used to prevent too frequent exposure to radiation in patients in whom regular screening is required, like healthcare providers.

115. ***a***
ACE inhibitors have numerous indications. Three are indicated in the first choice. ACE inhibitors are also indicated in patients who have renal insufficiency. However, ACE inhibitors can worsen renal insufficiency, so the patients must be monitored closely with lab tests for BUN, Cr, and potassium. Diabetes without proteinuria is not a specific indication for ACE inhibitors though, they are used by some healthcare providers in this way. This is an off-label use.

116. ***a***
This patient likely has iron deficiency anemia because she consumes limited quantities of iron in her diet. In addition to an iron supplement, she should be encouraged to eat liberal amounts of iron rich foods like dark green leafy vegetables (spinach is a good example), peas and beans such as lentils, black beans, red beans, and white beans. Coupling these foods with foods rich in vitamin C will enhance absorption of iron.

117. ***c***
Thalassemia, like iron deficiency anemia can be recognized or suspected by the finding of small, pale red cells on the peripheral smear of a CBC. The definitive diagnosis of thalassemia can be made by hemoglobin electrophoresis.

118. ***b***
The typical cluster headache lasts less than 3 hours; usually less than 90 minutes. Migraine headaches are usually 4-72 hours, more common in females. Cluster headaches are more common in males and are triggered by alcohol or nicotine intake. Migraines may be triggered by diet, skipping meals, sunlight, red wine, aged cheeses, or menses. Family history is the most common finding in patients who have migraine headaches.

119. ***d***
The diagnostic criteria for Alzheimer's disease (AD) was established by DSM V and other organizations. The criteria are similar. Criteria include a gradual onset of cognitive decline. A rapid onset usually indicates another etiology, perhaps, delirium. Other criteria include impairment of recent memory, difficulty with language or finding words, the inability to execute skilled motor activities, disturbances of visual processing or disturbances in executive function that includes abstract reasoning and concentration. Focal neurologic signs are consistent with a vascular dementia. Radiologic evidence is not a criterion for diagnosis, though it may support the diagnosis of AD. There is no laboratory evidence of AD.

120. ***c***
A therapeutic relationship with a patient can be established in many different ways. One way is to ask open-ended questions. This allows the patient to discuss what is most important to him; personal concerns may be vocalized by the patient. Telling the patient that he can trust you probably does little to establish trust. Actions that establish trust are more therapeutic than this statement. Touching the patient during the interview may be perceived as inappropriate by many patients. In contrast, touching the patient during the exam is different. Finally, telling the patient that you enjoyed taking care of him (if this was true) does little to establish trust.

121. ***a***
There are several risk factors for HIV transmission. Viral load is likely the greatest risk factor. The presence of STDs increases the risk of HIV transmission. Specifically, the presence of chlamydia increases the risk of acquiring HIV by 5 times. Lack of circumcision increases the risk of transmission.

122. ***b***
An urgent threat to this patient is the possibility of stroke from atrial fibrillation. A common presentation in older patients who have hyperthyroidism is atrial fibrillation. Unless she is anti-coagulated, she is at very high risk for stroke, especially as her hyperthyroidism is treated and she returns to a normal sinus rhythm. She probably will exhibit a systolic murmur, but this poses little threat to her. She should also be monitored for angina and heart failure. These are commonly found when patients present urgently to a clinic or emergency department.

123. ***c***
Sleep difficulty is a common complaint among patients with depression. Patients with difficulty falling asleep are often anxious. Frequent waking and early morning wakening are often complaints by patients with depression. There is no agreed on physiologic explanation, but, this is a common symptom.

124. ***c***
Patients who have gout exacerbations should avoid foods high in purines. A low purine diet can significantly reduce risk of gout. Uric acid is a byproduct of purine metabolism. Purines can be found in high concentrations in beef, pork, bacon, lamb, seafood, beer, bread, gravy, and most alcoholic beverages. Foods considered low in purines are fruits and fruit juices, green veggies, nuts, dairy products, chocolate.

125. ***b***
Several studies have demonstrated that erectile dysfunction (ED) was associated with use of thiazide diuretics, specifically chlorthalidone. When ED was evaluated in patients taking chlorthalidone, acebutolol, amlodipine, enalapril, and doxazosin (the major antihypertensive drug classes), the thiazide diuretic, chlorthalidone had the greatest incidence of ED. The other drugs in the study were no more likely to cause ED than a placebo. However, a common complaint of men on antihypertensive medications is ED. This should always be evaluated as a side effect of antihypertensive treatment.

126. ***b***
This is an example of secondary prevention. Secondary prevention is represented by screenings intended to identify early course of a disease. In this example, a mammogram is intended to identify early breast cancer.

127. ***c***
The primary goal of antiviral therapy in a patient diagnosed with shingles is to reduce the risk of or severity of post-herpetic neuralgia. Since she has been identified within 72 hours of onset of lesions, she can be treated with most benefit with an oral antiviral agent. Studies do not demonstrate that patients have reduction of pain or resolution of symptoms faster if oral steroids are given. They should be avoided in older patients because there is no identified benefit. Shingles can be very painful and so treatment for pain should be priority.

128. ***a***
The most common pathogen associated with pyelonephritis is E. coli. This is a gram negative pathogen which commonly inhabits the lower genitourinary (GU) tract. It also is the most common pathogen associated with urinary tract infections (UTI). Untreated or undertreated UTIs are the most common reason for pyelonephritis. Hence, it is reasonable for the pathogen to be similar. The other organisms listed are not common inhabitants in the lower GU tract.

129. ***d***
The incubation period for scabies is about 3-4 weeks after primary infection. Patients with subsequent infections with scabies will develop symptoms in 1-3 days. The classic symptom is itching that is worse at night coupled with a rash that appears in new areas over time.

130. ***a***
Many factors must be present for a patient to develop Lyme Disease from a tick bite. First, the tick must belong to Ixodes species. The tick must have been attached for at least 48-72 hours before disease can be spread. Time of year, stage of organism's development, and others all affect transmission. There is no need for prophylactic treatment in this case because the tick has not been present long enough, though, many patients will feel antibiotics are necessary.

131. ***b***
Hot water heaters are common sources of burns in homes of elderly patients and very young patients. Many safety organizations in the United States believe that burns can be prevented if hot water heaters are set to less than 120 degrees.

132. ***d***
Cranial nerve (CN) XII enables a patient to stick his tongue out and to move it from side to side in his mouth. CN III is partly responsible for eye movement. CN VII is responsible for the ability to close eyes tightly, wrinkle the forehead, and smile. CN X is partly responsible for speaking and tongue movement.

133. *d*
Arteriovenous nicking (AV nicking), or nipping, is commonly seen in patients who have hypertension. It represents retinal microvascular changes. These are typically early changes and usually reflective of current and past blood pressures. More severe damage can be seen when flame hemorrhages or cotton wool spots are identified. These often represent current blood pressure elevations since these tend to be more acute evidence of elevated blood pressure.

134. *c*
These nodules describe erythema nodosum. These are most common in women aged 15-40 years old. They are typically found in pretibial locations and can be associated with infectious agents, drugs, or systemic inflammatory disease like ulcerative colitis. They probably occur as a result of a delayed hypersensitivity reaction to antigens. It is not unusual to find polyarthralgia, fever, and or malaise that precede or accompany the skin nodules.

135. *c*
The class of medications known as triptans, which includes sumatriptan, is used as abortive agents, not for prophylaxis. The other classes mentioned can be used for prophylaxis. Some of these medications are used off-label for migraine prophylaxis. Other prophylactic agents include lithium, SSRIs, anticonvulsants, ACEs and ARBs.

136. *c*
The eyes are drained partly by the pre-auricular lymph nodes. They are palpated near the ear and can swell in response to eye infections, allergies, or foreign bodies in the eye.

137. *d*
This represents leakage of blood out of the ophthalmic vasculature. It is usually painless and can be the result of coughing, sneezing, hypertension, or trauma. This will resolve without treatment, but, aspirin or other agents that can produce bleeding should be discontinued until the etiology is determined.

138. *b*
There are a number of possible etiologies for her vomiting. Without knowing her last menstrual period (and even if she reported one), pregnancy must be ruled in or out. The other concern is her electrolyte status, especially her potassium.

139. *b*
Nearly all cases of pneumonia can be identified on chest x-ray by the presence of infiltrates. Patients with bronchitis have a normal chest x-ray unless there are other underlying pathologies. CBCs distinguish bacterial from viral infections. Sputum specimens are indicated when there is a need to identify organisms in the sputum. Pulmonary function tests are indicated in chronic lung diseases like COPD or asthma.

140. *d*
When an abnormal TSH is received, especially when a patient is not symptomatic, it

should be repeated. Sometimes there are periods of transient hypothyroidism, lab error, and missed doses that can cause changes in TSH levels.

141. ***b***
In 2010, CDC released its most recent guidelines for management of STDs. There was a major update for management of gonorrhea in Fall, 2012. Cefixime is no longer recommended as a cephalosporin for treatment of gonorrhea because of cephalosporin resistant strains of gonorrhea. 250 mg ceftriaxone should be given IM in conjunction with either azithromycin or doxycycline by mouth when gonorrhea is diagnosed. Treatment failure should be reported to CDC.

142. ***c***
This patient has an elevated mean corpuscular volume. This indicates a macrocytic anemia. Common macrocytic anemias are B12 deficiency and folate deficiency. These are common in older patients, especially if they consume large quantities of alcohol. This patient also has elevated triglycerides. Triglycerides are commonly elevated when patients are exposed to alcohol and carbohydrates. This patient's history indicates two elements that indicate alcohol abuse. He should be questioned regarding alcohol abuse.

143. ***a***
The most common cause of vaginal discharge in women of child-bearing age is bacterial vaginosis. The most common presentation is a complaint of vaginal discharge with a fishy odor, most noticeable after sexual intercourse. The vaginal discharge is cream colored and thin. Chlamydia produces a discharge but it is not reported as pruritic. Herpes does not produce a discharge. Syphilis produces a lesion.

144. ***b***
Plantar fasciitis is an inflammation of the ligaments in the plantar fascia. The fascia is a thick white tissue that begins at the heel and extends under the foot to the toes. It supports the foot during walking. Patients who are at increased risk are long-distance runners, dancers, people who are on their feet for long periods of time. This can be treated with rest, ice, NSAIDs short-term, stretching exercises, orthotics, and steroid injections.

145. ***a***
Thiazide diuretics have the secondary effect of increasing serum calcium by decreasing fluid. This makes more calcium available for absorption. This would not be used to treat a patient with osteoporosis, but, this mechanism of action could be helpful as an adjunct for patients who are receiving other forms of treatment for osteoporosis. The other agents listed would have no effect on osteoporosis. Calcium channel blockers impede movement of calcium into cells. This has no effect on available serum calcium.

146. ***b***
A polyneuropathy is a term that refers to a process that affects multiple nerves, usually peripheral. The distal nerves are more commonly affected. Symptoms described by patients are burning, weakness, or loss of sensation. Charcot-Marie-Tooth disease is a

rare, hereditary primary motor sensory neuropathy. Guillain-Barre is an acute autoimmune neuropathy that is primarily demyelinating. Urinary incontinence does not represent a common polyneuropathy in the elderly.

147. *b*
Saw palmetto is an extract of fruit of the American dwarf tree. It is commonly used to treat benign prostatic hypertrophy (BPH) but there is no objective data supporting its use. It is available over the counter and is purchased by men for BPH. It has an unknown mechanism of action but men with BPH report a subjective increase in urine flow rate when taking saw palmetto.

148. *c*
The description in the question describes a xanthelasma. It is slightly raised and is a well-circumscribed plaque on the upper eyelid usually. One or both lids may be affected. These are often associated with lipid disorders but may occur independent of any systemic or local disease. These plaques do not affect vision.

149. *c*
The period of time that risk of transmission is greatest is when the viral load is high. Many times this is before a patient has been diagnosed and so he is capable of transmitting this disease without knowledge that he is doing so. The highest viral load may occur during the earliest stages of HIV and before there is detectable antibody.

150. *b*
Osgood-Schlatter disease is an overuse syndrome that produces pain and tenderness at the tibial tuberosity. It is also called tibial tuberosity apophysitis. Although Osgood-Schlatter disease sounds ominous, it is very common during adolescence. It occurs generally in males ages 13-14, and ages 11-12 in females.

Family Exam #2 Questions

1. **A female patient who takes oral contraceptives has just completed her morning exercise routine. She complains of pain in her right calf. Her blood pressure and heart rate are normal. She is not short of breath. Her calf is red and warm to touch. What is NOT part of the differential diagnosis?**

    a. **Deep vein thrombosis**
    b. **Cellulitis**
    c. **Calf muscle strain**
    d. **Trochanteric bursitis**

2. **A one week-old infant has a mucopurulent eye discharge bilaterally. What explains the etiology of the discharge?**

    a. **The mother probably has an STD.**
    b. **The infant likely has a plugged tear duct.**
    c. **This is bacterial conjunctivitis.**
    d. **This is viral conjunctivitis.**

3. **A patient with eczema asks for a recommendation for a skin preparation to help with xerosis. What should the NP respond?**

    a. **Use a petroleum based product**
    b. **Use a hypoallergenic lotion**
    c. **Use any hypoallergenic product**
    d. **No particular product is better than another**

4. **Which patient below should be screened for osteoporosis?**

    a. **60 year-old male with rheumatoid arthritis**
    b. **50 year-old Caucasian female**
    c. **A 65 year-old male who is otherwise healthy**
    d. **A 62 year-old post menopausal female**

5. **A 3 year-old has fluid in the middle ear that does not appear infected. The eardrum appears normal. This is referred to as:**

    a. **serous otitis media.**
    b. **acute otitis media.**
    c. **otitis media with effusion.**
    d. **middle ear effusion.**

6. Which set of symptoms is most likely in a patient infected with *C. difficile*?

a. **Headache, diarrhea, body aches**
b. **Body aches, fever, abdominal cramps**
c. **Fever, headache, diarrhea**
d. **Diarrhea, abdominal pain, nausea or vomiting**

7. A patient who presents with a complaint of sudden decreased visual acuity has a pupil that is about 4 mm, fixed. The affected eye is red. What might be the etiology?

a. **Stroke**
b. **Brain tumor**
c. **Glaucoma**
d. **Cataract**

8. Which statement about attention deficit disorder (ADD) is correct?

a. **This is more common in girls less than age 9 years.**
b. **Family history does not play a role in this disorder.**
c. **Hyperactivity must be present for this diagnosis.**
d. **DSM V is used to diagnose a child with ADD.**

9. Which of the following increases the prostate specific antigen (PSA) insignificantly?

a. **Digital rectal exam**
b. **Ejaculation**
c. **Prostatitis**
d. **Prostate biopsy**

10. A 4 year-old child with otitis media with effusion:

a. **needs an antibiotic.**
b. **probably has a viral infection.**
c. **probably has just had acute otitis media.**
d. **has cloudy fluid in the middle ear.**

11. Abuse during pregnancy:

a. **tends to occur throughout the pregnancy.**
b. **is more likely when pregnancies are planned.**
c. **is more prevalent in middle socio-economic populations.**
d. **is often acknowledged by the abusing spouse.**

12. A patient with COPD has been using albuterol with good relief of his shortness of breath. He is using it 3-4 times daily over the past 4 weeks. How should the NP manage this?

a. **Encourage its use**
b. **Add a long acting anticholinergic**
c. **Tell him to use it only once daily**
d. **Add an oral steroid**

13. A typical description of sciatica is:

a. **deep and aching.**
b. **worse at nighttime.**
c. **burning and sharp.**
d. **worse with coughing.**

14. An example of a short-acting beta agonist is:

a. **levalbuterol.**
b. **salmeterol.**
c. **mometasone.**
d. **beclomethasone.**

15. Which factor listed below increases the risk of ectopic pregnancy?

a. **Prior history of ectopic pregnancy**
b. **History of pre-term labor**
c. **Use of oral contraceptives**
d. **Young age**

16. A 40 year-old patient has the following laboratory values. How should they be interpreted?

HBsAg (-), HBsAb (+), HBcAb (+)

a. **The patient had hepatitis.**
b. **The patient has never had hepatitis.**
c. **The patient should consider immunization.**
d. **The patient has been immunized.**

17. A patient that you are caring for in your clinic has Medicare Part B. What does this mean?

a. **The federal government will pay for his visit to your clinic today.**
b. **His medicare benefit covers outpatient services.**
c. **He will have a co-pay for his visit today.**
d. **His prescriptions will be partly paid for today.**

18. A patient presents with costovertebral angle (CVA) tenderness, fever of 101 degrees. She is anorexic. What is her likely diagnosis?

a. **Diverticulosis**
b. **Renal stone**
c. **Pyelonephritis**
d. **Urinary tract infection**

19. A patient has a positive pregnancy test that she performed from an over the counter kit. It has been 6 weeks since her last menstrual period. What are the chances that she is pregnant?

a. **> 25%**
b. **> 50%**
c. **> 75%**
d. **> 90%**

20. Ipratropium is very widely used in the treatment of COPD. Which of the following statements about ipratropium is correct?

a. **It slows the progression of COPD.**
b. **It decreases parasympathetic tone and produces bronchodilation.**
c. **It has anti-inflammatory actions and reduces bronchoconstriction.**
d. **It is less effective than a beta agonist in producing bronchoconstriction.**

21. A patient being treated for trichomoniasis is given a prescription for metronidazole. What instructions should she be given?

a. **Take this medication with food.**
b. **Do not take this medication if you are pregnant.**
c. **Take this medication on an empty stomach.**
d. **This medication should not be taken with alcohol.**

22. Which activity does NOT place the pregnant patient at risk of contracting toxoplasmosis?

a. **Eating undercooked lamb, venison, or pork**
b. **Poor hand washing after gardening**
c. **Eating sushi**
d. **Cleaning a cat's litter box**

23. A 35 year-old patient who is HIV positive is diagnosed with thrush. A microscopic exam of this patient's saliva demonstrates:

a. **epithelial cells.**
b. **yeast.**
c. **spores.**
d. **red blood cells.**

24. You are volunteering at a clinic that cares for homeless patients. What's the most important aspect of a patient's first visit?

a. **A complete head to toe exam**
b. **Establish trust**
c. **Take an excellent history**
d. **Ask about problems with alcohol**

25. Which of the following medications may have an unfavorable effect on a hypertensive patient's blood pressure?

a. **Lovastatin**
b. **Ibuprofen**
c. **Fluticasone**
d. **Amoxicillin**

26. The agent commonly used to treat patients with scabies is permethrin. How often is it applied to eradicate scabies?

a. **Once**
b. **Once daily for 3 days**
c. **Twice daily for 3 days**
d. **Once daily for one week**

27. What is the proper technique to safely remove a tick from a human?

a. **Pull it off with tweezers**
b. **Use petroleum jelly**
c. **Use isopropyl alcohol**
d. **Use a hot match**

28. A patient has developed rapid loss of hearing over the past several weeks. What cranial nerve should be assessed?

a. **Cranial Nerve III**
b. **Cranial Nerve V**
c. **Cranial Nerve VIII**
d. **Cranial Nerve X**

29. A patient who has been treated for hypothyroidism presents for her annual exam. Her TSH is 14.1 (normal = 0.4- 3.8). She complains of weight gain and fatigue. How should the NP proceed?

a. **Ask what time of day she is taking her medication**
b. **Ask if she is taking her medication**
c. **Increase her dose of thyroid supplement**
d. **Repeat the TSH in 2-3 months**

30. If plantar fasciitis is suspected in a patient, how is this diagnosed?

a. **X-ray of the foot**
b. **CT scan**
c. **Physical exam**
d. **Bone scan**

31. Which mitral disorder results from redundancy of the mitral valve's leaflets?

a. **Acute mitral regurgitation**
b. **Chronic mitral regurgitation**
c. **Mitral valve prolapse**
d. **Mitral stenosis**

32. A mother of a 4 week-old infant visits your office. She states that her baby is vomiting after feeding and then cries as if he is hungry again. What should the nurse practitioner assess?

- a. **His abdomen for an olive shaped mass**
- b. **His rectum for patency**
- c. **His swallowing ability**
- d. **The position his mother uses when she feeds him**

33. A patient was diagnosed today with pregnancy. Her last pregnancy was 3 years ago. At that time she had a protective rubella titer. What should be done about evaluating a rubella titer today?

- a. **There is no need to get one since she has been pregnant before.**
- b. **It should be evaluated to make sure it is still protective.**
- c. **She should be vaccinated now to insure protection.**
- d. **She does not need one because it was protective 3 years ago.**

34. A patient reports that she takes kava kava regularly for anxiety with good results. What should the NP evaluate?

- a. **Liver function studies**
- b. **Risk of bleeding**
- c. **Thyroid function**
- d. **Colon polyps**

35. When examining the vessels of the eye:

- a. **the veins are smaller than the arteries.**
- b. **the arteries are smaller than the veins.**
- c. **the arteries are dark red.**
- d. **the arteries pulsate.**

36. A 70 year-old male has a yellowish, triangular nodule on the side of the iris. This is probably:

- a. **a stye.**
- b. **a chalazion.**
- c. **a pinguecula.**
- d. **subconjunctival hemorrhage.**

37. Which suggestion below is the standard for treating iron deficiency anemia in infants and children?

a. **Iron supplementation in divided doses between meals with orange juice**
b. **Iron supplementation once daily with the largest meal**
c. **Meat >5 servings per week with citrus juice**
d. **Iron supplementation with orange juice 5 times weekly**

38. Hyperemesis gravidarum is:

a. **morning sickness.**
b. **persistent, intractable vomiting during pregnancy.**
c. **always occurs with hydatiform mole.**
d. **indicative of multiple gestation.**

39. A 28 year-old female presents with a slightly tender 1.5 cm lump in her right breast. She noticed it two days ago. She has no associated lymphadenopathy and there is no nipple discharge. How should she be managed?

a. **Mammogram**
b. **Ultrasound and mammogram**
c. **Re-examination after her next menses**
d. **Clinical exam only**

40. A common, early finding in patients with chronic aortic regurgitation (AR) is:

a. **an hypertrophied left ventricle.**
b. **atrial fibrillation.**
c. **pulmonary congestion.**
d. **low systolic blood pressure.**

41. The test of choice to confirm and assess developmental dysplasia of the hip (DHH) in a 3 month old is:

a. **frog leg x-rays.**
b. **plain hip x-rays.**
c. **ultrasound of the hip.**
d. **CT of the hip.**

42. The usual clinical course of mitral valve prolapse:

a. **is benign.**
b. **results in sudden cardiac death.**
c. **results in congestive heart failure.**
d. **is associated with multiple episodes of emboli.**

43. What should be avoided in a patient being treated with metronidazole for trichomonas?

a. **Direct sunlight**
b. **Alcohol**
c. **Tea**
d. **Penicillin**

44. A pregnant patient took L-thyroxin prior to becoming pregnant. What should be done about the L-thyroxin now that she is pregnant?

a. **It should be discontinued during pregnancy.**
b. **She should continue it and have monthly TSH levels.**
c. **She should be switched to a supplement with a category B rating.**
d. **She can continue it during pregnancy without concern.**

45. The most common place for basal cell carcinoma to be found is the:

a. **scalp.**
b. **face.**
c. **anterior shin.**
d. **upper posterior back.**

46. Where would the murmur associated with mitral regurgitation best be auscultated?

a. **Aortic listening point**
b. **Mitral listening point**
c. **Pulmonic listening point**
d. **Tricuspid listening point**

47. A 74 year-old is diagnosed with shingles. The NP is deciding how to best manage her care. What should be prescribed?

a. **An oral antiviral agent**
b. **An oral antiviral agent plus an oral steroid**
c. **An oral antiviral agent plus a topical steroid**
d. **A topical steroid only**

48. A 4 year-old was brought into the clinic by her mother who reports that she pulled her arms upward to pick her up and now the child won't use her right arm. A nursemaid's elbow is suspected. Which statement below is correct?

a. **The child is crying because her arm hurts.**
b. **She will need to be admitted to the hospital for fracture reduction.**
c. **Her arm is slightly flexed and held close to her body.**
d. **Her elbow is held straight at her side and her fingers are in a fist.**

49. The diagnosis of mitral valve prolapse can be confirmed by:

a. **physical examination.**
b. **electrocardiography.**
c. **echocardiography.**
d. **chest x-ray.**

50. The incidence of pyelonephritis is:

a. **more common in children.**
b. **less common than urinary tract infections.**
c. **always associated with urinary tract infections.**
d. **more likely in elderly males.**

51. A patient complains of "first step in the morning" pain in his heel. He states that it has progressed to "end of the day" heel pain. What probably has contributed to this most?

a. **Driving a vehicle long distances**
b. **Walking in new tennis shoes**
c. **Riding a bicycle**
d. **Pes planus**

52. A patient who has diabetes presents with pain when he walks and pain resolution with rest. When specifically asked about the pain in his lower leg, he likely will report pain:

a. **in and around the ankle joint.**
b. **in the calf muscle.**
c. **radiating down his leg from the thigh.**
d. **pain in his lower leg which waxes and wanes.**

53. The two tests which can indicate with certainty that a patient has hepatitis B at present are:

a. **hepatitis B surface antigen and antibody.**
b. **hepatitis B surface antigen and IgM.**
c. **hepatitis B surface antibody and core antibody.**
d. **positive IgG and positive core antibody.**

54. A pregnant patient asks why she must take calcium during pregnancy. The nurse practitioner replies that:

a. **it will strengthen the bones and teeth in your fetus.**
b. **it may prevent pregnancy induced hypotension.**
c. **it is to keep you from having dental problems.**
d. **it will help strengthen your bones.**

55. A patient has non-fasting glucose values of 110 mg/dL and 116 mg/dL. This patient:

a. **can be diagnosed with Type 2 diabetes.**
b. **has impaired fasting glucose.**
c. **should have a Hgb A1C performed.**
d. **has normal glucose values.**

56. Which of the following characteristics is always present in a patient with COPD?

a. **Productive cough**
b. **Obstructed airways**
c. **Shortness of breath**
d. **Hypercapnia**

57. A male child has a swelling in the upper thigh below the inguinal ligament with cramping and abdominal pain. What is in the NP's differential diagnosis?

a. **Testicular torsion**
b. **Femoral hernia**
c. **Varicocele**
d. **Hydrocele**

58. In a patient with mononucleosis, which laboratory abnormality is most common?

a. **Lymphocytosis and atypical lymphocytes**
b. **Elevated monocytes**
c. **A decreased total white count**
d. **Elevated liver enzymes**

59. A 65 year-old male is diagnosed with an initial episode of gout. It is likely that he:

a. will have elevated uric acid levels.
b. is consuming too much meat.
c. will have involvement in a joint like the hip or shoulder.
d. will have severe inflammation in a single joint.

60. A 24 year-old female presents with abdominal pain. On exam, she is found to have cervical motion tenderness. What finding supports a diagnosis of pelvic inflammatory disease (PID)?

a. A positive pregnancy test
b. Vaginal discharge
c. Positive RPR
d. Oral temperature 102F

61. A male patient who injured his back lifting a heavy object reports that he has low back pain. He is diagnosed with a lumbar strain. He is afraid to continue activities of daily living and especially walking because he has pain with these activities. What statement below is true?

a. Stop doing any activities that produce pain in your lower back.
b. Continue your activities of daily living, but stop walking, except to go to the bathroom.
c. Bedrest will help your back pain.
d. Continue your activities of daily living and walking.

62. A seven year-old entered the clinic one month ago. There was no evidence that he had any immunizations. He was given hepatitis B, DTaP, IPV, varicella, and MMR. If he returns today, which immunizations can he receive?

a. Hepatitis B, Td, Hib, polio, MMR
b. Hepatitis B, Td, IPV, MMR, varicella
c. IPV only
d. Hepatitis B, DTaP, IPV, MMR

63. A 63 year-old male has been your patient for several years. He is a former smoker who takes simvastatin, ramipril, and an aspirin daily. His blood pressure and lipids are well controlled. He presents to your clinic with complaints of fatigue and "just not feeling well" for the last few days. His vital signs and exam are normal. What should be done next?

a. Order a CBC and consider waiting a few days if normal.
b. Inquire about feelings of depression and hopelessness.
c. Order a CBC, metabolic panel, TSH, and urine analysis.
d. Order a B12 level, TSH, CBC, and chest x-ray.

64. MMR immunization is safe in children:

- a. who are allergic to eggs.
- b. less than one year of age.
- c. when given every 5 years.
- d. if they are at least 5 years of age.

65. A pregnant patient is found to have positive leukocytes and positive nitrites in her urine. What medication should be given?

- a. Doxycycline
- b. Trimethoprim-sulfamethoxazole (TMPS)
- c. Ciprofloxacin
- d. Nitrofurantoin

66. A 25 year-old female presents with lower abdominal pain. Which finding below would likely indicate the etiology as pelvic inflammatory disease?

- a. Presence of hyphae
- b. Hematuria
- c. Temperature >101F
- d. Normal sedimentation rate

67. A patient has had an anaphylactic reaction to eggs. She should avoid immunization with:

- a. varicella.
- b. hepatitis B.
- c. IPV.
- d. influenza.

68. A 70 year-old male who is diabetic presents with gait difficulty, cognitive disturbance, and urinary incontinence. What is part of the nurse practitioner's differential diagnosis?

- a. Diabetic neuropathy
- b. Normal pressure hydrocephalus
- c. Parkinson's Disease
- d. Multiple sclerosis

69. A 5 year-old female's playmate has been diagnosed with pinworms. The mother brings her child in for an exam. The 5 year-old denies rectal itching. How should the NP proceed?

- a. **Reassure the mother that if the child develops symptoms, she will need to be treated.**
- b. **Visually assess the child's rectum for redness or presence of worms.**
- c. **Have the mother collect a stool specimen and send it to the laboratory.**
- d. **Perform the "scotch tape" test and look at the collection under the microscope.**

70. The lipid particle with the greatest atherogenic effect is:

- a. **total cholesterol.**
- b. **HDL.**
- c. **LDL.**
- d. **triglycerides.**

71. The gold standard for diagnosing pneumonia on chest x-ray is the presence of:

- a. **infiltrates.**
- b. **interstitial fluid.**
- c. **cavitation.**
- d. **"pooling".**

72. An immune response to Group A Streptococcal infections involving the heart is:

- a. **Kawasaki syndrome.**
- b. **rheumatic fever.**
- c. **hemolytic disease.**
- d. **pericarditis.**

73. A 74 year-old patient has a pill-rolling tremor. With what disease is this often associated?

- a. **Psychosomatic disorder**
- b. **Multiple sclerosis**
- c. **Parkinson's disease**
- d. **Benign essential tremor**

74. Pharmacologic treatment for children with hypertension should be initiated for:

- a. **those who are obese.**
- b. **Stage 1 hypertension.**
- c. **diabetics with hypertension.**
- d. **asymptomatic Stage 1 or Stage 2 hypertension.**

75. Which statement below is true regarding NSAIDs for low back pain?

a. **They are as equally efficacious as acetaminophen for pain.**
b. **They are associated with more side effects than acetaminophen.**
c. **They provide superior relief of symptoms at one-week post injury.**
d. **They should not be used to treat acute low back pain.**

76. A pregnant patient is in her first trimester in October. How should a flu immunization be handled for her?

a. **Do not give an influenza immunization during pregnancy.**
b. **Give the influenza immunization after the first trimester.**
c. **Give the influenza immunization without regard to trimester.**
d. **Only give the intranasal influenza immunization.**

77. Mycoplasma pneumoniae is:

a. **a diagnosis of exclusion.**
b. **a typical respiratory pathogen.**
c. **only identifiable on chest x-ray.**
d. **a disease with extrapulmonary manifestations.**

78. Most hypertension in pre-adolescents and children is:

a. **obesity related.**
b. **primary hypertension.**
c. **secondary hypertension.**
d. **endocrine related.**

79. The most common cause of diarrhea in adults is:

a. ***E. coli.***
b. ***Salmonella.***
c. ***C. difficile.***
d. **viral gastroenteritis.**

80. A 55 year-old male is obese, does not exercise, and has hyperlipidemia. He is diagnosed with Stage 1 hypertension today. How should he be managed?

a. **He should be given low dose thiazide diuretic.**
b. **An ACE inhibitor is appropriate.**
c. **Lifestyle modifications are appropriate.**
d. **He should receive an ACE inhibitor and thiazide diuretic.**

81. A patient recently received an antibiotic for 10 days for pneumonia. His respiratory symptoms have resolved but today he calls the office. He reports having severe watery diarrhea, abdominal cramping, and low-grade fever. What should be done?

a. **Give an anti-diarrheal agent**
b. **Encourage the patient to force fluids**
c. **Order a stool specimen**
d. **Wait 24 hours for resolution of symptoms**

82. The three most common causes of bacterial diarrhea in the US are Salmonella, Campylobacter, and:

a. ***E. coli.***
b. ***Enterovirus.***
c. ***Yersinia.***
d. ***Shigella.***

83. A patient has been diagnosed today with Type II diabetes. A criterion for diagnosis is:

a. **an abnormal random blood glucose.**
b. **proteinuria.**
c. **a fasting glucose $\geq$ 126 and confirmed on a previous day.**
d. **an abnormal post-prandial glucose.**

84. A medication considered first line for a patient with allergic rhinitis is a:

a. **decongestant.**
b. **non-sedating antihistamine.**
c. **a leukotriene blocker.**
d. **topical nasal steroid.**

85. A female patient reports fatigue. She is found to have an iron deficiency anemia. An iron supplement is best taken:

a. **in the morning.**
b. **with food.**
c. **with a food rich in Vitamin D.**
d. **on an empty stomach.**

86. Testicular torsion can produce:

a. penile erythema.
b. scrotal edema.
c. scrotal erythema.
d. penile edema.

87. A 20 year-old male reports nocturnal headaches of recent onset. What is NOT part of the differential diagnosis in this patient?

a. Migraine headache
b. Brain tumor
c. Hydrocephalus
d. Cluster headache

88. A pregnant patient in her second trimester will probably have a decrease in her:

a. blood pressure.
b. respiratory rate.
c. heart rate.
d. cardiac output.

89. Serotonin is thought to play a role in the etiology of:

a. depression.
b. multiple myeloma.
c. multiple sclerosis.
d. ulcerative colitis.

90. Mild persistent asthma is characterized by:

a. limitation in activity due to bronchoconstriction.
b. symptoms occurring more than twice weekly.
c. wheezing and coughing during exacerbations.
d. shortness of breath with exercise.

91. A 37 year-old overweight male is diagnosed today with Type II diabetes. His fasting glucose is 159 mg/dL. He is hyperlipidemic (LDL = 210 mg/dL) and hypertensive (146/102). What medications should be initiated today?

a. Metformin, ASA, and pravastatin
b. Metformin, niacin, Monopril
c. Glimepiride, ASA, fosinopril
d. Metformin, atorvastatin, ramipril, ASA

92. A patient with allergic rhinitis developed a sinus infection 10 days ago. He takes fexofenadine daily. What should be done with the fexofenadine?

a. **Stop the fexofenadine.**
b. **Stop the fexofenadine and add a nasal steroid.**
c. **Continue the fexofenadine and prescribe an antibiotic.**
d. **Continue the fexofenadine and add a decongestant.**

93. An 18 year-old female patient has iron deficiency anemia. If this anemia has occurred in the past 3-4 months, what might be expected?

a. **An increased RDW**
b. **A decreased RDW**
c. **An elevated serum ferritin**
d. **A decreased total iron binding capacity**

94. A 17 year-old presents with complaints of dysmenorrhea. What finding below suggests that this is secondary dysmenorrhea?

a. **Normal pelvic exam**
b. **Dysmenorrhea is not limited to menses**
c. **Unpredictable menses**
d. **Nausea with menses**

95. A medication belonging to the class of triptans could be used to treat a patient with migraine headaches and:

a. **tension headaches.**
b. **cluster headaches.**
c. **serotonin abnormalities.**
d. **depression.**

96. A nurse practitioner is taking care of a patient with health insurance and allergic complaints. The NP is aware that the patient is not using the prescribed allergy medication for her. Instead, the patient is giving the medication to her husband because he does not have insurance. What should the NP do?

a. **Continue to prescribe the medication**
b. **Stop prescribing the medication for the patient**
c. **Only prescribe the medication if the patient promises to use it**
d. **Prescribe the medication only once more**

97. Which study listed below is considered an experimental study?

a. Case series
b. Cross-sectional study
c. Cohort study
d. Meta-analysis

98. The preferred medication class to treat patients with an initial episode of depression is:

a. tricyclic antidepressants.
b. monoamine oxidase inhibitors.
c. selective serotonin reuptake inhibitors.
d. any class. There is no preferred class.

99. A pregnant patient in her first trimester is found to have chlamydia. How should this be managed?

a. Treat with azithromycin
b. Treat with ceftriaxone by injection
c. Treat with doxycycline
d. Do not treat in the first trimester

100. A B-12 deficiency can produce:

a. a microcytic anemia.
b. pernicious anemia.
c. sideroblastic anemia.
d. insomnia.

101. Serotonin syndrome may result from taking an SSRI and:

a. dextromethorphan.
b. loratadine.
c. pravastatin.
d. niacin.

102. What would be the study of choice to determine the cause of a cluster of pediatric leukemia cases found in an isolated area of a rural state?

a. Randomized clinical trial
b. Cohort study
c. Case series
d. Case control

103. An elderly male diagnosed with a microcytic, hypochromic anemia:

- a. should be worked up for a malignancy.
- b. might be consuming excessive amounts of alcohol.
- c. will have a increased RBC count.
- d. may have a GI bleed.

104. The early signs and symptoms of appendicitis in an adult:

- a. are subtle.
- b. produce marked pain in the lower right abdominal quadrant.
- c. produce symptoms in the periumbilical region only.
- d. include fever, nausea and vomiting.

105. An 80 year-old female has blood pressure of 176/80. How should she be managed pharmacologically?

- a. Thiazide diuretic
- b. ACE inhibitor
- c. Calcium channel blocker
- d. Angiotensin receptor blocker

106. A patient with diabetes has a right lower leg that has recently become edematous, erythematous, and tender to touch over the anterior shin. There is no evidence of pus, but the leg is warm to touch. What is the most likely diagnosis to consider?

- a. Deep vein thrombosis (DVT)
- b. Buerger's disease
- c. Cellulitis
- d. Venous disease

107. Which medication used to treat diabetes is associated with diarrhea and flatulence?

- a. Pioglitazone
- b. Insulin
- c. Metformin
- d. Glimepiride

108. A patient has a penicillin allergy. He describes an anaphylactic reaction. Which medication class should be specifically avoided in him?

- a. Quinolones
- b. Macrolides
- c. Cephalosporins
- d. Tetracyclines

109. A serum ferritin level:

a. **could indicate thalassemia in a patient.**
b. **demonstrates the amount of iron in storage.**
c. **indicates when a patient has iron deficiency anemia.**
d. **confirms a low hemoglobin and hematocrit.**

110. Which imaging study of the abdomen would be LEAST helpful in diagnosing an acute appendicitis?

a. **Ultrasound**
b. **CT scan**
c. **MRI**
d. **X-ray**

111. What component of a prenatal vitamin is intended to prevent neural tube defects?

a. **Iron**
b. **Vitamin C**
c. **Folic acid**
d. **Niacin**

112. A sexually active male patient presents with epididymitis. What finding is likely?

a. **Abnormal urinalysis**
b. **Dysuria**
c. **Recent history of heavy physical exercise**
d. **Scrotal edema**

113. A 76 year-old depressed patient is started on an SSRI. When should another antidepressant be tried if there is no response?

a. **3-7 days**
b. **2-3 weeks**
c. **4-6 weeks**
d. **8-12 weeks**

114. A 42 year-old hypertensive patient was given a thiazide diuretic 4 weeks ago. On his return visit today, he reports feeling weak and tired. What should the NP consider to evaluate the weakness and fatigue?

a. **Blood pressure**
b. **Potassium level**
c. **CBC**
d. **Cr/BUN**

115. A 10 year-old has thick, demarcated plaques on her elbows. Which features are suggestive of psoriasis?

a. **Scaly lesions on the scalp**
b. **Pruritis around the lesions**
c. **A scaly border around the plaques**
d. **Silvery scales that are not pruritic**

116. A 52 year-old presents with symptoms of diabetes today. His glucose is 302 mg/dL. How should this be managed today?

a. **Have him return tomorrow to recheck his blood glucose**
b. **Start metformin**
c. **Start insulin**
d. **Start metformin plus pioglitazone**

117. Swimmer's ear is diagnosed in a patient with tragal tenderness. What other symptom might he have?

a. **Otitis media**
b. **Hearing loss**
c. **Otic itching**
d. **Fever**

118. A patient has heavy menses. Which lab value below reflects an iron deficiency anemia?

a. **Increased TIBC**
b. **Decreased TIBC**
c. **Normal serum iron**
d. **Decreased RDW**

119. A man fell off a 3-foot step ladder while working at home. He presents to your office with complaints of foot pain. He has point tenderness over the lateral malleolus, swelling, but he is able to ambulate. How should this be managed initially?

- a. ACE wrap and rest
- b. Rest, ice, compression, and elevation
- c. X-ray of the ankle
- d. Non-weight bearing for 3-7 days

120. An initial pharmacologic approach to a patient who is diagnosed with primary dysmenorrhea could be:

- a. acetaminophen.
- b. NSAIDs at the time symptoms begin or onset of menses.
- c. NSAIDs prior to the onset of menses.
- d. combination acetaminophen and NSAIDs.

121. A patient complains of right leg numbness and tingling following a back injury. He has a diminished right patellar reflex and his symptoms are progressing to both legs. What test should be performed?

- a. Lumbar x-rays
- b. Lumbar CT scan
- c. Lumbar MRI
- d. Lumbar MRI with contrast

122. Routine screening for gestational diabetes should take place:

- a. at 12-16 weeks.
- b. 16-20 weeks.
- c. 24-28 weeks.
- d. anytime after the first trimester.

123. A 73 year-old patient is thought to have benign prostatic hyperplasia. What would be part of the initial workup?

- a. Digital rectal exam (DRE) only
- b. DRE, urinalysis, PSA
- c. PSA only
- d. PSA, DRE, BUN, Cr

124. The cranial nerve responsible for vision is Cranial Nerve:

- a. I.
- b. II.
- c. III.
- d. IV.

125. The research design that provides the strongest evidence for concluding causation is:

- a. randomized controlled trials.
- b. cohort studies.
- c. case control studies.
- d. prospective studies.

126. The clinical difference between minor depression and major depression is:

- a. the length of time symptoms have lasted.
- b. the number of symptoms present.
- c. the severity of the symptoms.
- d. presence of suicidal ideations.

127. A characteristic of an ACE inhibitor induced cough is that it:

- a. is mildly productive.
- b. is worse at nighttime.
- c. usually begins within a week of starting therapy.
- d. is more common in men.

128. Which description is more typical of a patient with acute cholecystitis?

- a. The patient rolls from side to side on the exam table.
- b. The patient is ill appearing and febrile.
- c. An elderly patient is more likely to exhibit Murphy's sign.
- d. Most are asymptomatic until a stone blocks the bile duct.

129. A nurse practitioner has decided to initiate insulin in a patient who takes oral diabetic medications. How much long acting insulin should be initiated in a patient who weighs 100 kg?

- a. About 5 units
- b. 10 units
- c. 15 units
- d. 20 units

130. The throat swab done to identify Streptococcal infection was negative in a 12 year-old female with tonsillar exudate, fever, and sore throat. What statement is true regarding this?

a. **A second swab should be done to repeat the test.**
b. **The patient does not have Strept throat.**
c. **The patient probably has mononucleosis.**
d. **A second swab should be collected and sent to microbiology.**

131. A patient demonstrates leukocytosis. This means:

a. **he has a bacterial infection.**
b. **he has a viral infection.**
c. **he has an infection of unknown origin.**
d. **he does not have an infection.**

132. An adolescent has suspected varicocele. He has dull scrotal pain that is relieved by:

a. **standing.**
b. **recumbency.**
c. **having a bowel movement.**
d. **elevation of the testicle.**

133. A female with complaint of dysuria has a urine specimen that is positive for leukocytes and nitrites. There is blood in the specimen. An appropriate diagnosis is:

a. **urinary tract infection.**
b. **asymptomatic bacteriuria.**
c. **UTI with hematuria.**
d. **UTI or chlamydia.**

134. The classic presentation of placenta previa is:

a. **painless bleeding in the first trimester.**
b. **painful bleeding in the third trimester.**
c. **painless vaginal bleeding after the 20th week.**
d. **painful vaginal bleeding before the 30th week.**

135. A patient is found to have eosinophilia. An expected finding is:

a. **asthma exacerbation.**
b. **bronchitis.**
c. **hepatitis.**
d. **osteoporosis.**

136. A 3 year-old has been recently treated for an upper respiratory infection (URI) but drainage from the right nostril persists. What should the NP suspect?

a. **Allergic rhinitis**
b. **Presence of a foreign body**
c. **Unresolved URI**
d. **Dental caries**

137. A 4 year-old presents with fever, rhinorrhea, and paroxysmal, high-pitched whooping cough. This is:

a. **bronchiolitis.**
b. **croup.**
c. **pertussis.**
d. **epiglottitis.**

138. A nurse practitioner is volunteering in a homeless clinic to gain clinical experience. Which statement is true about this?

a. **Malpractice insurance is not needed because this is volunteer work.**
b. **Volunteerism negates susceptibility to lawsuits.**
c. **Malpractice insurance is needed by the nurse practitioner.**
d. **Coverage will be provided by the state where the clinic is located.**

139. The most common symptoms associated with gastroesophageal reflux disease (GERD) are heartburn and:

a. **cough.**
b. **regurgitation and dysphagia.**
c. **cough and hoarseness.**
d. **belching and sore throat.**

140. Niacin is known to:

a. **increase fasting glucose levels.**
b. **produce hypertension.**
c. **decrease triglycerides.**
d. **decrease HDLs.**

141. An example of a first generation cephalosporin used to treat a skin infection is:

a. **cephalexin.**
b. **cefuroxime.**
c. **cefdinir.**
d. **ceflamore.**

142. **A patient has been prescribed pioglitazone. The nurse practitioner must remember to:**

   a. check a hemoglobin A1C in 3 months.
   b. order liver function studies in about 2-3 months.
   c. screen for microalbuminuria.
   d. wean off metformin.

143. **A patient has been diagnosed with mononucleosis. Which statement is correct?**

   a. He is likely an adolescent male.
   b. Splenomegaly is more likely than not.
   c. He cannot be co-infected with Strept.
   d. Cervical lymphadenopathy may be prominent.

144. **Which statement is true about Vitamin B-12?**

   a. It is easily absorbed through the gastrointestinal tract.
   b. Deficiencies are seen in elderly patients only.
   c. Low levels can result in elevated lipid levels.
   d. Inadequate amounts can produce cognitive changes.

145. **A patient who has hyperlipidemia should have:**

   a. a statin daily.
   b. a thyroid stimulating hormone (TSH) level.
   c. a second measurement to confirm diagnosis.
   d. a stress test done.

146. **An adolescent athlete has sprained his ankle. What instruction should be given to him regarding activity?**

   a. He can resume regular activities in about one week.
   b. He should be able to walk pain-free before he starts to run.
   c. His ankle should be taped prior to competition.
   d. He can resume activity when the edema has resolved.

147. **An adolescent female has had normal menses for almost 2 years. She has not had menses in 3 months. She is diagnosed with polycystic ovarian syndrome (PCOS). What else is a common finding?**

   a. Obesity
   b. Elevated insulin levels
   c. Positive pregnancy test
   d. Elevated blood pressure

148. Clue cells are found in patients with:

a. **leukemia.**
b. **bacterial vaginosis.**
c. **epidermal fungal infections.**
d. **pneumonia.**

149. A 26 year-old female present with flank pain that waxes and wanes. Her urine specimen indicates the presence of:

a. **blood.**
b. **nitrites.**
c. **leukocytes.**
d. **calcium.**

150. A positive Tinel's test can be used to assess carpal tunnel syndrome. What other test can be used to assess for this?

a. **Patrick's test**
b. **Finkelstein's test**
c. **Phalen's test**
d. **Allen's test**

Family Exam #2 Answers

1. *d*

Trochanteric bursitis does not produce pain in the calf. Pain is concentrated in the affected hip. While it is not likely that someone who exercises regularly would have a DVT, this patient does take oral contraceptives. Therefore, DVT should always be part of the differential given the potential risks associated with untreated DVT (pulmonary embolism).

2. *a*

A mucopurulent eye discharge bilaterally in a one week-old infant sounds like genitourinary in origin. The mother may have Chlamydia. If the infant is delivered vaginally and the mother is infected with Chlamydia, symptoms will appear 1-2 weeks post-delivery in the infant. The discharge is mucopurulent and would not be confused with the discharge associated with a plugged tear duct. Other STDs like gonorrhea could produce symptoms 2-4 days post vaginal delivery.

3. *a*

Xerosis is dry skin. It is common in patients who have eczema. Using thick creams or ointments can prevent xerosis. Lotions should be avoided because they have high water content that promotes evaporation of water from the skin. Hypoallergenic refers to the allergenicity of a product. This is not related to the water content of products.

4. *a*

Routine screening for osteoporosis is not recommended in males unless risk factors are present. Screening in women is recommended starting at age 65. If risk factors are present in a female, screening is recommended at an earlier age. Screening is usually performed by bone mineral density using a dual energy x-ray absorptiometry (DXA) scan.

5. *d*

Middle ear effusion refers to the presence of fluid in the middle ear. This is present in both otitis media with effusion and acute otitis media. Since the eardrum appears normal and the fluid does not appear infected, there is no reason to suspect otitis media, acute or with effusion. Another name for otitis media with effusion is serous otitis media. Other terms for this are secretory or nonsuppurative otitis media.

6 *d*

The classic symptoms that patients with C. difficile experience are described in choice D. This patient should be treated because symptoms are present. If no symptoms or mild symptoms are present, treatment can be delayed until symptoms develop or worsen. All patients who are infected do not exhibit symptoms. They do not need treatment.

7. ***c***
This patient needs urgent referral to ophthalmology. While this is a relatively unusual patient in primary care, the primary care clinician must be able to recognize this patient and the need for urgent referral. In a patient with acute angle closure glaucoma, the patient is usually ill appearing, may have nausea and vomiting. This scenario should prompt urgent referral.

8. ***d***
ADD and ADD with hyperactivity are two separate diagnoses. This disorder is more common in boys (5:1) and symptoms must be present by age 7 for at least 6 months before diagnosis can be made. DSM V should be used to diagnose children. Parents and/or teachers should establish specific elements. Examples include fidgeting, difficulty remaining in seat, excessive talking, impatient when asked to wait their turn, blurting out answers before time, and interrupting conversation. These must be established in more than one environment.

9. ***a***
Digital rectal exam (DRE) leads to a clinically insignificant increase of 0.26-0.4 ng/ml for about 48-72 hours afterwards. Prostate biopsy increases the PSA about 8 ng/ml for up to 4 weeks following biopsy. Prostate infection and ejaculation both can increase the PSA levels.

10. c
Otitis media with effusion (OME) frequently precedes or follows an episode of acute otitis media. This condition should not be treated with an antibiotic since the middle ear fluid is not infected. However, the fluid acts as a medium for bacterial growth.

11. ***a***
Unfortunately, pregnant women are more likely to be abused than non-pregnant ones. When women are abused prior to becoming pregnant, abuse generally escalates during pregnancy. Abuse is not specific to a certain trimester. Abuse during pregnancy tends to occur throughout pregnancy. Because of this, it is important to keep vigilant and re-assess at each prenatal visit.

12. ***b***
The patient is using albuterol too frequently. It should be used only a few times weekly because if it is used too frequently, it will lose its effectiveness over time. This medication should be used as a rescue medication only, but you cannot tell a patient to use it only once daily. This patient's medication regimen needs adjusting. The best choice is to consider adding a long acting anticholinergic and have him use albuterol as a rescue medication. Another consideration is a short-acting anticholinergic in combination with his albuterol for symptom management.

13. ***c***
Sciatica represents irritation of the nerve root. Patients usually complain of sharp, burning pain that can be accompanied by numbness, tingling and radiating pain down

the posterior aspect of one leg. Disc herniation, which could cause sciatica, produces increased pain with coughing, sneezing, or the Valsalva maneuver.

14. ***a***
An example of a short-acting beta agonist is albuterol, levalbuterol, pirbuterol, or bitolterol. These provide rapid dilation of the bronchioles and can give immediate relief; hence the term for this class of medications: rescue medications. Salmeterol is a long-acting beta agonist. These should never be used without an inhaled steroid to treat a patient who has asthma. Mometasone and beclomethasone are steroids commonly used to treat patients with asthma.

15. ***a***
In an ectopic pregnancy, the developing embryo becomes implanted outside the uterus. A common site is the fallopian tube. Young age is a low risk factor for ectopic pregnancy. A past history of ectopic pregnancy confers a high risk of future ectopic pregnancies. Other high risk factors are previous tubal surgery or pathology, tubal ligation, and in utero DES exposure.

16 ***a***
This patient has a negative hepatitis B surface antigen (HBsAg). Therefore, he does not have hepatitis B. The patient has a positive hepatitis B surface antibody (HBsAb). Therefore, he is considered immune. The patient also has a positive hepatitis B core antibody (HBcAb). Therefore, he is immune because he has had hepatitis B. The correct answer is choice A.

17. ***b***
Part B pays the examiner (NP, PA, MD, etc.). Part B of Medicare pays for outpatient care, ambulatory surgery services, x-rays, durable medical equipment, laboratory, and home health. Part B is an option that Medicare recipients can pay for with a monthly option. This charge is based on income. Since there is an initial co-pay, the federal government's insurance plan may NOT pay for his visit to your clinic today.

18. ***c***
CVA tenderness is typical of patients who have pyelonephritis. Additionally, the most common symptom associated with pyelonephritis is fever. A patient who presents with this scenario has to be considered to have pyelonephritis until proven otherwise.

19. ***d***
The over the counter urine pregnancy kits have very high sensitivity and specificity. Consequently, their results can be trusted. A positive urine tests will correlate with the serum results. The tests identify hCG in the specimen.

20. ***b***
Ipratropium is the most widely studied anticholinergic medication used to treat patients with COPD. It produces its helpful effects by reducing cholinergic tone in the lungs. It should not be used with a beta agonist unless shortness of breath is present because beta

agonists increase side effects like tachycardia and tremor and do not improve efficacy.

21. ***d***

Metronidazole may be associated with a disulfiram reaction when mixed with alcohol. Advice that should be given to all patients who take metronidazole is to avoid alcohol entirely while this medication is being taken. Additionally, alcohol should be avoided for 72 hours after the last dose of medication. The disulfiram reaction is characterized by fever, abdominal pain, nausea, vomiting, and headache. This reaction is called the "Antabuse" reaction.

22. ***c***

Toxoplasmosis is an infection caused by the parasite Toxoplasma gondii. Toxoplasmosis can result in fetal demise. It is recommended that pregnant patients avoid contact with cats and particularly feline feces. The eggs from the parasite are abundant in feces. Toxoplasmosis can also be acquired by eating undercooked meats like lamb, venison, or pork. Since cats often defecate in soil, gardening could present a risk to the pregnant patient too.

23. ***b***

The visualization of yeast in saliva usually indicates Candida species. Yeast are commonly seen in patients who have thrush, vaginitis secondary to yeast, or intertrigo. While thrush is uncommon in adults, it is not uncommon in patients who are immunocompromised, such as a patient with HIV.

24. ***b***

The most important aspect of the initial visit is to establish trust. Many patients will not be willing to disclose a complete history to the examiner; especially one regarding alcohol or illegal drugs. A complete head to toe exam might be important, but most homeless patients are driven to care based on episodic illness. They will be interested in care for the problem that brought them in on the day of the exam. Additionally, resources may be limited which would not allow for a complete head to toe exam on each patient, but instead, a focused visit.

25. ***b***

Ibuprofen is an NSAID. NSAIDs produce sodium retention and hence, water retention. This produces many systemic effects such as an increase in blood pressure, lower extremity edema, increased workload of the heart, and inhibition of prostaglandin synthesis. Patients with hypertension and chronic heart failure should use NSAIDs cautiously. Neither lovastatin nor fluticasone would be expected to increase or decrease blood pressure. Amoxicillin is an antibiotic. These do not increase blood pressure.

26. ***a***

A single whole body application of permethrin is usually successful in eradicating infection with scabies. It is applied over the entire body from the neck down. The lotion is left on and then showered off 8-12 hours later. All contacts must be treated at the same time and all potential fomites (bed linen, mattresses, cloth furniture, etc.) must be

treated as well. Permethrin can be sprayed on cloth fomites or they can be bagged for several days, washed and dried in washing machine and dryer. Ironing clothes after washing them is acceptable.

27. ***a***
If tweezers are not available, protected fingers should be used. The person removing the tick should take care NOT to crush the tick because it may contain infectious organisms. After the tick is removed, the skin should be washed well with soap and water. If mouth parts remain after the tick has been removed, they should NOT be removed. The area should be monitored for 30 days for erythema migrans.

28. ***c***
Cranial Nerve (CN) VIII is the CN responsible for hearing. When assessing CN VIII, each ear should be assessed individually. The Weber and Rinne are usually used to distinguish conductive and sensorineural hearing loss. An audiogram gives more reproducible results than the Weber and Rinne tests.

29. ***b***
Her TSH is elevated. This is usually caused by insufficient supplementation in a patient with hypothyroidism. If the TSH was within normal range following her last annual exam, something has changed. The first point that must be established is whether the patient is still taking her medication. If she is still taking her medication, determining when she is taking it is very important. It should be taken on an empty stomach for absorption. These two important facts must be established BEFORE increasing her current dose. The TSH is usually repeated when an abnormal value is measured, but, this patient has symptoms of an abnormal TSH.

30. ***c***
The easiest way to diagnose plantar fasciitis is to dorsiflex the patient's toes and palpate with the thumb along the fascia starting at the heel progressing toward the forefoot. The patient will experience pain with palpation. In fact, the pain is reproducible as the "exact same" pain that is experienced when the patient steps out of bed or performs another activity that recreates the pain.

31. ***c***
Mitral valve prolapse (MVP) is the most common adult murmur. It is a result of redundancy of the mitral valve leaflets and subsequent degeneration of the mitral tissue. The posterior leaflet is more commonly affected than the anterior leaflet. The valve's annulus becomes enlarged in conjunction with elongation of the chordae tendineae.

32. ***a***
The symptoms sound like pyloric stenosis. The most common time for this to occur is 3-6 weeks. It rarely occurs after 12 weeks of age. Babies who have episodes of projectile vomiting and who demand to be re-fed are called "hungry vomiters" and a diagnosis of pyloric stenosis should be considered. The olive shaped mass, if found, probably

represents hypertrophy of the lateral edge of the rectus abdominus muscle. It is most easily felt immediately after vomiting. This diagnosis is made much earlier now than it used to be, so problems with dehydration are not as common as decades ago.

33. ***d***
Standard practice across the United States is to insure that a protective rubella titer exists in women who are pregnant now. If a pregnant patient had a protective rubella titer in a previous pregnancy, re-evaluation is not necessary. A protective titer is usually 1:10 or greater. If she was found at any time during pregnancy to have a negative rubella titer, she should be vaccinated AFTER delivery.

34. ***a***
Kava kava is an herb from the South Pacific that is used to treat anxiety, fibromyalgia, and hyperactivity, attention deficit disorder. Hepatotoxicity has been reported with kava kava use, especially when consumed as tea. Liver toxicity should be reviewed in this patient. If she is not willing to use another agent for treatment of her anxiety, liver function studies should be monitored periodically.

35. ***b***
The arteries are 2/3 to 4/5 the diameter of the veins. The arteries appear as light red in color; veins are darker red. Interestingly, the veins in the eyes pulsate, the arteries do not. Loss of venous pulsations can be identified in patients with head trauma, meningitis, or elevated intracranial pressure.

36. ***c***
Pinguecula are common as patients age. They usually appear on the nasal side first and then on the temporal side. This is a completely benign finding. A stye is also called a hordeolum. It is a tender, painful infection of a gland at the eyelid margin. These are self-limiting. A chalazion is a non-tender enlargement of a meibomian gland. A subconjunctival hemorrhage is a blood red looking area on the sclera that does not affect vision. It occurs and resolves spontaneously.

37. ***a***
Generally, infants and children need about 3-4 mg/kg/day of elemental iron in divided doses. Since iron is better absorbed in an acidic environment, orange juice is recommended. Iron is better absorbed on an empty stomach, so the preference is to take it between meals. However, oral ferrous sulfate is poorly tolerated by some patients and may be better tolerated with food. If this is the case, a rise in hemoglobin will be at a decreased rate.

38. ***b***
Hyperemesis gravidarum (HEG) is a severe form of nausea and vomiting which occurs during pregnancy. In contrast, morning sickness is milder. A common definition used to define HEG is persistent vomiting which produces a weight loss exceeding 5% of pre-pregnancy body weight. The etiology of morning sickness and HEG is unknown.

39. *c*

Women who are less than age 35 years, who have no associated suspicious findings of breast cancer are probably advised to wait to be re-examined 3-10 days after the last menstrual period to determine whether the lump changes in size or becomes non-palpable. If there are associated suspicious findings on exam like palpable nodes, a large lump (>2.0 cm), or nipple discharge, then diagnostic evaluation should not be delayed. If management involved a return visit for re-examination after menses, and the lump is unchanged, ultrasound is certainly advised. Mammogram may not yield good information in a 28 year-old because of the density of the breast tissue. Baseline mammogram may be advised. Direction from a radiologist or breast surgeon should be sought.

40. *a*

The left ventricle enlarges as blood regurgitates from the aorta. Atrial fibrillation is not typical or usual in aortic regurgitation (AR) since neither atrium is affected. Pulmonary congestion is seen later in the pathogenesis of AR. The blood pressure in patients with AR is characterized by an elevated systolic and decreased diastolic pressure. This is termed a wide pulse pressure.

41. *c*

The primary imaging technique for assessing DHH in the first 3-4 months of life is ultrasound. The biggest limitation is the experience of the ultrasonographer. X-rays are of little benefit in the first few months of life because the femoral head is mostly cartilaginous and unossified. After 3-4 months of age, AP x-rays of the hip are more valuable. The frog leg view of the pelvis provides the lateral view of the femoral heads. During treatment or to confirm reduction post-operatively, a CT may be valuable.

42. *a*

The usual course of mitral valve prolapse (MVP) is benign and most patients who have MVP are asymptomatic. In a minority of patients, symptoms of heart failure or sudden death may occur. When congestive heart failure results, it is usually a result of mitral regurgitation. Embolization may occur, but, this is not common or usual in the majority of patients.

43. *b*

A disulfiram reaction can take place in a patient who combines alcohol and metronidazole. The disulfiram reaction is described as elevation in body temperature, abdominal cramps, diarrhea, headache, and nausea/vomiting.

44. *b*

L-thyroxin is thyroid supplement used to treat patients with hypothyroidism. It is safe to use during pregnancy and should be continued. However, during pregnancy, thyroid hormone needs increase and so she will need frequent monitoring because if levels drop to a hypothyroid state, growth of the fetus can be severely affected.

45. ***b***
The most common presentation of basal cell carcinoma (BCC) is on the face. This is probably because BCC occurs secondary to sun damage. The most common sun exposure occurs on the face. In fact, 70% of BCC occurs on the face, 15% is found on the trunk.

46. ***b***
The mitral listening point is where the murmur associated with mitral regurgitation (MR) can be heard loudest. Murmurs tend to be loudest at the point where they originate. In this case, that is the mitral listening point. As the left ventricle enlarges secondary to MR, the apical impulse becomes displaced left and laterally and becomes diffuse.

47. ***a***
An oral antiviral agent such as acyclovir, famciclovir, valacyclovir should be prescribed, especially if it can be initiated within 72 hours after the onset of symptoms. The addition of oral corticosteroids to oral antiviral therapy demonstrates only modest benefit. Adverse events to therapy are more commonly reported in patients receiving oral corticosteroids. There is no evidence that corticosteroid therapy decreased the incidence or duration of post-herpetic neuralgia or improved quality of life. Corticosteroids should be limited to use in patients with acute neuritis who have not derived benefit from opioid analgesics.

48. ***c***
Nursemaid's elbow is a subluxation of the radial head. The typical position of the affected arm is as described in the answer above. The patient is usually not in pain unless someone attempts to move the elbow. Reduction of the elbow can be done in an ER with the child seated in the caregiver's lap by hyper pronation of the forearm. It is painful but very brief. No treatment is necessary after reduction.

49. ***c***
The best means to identify mitral valve prolapse (MVP) is with 2D echocardiography. It will identify bulging of either, or both, of the leaflets (anterior or posterior) into the left atrium. Approximately 1-2% of the US population is identified to have MVP. A chest x-ray will not enable visualization of the mitral leaflets. Electrocardiography identifies the heart's rhythm. A physical exam may provide great clues to MVP, but in the absence of definitive mid to late systolic clicks, a diagnosis cannot be confirmed.

50. ***b***
The incidence of pyelonephritis in the US is much less common than urinary tract infections (UTIs). It is less likely in males, but is most common in females aged 15-29 years. Factors associated with pyelonephritis are frequent sexual intercourse, UTI within the last year, presence of diabetes, and presence of stress incontinence within the previous 30 days.

51. ***d***
This patient's symptoms are descriptive of plantar fasciitis. Pain usually begins as only pain in the morning with resolution after several steps and the passage of time. As plantar fasciitis worsens, patients complain of heel pain during the day, after sitting for a while, and at the end of the day. The most important contributor to this is pes planus, "flat feet". Approximately 70% of patients with plantar fasciitis have pes planus.

52. ***b***
This patient's symptoms are typical of arteriosclerosis. The term for this symptom is intermittent claudication. When there is compromised arterial blood flow in the lower legs, a common complaint is reproducible pain in a specific group of muscles. The pain occurs because there is an incongruence between blood supply and demand. This produces pain that causes a patient to stop exercising in order to obtain relief of pain.

53. ***b***
The earliest serologic marker that indicates acute hepatitis B infection is the hepatitis B surface antigen. It becomes positive about 2-6 weeks after infection, but before symptom onset. A positive IgM indicates acute infection at this time. The finding of a positive hepatitis B core antibody identifies with certainty, hepatitis B infection (either at present or in the past). It does not indicate timing of infection.

54. ***a***
Calcium supplementation during pregnancy is for the fetus, not the pregnant mother. Calcium supplementation will provide extra calcium that is needed during fetal development. It is hypothesized that adequate amounts of calcium will reduce the risk of pregnancy-induced hypertension. Generally, 1000 mg daily is recommended.

55. ***d***
Non-fasting glucose values less than 125 mg/dL are considered normal values.

56. ***b***
COPD, chronic obstructive pulmonary disease, is characterized by obstructed airways. The obstruction is NOT completely reversible. Asthma is completely reversible. This is the reason many learned authorities do not consider asthma to be part of the COPD umbrella. Productive cough is likely present in patients with acute bronchitis. Shortness of breath does not have to be present (or perceived in patients with COPD). Hypercapnia is more prevalent in patients with emphysema since air trapping occurs.

57. ***b***
This is a femoral hernia. Testicular torsion is a medical emergency. The testicle is swollen, not the upper thigh. Varicocele and hydrocele are both confined to the scrotum. Hydrocele is evidenced by scrotal swelling, is painless, and is easily transilluminated. The varicocele is confined to the scrotum too, but presents most commonly in the adolescent age group with a large, soft scrotal mass that decompresses when the child lies down.

58. *a*
Lymphocytosis, a predominance of lymphocytes, is the most common laboratory abnormality seen with infectious mononucleosis (mono). Atypical lymphocytes are a common finding too. An elevation in monocytes is often found, but does not occur with as high frequency as lymphocytosis. The total white count often is increased and may lie between 12,000-18,000/microL. Elevated liver enzymes, ALT and AST, are noted in the majority of patients but is a benign finding. These usually return to baseline within several weeks of onset of acute symptoms.

59. *d*
Patients with gout do not always have elevated uric acid levels. In fact, during an acute attack, uric acid levels can be normal. Meat contains purines that are known to contribute to attacks of gout, but it is not likely that this patient is consuming too much meat. It is more likely due to multiple factors in his diet. The initial episode of gout usually involves a lower extremity. The great toe is the most common joint affected. Joints like the hip or shoulder are rarely affected initially and usually are never affected because they are close to the trunk and are at higher body temperature than the toes and fingers.

60. *d*
PID is sometimes a difficult diagnosis to make. A high index of suspicion should exist in adolescents and young women who present with the symptoms indicated above. CDC recommends empiric treatment for PID in women who present with abdominal pain and one of these: cervical motion tenderness, fever > 101F, a shift to the left, abnormal vaginal discharge, presence of white cells in the vaginal secretions, and an elevated sed rate or C reactive protein.

61. *d*
Pain associated with a lumbar strain does produce pain with activity and walking. This patient should be educated that pain is some pain is expected and that it will not produce permanent injury. He should be encouraged to engage in activities of daily living and normal walking. Generally, this will speed his return to normal activities. Bedrest is no longer recommended. Patients feel better sooner and have fewer complications if bed rest is avoided.

62. *d*
The minimum length of time between Hepatitis B, DTaP, IPV, and MMR is one month. Therefore, he can receive all of these today. He should not receive another varicella today. The minimum length of time between immunizations is 3 months if he is less than 13 years of age.

63. *c*
Fatigue is a difficult complaint to assess and diagnose. This patient's exam and vital signs are normal. There is no reason to think that he is infected or is bleeding, so a lone CBC, offers little diagnostic help. However, in addition to a CBC, adding a metabolic panel, TSH, and urine (to screen for blood in this former smoker) is a more thorough

laboratory assessment of his fatigue.

64. ***a***
Egg allergy is no longer considered a contraindication for the MMR vaccine. The measles vaccine is grown in a chick embryo medium but several large studies have demonstrated efficacy and safety. The immunization is attenuated and considered safe if given at 12 months of age. It is repeated once at age 4-6 years.

65. ***d***
Nitrofurantoin would be a good choice to treat a UTI in a pregnant patient because it has good coverage of common urinary tract pathogens and it has a pregnancy Category B rating. Doxycycline is a category D; TMPS is a category C; and ciprofloxacin is a category C.

66. ***c***
Symptoms of pelvic inflammatory disorder (PID) include oral temperature > 101 F (38.8C), abnormal cervical or vaginal mucopurulent discharge, presence of abundant WBCs on microscopy or vaginal secretions, elevated sedimentation rate or C-reactive protein. CDC has indicated empiric treatment for PID if lower abdominal pain or pelvic pain is present concurrently with cervical motion tenderness or uterine/adnexal tenderness.

67. ***d***
Influenza is contraindicated for persons who have had anaphylactic reactions to eggs. The immunization is made from eggs and thus, the contraindication. There is an adult influenza immunization approved by the FDA in 2013 that is made without eggs.

68. ***b***
The classic triad of normal pressure hydrocephalus (NPH) is described above. Diabetic neuropathy would not be typical because this involves three different areas of complaint. Parkinson's Disease presents with tremor, gait disturbance, and bradykinesia. Multiple sclerosis almost never presents beyond the age of 50 years and would be unlikely in an elderly male. The incidence of NPH varies from 2-20 million people per year. It is more common in elderly patients and affects both genders equally. This is diagnosed demonstrated by the presence of enlarged ventricles on CT scan.

69. ***d***
The diagnosis of pinworms, Enterobiasis, is made by using a piece of scotch tape on a tongue depressor. It is touched against the child's rectum. The greatest yield of eggs will occur during the nighttime or early AM. Eggs will be found here if they are present. Worms and eggs are rarely found in stool specimens, so this is not a good plan. When the scotch tape is examined under a low power microscope, the eggs will be easily visualized since they are large and bean shaped. The finding of an adult worm would confirm the diagnosis. These are large enough to be seen with the naked eye.

70. *c*
LDL cholesterol promotes atherosclerosis via several different mechanisms. Consequently, LDL cholesterol tends to be the primary target when patients are treated pharmacologically for elevated lipid levels. Low HDL levels and elevated triglyceride levels have also shown to accelerate atherogenesis.

71. *a*
The finding of infiltrates on chest x-ray, in conjunction with clinical findings of fever, chest pain, dyspnea, and sputum production on clinical exam should direct the examiner to consider pneumonia as the diagnosis. Though not common, some patients with pneumonia exhibit gastrointestinal symptoms like nausea, vomiting, and diarrhea.

72. *b*
Rheumatic fever is the correct answer. The immune response involves not just the heart, but can affect the joints, skin, and central nervous system. 0.1- 0.3% of untreated or under treated infections involving Group A beta hemolytic Strept can result in rheumatic fever. More often than not, this involves an infection in the upper airways. The most common age group affected is 5-15 years. However, the residual effect of rheumatic fever is realized into the later decades of life.

73. *c*
The three cardinal symptoms of Parkinson's Disease are tremor, bradykinesia, and rigidity. The tremor is often described as a "pill-rolling" tremor. This is most noticeable when the body is at rest. Usually, the tremor disappears at night during sleep and may disappear with deliberate physical activities.

74. *c*
Pharmacologic treatment should be initiated for children who have both hypertension and diabetes, symptomatic hypertension, Stage 2 hypertension, end-organ damage, or Stage 1 hypertension that is resistant to lifestyle modifications. Obesity is a risk factor, but is not a sole indicator of treatment.

75. *b*
Which statement below is true regarding NSAIDs for low back pain?

76. *c*
An influenza immunization is considered safe to give to pregnant patients, even in the first trimester. It is considered a greater risk to have the flu during pregnancy than to get the influenza immunization. The intranasal influenza immunization is contraindicated during pregnancy because it contains live virus. Only the injectable immunization should be given.

77. *d*
Mycoplasma is an atypical pathogen and produces atypical pneumonia. It can be difficult to diagnose because symptoms can be varied and involve multiple body systems (extrapulmonary manifestations). Infection with Mycoplasma may present with a

normal white blood cell count, maculopapular rash, GI symptoms, tender joints and aches, and though rare, cardiac rhythm disturbances. Respiratory symptoms may not be pronounced. On chest x-ray there are some unique findings (peribronchial pattern) with Mycoplasma. These include thickened bronchial shadow, streaks of interstitial infiltration, and atelectasis. These are more likely to occur in the lower lobes.

78. ***c***
Most hypertension in children and pre-adolescents is secondary hypertension. 60-70% is due to renal parenchymal disease. Rarely does primary hypertension exist in this age group. However, 85-90% of adolescents have primary hypertension. General obesity is often associated with hypertension but is not the primary cause.

79. ***d***
Most cases of acute gastroenteritis are viral in origin. Severe diarrhea is usually caused by bacteria. This usually lasts longer than 3 days.

80. ***c***
According to JNC VII, a patient who is diagnosed with Stage I hypertension should have lifestyle modifications initiated for 3 months. If his blood pressure is not within normal range (< 140/90) after 3 months, a low dose diuretic is appropriate unless there is a compelling indication to give a different medication. Two medications should not be initiated for a patient with Stage I hypertension according to JNC VII.

81. ***c***
This history of recent antibiotic exposure suggests *C. difficile*. A stool specimen should be ordered to assess for *C. difficile*. Some clinicians will initiate treatment for *C. difficile* based on this history, especially if the patient's symptoms are severe or the patient is elderly.

82. ***d***
***Shigella* will be shed continuously in the stool and should be easily identified on stool culture. When bacterial gastroenteritis is suspected, a stool specimen could be ordered for confirmation. Generally, these three pathogens are easily identified if they are present.**

83. ***c***
Type II diabetes is diagnosed after a random fasting glucose $\geq$ 126 mg/dL and confirmed on a subsequent day. Other diagnostic criteria include a random blood glucose $\geq$ 200 mg/dL with polyuria, polydypsia, or polyphagia; or an A1C $\geq$ 6.5% (and confirmed on a subsequent day). A glucose tolerance test may also be used for diagnosis but this is usually reserved for pregnant women.

84. ***d***
Allergy and asthma guidelines in the US recommend topical nasal steroids first line for management of symptoms of allergic rhinitis. A non-sedating antihistamine can be added to manage unresolved symptoms after a nasal steroid has been initiated.

Antihistamines work well when the predominant symptoms are thin, clear nasal discharge. These can be safely used in combination for management. Decongestants are not recommended as lone agents because they have no effect on the underlying allergic mechanisms. They work well in combination with antihistamines and nasal steroids for congestion. Sedating antihistamines are usually avoided for allergic rhinitis because of safety concerns.

85. ***d***
Iron is best absorbed on an empty stomach. However, iron consumption on an empty stomach is usually not well tolerated and is often taken with a meal. Reduced absorption of the iron is expected if it is not taken on an empty stomach. Vitamin C enhances absorption of iron and so if iron is taken with food, a Vitamin C rich one should accompany it, not a Vitamin D rich food. An example of a vitamin C rich beverage is orange juice. Citrus fruits are typically rich in Vitamin C.

86. ***b***
Testicular torsion is an emergency because the testicle is deprived of normal blood supply. If blood supply is not resumed within 12 hours, irreversible damage is certain to occur. Ideally, ischemia is resolved within 4-6 hours. The penis is not affected during testicular torsion. Besides testicular torsion, epididymitis, trauma, and an inguinal hernia are other common causes of scrotal pain.

87. ***c***
Migraine headaches usually begin in the early morning and can awaken patients from sleep, but they may begin at any time, including nocturnally. Cluster headaches are very likely in this age and gender patient. A brain tumor must always be considered since intracranial pressure increases in a horizontal patient. Hydrocephalus produces headache, but it is not specific for nighttime.

88. ***a***
A decrease in blood pressure is commonly observed in pregnant women in their second trimester. This is part of the normal cardiovascular changes that take place during pregnancy. In fact, sometimes pregnant women can become symptomatic if their blood pressure drops below 80 or 90 mm Hg systolic.

89. ***a***
Serotonin (5-HT) is a neurotransmitter released in the brain. It is part of the monoamine oxidase system. These neurotransmitters are responsible for many emotional and behavioral disorders. Agents that cause more serotonin to be available in the brain have an ameliorating effect on symptoms of depression, anxiety, and obsessive-compulsive behavior.

90. ***b***
Mild intermittent asthma is characterized by symptoms that occur more than twice weekly but not daily; or 3-4 nocturnal awakenings per month due to asthma. It is treated with a daily inhaled steroid and a bronchodilator PRN for exacerbations. If

symptoms occur more than twice weekly, therapy should be stepped up. Generally, a long acting bronchodilator is added to the steroid.

91. ***d***
This patient needs several medications started today. American Diabetes Association recommends starting treatment with metformin. This should be initiated today. The drug class of choice for treatment of his LDL cholesterol is a statin. Dietary modifications are usually attempted for 3 months prior to initiation of a statin. However, considering this patient's LDLs of 210 mg/dL (goal of less than 100 mg/dL), strong consideration should be given to initiating therapy today with a statin. An ACE inhibitor is the preferred antihypertensive medication to treat blood pressure elevations in this patient. An aspirin should be initiated if there are no contraindications.

92. ***d***
This patient should continue his fexofenadine. This treats his allergies and although he has a sinus infection, he still needs treatment for his allergies. A topical nasal steroid can be added if poor control of allergies exists, otherwise, this probably just increases the cost of treatment of during this sinus infection. If his sinus infection has been present for 10 days, an antibiotic seems prudent at this point.

93. ***a***
RDW is the red blood cell distribution width. Another way to think of this is that the RDW is the variation in the size of the red blood cells. In a patient with recent onset iron deficiency anemia (the last 3-4 months), some red blood cells will be of normal size and some will be of decreased size (microcytosis). The variation in size of the red blood cells will be demonstrated by an increased RDW. Serum ferritin is a measure of the iron in storage. The total iron binding capacity is always increased in a patient with iron deficiency anemia.

94. ***b***
Primary dysmenorrhea has been attributed to prolonged uterine contractions that cause ischemia to the myometrium. Some females with secondary dysmenorrhea may have a normal pelvic exam, but they tend to have an enlarged irregularly shaped uterus, or tender uterus on exam. Most secondary dysmenorrhea is due to endometriosis. On physical exam, patients with secondary dysmenorrhea can have displacement of the cervix, cervical stenosis, adnexal enlargement, or nodular and/or tender uterosacral ligaments.

95. ***b***
The triptans are a class of medications that are helpful for many patients with migraine headaches because they produce cerebral vasoconstriction. This class is also helpful for patients who experience cluster headaches. The triptans are not helpful for patients with tension headaches. Some patients with cluster headaches use nasal oxygen at the onset of the cluster headache. Relief is usually realized in about 10 minutes or less.

96. ***c***
If the NP knowingly prescribes a medication for a patient other than the intended patient, the NP incurs medical liability and is deliberately diverting medications. This is illegal and constitutes theft in most states. The NP cannot legally continue to prescribe the medication if she knows that the intended patient is not the recipient of the medication.

97. ***d***
Observational studies are studies where subjects are observed. No intervention takes place with them. Examples of these are found in the first three choices. A meta-analysis takes published information from other studies and combines the information to arrive at a conclusion. Although a meta-analysis can use observational studies, these should be reported separately.

98. ***c***
The major classes of antidepressants used to treat depression are listed in this question. Multiple studies have concluded that there is no clear choice on selection of one class over another for efficacy. However, SSRIs are usually the first choice because they are associated with fewer side effects and there is less danger of suicide with an overdose. Monoamine oxidase inhibitors are involved with a number of drug-drug and drug-food interactions and so these are seldom chosen initially.

99. ***a***
Chlamydia is treated in a pregnant patient exactly as it is treated in a non-pregnant patient. Azithromycin is given as a single one gram dose. This patient should be screened for other STDs now, and all STDs again before delivery. Commonly, pregnant patients infected with an STD become re-infected before delivery.

100. ***b***
Pernicious anemia is the most common side effect of Vitamin B-12 deficiency. Pernicious anemia is characterized by a macrocytic anemia, not microcytic. Sideroblastic anemia is not related to B-12 deficiency. Insomnia is not a specific finding with B-12 deficiency.

101. ***a***
Serotonin syndrome is a potentially life-threatening condition. The syndrome occurs when there is too much serotonergic activity in the central nervous system. It can occur with an interaction between two medications, like an SSRI and dextromethorphan, an SSRI and a triptan, an intentional overdose, or with high doses of an SSRI in a particularly sensitive patient. Symptoms of serotonin syndrome include hyperreflexia, clonus, rigidity in the lower extremities, tachycardia, hyperthermia, hypertension, vomiting, disorientation, agitated delirium, or tremor. None of the other medications listed can precipitate serotonin syndrome.

102. ***d***
A case control study would be ideal for discovering the cause of this situation. Case

control looks at "what happened"? It would identify those subjects who have leukemia and would identify a control group of children from the area who did not have leukemia. Both groups would be analyzed for characteristics or risk factors that were present in the "case" group but not the "control" group. This is an observational study.

103. ***d***
A microcytic, hypochromic anemia is typical in a patient with iron deficiency anemia; less common in patients with chronic disease, and even less common in patients with a malignancy. Excessive consumption of alcohol would result in a patient with a macrocytic anemia, not microcytic. RBC counts would be expected to be decreased in this patient. In an adult male, the most common place for loss of blood is the GI tract. This should be investigated initially. It is certainly possible that he has a malignancy---possibly leukemia, but this is not as common as a GI bleed in an elderly adult.

104. ***a***
The most consistent findings in adults with early presentation of acute appendicitis are very subtle and difficult to identify. Symptoms may be as vague as indigestion, flatulence, a feeling of ill-being. Initially, pain can be in the general abdomen, then become periumbilical, and finally localize to the lower right quadrant. Early symptoms are difficult to identify, especially in older adults.

105. ***c***
This patient has isolated systolic hypertension (ISH). This is common in older adults and is associated with tragic cardiac and cerebrovascular events. The drug class of choice to treat these patients is a long-acting calcium channel blocker. The class of calcium channel blockers recommended for ISH has the suffix "pine" (amlodipine, felodipine, etc).

106. ***c***
This description is one of cellulitis. Cellulitis involves an infection of the subcutaneous layers of the skin. It must be treated with an oral antibiotic. This is particularly important to identify early, and aggressively treat in a diabetic because elevated blood sugar levels will make eradication more difficult. Buerger's disease involves inflammation of the medium sized arteries and does not present on the anterior shin only. DVT seldom presents on the anterior shin. Venous disease does not present acutely as in this situation.

107. ***c***
Metformin is associated with these symptoms---especially in the first two weeks of use. These symptoms can also be seen with increases in the dose of metformin. The other medications listed do not produce lower gastrointestinal symptoms. If the medication can be continued for a couple of weeks, generally, GI symptoms will resolve. Metformin is known to decrease morbidity and mortality associated with diabetes.

108. ***c***
This patient should never have a cephalosporin prescribed for him because of the risk

of cross-reactivity between the penicillin and cephalosporin classes. This could potentially give rise to another anaphylactic reaction to the cephalosporin prescribed. A good rule to follow if a patient has had an anaphylactic reaction to a penicillin is to NEVER prescribe a cephalosporin. Although the risk is small, it should not be taken.

109. ***b***
A serum ferritin level is helpful in evaluating a patient being treated for iron deficiency anemia. When these levels rise to normal levels and the anemia has been corrected, it is considered appropriate to stop iron supplementation, as it is no longer needed.

110. ***d***
X-rays are usually not helpful in diagnosing appendicitis, however, some findings on radiograph can be associated with appendicitis: ileus, free air, right lower quadrant appendicolith or soft tissue density, or a deformity of the cecal outline. A CT scan is considered more accurate than an ultrasound, but, ultrasound and CT are the most commonly used tests. The sensitivity and specificity with CT scan are 94 and 95% respectively. With an ultrasound, the sensitivity and specificity are 86 and 81% respectively. MRI is generally not used because it is more expensive, takes more time to complete, and is not as readily available.

111. ***c***
Folic acid is contained in every prenatal vitamin (PNV) in the United States. The usual dose is at least 0.4 mg, but one gram is usually incorporated into PNVs. Folic acid deficiencies in the first trimester are teratogenic. Folic acid is also helpful in preventing some chromosomal abnormalities. It is usually taken throughout pregnancy.

112. ***c***
The typical presentation of an adult male with epididymitis is gradual development of scrotal pain. There is no scrotal edema. This is more typical in hydrocele. Common precipitants are sexual activity, heavy physical exertion as described in the question, and bicycle or motorcycle riding. In sexually active males under age 35 years, a common cause is an STD.

113. ***d***
Most learned authorities agree that if there is no response by 8-12 weeks at a maximal therapeutic dose, a different antidepressant should be tried. The 8-12 week period is the correct time frame because it will take this long to increase the dose and attempt to reach maximal dose for therapeutic response. 4-6 weeks is nearing the appropriate time frame, but this may be too short a period of time to reach and evaluate therapeutic dose.

114. ***b***
This patient has classic symptoms of hypokalemia associated with potassium loss from the thiazide diuretic. A potassium level should be measured and he should be supplemented if it is low. Generally, muscle weakness occurs as potassium levels drop below 2.5 mEq/L. If his potassium is low, strong consideration should be given to a

thiazide diuretic in combination with a potassium sparing diuretic. In fact, this should be considered when the thiazide is initially prescribed.

115. ***d***
There are many different presentations of psoriasis. Plaque psoriasis, which is described in this question, is usually found in a symmetrical distribution on the scalp, elbows, knees, and/or back. The size of the lesions ranges from 1-10 cm in diameter. Usually the plaques are asymptomatic, but may be mildly pruritic. Scaly lesions found on the scalp are not specific to psoriasis and could be seborrheic dermatitis. A scaly border around the plaque could describe the lesions associated with pityriasis rosea.

116. ***c***
This patient can be diagnosed with diabetes today because his glucose exceeds 200 mg/dL and he is symptomatic. Most learned authorities would describe him as glucose toxic. Oral agents will have little effect on his glucose and it should be lowered. Insulin is the best agent to reduce the blood sugar so that oral agents can be given a chance. He should return tomorrow for a recheck of blood glucose and adjustment of his medication.

117. ***c***
Swimmer's ear is termed otitis externa. It represents an infection of the external canal. This is characterized by tragal tenderness with light touch of the tragus on the affected side. Fever does not occur because this is a superficial infection. It is treated with a topical agents: an antibiotic and steroid placed in the external canal.

118. ***a***
Iron deficiency anemia is characterized by a reduced RBC count and decreased hemoglobin and hematocrit. During an iron deficiency anemia the TIBC (total iron binding capacity) is increased. This finding demonstrates the low circulating levels of serum iron. The RDW would be expected to be increased. This demonstrates a > 15% variation in the size of the RBCs.

119. ***c***
This patient suffered trauma to his foot and/or ankle after a fall. A sprain is in the differential, but a fracture must be ruled out before this patient is allowed to continue to ambulate. An x-ray is needed now and he must be kept non-weight bearing until this is ruled out. A fracture should be suspected since the stem of the question indicates "point tenderness".

120. ***b***
Pain associated with dysmenorrhea is likely due to prostaglandins that can cause prolonged contraction of the uterus. This produces uterine ischemia, sometimes termed "uterine angina". NSAIDs (non-steroidal anti-inflammatory drugs) are prostaglandin synthesis inhibitors. These are usually started at the onset of menses or onset of symptoms and continued for 2-3 days depending on the symptom pattern of the patient. There is no demonstrated increase in efficacy when acetaminophen is added or given

alone.

121. ***c***
This patient has symptoms that could indicate an urgent neurological situation. Acute radiculopathy could indicate the need for intervention by a neurosurgeon. An MRI is a superior study because it provides excellent information about the soft tissues, like the lumbar discs. Contrast might be used in this patient if he had a history of previous back surgery. Then, contrast would be helpful to distinguish scar tissue from discs.

122. ***c***
The ideal time to screen for gestational diabetes (GD) is in the second trimester at 24-28 weeks. This is the time GD is most likely to be identified. The placenta produces hormones that cause insulin insensitivity in the mother. She should be screened with a 75-gram glucose load without regard to meals. If this is positive, she should have a diagnostic test. Elevated glucose levels during pregnancy can severely affect growth of the fetus.

123. ***b***
Many tests can be used to evaluate an elderly patient with suspected BPH. The value of DRE is to evaluate the size, consistency and assess for malignancy of the prostate gland. Urinalysis is done to detect blood or infection, but hematuria is common in patients with BPH. The PSA is done as a screening test for prostate cancer in men. A serum creatinine can be part of the initial screening. This would help identify bladder outlet obstruction, renal, or prerenal disease. A BUN is not necessary. Of course, the patient's history will dictate other exams for a complete evaluation.

124. ***b***
Cranial nerve II evaluates vision. Cranial nerve I evaluates the ability to smell. Cranial nerve III evaluates eye movements, pupillary constriction, and accommodation. Cranial nerve IV, the trochlear nerve is partly responsible for eye movement. Cranial nerves III, IV, and VI are responsible for eye movement.

125. ***a***
A randomized clinical trial (RCT) is the epitome of all research designs. Subjects are randomly assigned to treatment groups. This type study provides the best evidence that the results were due to the intervention and not something else. A RCT is an experimental design, not an observational one.

126. ***b***
Major depression is diagnosed when at least 5 symptoms out of nine symptoms (that characterize depression) are identified by the examiner. Minor depression is characterized by the presence of 2-4 of the nine symptoms. Symptoms must be present for at least 2 weeks and must be present most of the day nearly every day. One symptom that must be present is depressed mood. The 9 criteria are identified by the DSM V manual.

127. *c*
The cough associated with use of an ACE inhibitor is typically dry and non-productive. It is more common in women than men and is thought to be due to the buildup of bradykinin. Bradykinin is partly degraded by ACE (angiotensin converting enzyme). When degradation is impaired, bradykinin can accumulate and cough can ensue.

128. *b*
A patient with acute cholecystitis usually complains of abdominal pain in the upper right quadrant or epigastric area. Many patients complain of nausea. The patient lies very still on the exam table because cholecystitis is associated with peritoneal inflammation that is worse with movement. Elderly patients are more likely to NOT exhibit Murphy's sign and thus are more likely to suffer from complications of acute cholecystitis. Patients who are asymptomatic have cholelithiasis, not acute cholecystitis.

129. *d*
A patient who will be starting insulin can have his daily insulin needs calculated by multiplying his weight in kilograms by 0.2. In this patient, (100 x 0.2= 20 units) 20 units could be used for insulin initiation. Once insulin has been initiated, 3 days of AM fasting glucose measurements should be collected and the insulin dose adjusted so that the AM fasting glucose levels are about 100-120 mg/dL. Giving fewer than 20 units will probably be too little to meet this patient's needs.

130. *d*
A second swab is collected, but it is not used to repeat the test. The second swab is sent to microbiology for culture. The sensitivity varies in office Strept tests. Some are as low as 50% and a second swab should be collected. If beta-hemolytic Strept organisms are grown out, then the patient can be diagnosed with Streptococcal infection.

131. *c*
A patient with leukocytosis has a predominance of white cells in the blood. Leukocytes can elevate in response to viral or bacterial infections. Possible clarification of the type of infection could be determined by looking at the number of lymphocytes and neutrophils.

132. *b*
Varicocele may be asymptomatic but more commonly is accompanied by scrotal pain described as a dull ache. It becomes more noticeable with standing and is relieved by lying down. This occurs because lying down relieves dilation of the spermatic veins. This is present in about 15-20% of post-pubertal males and may be referred to as "a bag of worms" because of the scrotum's appearance. Wearing a scrotal supporter may also provide relief.

133. *c*
UTI is a common abbreviation for urinary tract infection. The presence of leukocytes and nitrites in the urine indicates a very likely infection in the bladder. The presence of blood is common when a patient has a urinary tract infection. This is termed

hematuria. A diagnosis of chlamydia cannot be made based on symptoms or these urinalysis results. Asymptomatic bacteriuria is the diagnosis given to patients who are found to have bacteria in the urine and who are asymptomatic. This patient has complaints of dysuria.

134. ***c***
Painless vaginal bleeding occurs after the 20th week. Bleeding is likely at this time because the lower uterine segment develops and uterine contractions occur. At this time, the cervix dilates and effaces. The placenta can become detached and bleeding can occur. In women who are identified to have placenta previa, coitus and vaginal exam are contraindicated because both can cause separation and further bleeding.

135. ***a***
Eosinophilia can be found in patients who have a predominance of eosinophils in the blood. An increase in eosinophils may be found in patients with allergic reactions or parasitic infections. In this instance, an asthma exacerbation could be due to an allergic response and so, could elicit the increase in circulating eosinophils.

136. ***b***
Two clinical clues should make the examiner suspect a foreign body. First, the patient has continued drainage despite treatment. Second, the drainage is unilateral. Unilateral drainage from a nostril should prompt the examiner to visualize the turbinates. In this case, a foreign body could probably be visualized.

137. ***c***
Pertussis is also called "whooping cough". This is a highly communicable respiratory disease caused by Bordetella pertussis. There are three recognized stages of pertussis: the catarrhal phase, the paroxysmal phase, and convalescence. Generally, children who are immunized do not get the disease. Since the outbreak of pertussis in Iowa in 2005, diminished titers were recognized and adolescents are being given a booster with tetanus booster.

138. ***c***
Malpractice insurance is needed in any situation where patients are treated by a nurse practitioner. Some states have a "good Samaritan" law that protects professional volunteers from being sued. Unless specifically provided by state law, a nurse practitioner should have professional liability insurance in the event the NP is sued.

139. ***b***
The three most commonly associated symptoms of GERD are heartburn, especially post-prandial, regurgitation, and dysphagia, especially after long-standing heartburn. Other common symptoms are chest pain, nausea, and odynophagia (painful swallowing).

140. ***a***
Niacin can decrease glucose tolerance. It should be used cautiously in patients with

impaired fasting glucose. In the United States, niacin is primarily used to increase HDL levels. However, niacin is poorly tolerated by many patients who take it. The most common side effects are flushing, hypotension, and occasionally gout flares. Niacin should be taken in the evening with an aspirin to minimize side effects. Tolerance improves over time.

141. ***a***
Two common first generation cephalosporins used to treat skin and skin structure infections are cephalexin and cefadroxil. These are taken 2-4 times daily and are generally well tolerated. These antibiotics provide coverage against *Staphylococcus* and *Streptococcus,* common skin pathogens.

142. ***b***
Pioglitazone belongs to a class of medications that can cause hepatotoxicity. Therefore, assessment of liver function studies, particularly AST and ALT, should be performed in 1-3 or 4 months after initiation of this medication. The manufacturer has not suggested an ideal schedule to check AST and ALT. Depending on patient history and concurrent medications, a check of the AST and ALT may be prudently done in 1-3 months.

143. ***d***
Mononucleosis is a common viral infection in adolescents and early twenty year olds. Splenomegaly occurs in about 50% of patients with mononucleosis. While it is not common, it is possible to be co-infected with *Streptococcus* in the throat. If this is the case, treatment with penicillin should be avoided because of the possibility of an "ampicillin" rash. The most prominent symptoms are fever, fatigue, pharyngitis, and lymphadenopathy.

144. ***d***
Vitamin B-12 is absorbed through the gastrointestinal (GI) tract from foods that are consumed daily. Deficiencies are usually seen in patients who have difficulty absorbing B-12. Consequently, supplementation through the GI tract is not an efficient means to correct deficiencies. The most efficient way to supplement with B-12 is via intramuscular injection. Injections are usually needed lifelong once deficiency is diagnosed. Deficiencies are often seen in elderly patients and in patients who consume alcohol in excess.

145. ***b***
If a patient's lipids are elevated, a TSH should be performed. If the TSH is elevated, it may be the secondary cause of the elevated lipids. It is considered safe practice to NOT treat elevated lipid levels until the TSH level has decreased to at least 10 mU/L. If the lipids are still elevated, they should be treated at that time.

146. ***b***
A sprained ankle is a common orthopedic injury in athletes. Resumption of regular activities can take place when he is able to walk pain-free. His ankle does not necessarily need taping prior to competition but it may need support with an orthotic

device. The edema may take weeks to completely resolve. In fact, edema after resumption of athletic activities is common.

147. ***b***
PCOS is a systemic disease characterized by multiple cysts about the ovaries. Overweight states are common but not obesity. Normal weight is also seen in these patients. This patient will not have a positive pregnancy test unless she is pregnant. There is no indication from the information that this is the case. She likely has had not had menses because of anovulation. There is no associated blood pressure elevation, though this should be watched closely. Elevated insulin levels are usual findings in patients who have PCOS.

148. ***b***
The hallmark finding in a patient with bacterial vaginosis (BV) is clue cells on microscopic exam. Clue cells are epithelial cells with adherent bacteria. The most common clinical feature is an unpleasant, "fishy" smelling discharge that is more noticeable after sexual intercourse. BV can produce a cervicitis. It is a risk factor for HIV acquisition and transmission. Metronidazole is the most successful therapy. The usual oral regimen is 500 mg twice daily for 7 days. Alcohol should be avoided.

149. ***a***
These symptoms describe a patient who has a kidney stone, urolithiasis. The cause of the pain is usually urine obstruction. Blood is almost always expected in the urine specimen of these patients. Nitrites and leukocytes are indicative of a urinary tract infection (UTI). UTI can present at the same time as stone. Calcium is usually not found in the urine, though it may be a component of the stone if recovered.

150. ***c***
The other test commonly used to assess a patient with suspected carpal tunnel syndrome is Phalen's test. This test is also called the "backward praying test". It asks the patient to put the back of his hands together with flexion of the wrists. This narrows the carpal tunnel and may reproduce symptoms in a patient with carpal tunnel syndrome. The symptoms likely to be reproduced are paresthesias in the affected hand.

Family Exam #3 Questions

1. **A patient with diarrhea has a positive enzyme immunoassay for C. difficile. He is on clindamycin for a tooth abscess. How should he be managed?**

    a. **Stop the clindamycin, treat the diarrhea**
    b. **Treat the diarrhea, give metronidazole**
    c. **Stop the clindamycin if possible, give metronidazole**
    d. **Give metronidazole**

2. **A patient presents to clinic with a complaint of a red eye. Which assessment below rules out the most worrisome diagnoses?**

    a. **Usual visual acuity**
    b. **Normal penlight exam**
    c. **Normal fundoscopic exam**
    d. **Negative photophobia**

3. **A young male patient with a herniated disc reports bilateral sciatica and leg weakness. If he calls the NP with complaints of urinary incontinence, what should be suspected?**

    a. **Opioid overuse**
    b. **Medial or lateral herniation**
    c. **Rupture of the disc**
    d. **Cauda equina syndrome**

4. **The Medicaid funded health program is:**

    a. **funded with premiums from participants.**
    b. **unlimited on the number of adult visits.**
    c. **funded by both state and federal governments.**
    d. **basically the same from state to state.**

5. **A 6 year-old complains that his legs hurt. His mother states that he has complained for the past 2 weeks, and she thought it was from "playing outside too much". When asked to identify the painful areas, the child points to the midshaft of the femurs. He grimaces slightly when asked to walk. What should be part of the differential diagnosis?**

   a. **Osgood–Schlatter disease**
   b. **Growing pains**
   c. **Acute lymphocytic leukemia (ALL)**
   d. **Psychogenic pain**

6. **A topical treatment for basal cell carcinoma is:**

   a. **sulfacetamide lotion.**
   b. **5-fluorouracil.**
   c. **tetracycline lotion.**
   d. **trichloroacetic acid.**

7. **The first step in evaluating a breast lump is:**

   a. **history and physical exam.**
   b. **mammogram.**
   c. **ultrasound.**
   d. **MRI.**

8. **Which beverage below does not increase the risk of gout in a male who is prone to this condition?**

   a. **Vodka**
   b. **Beer**
   c. **Wine**
   d. **Bourbon**

9. **The first sign that a male child is experiencing sexual maturation is:**

   a. **increase in testicular size.**
   b. **enlargement of the scrotum.**
   c. **increase in length of the penis.**
   d. **scrotal and penile changes.**

10. **A patient has suspected plantar fasciitis. The plantar fascia is best examined:**

    a. **with the great toe dorsiflexed.**
    b. **with the foot in neutral position.**
    c. **while the patient stands.**
    d. **with the ankle at a 90 degree angle.**

11. A 19 year-old female presents with lower abdominal pain that began about 12 hours ago. She is febrile. She denies vaginal discharge. Which choice below is the least likely cause of her symptoms?

a. **Appendicitis**
b. **Urinary tract infection**
c. **Renal stone**
d. **Ovarian cyst**

12. A 74 year-old patient has peripheral artery disease (PAD). Which item listed below is the most important risk factor for PAD?

a. **Cigarette smoking**
b. **Hyperlipidemia**
c. **Diabetes**
d. **Alcohol consumption**

13. Which statement below is true of infants with developmental dysplasia of the hip?

a. **They usually have other orthopedic ailments.**
b. **Most have some congenital orthopedic anomaly.**
c. **There is often pain in the hip when the infant's diaper is changed.**
d. **A palpable clunk is considered diagnostic.**

14. A pregnant patient is likely to have:

a. **a venous hum murmur and an S3.**
b. **mitral stenosis and an S3.**
c. **mitral valve prolapse and an S4.**
d. **aortic regurgitation and an S4.**

15. The most common symptom associated with acute bronchitis is:

a. **fever.**
b. **cough.**
c. **pharyngitis.**
d. **purulent sputum.**

16. A young athlete is found to have a depression of the longitudinal arch of both feet. He complains of heel pain bilaterally. The rest of his foot is normal, and he has continued with his activities. What could be recommended for his heel pain?

a. **An x-ray of the foot is needed first.**
b. **He needs some heel support in his shoes.**
c. **NSAIDs should be used initially.**
d. **Rigid orthotics could be ordered for his shoes.**

17. A mother reports that her child is not allergic to chickens but is allergic to ducks and duck feathers. The child is 4 years-old today. Which immunizations should he receive?

a. **Avoid flu, but all others OK**
b. **Avoid hepatitis B**
c. **MMR and tetanus are contraindicated**
d. **None are contraindicated**

18. A mother has a negative rubella titer. She is not pregnant but is breastfeeding her 4 month-old infant. Is she able to safely receive the MMR immunization today?

a. **No, her infant is too young for her to receive the MMR.**
b. **Yes, the immunization offers no risk to her infant.**
c. **No, she will shed rubella in her breast milk.**
d. **Yes, the immunization at this time will preclude the need for MMR in her infant.**

19. A 40 year-old patient who has aortic stenosis wants to know what symptoms indicate worsening of his stenosis. The nurse practitioner replies:

a. **palpitations and weakness.**
b. **ventricular arrhythmias.**
c. **shortness of breath and syncope.**
d. **fatigue and exercise intolerance.**

20. Which of the following is appropriate for initiation of an 8 week-old with gastroesophageal reflux?

a. **Small, frequent thickened feedings**
b. **Cimetidine every 6 hours**
c. **Change formula to soy based**
d. **Place infant on left side after eating**

21. A patient with mononucleosis has pharyngitis, fever, and lymphadenopathy. His symptoms started 3 days ago.

a. **He will have a positive "Monospot".**
b. **He will have a normal CBC.**
c. **He could have negative "Monospot".**
d. **He could have a positive Monospot and a normal CBC.**

22. A patient has a positive hepatitis B surface antibody. His core antibody is negative. This indicates:

a. **he has acute hepatitis B and needs immunization.**
b. **he has chronic hepatitis B.**
c. **he is immune to hepatitis B.**
d. **he needs immunization to hepatitis B.**

23. A patient taking an ACE inhibitor should avoid:

a. **strenuous exercise.**
b. **potassium supplements.**
c. **protein rich meals.**
d. **grapefruit juice.**

24. A patient with mitral regurgitation (MR) has developed the most common arrhythmia associated with MR. The intervention most likely to prevent complications from this arrhythmia is:

a. **immediate referral for a pacemaker.**
b. **anticoagulation.**
c. **beta-blocker administration.**
d. **valve replacement.**

25. When do the clinical manifestations of an ectopic (fallopian tube) pregnancy typically appear?

a. **4 weeks after the LMP**
b. **6-8 weeks after the LMP**
c. **10-12 weeks after conception**
d. **Late first trimester**

26. The initial step in the management of encopresis is:

a. **client and family education.**
b. **bowel cleansing.**
c. **dietary changes.**
d. **psychosocial evaluation.**

27. LFTs should be checked initially in patients who take:

a. **niacin, atorvastatin, simvastatin.**
b. **naproxen, metformin, aspirin.**
c. **cimetidine, pravastatin, and propanolol.**
d. **ketoconazole, simvastatin, iron.**

28. A 3 year-old healthy child is diagnosed with pneumonia. He is febrile but in no distress. What is the preferred treatment for him?

- **a. Supportive measures, it is probably viral**
- **b. Amoxicillin, doses 80-100 mg/kg/d**
- **c. Azithromycin**
- **d. Doxycycline**

29. A patient with mitral valve prolapse (MVP) reports chest pain and frequent arrhythmias. In the absence of other underlying cardiac anomalies, the drug of choice to treat her symptoms is a(n):

- **a. ACE inhibitor.**
- **b. beta blocker.**
- **c. calcium channel blocker.**
- **d. diuretic.**

30. A patient with pneumonia reports that he has rust colored sputum. What pathogen should the nurse practitioner suspect?

- **a. *Mycoplasma pneumoniae***
- **b. *Chlamydophila pneumoniae***
- **c. *Staphylococcus aureus***
- **d. *Streptococcus pneumoniae***

31. A 6 year-old being treated for community-acquired pneumonia (CAP) has been taking azithromycin in therapeutic doses for 72 hours. His temperature has gone from 102F to 101F. What should be done?

- **a. Continue the same dose and monitor his status**
- **b. Increase the dose to high dose azithromycin**
- **c. Change antibiotics to a penicillin**
- **d. This is probably viral, stop the antibiotic**

32. Head circumference should be measured until a child has attained:

- **a. 12 months of age.**
- **b. 18 months of age.**
- **c. 24 months of age.**
- **d. 36 months of age.**

33. **Niacin can:**

    a. **decrease total cholesterol and triglycerides.**
    b. **decrease serum glucose and LDLs.**
    c. **cause flushing and hypertension.**
    d. **increase liver enzymes.**

34. **A nurse practitioner is assessing a 3 day old infant's head. What would be a normal observation in a healthy 3 day old infant who is crying?**

    a. **There are pounding pulsations over the anterior fontanel.**
    b. **There are palpable pulsations over the anterior fontanel.**
    c. **There is a palpable nodule near the posterior fontanel.**
    d. **The fontanel is depressed.**

35. **A pregnant patient with urinary frequency is found to have a UTI. What drug is safest to treat this?**

    a. **Doxycycline**
    b. **Amoxicillin**
    c. **Ciprofloxacin**
    d. **Nitrofurantoin**

36. **A 7 seven year-old has a complaint of ear pain. If he has otitis externa, which complaint is most likely?**

    a. **He has tragal pain.**
    b. **He has difficulty hearing the TV.**
    c. **He has fever.**
    d. **He has a concurrent upper respiratory infection.**

37. **A 48 year-old patient has the following laboratory values. How should they be interpreted?**

    HCV IgG (+), RIBA (radio immuno blot assay) (+)

    a. **The patient has hepatitis C.**
    b. **The patient does not have hepatitis C.**
    c. **The patient should consider immunization.**
    d. **The results are indeterminate.**

38. The major laboratory abnormality noted in patients with pneumonia is:

a. **eosinophilia.**
b. **leukocytosis.**
c. **Gram stain positive.**
d. **leukopenia.**

39. Which patient is most likely to have mitral valve prolapse?

a. **An adolescent male with no cardiac history**
b. **A 25 year-old male with exercise intolerance**
c. **A 30 year-old female with no cardiac history**
d. **A 65 year-old male with shortness of breath**

40. A 4 year-old was diagnosed and treated for left acute otitis media 4 weeks ago. She is here today for a well-child visit. There is an effusion in the left ear. She denies complaints. How should this be managed?

a. **This should be monitored.**
b. **She should be given another antibiotic.**
c. **She should be evaluated with pneumatic otoscopy.**
d. **She needs a tympanogram.**

41. A 63 year-old male has been your patient for several years. He is a former smoker who takes simvastatin, ramipril, and an aspirin daily. His blood pressure and lipids are well controlled. He presents to your clinic with complaints of fatigue and "just not feeling well" for the last few days. His vital signs and exam are normal. His CBC, TSH, urine analysis are normal. His liver enzymes are six times the upper limits of normal. What should be done next?

a. **Order a hepatitis panel and stop his medications**
b. **Refer to gastroenterology**
c. **Refer for a toxicology evaluation**
d. **Order a hepatitis panel and stop his simvastatin and aspirin**

42. A full-term newborn is diagnosed with hyperbilirubinemia. When would his bilirubin level be expected to peak?

a. **1-2 days**
b. **3-4 days**
c. **5-7 days**
d. **7-10 days**

43. Group A Strept pharyngitis:

- **a. is characterized by a single symptom.**
- **b. can be accompanied by abdominal pain.**
- **c. usually does not have exudative symptoms.**
- **d. is commonly accompanied by an inflamed uvula.**

44. The most common presentation of Parkinson's Disease is:

- **a. muscular rigidity.**
- **b. tremor.**
- **c. falling.**
- **d. bradykinesia.**

45. The most common indicator of end-organ damage in children with hypertension is:

- **a. left ventricular hypertrophy.**
- **b. seizure.**
- **c. renal dysfunction.**
- **d. renal artery damage.**

46. A 44 year-old non-smoker is diagnosed with pneumonia. He is otherwise healthy and does not need hospitalization at this time. Which antibiotic can be used for empirical treatment according to the 2007 Infectious Diseases Society of America/American Thoracic Society?

- **a. Erythromycin**
- **b. Levofloxacin**
- **c. Azithromycin**
- **d. Amoxicillin**

47. A patient is diagnosed with thrush. A microscopic exam of this patient's saliva demonstrates:

- **a. budding yeasts, pseudohyphae.**
- **b. cocci.**
- **c. spores.**
- **d. rods, spores, cocci.**

48. The most common pathogen found in patients with pyelonephritis is:

- **a. *Pseudomonas.***
- **b. *Streptococcus.***
- **c. *E. coli.***
- **d. *Klebsiella.***

49. A 45 year-old patient has the following laboratory values. How should they be interpreted?

HBsAg (+), HBsAb (-), HBcAb (+)

a. **The patient has hepatitis.**
b. **The patient had hepatitis.**
c. **The patient should consider immunization.**
d. **The results are indeterminate.**

50. Tables for determination of maximum blood pressure values for children are based on:

a. **height percentile, body mass index, and gender.**
b. **gender and age.**
c. **height percentile, gender, and age.**
d. **body mass index and gender.**

51. A 63 year-old male has been your patient for several years. He is a former smoker who takes simvastatin, ramipril, and an aspirin daily. His blood pressure and lipids are well controlled. He presents to your clinic with complaints of fatigue and "just not feeling well" for the last few days. His vital signs and exam are normal. His hepatitis panel is negative for infectious hepatitis. What is the most likely cause of his elevated liver enzymes?

a. **He has received a generic version of simvastatin**
b. **He is an alcoholic in denial**
c. **Daily grapefruit consumption for the past 10 days**
d. **Rare liver toxicity from a usual dose of simvastatin**

52. Which patient has NO indication for further evaluation of his diarrhea? One with:

a. **bloody diarrhea.**
b. **temperature > 101.3F.**
c. **duration of illness >48 hours.**
d. **watery diarrhea and fever.**

53. A patient has suspected serotonin syndrome. How can this be diagnosed?

a. **CT scan of the brain**
b. **Elevated white count and C-reactive protein**
c. **Elevated CK**
d. **Clinical exam and index of suspicion**

54. The Framingham study of cardiovascular disease initiated in the early 1970s is an example of a:

a. randomized clinical trial.
b. cohort study.
c. case control study.
d. sequential control study.

55. A 20 year-old female patient presents with tenderness at McBurney's point. Appendicitis is considered. What laboratory test would be LEAST helpful to the nurse practitioner in excluding appendicitis as part of the differential?

a. CBC with elevated white count
b. Urinalysis with leukocytes
c. Positive serum pregnancy
d. Positive pelvic cultures

56. A 40 year-old complains of back pain after heavy lifting. This began 2 weeks ago. He has had little improvement in his pain. Which statement is true regarding plain x-rays in this patient?

a. They should be gotten since 2 weeks have passed without improvement.
b. X-rays will be of benefit in diagnosis.
c. X-rays usually detect findings unrelated to symptoms.
d. X-rays can detect herniated discs.

57. A patient has hepatitis B. He probably has a predominance of:

a. leukocytes.
b. lymphocytes.
c. neutrophils.
d. eosinophils.

58. An elderly patient with urinary frequency is found to have a UTI. What medication could produce arrhythmias in her?

a. Doxycycline
b. Amoxicillin
c. Ciprofloxacin
d. Macrodantin

59. A patient with aortic stenosis has been asymptomatic for decades. On routine exam he states that he has had some dizziness associated with activity but no chest pain or shortness of breath. The best course of action for the nurse practitioner is to:

a. **monitor closely for worsening of his status.**
b. **refer to cardiology.**
c. **consider a non-cardiac etiology for dizziness.**
d. **assess his carotid arteries for bruits.**

60. Which choice below characterizes a patient with aortic regurgitation?

a. **Long asymptomatic period followed by exercise intolerance, then dyspnea at rest**
b. **An acute onset of shortness of breath in the fifth or sixth decade**
c. **Dyspnea on exertion for a long period of time before sudden cardiac death**
d. **A long asymptomatic period with sudden death usually during exercise**

61. A 16 year-old has been diagnosed with Lyme disease. Which drug should be used to treat him?

a. **Doxycycline**
b. **Amoxicillin-clavulanate**
c. **Trimethoprim-sulfamethoxazole**
d. **Cephalexin**

62. The most appropriate time to begin screening for renal nephropathy in a patient with Type II diabetes is:

a. **at diagnosis.**
b. **once year after diagnosis.**
c. **2-3 years after diagnosis.**
d. **5 years after diagnosis.**

63. An example of a drug that targets the renin-angiotensin-aldosterone system is:

a. **an ACE inhibitor.**
b. **a beta blocker.**
c. **a calcium channel blocker.**
d. **a diuretic.**

64. A patient taking an angiotensin receptor blocker inhibitor should avoid:

- **a. strenuous exercise.**
- **b. potassium supplements.**
- **c. protein rich meals.**
- **d. grapefruit juice.**

65. A skin disorder has a hallmark finding of silvery scales. What word below describes this common condition?

- **a. Chronic**
- **b. Infectious**
- **c. Contagious**
- **d. Acute**

66. A patient has a urinary tract infection. What findings on a urine dipstick best describe a typical urinary tract infection?

- **a. Positive leukocytes**
- **b. Positive nitrates**
- **c. Positive leukocytes, positive nitrites**
- **d. Positive nitrates and hematuria**

67. A patient with mononucleosis would most likely have:

- **a. lymphocytosis.**
- **b. eosinophilia.**
- **c. leukocytosis.**
- **d. monocytosis.**

68. A female patient has the following characteristics. Which one represents a risk factor for Type II diabetes?

- **a. Hyperlipidemia**
- **b. History of gestational diabetes**
- **c. Infrequent, regular exercise**
- **d. Family history of Type I diabetes**

69. A patient with iron deficiency anemia takes iron supplementation daily. What should he be advised to avoid within a couple of hours of taking iron?

- **a. An antacid**
- **b. Heavy exercise**
- **c. Potassium supplements**
- **d. Grapefruit juice**

70. A patient with anemia of chronic disease probably has a:

a. macrocytic anemia.
b. normocytic anemia.
c. hypochromic anemia.
d. hyperchromic anemia.

71. A patient has 2 fasting glucose values of 101 mg/dL and 114 mg/dL that were measured on 2 separate days in the same week. This patient:

a. can be diagnosed with Type 2 diabetes.
b. has impaired fasting glucose.
c. should have further glucose testing done for diagnosis.
d. should have a Hgb A1C performed.

72. What choice below has no precautions for oral contraceptive pill use?

a. Gallbladder disease
b. 5 months post-partum and lactating
c. Blood pressure 160/100
d. Varicose veins

73. A patient has nasal septal erosion with minor, continuous bleeding. There is macerated tissue. What is a likely etiology?

a. Improper use of a nasal steroid
b. Chronic sinusitis
c. Severe allergic rhinitis
d. Cocaine abuse

74. Which form of birth control presents the highest risk to a female patient if she is exposed to a sexually transmitted disease (STD)?

a. Intrauterine device
b. Progestin only pill
c. Diaphragm
d. Oral contraceptives

75. Patients with asthma:

a. all wheeze.
b. all cough.
c. can cough or wheeze.
d. have dyspnea.

76. A patient is examined and found to have positive Kernig's and Brudzinski's signs. What is the most likely diagnosis?

- **a. Hepatitis**
- **b. Encephalitis**
- **c. Meningitis**
- **d. Pneumonitis**

77. Most cases of atopic dermatitis exacerbation are treated with:

- **a. emollients.**
- **b. topical steroids.**
- **c. antihistamines.**
- **d. antibiotics.**

78. A patient presents with severe toothache. She reports sensitivity to heat and cold. There is visible pus around the painful area. What is this termed?

- **a. Pulpitis**
- **b. Caries**
- **c. Gingivitis**
- **d. Periodontitis**

79. A college-age basketball player landed awkwardly on his foot and ankle after jumping during practice yesterday. He states that he sprained his ankle. He complains of ankle pain and foot pain but is able to limp into the exam room. How should he be managed?

- **a. Rest, ice, compression, elevation**
- **b. Non-weight bearing until fracture is ruled out**
- **c. Short leg splint**
- **d. NSAIDs and rest with partial non-weight bearing**

80. Which form of birth control would be the best choice in a lactating mother who wanted to insure that she did not become pregnant?

- **a. Injectable progestin**
- **b. Oral progesterone**
- **c. Oral contraceptives**
- **d. Natural family planning**

81. A child and father live in an old house. They both are found to be lead toxic. What type anemia is typically observed in patients who are lead toxic?

a. **Pernicious anemia**
b. **Iron deficiency anemia**
c. **Lead anemia**
d. **Anemia of chronic disease**

82. A characteristic that is true of tension headaches but not of cluster headaches is:

a. **cluster headaches are always bilateral.**
b. **tension headaches are always bilateral.**
c. **cluster headaches always cause nausea.**
d. **tension headaches cause photosensitivity.**

83. In a private NP clinic, a patient presents with trichomonas. State law requires reporting of STDs to the public health department. The patient asks the NP not to report it because her husband works in the public health department. How should this be managed by the NP?

a. **Respect the patient's right to privacy and not report it.**
b. **Tell the patient that it won't be reported, but report it anyway.**
c. **Report it to public health as required by law.**
d. **Report it to public health but don't divulge all the details.**

84. A patient reports to the minor care area of the emergency department after being bitten by a dog. The patient states that the dog had a tag around his neck and had been seen roaming around the neighborhood. The dog did not exhibit any odd behavior. How should this be managed?

a. **If the bites are only minor, do not mention rabies prophylaxis to the patient.**
b. **Give the patient tetanus immunization only. Don't call animal control.**
c. **Clean the wounds, provide tetanus and rabies prophylaxis.**
d. **Report the bite to animal control and administer appropriate medical care.**

85. A neurologic disease that produces demyelination of the nerve cells in the brain and spinal cord is:

a. **Parkinson's disease.**
b. **late stage Lyme disease.**
c. **multiple sclerosis.**
d. **amyotrophic lateral sclerosis.**

86. Which of the following statements regarding HIV is correct?

a. **There are few conditions that cause depletion of CD4 cells other than HIV.**
b. **CD4 cell counts vary very little in individuals infected with HIV.**
c. **A normal CD4 count is < 200/mm^3.**
d. **CD4 counts are the first abnormality seen in patients with HIV.**

87. A patient has been diagnosed with MRSA. She is sulfa allergic. Which medication could be used to treat her?

a. **Augmentin**
b. **Trimethoprim-sulfamethoxazole (TMPS)**
c. **Ceftriaxone**
d. **Doxycycline**

88. Women who use diaphragms for contraception have an increased incidence of:

a. **sexually transmitted diseases.**
b. **pregnancy.**
c. **urinary tract infection.**
d. **pelvic inflammatory disease.**

89. What is the effect of digital rectal examination (DRE) on a male's PSA (prostate specific antigen) level if it is measured on the same day as DRE?

a. **The change is insignificant.**
b. **A decrease in the PSA will occur.**
c. **An increase in the PSA will occur.**
d. **There will be a change, but it is not predictable.**

90. Papilledema is noted in a patient with a headache. What is the importance of papilledema in this patient?

a. **It is not related to this patient's headache.**
b. **It is an incidental finding in patients with migraines.**
c. **It could be an important finding in this patient.**
d. **This is a common finding in patients with headaches.**

91. Syphilis may present as:

a. **a discharge.**
b. **a rash.**
c. **a painful lesion.**
d. **dysuria.**

92. Depression is diagnosed on clinical presentation. What time frame is important for distinguishing between depressed mood and clinical depression?

a. 1 week
b. 2 weeks
c. 3 weeks
d. 4 weeks

93. A patient with bipolar disease has purchased a $10,000 baby grand piano. He does not play the piano. Consistent with a manic episode in bipolar disease, this is an example of:

a. grandiosity.
b. poor judgment.
c. racing thoughts.
d. psychosis.

94. Patients with cough variant asthma:

a. all exhibit wheezing.
b. all exhibit cough.
c. may exhibit cough or wheeze.
d. have dyspnea.

95. An older patient presents with left lower quadrant pain. If diverticulitis is suspected, how should the NP proceed?

a. Order a chest and abdominal x-ray
b. CT scan with IV and oral contrast
c. Barium enema
d. Ultrasound of the abdomen

96. A patient has fatigue, weight loss, and a TSH of .05. What is his likely diagnosis?

a. Hypothyroidism
b. Hyperthyroidism
c. Subclinical hypothyroidism
d. More tests are needed to establish his diagnosis.

97. A female should be told to take her OCP at bedtime if she experiences:

a. weight gain.
b. headaches.
c. nausea.
d. spotting.

98. The following PSA levels have been observed in a patient. What conclusion can be made following these annual readings?

Year 1: 3.2 ng/mL
Year 2: 3.8 ng/mL
Year 3: 4.2 ng/mL

a. **They are all within normal range.**
b. **None are within normal range.**
c. **There is a steady increase that is worrisome.**
d. **There is a steady increase but not worrisome.**

99. A patient asks the NP's advice about an herb to help with her hot flashes. The NP knows these:

a. **are safe to use in all patients.**
b. **may be contraindicated in patients with history of breast cancer.**
c. **substances have a mild estrogenic effect and will halt hot flashes.**
d. **help prevent osteoporosis.**

100. A 15 year-old female has never menstruated. She and her mother are concerned. What is most important for the NP to assess?

a. **Stature**
b. **Tanner stage**
c. **Anemia**
d. **Family history of amenorrhea**

101. A female patient has the following characteristics. Which one represents a risk factor for Type II diabetes?

a. **BMI 31**
b. **Osteopenia**
c. **Mediterranean decent**
d. **Hypothyroidism**

102. What finding characterizes shingles?

a. **Pain, burning, and itching**
b. **Unilateral dermatomal rash**
c. **Grouped vesicles**
d. **Resolution of rash and crusting**

103. A 45 year-old patient starting taking paroxetine one week ago for depression. She calls to report intermittent headache and nausea. What is a likely etiology?

a. **Gastroenteritis**
b. **Viral infection**
c. **Drug side effect**
d. **Depression**

104. A male with gonorrhea might complain of:

a. **dysuria.**
b. **a penile lesion.**
c. **abdominal pain.**
d. **fatigue.**

105. What medication used to treat patients who have GERD provides the fastest relief of heartburn symptoms?

a. **Calcium carbonate**
b. **Ranitidine**
c. **Amantadine**
d. **Pantoprazole**

106. A patient exhibits petechiae on both lower legs but has no other complaints. How should the NP proceed?

a. **Refer to hematology**
b. **Order a CBC**
c. **Order blood cultures**
d. **Stop aspirin and re-assess in one week**

107. A vitamin B-12 deficiency might be suspected in an older patient with what complaints?

a. **Fatigue and restless legs**
b. **Memory issues and glossitis**
c. **Painful legs with exercise**
d. **Insomnia and anorexia**

108. Which drug listed below is NOT associated with weight gain?

a. **Insulin**
b. **Pioglitazone**
c. **Citalopram**
d. **Metoprolol**

109. The primary therapeutic intervention for patients who present with hives is:

a. steroids.
b. anti-histamines.
c. calcium channel blockers.
d. topical steroid cream.

110. Kegel exercises may be helpful for patients with what type of incontinence?

a. Stress
b. Urge
c. Mixed
d. Overflow

111. A 52 year-old patient presents with an acute drooping right eye and drooping right upper lip. The right side of her face is numb. She is otherwise healthy. Based on the most likely etiology, how should she be managed?

a. Steroids plus an antiviral agent
b. Immediate referral to the emergency department
c. Antihistamines and steroids
d. Steroids only

112. A patient presents to the NP clinic with a complaint of nocturnal paresthesias. What is the likely underlying etiology?

a. De Quervain's tenosynovitis
b. Carpal tunnel syndrome
c. Ulnar radiculopathy
d. Medial epicondylitis

113. What is the recommendation from American Cancer Society for assessment of the prostate gland in a man who is 45 years old and of average risk for development of prostate cancer? He should have:

a. screening starting at 50 years of age.
b. prostate specific antigen (PSA) now.
c. PSA and digital rectal exam now.
d. digital rectal exam only.

114. A 24 year-old female patient who is sexually active complains of vaginal itching. If she has bacterial vaginosis, she might complain of:

- a. a "fishy" vaginal odor after coitus.
- b. a truncal rash.
- c. copious vaginal discharge.
- d. midcycle bleeding.

115. A patient is diagnosed with mild chronic heart failure (CHF). What drug listed below would be a good choice for managing his symptoms and improving long-term outcomes?

- a. Verapamil
- b. Digoxin
- c. Furosemide
- d. Metoprolol

116. A patient who has been in the sun for the past few weeks is very tanned. He has numerous 3-6 mm light colored flat lesions on his trunk. What is the likely etiology?

- a. Tinea corporis
- b. Tinea unguium
- c. Tinea versicolor
- d. Human papilloma virus

117. A patient has been diagnosed with anxiety. What sleep disturbance might she have?

- a. Early morning wakening
- b. Difficulty remaining asleep
- c. Difficulty falling asleep
- d. Never feeling tired

118. A female patient complains of dysuria with vaginal discharge. How should she be managed?

- a. Order a urinalysis
- b. Order a urine culture
- c. Perform a pelvic exam
- d. Perform an abdominal exam, urinalysis, and pelvic exam

119. Ankle inversion is a common complaint from a patient with a:

a. medial ankle sprain.
b. lateral ankle sprain.
c. severely torn ligament.
d. fracture of the medial malleolus.

120. A 60 year-old has been on NSAIDs for the past week for shoulder pain. He has complaints of blood on toilet tissue when wiping after a bowel movement. What should be suspected?

a. He has a GI bleed from NSAIDs.
b. He could have hemorrhoids.
c. He does not have a GI bleed. The bleeding is from tissue friability from NSAIDs.
d. This is unrelated to the NSAIDs.

121. A 65 year-old patient has a firm, non-tender, symmetrical enlarged prostate gland on examination. His PSA is 3.9 ng/mL. This probably indicates:

a. prostate cancer.
b. benign prostatic hypertrophy (BPH).
c. prostate infection.
d. a perfectly normal prostate gland.

122. A contact lens wearer presents with an erythematous conjunctiva. He denies blurred vision. There is scant drainage and crusting around the eye. He reports that there was crusting when he woke up this morning. How should the exam begin?

a. The patient should wash his hands.
b. His visual acuity should be measured in each eye.
c. Fluorescein staining should be assessed.
d. Extraocular eye movements should be assessed.

123. The hearing loss associated with aging involves:

a. the 8th cranial nerve.
b. sensorineural hearing loss.
c. conductive hearing loss.
d. noise damage.

124. In a research study, the difference between the smallest and largest observation is the:

- a. standard deviation.
- b. first degree of freedom.
- c. range.
- d. absolute value.

125. Nagel's rule estimates:

- a. the age of the fetus.
- b. days past conception.
- c. timing of prenatal interventions.
- d. date of confinement (EDC).

126. A patient presents with symptoms of influenza during influenza season. What should be used to help diagnose influenza in him?

- a. A nasal culture
- b. A nasal swab
- c. CBC
- d. Based on symptoms

127. A patient who is taking long acting insulin basal insulin has elevated blood sugars. Which blood sugars are important to review in order to increase the dose of insulin?

- a. AM fasting
- b. 2 hour post prandial
- c. Pre-prandial
- d. Bedtime

128. A patient with sciatica is most likely to describe relief of symptoms with:

- a. sitting.
- b. standing.
- c. side lying or standing.
- d. walking.

129. A patient with asthma presents with chest tightness, wheezing, coughing, and fever. He is wheezing in the upper right lobe. His cough is non-productive, and he denies nasal symptoms. Which symptoms are not likely related to his asthma?

a. **Fever**
b. **Coughing**
c. **Wheezing**
d. **Chest tightness**

130. A 60 year-old female presents with history of low back pain of recent origin. Her gait is antalgic and she reports loss of bladder function since the onset of back pain this morning. What should be done?

a. **Order physical therapy**
b. **Refer to the emergency department**
c. **Refer to a neurologist**
d. **Keep non-weight bearing until x-rays are completed**

131. After a vaginal exam, a patient received a prescription for metronidazole. What was her likely diagnosis?

a. **Syphilis**
b. **Trichomonas**
c. **Chlamydia**
d. **Gonorrhea**

132. A patient presents with small vesicles on the lateral edges of his fingers and intense itching. On close inspection, there are small vesicles on the palmar surface of the hand. What is this called?

a. **Seborrheic dermatitis**
b. **Dyshidrotic dermatitis**
c. **Herpes zoster**
d. **Varicella zoster**

133. A patient has a "herald patch" and is diagnosed with pityriasis rosea. Where is the "herald patch" found?

a. **On the affected limb**
b. **On the chest**
c. **Close to the scalp**
d. **Behind one of the ears**

134. A patient with environmental allergies presents to your clinic. She takes an oral antihistamine every 24 hours. What is the most effective single maintenance medication for allergic rhinitis?

a. **Antihistamine**
b. **Decongestant**
c. **Intranasal glucocorticoids**
d. **Leukotriene blockers**

135. A patient presents with tragal pain. What is the most likely diagnosis?

a. **Otitis media**
b. **Otitis externa**
c. **Presbycusis**
d. **Mastoiditis**

136. A patient has been diagnosed with viral gastroenteritis. He has nausea, vomiting, and has started having lower abdominal cramps. What is the most effective intervention for him?

a. **An anti-diarrheal agent**
b. **An anti-emetic**
c. **An antispasmodic**
d. **Oral rehydration**

137. A characteristic of rheumatoid arthritis not typical in osteoarthritis is:

a. **weight loss.**
b. **morning stiffness.**
c. **symmetrical joint involvement.**
d. **the presence of Bouchard's nodes.**

138. A patient with migraine headaches and hypertension should receive which medication class with caution?

a. **Beta-blockers**
b. **Triptans**
c. **Pain medications**
d. **ACE inhibitors**

139. A female patient who is 45 years old states that she is having urinary frequency. She describes episodes of "having to go right now" and not being able to wait. Her urinalysis is normal. What is part of the differential?

a. **Diabetes**
b. **Lupus**
c. **Stress incontinence**
d. **Asymptomatic bacteriuria**

140. A 30 year-old male who is sexually active presents with pain during bowel movements. He is negative when checked for hemorrhoids, but has a tender prostate gland. What should be suspected?

a. **Acute bacterial prostatitis**
b. **Prostate cancer**
c. **Benign prostatic hyperplasia**
d. **Gonorrhea**

141. Which of the following can NOT be a microcytic anemia?

a. **Vitamin B12**
b. **Anemia of chronic disease**
c. **Iron deficiency anemia**
d. **Thalassemia**

142. A patient reports that her knee "locks" sometimes and feels like it will "give out". She denies injury. She has no complaint about her other knee. What is her likely problem?

a. **Torn anterior cruciate ligament**
b. **Knee effusion**
c. **Premature osteoarthritis**
d. **Meniscal tear**

143. A nurse practitioner has not increased the dosage of an antihypertensive medication even though the patient's blood pressure has remained 140/90. This might be described as:

a. **clinical inertia.**
b. **malpractice.**
c. **resistant hypertension.**
d. **lackadaisical attitude.**

144. Which choice below would be the best choice for an 80 year-old patient whose blood pressure is 172/72 mm Hg?

a. **Chlorthalidone**
b. **Amlodipine**
c. **Monopril**
d. **Acebutolol**

145. A patient who is diagnosed today with diabetes has microalbuminuria. What can be concluded about this finding?

a. **The patient has diabetic nephropathy.**
b. **There is renal damage.**
c. **The patient should have a repeat test in one month.**
d. **The patient might have been diabetic for a long time before diagnosis.**

146. A patient with bulimia nervosa probably has concurrent:

a. **hypothyroidism.**
b. **malnutrition.**
c. **anxiety.**
d. **hypoalbuminemia.**

147. What symptom listed below might be seen in a male patient with benign prostatic hyperplasia?

a. **Dysuria**
b. **Nocturia**
c. **Low back pain**
d. **Pain with bearing down**

148. A nurse practitioner performs a fundoscopic exam. He identifies small areas of dull, yellowish-white coloration in the retina. What might these be?

a. **Cotton wool spots**
b. **Microaneurysms**
c. **Hemorrhages**
d. **Exudates**

149. A patient with intermittent asthma is using his "rescue" medication once daily. How should this be managed? He must receive a prescription for:

a. **a bronchodilator.**
b. **an inhaled steroid.**
c. **a long-acting beta agonist.**
d. **a leukotriene blocker.**

150. Which medication should be avoided in a patient with a sulfa allergy?

a. **Sulfonylurea**
b. **Sulfamethoxazole**
c. **Naproxen**
d. **Cefazolin**

Family Exam #3 Answers

1. *c*
The most important step in treating infection with C. difficile is stopping ingestion of the offending antibiotic. In this case, stopping the clindamycin, if possible, is the most important part of treatment. Metronidazole is recommended initially for non-severe infection. If the antibiotic cannot be stopped, treatment for C. difficile should be continued as long as the patient must take the offending antibiotic.

2. *a*
This is a test that should be done on every patient who presents with an eye complaint; especially if the eye is red. It is not necessary to determine exactly what the visual acuity is; it is necessary to establish that vision is usual. If this is the case, the most worrisome diagnoses can be ruled out: infectious keratitis, iritis, and angle closure glaucoma.

3. *d*
Cauda equina is a medical emergency. It is characterized by compression of the spinal cord. A common manifestation of this is bowel or bladder dysfunction. This patient needs immediate neuro or orthopedic referral.

4. *c*
Medicaid is state run and specific to each state. The state programs are funded by a combination of state and federal funds. Most states have limits on the number of adult visits. Some states have no limits on visits for children. Participants generally do not pay premiums like Medicare recipients pay.

5. *c*
Bone pain is common in children, especially adolescents. However, a six year-old with complaints of mid-bone pain should be evaluated for ALL. Osgood-Schlatter produces pain in the knees. Growing pain usually occurs at nighttime. There is no information from history to suggest psychogenic pain, but ALL must always be considered since it is the most common malignancy in children. The child should be assessed for lymphadenopathy since this accompanies bone pain in ALL at least 50% of the time.

6. *b*
Several treatments exist for basal and squamous cell carcinoma. The majority are simple procedures like cryotherapy, electrodessication, surgical excision, and a topical treatment like 5-fluorouracil (5-FU). The other agents listed are not used to treat basal or squamous cell carcinoma. 5-FU works by inhibiting DNA synthesis. It is effective if used for superficial basal cell carcinomas. It is available in cream and solution and is usually applied twice daily for 3-6 weeks.

7. *a*
Although most patients will need further work-up of a breast mass, historical information is critically important in directing the health care provider to the next step. Historical information that should be ascertained is the location of the lump, how and when it was first noticed, whether there is nipple discharge, and whether it changes in size related to menses. Other historical information is the patient's personal and family history of breast cancer and/or history of breast biopsies.

8. *c*
Alcohol is known to be a contributing factor in development of gouty arthritis. Males are more prone to gout than females, and alcohol consumption increases the likelihood of gout development. Of all alcohols, wine contributes least to the development of gout. Consumption of meat and fish increase the concentration of uric acid and thus, the risk of developing gout.

9. *a*
A male in Tanner Stage II will have an increase in testicular volume from 1.5 ml or less, to up to 6 ml. The skin on the scrotum will begin to thin, redden, and enlarge. The penile length will remain the same.

10. *a*
When the great toe is dorsiflexed, the plantar fascia is easy to palpate because it tightens and can be easily palpated on the sole of the foot. Anterior heel pain is usually easily appreciated when the patient has plantar fasciitis.

11. *c*
A renal stone can produce lower abdominal pain, but is unlikely to produce fever. Fever can be associated with the presence of a stone if pyelonephritis also accompanies this. However, this is not nearly as likely as the other diagnoses listed. Another diagnosis that must be considered because of her age, is pelvic inflammatory disease. In this case, a pelvic exam should be performed.

12. *a*
Cigarette smoking is considered the most important risk factor for PAD. Stopping cigarette smoking reduces the progression of PAD and is associated with lower rates of amputation, and improves rest ischemia and pain in patients who experience this. The other major risk factors for PAD are presence of diabetes, hypertension, hyperlipidemia. Alcohol consumption actually reduces the risk of PAD but can increase the risk of many other diseases.

13. *d*
Several maneuvers may be attempted to elicit the dislocation. The physical exam techniques used to identify hip dislocation are Ortolani's and Barlow's maneuvers. Both attempt to dislocate or reduce the hip. There is a distinct "clunk" which can be felt by the examiner and sometimes heard as well. Each hip should be assessed individually and several times.

14. *a*

Many changes occur in the cardiovascular system when patients are pregnant. Nearly all pregnant women have a venous hum murmur. A higher basal heart rate, louder heart sounds and a systolic ejection murmur. An S3 is commonly present probably related to increased fluid. An S4 is rarely heard. Mitral stenosis and aortic regurgitation are diastolic murmurs and these are abnormal in pregnant patients.

15. *b*

Fever is an unusual symptom associated with acute bronchitis. Cough is the most common symptom associated with acute bronchitis. Purulent sputum is identified in more than 50% of patients with acute bronchitis. The color imparted to the sputum is usually due to sloughing of epithelial cells, not bacterial infection. Concurrent upper respiratory symptoms are typical of acute bronchitis. Pharyngitis is very common.

16. *b*

A description of functional flat foot is described in this question. It is common among athletes. Although pain is not always present with this finding, it may accompany the finding but is usually not severe enough to inhibit activity. The treatment deemed to be best is a well supported heel counter. The heel counter is the rigid part of the shoe that supports the heel. A radiograph is not needed unless the patient presents with other symptoms or fails to derive relief from the heel counter. NSAIDs may help symptoms of pain, but they will not correct the underlying problem. Orthotics may increase his pain. These are more helpful in patients with more severe pes planus.

17. *d*

Allergy to duck meat, duck feathers is not a contraindication to any allergy even if the child has had an allergic reaction to chicken eggs. He should receive all needed immunizations today.

18. *b*

There is no risk of transmitting measles, mumps, or rubella to her young infant through respiration or breast milk. The mother should be immunized and so should the infant when he attains 12 months of age.

19. *c*

The three most common symptoms associated with aortic stenosis are angina, syncope, and congestive heart failure evidenced by dyspnea. Syncope is usually exertional. Angina may be due to aortic stenosis, but, underlying coronary artery disease accounts for half of anginal symptoms in these patients. There is usually a prolonged asymptomatic phase, but the presence of symptoms usually indicates a need for valve replacement. Without replacement, there is a rapid decline in the patient's status and death will ensue.

20. ***a***
Two strategies should be tried initially. First, avoidance of overfeeding is recommended. Hence, small, frequent feedings. Second, milk thickening agents appear to improve symptoms in infants who experience gastroesophageal reflux (GER). Thickened feedings significantly decrease frequency of reflux in most infants. Also, caloric content is increased and this may be helpful for patients who are underweight because of persistent GER. Generally, when medications are used, proton pump inhibitors are preferred over an H2 blocker like cimetidine. Changing formula generally does not help, however, a milk-free diet may help since 40% of infants with GER are sensitive to cow's milk protein. Thus, soy would not help. Positioning seems to be ineffective in relieving symptoms in infants.

21. ***c***
The "Monospot" detects the presence of heterophile antibodies in mononucleosis (mono). If the "Monospot" is performed too early in the course of the illness, it will be negative even though the patient has mono. If the patient has persistent symptoms suspicious of mono, a "Monospot" should be repeated. It is likely that in several days after a negative result, a positive result will be obtained. Lymphocytosis characterizes mononucleosis; therefore, a patient will not have a normal CBC if he has mono.

22. ***c***
This patient is immune to hepatitis B because he has a positive hepatitis B surface antibody. He does not need immunization. His immunity is due to immunization because he has a negative core antibody. The finding of a positive surface antibody and a negative core antibody in this patient indicates immunity from hepatitis B from immunization. If his immunity had been derived from infection, his core antibody would have been positive.

23. ***b***
An ACE inhibitor potentially can produce hyperkalemia because its mechanism of action is in the renin-angiotensin-aldosterone system where potassium is spared. If potassium is taken in the form of potassium supplements, the effect will be additive and the risk of hyperkalemia can be great.

24. ***b***
The most common arrhythmia associated with mitral regurgitation (MR) is atrial fibrillation. Anti-coagulation with warfarin will help prevent arterial embolism that can result in stroke or myocardial infarction. Atrial fibrillation occurs because the fibers in the atrium are stretched as the atrium dilates. The stretch results in conduction defects, notably, atrial fibrillation.

25. ***b***
Clinical manifestations usually occur 6-8 weeks after the last menstrual period. The classic symptoms are vaginal bleeding, abdominal pain, and amenorrhea. If shoulder pain accompanies these symptoms, fallopian tube rupture must be considered. The risk of maternal morbidity is increased.

26. ***a***

Encopresis is repetitive soiling of stool by a child who is 4 years of age or older who should be potty trained. The patient and caregivers of a child with encopresis need education about the underlying cause, usually chronic constipation. The initial step is to remove negative attributions regarding soiling. The caregivers should be educated about changing the child's chronic behavior patterns. The child should not be scolded. The next step after education is to relieve the constipation with a goal of one soft bowel movement daily.

27. ***a***

Patients who take niacin and the statins should have liver enzymes measured prior to initiation. The need for periodic monitoring of liver enzymes with the statins is no longer required. However, baseline values are prudently measured. There is no need to do this routinely with aspirin, cimetidine, propanolol, or iron in patients without risk factors. There are more than 600 commonly prescribed drugs that can produce liver enzyme elevations. Care with prescribing is always warranted.

28. ***b***

In this age group, specifically 4 months to 4 years, the most common pathogen is *Streptococcus pneumoniae*, therefore, amoxicillin is the preferred agent. It is usually chosen first for its efficacy, cost, and tolerability. The higher dose (80-100 mg/kg/d) is chosen because of the prevalence of resistant *Streptococcus pneumoniae.* Azithromycin would be chosen if an atypical pathogen was suspected. Doxycycline is not an appropriate choice because it has poor Strept coverage and it is contraindicated in children younger than 8 years.

29. ***b***

Beta blockers are recommended to alleviate atrial or ventricular arrhythmias associated with mitral valve prolapse. However, long-term effectiveness of beta-blockers is uncertain. Most patients with MVP who do not have symptoms of arrhythmias or ectopy at rest, usually do not require further evaluation. However, they should be monitored at least annually for a change in their condition.

30. ***d***

Clinical descriptions of mucus do not really help in clinical decision-making regarding pneumonia, but certain clinical characteristics are associated with specific types of pneumonia. Strept pneumonia, also known as pneumococcal pneumonia, is associated with rust colored sputum. Scant or watery sputum is associated with atypical pathogens like *Mycoplasma* and *Chlamydophila* pneumonia. Thick, discolored sputum may be associated with bacterial pneumonia.

31. ***c***

A 6 year-old with CAP should show improvement in symptoms in 24-48 hours if he is on appropriate antibiotic therapy. Azithromycin treats atypical pathogens like Mycoplasma and Chlamydia, but, has poor Strept coverage. The most likely pathogen in this age group that causes pneumonia is an atypical pathogen, but, at this point the

most common typical pathogen, Strept pneumo, must be considered. The best choice is to consider Strept as the pathogen and treat with a penicillin. Specifically, this patient should receive high dose amoxicillin because of the increased incidence of resistant Strept pneumo.

32. ***d***

A child's head is usually measured at each periodic well child visit until he has attained the age of 3 years old. During the first three years of life, the head grows and its growth should be monitored for adequacy. The tape measure should encircle the head at the largest point above the ears. These measurements are recorded on a growth chart so that changes in head circumference can be followed and percentile for age and rate of growth can be determined.

33. ***d***

Niacin is used to decrease total cholesterol, LDLs, and increase HDLs. Liver function studies should be monitored prior to, with dosage increases, and periodically during consumption of niacin because elevations can occur. Glucose levels should be monitored as well because glucose levels can increase slightly in some patients who take niacin. Monitor for myalgias and rhabdomyolysis as with the statins. Niacin commonly causes flushing in patients, but, not hypertension. Hypotension is common in patients who take niacin.

34. ***b***

Palpable or visible pulsations are common if the infant is crying or is agitated. Normally, the anterior fontanel is slightly depressed, but a depressed fontanel is indicative of a dehydrated or malnourished infant. Pounding pulsations are indicative of increased intracranial pressure. A palpable nodule near the posterior fontanel is an abnormal finding possibly indicative of a calcium deposition or bony abnormality.

35. ***d***

Medication safety during pregnancy is of utmost concern. Therefore, medications are rated according to safety for the developing fetus. In the current rating system, Nitrofurantoin is the safest and most efficacious medication listed. Amoxicillin is as safe as nitrofurantoin, but has a lower efficacy against typical urinary tract pathogens. Doxycycline is associated with fetal tooth discoloration and so it should be avoided. Ciprofloxacin is not recommended during pregnancy due to potential problems with bone and cartilage formation.

36. ***a***

A patient with otitis externa has swimmer's ear; an infection of the external canal. The classic complaint is tragal pain or even pinnae pain. If there is such significant edema in the external canal, hearing may be impaired, but, the most common complaint is tragal pain. Systemic complaints do not accompany swimmer's ear unless a second diagnosis is present simultaneously. Fever and upper respiratory infection are not likely.

37. ***a***
This patient has hepatitis C. He has a positive HCV IgG. This is a positive screen for hepatitis C. The confirmatory RIBA is positive. When both the HCV IgG and RIBA are positive, the patient can be diagnosed with hepatitis C. At this time, there is no immunization for hepatitis C.

38. ***b***
An increased white count is typical in patients with pneumonia. This is more commonly seen in bacterial pneumonia. Eosinophils can be increased in patients who develop pneumonia secondary to exposure to a very irritating substance like a toxic gas. Gram stain can demonstrate gram positive or negative pathogens. Leukopenia is an ominous finding, especially in older patients. This indicates a poor prognosis because it means that the immune system is not responding to a potentially fatal pathogen.

39. ***c***
Mitral valve prolapse (MVP) is most common in women aged 14-30 years of age. However, it can be found in children (though not usually) or in older adults. The symptoms most commonly associated with MVP are arrhythmias, both atrial and ventricular, and chest pain. However, most patients with MVP are asymptomatic.

40. ***a***
About 40% of children have effusion at 4 weeks post-acute otitis media. This should be monitored and not treated with another antibiotic. Effusion is a stage in the resolution of otitis media. Pneumatic otoscopy will identify the presence of fluid or pus behind the TM, but will not help in diagnosis or treatment once an effusion has been established. A tympanogram will establish that her hearing is diminished, a fact which should be assumed since there is fluid in the middle ear.

41. ***d***
This patient has very probable damage to his liver, as evidenced by his elevated liver enzymes. Elevations in liver enzymes can be a direct result of hepatic injury or something else. 2 important notes: first, these enzymes are not specific for the liver, although, the highest ALT content is in the liver. ALT and AST can be found in the heart, skeletal muscle, pancreas, kidney, brain, and in white and red blood cells. Second, normal ALT/AST levels can be found in the setting of hepatic injury. This is common in patients with chronic hepatitis C and in patients with cirrhosis because of the absence of continuing injury. Because the liver is responsible for making clotting factors, stopping the aspirin is prudent until the etiology of has been determined.

42. ***b***
In full-term infants, the bilirubin level peaks at 3-4 days. In premature infants, the level peaks at 5-7 days. This is diagnosed when the bilirubin level exceeds 5 mg/dL. It occurs in more than 60% of full-term infants.

43. ***b***
Group A Streptococcus is usually characterized by multiple symptoms with an abrupt onset. Sore throat is usually accompanied by fever, headache. GI symptoms are common too; nausea, vomiting and abdominal pain are usual. Even without treatment, symptoms usually resolve in 3-5 days.

44. ***b***
Approximately 70% of patients with Parkinson's Disease have tremor as the presenting symptom. The tremor typically involves the hand but can involve the legs, jaw, lips, tongue. It seldom involves the head.

45. ***a***
The most common manifestation of end-organ damage in hypertensive children is left ventricular hypertrophy (LVH). According to the "National high blood pressure education program working group on high blood pressure in children and adolescents", as many as 41% of children who have hypertension, have LVH identifiable on ECG.

46. ***c***
The guidelines recommend macrolide use or doxycycline for initial treatment of uncomplicated pneumonia in outpatients who are otherwise healthy and have not had recent antibiotic exposure. The initial choices can be any of these: azithromycin, clarithromycin, or doxycycline. These agents are chosen because they cover atypical pathogens, the most likely pathogen in this population. Fluoroquinolones are commonly used first line in these patients; however, the guidelines strongly recommend using fluoroquinolones for patients with co-morbidities or those who have recent antibiotic exposure.

47. ***b***
The visualization of yeasts and/or pseudohypha in saliva indicates a fungal infection, often Candida species. Budding is a process by which yeasts reproduce.

48. ***c***
The most common pathogen in upper and lower urinary tract infections is E. coli. Approximately 70-95% of infection can be attributed to E. coli. As patients age, the incidence of E. coli declines (though it is still the most common pathogen), the incidence of Klebsiella increases.

49. ***a***
This patient has a positive hepatitis B surface antigen (HBsAg). Therefore, he has hepatitis B. A positive HBcAb is found in patients who either have hepatitis now or who have had it. The surface antibody (HBsAb) would be expected to be negative in a patient with positive surface antigen (HBsAg) because these 2 markers will not be positive at the same time.

50. ***c***
Body size is an important determinant in blood pressure in children. Blood pressure

tables are NOT based on body mass index. The tables include 50th, 90th, 95th, and 99th percentiles based on age, height, and gender. At least 3 separate elevated blood pressure readings on separate visits are required for diagnosis.

51. *c*
Grapefruit is a potent inhibitor of the cytochrome P450 enzyme system. Statins and calcium channel blockers are two infamous drug interactions that occur with grapefruit and grapefruit juice. Because they inhibit metabolism of the statin, the patient continues to have statin in circulation because he cannot significantly metabolize the medication. When the next day's dose is taken, its effect is coupled with the effect of the previous day's dose. The effect is cumulative. Hepatoxicity can quickly develop. The simvastatin must be stopped immediately! The liver enzymes must be followed until they return to normal; which could take weeks, months or even longer.

52. *d*
Diarrhea is extremely common. Evaluation of diarrhea should take place when specific criteria suggest severe illness. In addition to those listed, some conditions which indicate further work-up are: profuse watery diarrhea with signs of hypovolemia, passage of >6 unformed stools per 24 hours or a duration of illness > 48 hours, recent antibiotic use or recent hospitalization, and diarrhea in a patient ≥ 70 years old.

53. *d*
Serotonin syndrome is a clinical diagnosis characterized by too much serotonergic activity in the central nervous system. There is no way to measure serotonin levels at this time. Therefore, no clinical laboratory or imaging study can identify this syndrome. However, these studies may rule out other conditions.

54. *b*
The Framingham study was initiated in Framingham, Massachusetts in the early 1970s. The participants agreed to follow-up study (interviews and physical exam) every 2 years in a long-term study. This cohort study has examined what happens to disease over time. These are termed prospective studies because the events of interest occur after the study has begun.

55. *a*
CBC with an elevated white count simply indicates that an infection is likely. It is not specific for the location of the infection. Urinalysis should be performed to rule out a UTI. Symptoms can mimic an appendicitis. Serum pregnancy test must be performed since this patient could have an ectopic pregnancy. Positive pelvic cultures could indicate pelvic inflammatory disease as the cause of the pain.

56. *c*
X-rays are of little benefit in patients with back pain unless the underlying etiology is infection, fracture, malignancy, disc space narrowing, degenerative changes, or spondylolisthesis. They do not detect herniated discs and are generally of little benefit. If they are obtained, it is usually done after back pain of 4 weeks duration.

57. *b*
Lymphocytes tend to be the predominant white cell present during viral infections. Hepatitis B is a viral infection. The total white count will likely be decreased. This happens very often in the presence of viral infections. A bacterial infection is frequently evidenced by an elevated leukocyte count, a increased neutrophil count, and a decreased lymphocyte count.

58. *c*
Ciprofloxacin is a quinolone antibiotic. All quinolones have the potential to produce prolongation of the QT interval. It should be prescribed with caution in older adults.

59. *b*
In a patient with known aortic stenosis (AS) who has been asymptomatic for decades, one should be alert for symptoms that will precede angina, CHF, and syncope. Dizziness precedes syncope in these patients and so this is an early indication that the patient is becoming symptomatic from his AS. Once symptoms develop, there is a rapid downhill course. Therefore, being alert for dizziness, chest discomfort, or exercise intolerance are very important symptoms to assess in previously asymptomatic patients who have aortic stenosis.

60. *a*
The natural course of aortic regurgitation (AR) is that the patient has a long asymptomatic period with slowing of activities but remains essentially asymptomatic. Then, shortness of breath develops with activity and finally, shortness of breath at rest. The left ventricle eventually fails unless the aorta is replaced.

61. *a*
Doxycycline is frequently chosen first line to treat Lyme Disease. However, numerous studies have demonstrated that amoxicillin and cefuroxime have equal efficacy as doxycycline in treatment of early Lyme Disease. These drugs are recommended in patients who exhibit erythema migrans. Doxycycline is not recommended in children less than 9 years of age.

62. *a*
Patients with Type II diabetes should be screened for renal nephropathy at diagnosis. Nephropathy takes several years to develop but develops in about 30% of patients with diabetes. Diabetic nephropathy is defined as the presence of diabetes and more than 300 mg/d of albuminuria on at least 2 occasions separated by 3-6 months. Screening should take place annually.

63. ***a***
Examples of drugs that target the renin-angiotensin-aldosterone system are angiotensin converting enzyme (ACE) inhibitors and angiotensin receptor blockers (ARBs). These drugs are particularly beneficial to patients with diabetic nephropathy because they may prevent and treat diabetic nephropathy. Additionally, these agents also lower blood pressure that may be reno-protective. Management of glucose levels and hypertension is especially important in preventing diabetic nephropathy.

64. ***b***
An ARB potentially can produce hyperkalemia because its mechanism of action is in the renin-angiotensin-aldosterone system where potassium is spared. If potassium is taken in the form of potassium supplements, the effect will be additive and the risk of hyperkalemia can be great.

65. ***a***
"Silvery scales" describes the hallmark finding in psoriasis. This is a chronic condition. It is not infectious, contagious, or acute. There are several variants, but "silvery scales" is the most common.

66. ***c***
Classic findings in a urinary tract infection (UTI) are positive leukocytes and nitrites. Leukocytes indicate the presence of white cells in the urine. Nitrates are a normal finding in a urine specimen. Nitrites are not normal in the urine. Positive nitrites indicate that an organism in the urine is consuming nitrates for nutrition. Hematuria indicates the presence of red blood cells in the urine. This is not unusual in the presence of a UTI.

67. ***a***
Mononucleosis (mono) is a viral infection. This is usually characterized by a predominance of lymphocytes. Eosinophilia is typical in parasitic infections and allergic reactions. Leukocytosis is a predominance of white cells but is not specific for mono. Monocytes can rise in mono, but their presence is not specific to mono.

68. ***b***
History of gestational diabetes conveys an 83% chance of developing Type II diabetes (within 17 years of delivery). Hyperlipidemia by itself is not a risk factor for diabetes, though it is commonly seen in conjunction with diabetes. Infrequent, regular exercise increases the risk of increased BMI, but by itself is not a risk factor for Type II diabetes. A family history of Type II diabetes increases the risk of developing it, but this is not true of Type I diabetes.

69. ***a***
Antacids should be avoided because they will inhibit absorption of iron. Other substances that should be avoided an hour before or 2 hours after iron supplementation are tetracyclines and dairy products. Foods that are rich in vitamin C, such as grapefruit juice should be encouraged because they enhance iron absorption. Potassium

supplements have no known effect on iron absorption. Heavy exercise does not inhibit iron absorption.

70. ***b***

Anemia of chronic disease is usually a normocytic, normochromic anemia. In about 30% of cases, it is microcytic. The red blood cells that characterize anemia of chronic disease tend to be normal in size and hemoglobin content. Hence, the term for anemia of chronic disease, normocytic normochromic anemia.

71. ***b***

This patient has impaired fasting glucose. This is diagnosed when 2 fasting glucose values are between 100 mg/dL and 125 mg/dL. There is no need for further testing. At this time, this patient does not meet the criteria for diabetes and does not need further testing to arrive at a diagnosis.

72. ***d***

One of the major components of gallstones is estrogen. A patient with underlying gallbladder disease should not receive oral contraceptives (OC) since they will increase estrogen exposure and theoretically, formation of gallstones. Patients who are less than 6 months post-partum should avoid OCs until they are 6 months post-partum because OCs can decrease the quantity of breast milk produced. Hypertension is a contraindication to OC use because of the increased risk of stroke. Varicose veins are not a contraindication.

73. ***d***

The nasal septum separates the right from left nostrils. It is made of thick cartilage and is covered with mucous membrane. It can be injured from foreign substances that contact it, like cocaine. A nasal septal erosion or perforation should always be assumed to have been from sniffing toxic substances in the nose, not nasal steroids.

74. ***a***

Exposure to an STD always increases the likelihood of contracting an STD. However, the patient is at very high risk of developing pelvic inflammatory disease when there is an implanted foreign body. An example of this is an intrauterine device (IUD). The risk is also increased with a diaphragm, but, because it is not implanted for long periods at a time, the risk is less than with an IUD.

75. ***c***

The second leading cause of cough in adults is asthma. Cough due to asthma is often accompanied by episodic wheezing or dyspnea, though some patients with asthma only cough. This is termed "cough variant asthma". The clinical presentation of asthma varies but hyper responsiveness of the airways is a typical finding.

76. ***c***
The findings of positive Kernig's and Brudzinski's signs are highly suggestive of meningitis. Kernig's sign is elicited by leg extension; then observing for neck pain and flexion. Brudzinski's sign is elicited by passively flexing the neck and observing for flexion of the legs.

77. ***b***
An exacerbation of atopic dermatitis is termed eczema. Under normal conditions, the skin should be kept well lubricated with emollients. These should be used liberally as often as needed to prevent skin from becoming dry. Dry skin is more prone to exacerbations. When an exacerbation occurs, topical steroids are very effective and are commonly used. The lowest potency steroid that resolves the exacerbation should be used.

78. ***a***
The predominant symptom of patients who exhibit pulpitis is pain especially elicited by thermal changes, cold and hot. The pain can become severe and patients are ill appearing. Pus may be seen around the gum area or may be restricted to the pulp cavity. Caries and gingivitis do not produce pus. Periodontitis is characterized by gingival inflammation and pain. Pus is not present in this disease. A periodontal abscess produces pain and pus, but the pus is usually only expressed after probing.

79. ***b***
The mechanism of injury suggests a possible ankle sprain or fracture. However, the foot pain is suspicious of a possible 5th metatarsal fracture, the most common fracture occurring with an ankle sprain. He should receive an x-ray of the foot and ankle and should be kept non-weight bearing until the fracture is ruled out.

80. ***a***
The highest rate of pregnancy prevention occurs with injectable progestin. The rate is about 99.7% prevention. The prevention rate with the progestin only pill is about 97-99%. The theoretical rate of effectiveness with oral contraceptives is 99.7%, but the actual rate is 90-96%. With natural family planning, pregnancy is prevented about 79% of the time.

81. ***b***
In patients with lead toxicity, many metabolic changes can occur. Some patients develop pica; many develop a sideroblastic anemia. This occurs because iron is unable to be incorporated into the heme molecule. An iron deficiency anemia results. This is treated by eliminating the patient's exposure to lead, increasing iron in the diet, and supplementing with iron.

82. ***b***
Cluster headaches are always unilateral. The affected side produces a red, teary eye with nasal congestion on the affected side. Tension headaches are always bilateral with no nausea or photosensitivity associated with them.

83. *c*
If state law requires reporting of the STD, it should be reported. Patient names or other identifying data are not part of the reporting process and so, the NP's patient should not worry about being identified and associated with this finding. If the NP does not report it, she has violated state law. If she reports it but doesn't tell the patient, she is not being honest with the patient. Reporting data to public health with deliberate elimination of required illness details is inaccurate reporting and doesn't meet state law.

84. *d*
All 50 states require reporting of animal bites to animal control or the state's appropriate authority for reporting animal bites. It sounds unlikely that the dog could be infected with rabies, but rabies prophylaxis must be considered after all history and information has been taken.

85. *c*
Multiple sclerosis is a disease of the central nervous system characterized by demyelination of the nerve cells. This produces varied neurological symptoms and deficits. This disease is typical in women between the ages of 16 and 40 years. It is rarely diagnosed after age 50 years.

86. *a*
HIV specifically attacks the number of circulating CD4 cells. There is very little variability in CD4 counts. There are a number of factors that will cause minor fluctuation in counts. These include things like seasonal and diurnal variations, infections, and steroid intake. The normal CD4 cell count ranges from 800-1050/mm^3. Every year after infection with HIV, the CD4 cell count decreases by about 50/ mm^3 per year. There is great variation in individual decreases. Some individuals experience very little decrease in counts, other patients experience great decreases in counts. Oral antiretroviral agents slow down the CD4 decreases.

87. *d*
MRSA is methicillin resistant Staph aureus. This is very common in the community and is typically treated with sulfa medications like TMPS (Bactrim DS and Septra DS). If the patient is sulfa allergic, this could not be used. A narrow spectrum antibiotic that can be used is doxycycline or minocycline. It is given twice daily and is generally well tolerated. MRSA is resistant to the antibiotics mentioned and so they should NOT be used to treat it.

88. *c*
The exact mechanism for increased urinary tract infections is unknown, but it is believed to be due to nonoxynol-9 induced changes in vaginal flora. Another consideration is the possible contamination that might accompany insertion before each episode of coitus. Care and cleaning of the diaphragm must take place, or that could be a contributor to increased bacteria.

89. ***a***
There is an inconsequential rise in PSA levels within 72 hours after DRE. DRE should not prevent a patient from having a PSA level measured at any time.

90. ***c***
Papilledema represents swelling of the optic nerve head and disc secondary to increased intracranial pressure (ICP). It is not a common finding in patients with headaches; only those with headache secondary to ICP. The pressure disrupts fluid flow within the nerve and swelling results. The cardinal symptom of ICP is a headache; papilledema is a secondary finding.

91. ***b***
Secondary syphilis can present as a rash on the body, but more commonly as rash on the palms of the hands or soles of the feet. This can persist for up to 6 weeks. It will resolve without treatment, however the patient will still be infected with syphilis. Primary syphilis is characterized by a chancre. This is a painless lesion that can persist for 1-5 weeks. It will resolve without treatment.

92. ***b***
Screening tests for depression include questions about depressed mood or other symptoms that have lasted at least two weeks. This is an important time frame. Typical screening questions ask: "in the past 2 weeks, have you felt little interest or pleasure in doing things" or "in the past 2 weeks, have you felt down, depressed, or hopeless"?

93. ***a***
During a period of mania, common symptoms are inflated self-esteem and grandiosity (like a buying a baby grand piano), decreased need for sleep, hyper verbosity (excessive talking), racing thoughts and flight of ideas, distractibility, and excessive involvement in pleasurable activities that can be associated with very painful consequences later.

94. ***b***
The second leading cause of cough in adults is asthma. Cough due to asthma is often accompanied by episodic wheezing or dyspnea, though some patients with asthma only cough. This is termed "cough variant asthma". The clinical presentation of asthma varies but hyper responsiveness of the airways is a typical finding.

95. ***b***
CT scan of the abdomen is the diagnostic test of choice for this patient with suspected diverticulitis. The CT scan is able to demonstrate inflammatory changes in the colonic wall, colonic diverticula, thickening of the bowel wall, fistula formation, peritonitis, and other complications associated with diverticulitis. A chest and abdominal x-rays are commonly ordered and can help exclude other causes of abdominal pain, but do not help diagnose diverticulitis. Barium enema would be contraindicated if there were a potential for perforation. Ultrasound is much less widely used than CT.

96. ***b***
This patient has hyperthyroidism. The symptoms of fatigue are present in patients with both hypo and hyperthyroidism. The very low TSH measurement in the presence of weight loss very likely indicates a patient who has hyperthyroidism. The TSH should be evaluated on a different day and a T4 should be measured too.

97. ***c***
A common side effect of oral contraceptives is nausea. This is probably related to increased hormone levels (estrogen and progesterone). An easy way to combat nausea is to take the pill before going to sleep at night. Most patients will sleep through the symptom of nausea.

98. ***c***
Generally, a PSA measurement less than 4 ng/mL is considered normal. However, the PSA velocity (the rate of PSA change over time), is concerning. A PSA velocity > .35 ng/mL per year is associated with high risk of death from prostate cancer. This patient should have prostate biopsy by a urologist.

99. ***b***
The herb that the patient is asking about is probably black cohosh, Actaea racemosa. It is a phytoestrogen. This means that it provides estrogen from a plant source. If estrogen is contraindicated in a patient, then it does not matter whether it comes from plants or is produced synthetically. There is a potential safety concern in using black cohosh in women with breast cancer or who are at high risk of breast cancer because of the estrogenic effects that are possible on the breasts.

100. ***b***
Tanner staging, or sexual maturity ratings, are very predictable changes that occur with puberty. These should be assessed. In females, breasts and pubic hair signify specific pubertal changes that constitute maturation. These are not age specific, but at 15 years a Tanner Stage 3 or more would be characteristic of expected maturation. Menses should follow soon.

101. ***a***
A BMI of 26 or higher does increase the risk of developing Type II diabetes. Mediterranean decent does not impart a specific risk factor for development of Type II diabetes, but African-Americans and Asian-Americans are at increased the risk of developing Type II diabetes. Hypothyroidism may be found in some patients with diabetes, but this does not increase the risk.

102. ***b***
Shingles is herpes zoster. It characteristically affects a single dermatome. Grouped vesicles on an erythematous base can be seen in some patients with shingles, but this is not unique to shingles. In fact, it is typical in many viral infections. Crusting may be seen with shingles, chicken pox, or impetigo. Pain, burning, and itching describes the symptoms that some patients have with shingles, but not all patients report itching with

shingles.

103. ***c***
Paroxetine is a selective serotonin reuptake inhibitor (SSRI). Nausea, headache, diarrhea are not unusual symptoms observed in patients who take SSRIs. The symptoms are more common with initiation of therapy and with dose increases. The symptoms tend to subside after a week or so.

104. ***a***
In males, gonorrhea can have a varied presentation. Gonorrhea produces a purulent inflammation of the mucous membranes, urethral discharge, and dysuria. It can be diagnosed with a urethral culture, a urine screen, or nucleic acid tests. Urine screens are not preferred, but are commonly used for people who are difficult to screen, like adolescents or pediatric patients.

105. ***a***
Calcium carbonate is an antacid. It provides rapid changes in gastric pH. This provides relief that can be noticed immediately. The increase in pH lasts for about 30 minutes. Ranitidine is an H2 blocker. It provides relief in 1-2 hours. This usually lasts for about 6-12 hours. Amantadine is an antiviral not used to treat GERD. Pantoprazole is a proton pump inhibitor. This provides relief after several hours or days of daily consumption.

106. ***b***
The presence of petechiae on the lower legs (or anywhere on the body) should prompt the NP to consider a problem that is platelet related. A CBC should be checked to assess the platelet count and any evidence of anemia from blood loss. If the platelet count is found to be low, referral to hematology should be done. Blood cultures are of no value in this patient who has no other complaints.

107. ***b***
Vitamin B-12 deficiency is identified much earlier now because it is suspected earlier in older patients. However, patients do not always present with macrocytosis and anemia. Unexplained neurological symptoms like memory issues, weakness, paresthesias, should prompt suspicion and subsequent measurement of vitamin B-12 levels. Glossitis is an inflammation of the tongue that is associated with pernicious anemia. Glossitis as a lone finding should prompt measurement of B-12.

108. ***d***
Metoprolol is a beta-blocker and is NOT associated with weight gain. Unfortunately, most drugs used to treat Type 2 diabetes are associated with weight gain. Most patients with Type 2 diabetes are overweight and so weight loss is difficult.

109. ***b***
The primary cause of pruritis associated with hives is histamine. Histamine is released from mast cells with other substances of anaphylaxis. Anti-histamines are the primary

therapeutic intervention. Since both H1 and H2 receptors participate in allergic inflammation, both H1 and H2 blockers are helpful in relieving symptoms in these patients. Topical steroid is not helpful. Calcium channel blockers (nifedipine) are used as a "last resort" for refractory cases of urticaria. Steroids do not inhibit mast cell degradation and so are less helpful than thought. Steroids can be used for persistent attacks of acute urticaria if antihistamines are not helpful.

110. ***c***
Kegel exercises are exercises used to strengthen the pelvic muscles. The usual recommendation is 3 sets of 8-12 slow velocity contractions sustained for 6-8 seconds each. These should be performed 3-4 times weekly for about 3-4 months. Kegel exercises are now known to help patients who have mixed incontinence.

111. ***a***
This patient probably has Bell's palsy that affects the facial nerve. This is an acute event affecting only a single side of the face. Stroke must always be considered in the differential but is unlikely in a patient who is otherwise healthy. Early treatment with oral steroids like prednisone (60-80 mg/d and tapered over 7-14 days) should be started within 72 hours of the onset of symptoms. This has been found to decrease the risk of permanent facial paralysis. Oral antiviral agents may be of benefit because of the likely possibility of Bell's palsy having an herpetic etiology.

112. ***b***
Nocturnal paresthesias are typical in patients who have carpal tunnel syndrome. A patient will complain of nighttime numbness, tingling, or "sleeping" hands and arms. This is a result of compression of the median nerve that traverses through the carpal tunnel. If the nerve is compressed, the symptoms (nocturnal paresthesias) usually result. With surgical decompression, symptoms usually abate.

113. ***a***
At age 50 years, males of average prostate cancer risk should have PSA measurement with or without digital rectal exam (DRE). If they are deemed to be of high risk because of a family history (first degree relative with prostate cancer before age 65 years) or race (African American), screening discussions should take place at age 40-45 years. If initial PSA is ≥ 2.5 ng/mL; annual testing should take place. If the initial PSA is < 2.5 ng/mL; test every 2 years.

114. ***a***
Bacterial vaginosis is a clinical syndrome where high concentrations of anaerobic bacteria replace normal vaginal flora. This produces many symptoms that cause complaints in women. The typical symptoms are a "fishy" odor emanating from the vagina, itching, and vulvovaginal pruritis and burning. A typical complaint is an unpleasant odor after coitus.

115. ***d***
Metoprolol is a beta blocker. Beta blockers are known to reduce morbidity and

mortality associated with CHF. Verapamil is a calcium channel blocker. These are contraindicated because they decrease contractility of the heart. Furosemide and digoxin will improve symptoms but not long-term outcomes. Their main benefit is in treating symptomatic patients.

116. ***c***
Tinea versicolor is typically visualized during the spring and summer months when a patient has become tanned. The areas that are infected do not tan and so become very noticeable. The chest and back are common areas to observe tinea versicolor. There can be 100 or more in some infections. This can be treated with topical selenium sulfide or an oral antifungal agent.

117. ***c***
Patients with anxiety complain that they have difficulty falling asleep. Patients with depression complain of early morning awakening and difficulty remaining asleep. A manic patient may state that he never feels tired.

118. ***d***
A patient with dysuria and vaginal discharge should be assumed to have an STD until proven otherwise. She could have only an STD, or an STD and a UTI. She should have a vaginal exam with cultures and swab for trichomoniasis. The abdomen should be assessed because of the potential for pelvic inflammatory disease if STDs are present. A urinalysis can exclude a urinary tract infection.

119. ***b***
An ankle inversion causes the sole of the foot to roll into the body. This produces stretching of the lateral malleolar ligaments of the ankle and a lateral ankle sprain. Injury to the medial ligaments is a more serious injury and can produce a medial ankle sprain or an avulsion fracture. No information in the stem of the question suggests a fracture or tear of the ligament, though all sprains produce varying degrees of ligament tears.

120. ***b***
He could have hemorrhoids. It is unusual for a patient to have lower GI bleeding from one week's use of an NSAID. He is more likely to have upper GI symptoms (or bleeding) because of prostaglandin synthesis inhibition. This patient needs a colonoscopy to determine the etiology of the bleeding. The NSAID should be stopped.

121. ***b***
This probably indicates BPH. These findings of the prostate gland do not rule out prostate cancer. A prostate infection usually produces greater elevations in PSA as well as a tender gland. A PSA > 2.5 ng/mL in this instance may reflect PSA changes seen with BPH. An important historical note would be the value of his last PSA for comparison as well as to assess for PSA velocity.

122. ***b***
This patient's symptoms indicate that he could have conjunctivitis. Assessment of patients with eye complaints should always begin with assessment of vision in each eye. This should be documented.

123. ***b***
Hearing loss associated with aging is termed presbycusis and is a form of sensorineural hearing loss. This can be influenced by a number of factors including heredity. Conductive hearing loss involves the external canal and the middle ear. Sound cannot travel beyond the middle ear. The 8th cranial nerve and the inner ear are involved in sensorineural hearing loss. Noise damage can produce a sensorineural hearing loss. This usually occurs over time but is not necessarily associated with aging.

124. ***c***
The range is the difference between the smallest and the largest observation in a group of values.

125. ***d***
Nagel's rule estimates a woman's due date based on the date of the last menstrual period. Three months are subtracted from the last menstrual period, 7 days and one year are added. This predicts her due date. This is based on a pregnancy lasting 281-282 days.

126. ***b***
The flu is diagnosed based on the results of a flu swab and the patient's clinical presentation. A patient with influenza usually demonstrates Flu A (the most predominant strain during an outbreak) or Flu B (the strain identified occasionally during flu season but more often, throughout the rest of the year) if he is infected.

127. ***a***
Long acting insulin mimics the amount of insulin the pancreas produces at a steady rate throughout the day and night. Adjustments in doses of long-acting insulin are typically based on the AM fasting glucose values. The other blood sugars reflect blood sugars in relation to meals.

128. ***c***
Sciatica is caused by nerve root irritation. This produces a burning pain that usually radiates down the posterior aspect of the leg. The pain is often associated with numbness and tingling. Pain usually increases with coughing, sneezing, or straining. Relief of pain usually occurs in positions where nerve root irritation is minimized. These are commonly standing or side lying. It is usually worsened by sitting.

129. ***a***
Wheezing is typical of asthma, but one must consider pneumonia in an asthma patient who presents with wheezing in only the upper right lobe. Fever is not typical of asthma or an exacerbation.

130. ***b***
This patient has symptoms of cauda equina syndrome. This is a medical emergency. Urinary retention with overflow incontinence is typical. Other symptoms that can accompany this are saddle anesthesia, sciatica down both legs, and leg weakness, evidenced by the inability to support one's own weight on the affected side.

131. ***b***
Trichomonas can be treated with metronidazole orally. This is usually effective and is generally well tolerated as long as the patient avoids alcohol. Alcohol in the presence of metronidazole can produce a disulfiram reaction. Another medication used to treat trichomonas is tinidazole. The exact mechanism of tinidazole is unknown, but is an antiprotozoal.

132. ***b***
This dermatitis is intensely pruritic and involves the palms and soles and lateral aspects of the fingers. Over a couple of weeks, the vesicles desquamate. Recurrences are common. Seborrheic dermatitis affects only hairy areas of the body. The vesicles might raise suspicion of a viral infection, but this is not the case.

133. ***b***
The herald patch associated with pityriasis rosea is typically found on the trunk. It precedes the generalized Christmas tree pattern rash that is easily noted on the rest of the body. Because it appears round and has a darkened center, it looks like a ringworm. In fact, it is commonly mistaken for ringworm until the Christmas tree pattern rash appears. It would be unusual to identify the herald patch on a body part other than the trunk, but there are case reports of this.

134. ***c***
These agents are particularly effective in the treatment of nasal congestion and would be a good choice for the patient in this scenario. Intranasal glucocorticoids are effective in relieving nasal congestion, discharge, itching, and sneezing. A trial of stopping the oral antihistamine could be tried in this patient. Symptoms would determine whether the antihistamine should be resumed.

135. ***b***
Otitis externa is "swimmer's ear". It is characterized by tragal tenderness. Otitis externa is an infection of the external canal. When the tragus is tender, it will be difficult to insert a speculum to examine the ear.

136. ***d***
Patients with viral gastroenteritis should be treated symptomatically. The goal of therapy is to prevent dehydration and replace electrolyte losses. Loperamide can decrease abdominal cramping and symptoms of diarrhea but should only be used in adults. Careful use or avoidance is suggested in older adults and children less than age 5 years.

137. ***c***
Rheumatoid arthritis is characterized by pain, symmetrical involvement of multiple joints, morning stiffness lasting longer than one hour. Patients with osteoarthritis have morning stiffness lasting less than one hour, usually less than 30 minutes. Weight loss is not typical in either of these diseases. Bouchard's nodes are typical in osteoarthritis and represent enlargement of the proximal interphalangeal joint.

138. ***b***
The class of medications called "triptans" work to eradicate migraine headaches by producing vasoconstriction. This can produce a potentially serious drug-disease interaction in patients with hypertension. An episode of severe hypertension can result. Triptans may be used in patients with well-controlled hypertension, but a hypertensive episode can always occur.

139. ***a***
Patients with diabetes can present with polyuria. An assessment of the patient's risk factors should be done with strong consideration given to checking glucose levels. If this is normal, other diagnoses to consider are urge incontinence and vaginitis. The patient's medications should be reviewed for medications producing urgency, like diuretics or herbal supplements.

140. ***a***
This patient probably has acute bacterial prostatitis. A common presenting symptom is prostate tenderness, especially with bowel movements. A common cause in a 30 year-old male who is sexually active is infection with chlamydia or trichomonas. He should be screened for sexually transmitted diseases. If these are negative, a urinary pathogen is the likely cause. Penile and urine cultures should be collected.

141. ***a***
Vitamin B 12 produces a macrocytic anemia. This is characterized by large red cells. Anemia of chronic disease usually produces a normocytic anemia, but about 30% of the time produces a microcytic one. Thalassemia and iron deficiency produce microcytic anemias.

142. ***d***
A report of a knee "locking" is a classic complaint of a patient who has a meniscal tear. Sometimes a knee effusion accompanies this but not always. Often loss of range of motion secondary to pain is observed. Recollection of an injury is not always part of history, but it occurred during some event in the past. A meniscal tear represents a disruption of the pads between the femoral condyles and the tibial plateaus. Clinical exam and MRI are usually used to make the diagnosis.

143. ***a***
Clinical inertia ia an actual term used to describe healthcare providers who fail to intensify therapy despite patients not reaching goal. There are many reasons given as to

why this takes place, but healthcare providers can potentially modify these.

144. *b*
This patient has isolated systolic hypertension. According to JNC VII and other learned authorities, this is best treated with a long-acting calcium channel blocker, particularly the ones that end in "pine'. These belong to the class of calcium channel blockers termed dihydropyridines. Thiazide diuretics are not potent enough to decrease this patient's blood pressure into normal range and their effect is not additive with calcium channel blockers.

145. *d*
Microalbuminuria takes years to manifest after diabetes has developed. Microalbuminuria should never be diagnosed on a single reading because many factors can produce false microalbuminuria. Heavy exercise, elevated glucose levels, infection, and others can produce false positive microalbuminuria. The ideal time for microalbuminuria to be repeated is 3-6 months after the first abnormal measurement. This gives some time for glucose values to improve and can help rule out false positive results.

146. *c*
It is very common that other co-morbidities are present with eating disorders. Anorexia is commonly accompanied by anxiety, especially at mealtimes. Neurotransmitters are thought to play some role in the pathogenesis of anorexia nervosa. This is common in the United States in women especially between the ages of 15 and 30 years. It is relatively uncommon in males.

147. *b*
Men with benign prostatic hypertrophy (BPH) have some classic symptoms that include: hesitancy, urgency, post-void dribbling, and frequency. They will seek help for these symptoms. Although these symptoms are typical of BPH, prostate cancer can also present in the same way.

148. *a*
These are cotton wool spots. They are due to swelling of the surface layer of the retina. Swelling occurs because of impaired blood flow to the retina. The most common causes for cotton wool spots are diabetes and high blood pressure. A microaneurysm is the earliest manifestation of a diabetic retinopathy. These appear as small round dark red dots on the retinal surface. Exudates are an accumulation of lipid and protein. These are typically bright, reflective white or cream colored lesions seen on the retina.

149. *b*
The patient is using his bronchodilator ("rescue" medication) more than twice weekly. This is a signal to the healthcare provider that the patient's asthma is not well controlled and another medication needs to be used. The next step for this patient is a trial of an inhaled steroid. This should relieve his symptoms and decrease the use of his rescue medication. If an inhaled bronchodilator is overused, it will not continue to

produce bronchodilation over time.

150. ***b***
Sulfamethoxazole is the sulfa component in Bactrim DS. It is contraindicated in patients with a sulfa allergy. There is no allergic potential with the antihyperglycemic agents, sulfonylureas. Naproxen and cefazolin have no contraindications if a patient has a sulfa allergy. Some HIV protease inhibitors have the sulfonyl arylamine chemical group that is responsible for the allergic reaction.

Special Sections

Geriatrics

1. **Mrs. Jones is an 85 year old who has average blood pressures of 170/70. What agent would be a good starting medication to normalize her blood pressure?**

    a. **Fosinopril**
    b. **Losartan**
    c. **Amlodipine**
    d. **Hydrochlorothiazide**

2. **Mr. Bowers, a 97 year old, is not able to make an informed decision due to mental incapacity. He does not have advanced directives but only a durable power of attorney (DPA). How should the nurse practitioner proceed?**

    a. **Allow the family to make a decision regarding medical care.**
    b. **Allow the DPA to make a decision based on the patient's known values.**
    c. **Allow the nurse practitioner to make a decision if there is disagreement between the family and DPA.**
    d. **Have the family and DPA come to an agreement regarding care.**

3. **A criterion for medication choice in an older adult is:**

    a. **long half-life to prevent frequent dosing.**
    b. **dosing of 3-4 times daily.**
    c. **pill color and shape for easy identification.**
    d. **half-life less than 24 hours.**

4. **What pharmacokinetic factor is influenced by a decrease in liver mass in an elderly adult?**

    a. **Absorption**
    b. **Distribution**
    c. **Metabolism**
    d. **Elimination**

5. **Which screen for alcohol abuse has been validated in the elderly?**

    a. **GAGE**
    b. **CAGE**
    c. **MINE**
    d. **LIST**

1. *c*

This patient has isolated systolic hypertension (ISH), common in the elderly population. Long acting calcium channel blockers (CCB), specifically those with the suffix "pine", and thiazide diuretics, are recommended for starting treatment in patients with ISH. Amlodipine is probably a better choice in this patient because she needs a substantial decrease in her systolic blood pressure. Thiazide-type diuretics produce an average decrease of 5-15 points in the systolic blood pressure. The CCBs are more potent and a more significant decrease in blood pressure could be expected gradually.

2. *b*

An informed decision is determined by whether a patient is able to make and express personal preferences, comprehend risks, benefits, and implications, able to give reasons for alternatives, and has rational reasons for his choices. When an older adult is not able to make an informed decision, if a durable power of attorney is available, this makes the decision for direction of treatment.

3. *d*

Many factors go in to prescribing for older adults. Some important safety criteria include established efficacy, low adverse event profile, half-life less than 24 hours with no active metabolites. Active metabolites would produce a longer effect of the drug in the patient. Dosing of a medication 3-4 times daily invites dosing and medication errors. Once or twice daily dosing is ideal. Pill color and shape is never a criterion for prescribing. Patients who are cognitively able will recognize the color, shape, and size of pills they take on a regular basis.

4. *c*

As the liver decreases in mass and potentially has a decrease in blood flow, drug metabolism is decreased. Consequently, lower doses of medications in older adults may be as efficacious as higher doses in their younger counterparts.

5. *b*

CAGE is a screen for alcohol abuse that is validated in adults and older adults. The C stands for "have you ever felt you should CUT down" your alcohol consumption. The A stands for " does other's criticism of your drinking ANNOY you". G stands for "have you ever felt GUILTY about drinking". The E stands for "have you ever had an EYE opener to steady your nerves or get rid of a hangover". A positive response on any question constitutes a positive screen.

6. An octogenarian asks the nurse practitioner if it is OK for him to have an alcoholic beverage in the evenings. There is no obvious contraindication. How should the nurse practitioner respond?

a. **Yes, but not more that 4 days per week.**
b. **Yes, but not more than 1-2 drinks per day.**
c. **No, you will increase your risk of falling and injury.**
d. **It depends on the type of alcohol you would like to consume.**

7. Warfarin therapy is greatly influenced by a patient's food and medication intake. Which group listed can potentially decrease INR in an outpatient who takes warfarin?

a. **Alcohol and an aspirin**
b. **Flu vaccine and ketoprofen**
c. **Naproxen and celecoxib**
d. **Sucralfate and cholestyramine**

8. You are managing the warfarin dose for an older adult with a prosthetic heart valve. Which situation listed requires that warfarin be discontinued now?

a. **INR of 3, some bleeding**
b. **INR of 8, no significant bleeding**
c. **INR of 6, no significant bleeding**
d. **INR of 2 with serious bleeding**

9. The most common mental disorder in older adults is:

a. **alcohol abuse.**
b. **depression.**
c. **anxiety.**
d. **bipolar disorder.**

10. Mrs. Smith is worried about her eldest child who recently lost his job. She is unable to sleep at night because "she is just so worried she can't sleep." Which medication listed below should NOT be used to treat anxiety in an older adult?

a. **Buspirone**
b. **Lorazepam**
c. **Oxazepam**
d. **Zolpidem (Ambien®)**

6. ***b***
A good rule of thumb for alcohol consumption in older adults is no more than 1-2 drinks/day after age 65 years. If the patient is cognitively impaired, abstinence is recommended. The type of alcohol is not of great importance. Beer, wine, and hard liquor all contain alcohol with the potential to impair older adults. The reason alcohol should be limited or avoided is because of decreased lean body mass and decreased total body water in aging bodies.

7. ***d***
The drugs listed in choice D will decrease international normalized ratio (INR) in patients who take warfarin concurrently. Sucralfate and cholestyramine decrease absorption of warfarin. The drugs listed in the other choices will increase INR. Major interactions can occur with celecoxib, ketoprofen, and naproxen. These three NSAIDs are commonly taken by older adults and so, this should be part of education with a patient who takes warfarin.

8. ***d***
INR is a good measure of the clotting status in an outpatient who takes an oral anticoagulant like warfarin. When warfarin is overdosed and INR climbs, or when warfarin is overdosed because of food or medication that produces deleterious side effects, warfarin doses may be omitted or discontinued until the INR is in a more acceptable range. Warfarin should be discontinued when the INR is ≥ 9 or there is significant bleeding.

9. ***c***
Anxiety is very common in older adults. Depression is very common too, and may accompany anxiety in older adults. The prevalence of anxiety may be due in part to other physical illnesses or serious diseases or disorders, like cancer, Parkinson's disease. New onset anxiety should prompt the examiner to consider withdrawal of medication or side effects of medication being taken at therapeutic levels.

10. ***d***
Zolpidem is a sleep aid, not an anti-anxiety medication. If a benzodiazepine is prescribed, it should be short or intermediate duration. Since benzodiazepines are often abused and can produce cognitive impairment, they should be carefully prescribed. Additionally, they should be prescribed for short-term use only, preferably not more than 60-90 days.

11. The nurse practitioner caring for an independent 74 year old female who had acute coronary syndrome (ACS) about 6 weeks ago. What medications should be part of her regimen unless there is a contraindication?

   a. **ASA and beta-blocker**
   b. **ACE and beta-blocker**
   c. **ACE, ASA, and beta-blocker**
   d. **ACE, ASA, beta-blocker, and statin**

12. An 87 year old has history of symptomatic heart failure. He presents today with lower extremity edema and mild shortness of breath with exertion. In addition to a diuretic for volume overload, what other medication should he receive today?

   a. **ACE inhibitor**
   b. **Beta-blocker**
   c. **Calcium channel blocker**
   d. **Oxygen**

13. A 75 year-old patient with long-standing hypertension takes an ACE inhibitor and a thiazide diuretic daily. He has developed dyspnea on exertion and peripheral edema over the past several days. This probably indicates:

   a. **worsening hypertension.**
   b. **development of heart failure (HF).**
   c. **noncompliance with medication.**
   d. **fluid or sodium excess.**

14. Mr. Holbrook, a 75 year-old male, is a former smoker. He has come in today for an annual exam. He walks daily for 25 minutes, has had intentional weight loss, and has a near normal BMI. On examination, the patient is noted to have an absence of hair growth on his lower legs. Which statement is true regarding this patient?

   a. **This is a normal consequence of aging.**
   b. **This might indicate disease in the lower extremities.**
   c. **It might be from exercise initiation.**
   d. **This is from long-term smoking.**

15. Orthostatic hypotension can be diagnosed in an older adult if the systolic blood pressure decreases:

   a. **more than 20 points anytime after rising.**
   b. **more than 20 points within three minutes after rising.**
   c. **more than 20 points within one minute after rising.**
   d. **any degree drop if the patient becomes weak or dizzy.**

11. ***d***

After a myocardial event, an aspirin, ACE inhibitor, beta-blocker, and statin should be taken daily. The goal for statin dose is LDL measurement of less than 70-100 mg/dL. The aspirin will provide anticoagulation, and the ACE inhibitor and beta-blocker are associated with reduced morbidity and mortality if given soon after ACS. deleted

12. ***a***

This patient needs to begin a medication that will directly address his heart failure. ACE inhibitors have demonstrated reduced morbidity and mortality when given at target doses to patients with heart failure. A beta-blocker should be added when the patient is no longer symptomatic. A calcium channel blocker will worsen systolic dysfunction because it will decrease the force of contractions. Oxygen would be used if the patient were short of breath or having chest pain. Neither of these findings would be seen in someone who was stable. Oxygen is not needed today.

13. ***b***

The symptoms of dyspnea on exertion and peripheral edema are symptoms of mild HF. Long standing hypertension is a risk factor for HF. Noncompliance with medication and fluid or sodium excess might result in peripheral edema and development of heart failure.

14. ***b***

An absence of hair growth likely indicates peripheral artery disease in this patient. It is part of normal changes of aging that hair growth will diminish, but not become absent. His lower extremity pulses should be assessed, his cardiac risk factors should be assessed (he smoked for years), and he should be questioned about leg pain when he walks. An ankle-brachial index could be measured. If < 0.9, further assessment should be done. A normal ankle-brachial index should be greater than 0.9. Less than 0.4 is considered critical.

15. ***b***

Orthostatic hypotension, also called postural hypotension, is diagnosed in older adults when the systolic blood pressure drops 20 mm Hg or more within 3 minutes of moving to a more upright position. This can be from lying to sitting or sitting to standing. Additionally, if the systolic does not meet these criteria, but the diastolic drops by 10 mm Hg or more with a position change, postural hypotension can be diagnosed. Patients become symptomatic when this occurs and often report lightheadedness, weakness, dizziness, blurred vision, or decreased hearing.

16. Delirium differs from dementia because delirium:

a. often develops acutely.
b. is more likely if a patient has dementia.
c. is likely when a patient has hypertension.
d. occurs in debilitated adults, and dementia in less debilitated adults.

17. An 80 year old adult has begun to use over the counter diphenhydramine to help him fall asleep. What common side effect can occur in older adults with use of this medication?

a. Next day sleepiness
b. Bradycardia
c. Urinary incontinence
d. Anti-psychotic behavior

18. Mrs. Jopson is unable to name a familiar object. How is this described?

a. Anomia
b. Anosmia
c. Acanthosis
d. Incompetent

19. Mr. Williams has moderate cognitive deficits attributed to Alzheimer's disease and has been started on a cholinesterase inhibitor. The purpose of this drug is to:

a. decrease agitation.
b. increase anticholinergic stimulation of the brain.
c. improve depression.
d. slow progression of his cognitive deficits.

20. What statement describes depression in older adults?

a. Depression is common in older adults and is easily diagnosed.
b. They can be managed with some of the same medications as younger adults.
c. Evaluation by laboratory assessment is unnecessary in older adults.
d. This is a normal part of aging.

16. ***a***
Delirium is a change in consciousness or cognition. It may be accompanied by a physical diagnosis like urinary tract infection; or it may be due to consumption of a medication. Regardless, a change in cognition or consciousness needs immediate evaluation. The evaluation should include a medication review, physical exam and laboratory evaluation, and mental status exam.

17. ***a***
Diphenhydramine should be avoided in older adults. Diphenhydramine exhibits potent anti-cholinergic effects in patients who take this, but especially in older adults. Urinary retention is common (not incontinence) in older men with benign prostatic hyperplasia, but retention occurs in women too. Diphenhydramine is contraindicated in patients with glaucoma. The most serious side effect is cognitive impairment, like daytime sleepiness. Visual disturbances can occur as well as annoying side effects like dry mouth and constipation.

18. ***a***
Anomia is the difficulty in the naming of familiar objects. This is an example of mild impairment. Other evidence of mild impairment is recent recall problems, decreased insight, and difficulty managing finances. Many mildly impaired adults are not able to state today's date.

19. ***d***
This drug is a cholinesterase inhibitor. It will cause more acetylcholine to be available to neurons. Many patients show a slowing of cognitive decline when these medications are used for at least one year. A small percentage of patients, 10-25%, show significant improvement in symptoms. An anticholinergic medication would be contraindicated in these patients. There is no direct benefit on agitation or depression in patients who take this class of medications.

20. ***b***
Depression in older adults is difficult to diagnose because they may present with symptoms such as decreased energy, may associate depressive symptoms with "just getting older" and not mention them to healthcare providers, or they may present with somatic complaints. This last symptom is common in younger adults. Laboratory evaluation should include a CBC, TSH, B-12 level, electrolytes, urinalysis, and others as indicated by history. Many medications used to treat depression in younger patients are used in older patients. The dosages are usually decreased.

21. Tricyclic antidepressants may be safely used in older patients who have:

a. **glaucoma.**
b. **heart conduction defects.**
c. **ischemic heart disease.**
d. **hypothyroidism.**

22. Mr. Johnson is a 74 year old who presents with a pearly-domed nodular looking lesion on the back of the neck. It does not hurt or itch. What is a likely etiology?

a. **Basal cell carcinoma**
b. **Squamous cell carcinoma**
c. **Malignant melanoma**
d. **Actinic keratosis**

23. A 68 year old female adult with pendulous breasts complains of "burning" under her right breast. The nurse practitioner observes a malodorous discharge with mild maceration under both breasts. What is this?

a. **Intertrigo**
b. **Impetigo**
c. **Tinea corporis**
d. **Shingles**

24. An oral antifungal agent is commonly used to treat tinea unguium. The difficulty in treating an older adult with this is infection is:

a. **absorption of the medication.**
b. **applying the medication twice daily.**
c. **tolerability of the medication.**
d. **relative ineffectiveness of oral agents.**

25. A 70 year-old presents urgently to the nurse practitioner clinic with angioedema. This began less than an hour ago. He is breathing without difficulty. What medication may have caused this?

a. **Aspirin**
b. **Fosinopril**
c. **Penicillin**
d. **Metformin**

21. ***d***

Tricyclic antidepressants (TCA) are particularly UNSAFE in patients with conduction defects. Use of TCAs can induce bradyarrhythmias and thus can be deleterious for any patient, but especially in older adults who may be prone to this because of conduction defects and underlying myocardial ischemia. Patients with glaucoma and benign prostatic hyperplasia should avoid TCAs as well because of the anticholinergic effects. Selective serotonin reuptake inhibitors (SSRI) should be considered first line for most older patients with depression.

22. ***a***

Basal cell's classic description is "a pearly domed nodule with a telangiectatic vessel". It is commonly found on sun-exposed areas like the head or neck. Sending the patient to dermatology (since these represent skin cancer) best treats these lesions. Sometimes these lesions can be treated with a topical agent like 5-fluorouracil, but others require surgical intervention.

23. ***a***

This is not unusual in adults of any age. This is common in areas between skin folds, under the breasts, between the scrotum and inner thigh, or between the toes. These are moist lesions with maceration and possible skin loss. It is easily treated if the skin can be separated from touching the adjoining skin and the area can be kept dry. A topical powder with an antifungal would likely resolve this if used twice daily for 7-14 days. A diagnosis of diabetes should be considered if this is resistant to treatment or if it recurs.

24. ***c***

The most efficacious agents used to treat toenail fungus are the oral antifungal agents. They must be taken daily for 8-16 weeks (or longer) for adequate length of treatment. Additionally, the real difficulty lies in the ability of the elderly patient's liver to handle this medication. Oral anti-fungal agents require great amounts of the liver's resources for metabolism. A topical agent or toenail removal may be a better choice for an older adult.

25. ***b***

Angioedema is common in African American patients who take ACE inhibitors. It is an unpredictable event but once it occurs, the culprit medication must be discontinued and never prescribed again. This reaction has occured with many medications, but ACE inhibitors are classic culprits. Swelling that affects the lips, face, eyelids, tongue, and larynx characterizes angioedema. Not all reactions involve this severe a reaction, but any impairment in airway must be referred to the nearest emergency department.

26. A 69 year old adult with coronary artery disease is found to have hypothyroidism. Which dose of levothyroxine is considered appropriate for initial treatment?

a. **25 micrograms**
b. **50 micrograms**
c. **75 micrograms**
d. **100 micrograms**

27. A patient who is 73 years old was diagnosed with diabetes several years ago. His A1C has remained elevated on oral agents and a decision to use insulin has been made. What is the goal post prandial glucose for him?

a. **100- 120 mg/dL**
b. **120-150 mg/dL**
c. **175- 200 mg/dL**
d. **Less than 180 mg/dL**

28. A 79 year-old frail adult reports that she had a fall last week. She had no broken bones but is very sore. In evaluating this adult, what question is most important to ask?

a. **Do you have gait problems?**
b. **Have you had other falls this year?**
c. **Are you on any new medications?**
d. **Does your family know that you fell?**

29. According to the American Geriatric Society, symptoms of uncomplicated reflux disease in older adults should be treated:

a. **by referring for upper GI testing.**
b. **with empiric treatment.**
c. **ambulatory pH testing.**
d. **referral to gastroenterology.**

30. The most common reason that older adults develop peptic ulcer disease is:

a. **chronic NSAID use.**
b. ***H. pylori* infection.**
c. **acetaminophen abuse.**
d. **polypharmacy.**

26. *a*

When thyroid replacement is given to someone 50-60 years old, 50 mcg is the usual recommended starting dose. When the patient is older, and always if there are cardiac issues, 25 mcg is considered a prudent starting dose. The prescriber must recognize that all metabolic processes will increase after supplementation; and this includes myocardial oxygen demand, the potential for angina and arrhythmias. It is important to start this medication at a low dose and increase by 12.5 -25 mg increments every 4-6 weeks until therapeutic values are reached or cardiac symptoms occur.

27. *d*

In older adults, strong consideration must be given to the risk associated with hypoglycemic states. Falls, accidents, and stroke are more likely; and these are more deleterious in older adults than younger adults who have episodes of hypoglycemia. A1C levels should be < 7% for most older adults; > 7% for frail adults. Good clinical judgment must be exercised in setting a goal A1C for this patient due to age.

28. *b*

The assessment of falls in older adults is important. Providers should ask older patients about falls. If a single fall is reported, gait and balance should be evaluated. If there is no observable difficulty, continue to monitor. If the fall is NOT a single event, a fall assessment should be done. This would involve fall history, gait and balance, home hazards, physical factors like joint pain or neurologic disease, vision, a medication evaluation, and others depending on patient's history.

29. *b*

In older patients without signs of complicated GERD (choking, cough, shortness of breath, pain with swallowing or in the chest), empiric treatment is appropriate. Empiric treatment can take place using proton pump inhibitors or H2 blockers. If H2 blockers are used, famotidine and nizatidine are preferred because of their efficacy and low risk of drug-drug interactions. If symptoms of GERD persist despite initial treatment or if symptoms are severe, patients should have testing to rule out esophageal cancer, Barrett's esophagitis, or other conditions of the esophagus and throat.

30. *b*

The most common reason that older adults have peptic ulcer disease is infection with *H. pylori*. There are many regimens approved to treat *H. pylori* and most are well tolerated. NSAID use is the second most common reason older patients have PUD.

31. Which symptom is INCONSISTENT with irritable bowel syndrome in older adults?

- a. **Constipation**
- b. **Abdominal pain**
- c. **Bloating**
- d. **Onset after 50 years of age**

32. Older adults frequently complain of constipation. Which medication listed below does NOT increase chance of constipation in an older adult?

- a. **Diltiazem**
- b. **Hydrochlorothiazide**
- c. **Calcium supplements**
- d. **Metformin**

33. An 80 year-old is having difficulty hearing. When the nurse practitioner examines him, she is unable to visualize the tympanic membrane because of cerumen impaction. This produces what kind of hearing loss?

- a. **Tympanic**
- b. **Conductive**
- c. **Sensorineural**
- d. **Artificial**

34. What statement is true about anemia in older adults?

- a. **An evaluation should take place in older adults who present with hemoglobin less than 14 g/dL.**
- b. **Anemia may have more than one origin and co-exist in older adults.**
- c. **Faster return of hemoglobin to normal states in older adults.**
- d. **An evaluation should take place in an older adult who presents with an increase in hemoglobin > 1g/dl within one year.**

35. A 75 year old has isolated systolic hypertension. She started on amlodipine 4 weeks ago. She states that since then, she has developed urinary incontinence. What is the nurse practitioner's assessment?

- a. **This is unrelated to her new medication.**
- b. **It is coincidental.**
- c. **She may have underlying urinary tract pathology.**
- d. **It is probably related to amlodipine.**

31. ***d***

Irritable bowel syndrome (IBS) is common in adults and lasts into older adulthood but symptoms start prior to age 50 years. Typical symptoms of IBS are diarrhea and constipation intermittently, abdominal pain (one of the criteria for diagnosis), and bloating. Other symptoms that are inconsistent with IBS are associated weight loss, blood in the stool, rectal bleeding, nocturnal diarrhea. These are more indicative of inflammatory disease or carcinoma of the bowel.

32. ***d***

Constipation is a common complaint in older adults because of mediations they routinely consume and many diseases they often have. Some other examples of medications that can cause constipation are opiate analgesics, NSAIDs, and antacids. Some diseases and conditions that can produce constipation are hypothyroidism, colon cancer, electrolyte abnormalities, immobility, change in diet due to inability to chew food properly.

33. ***b***

This is a conductive hearing loss provided he is able to hear when the cerumen is removed. Anything that inhibits the ability of sound to enter the external canal and middle ear will produce a conductive hearing loss. Sensorineural hearing loss can be produced by aging, Meniere's disease, noise trauma, or cranial nerve VIII pathology.

34. ***b***

Older adults exhibit lower hemoglobin than their younger counterparts. Any decrease in hemoglobin in an older adult should be considered pathological until proven otherwise. Patients should be evaluated if their hemoglobin is less than 13 g/dL. It is common in older adults to have iron deficiency anemia co-existing with B-12 or folate deficiencies. Consequently, it is common in an adult with anemia to order folate, B-12, and iron in all cases.

35. ***d***

Amlodipine is a long-acting calcium channel blocker (CCB). Calcium is responsible for muscle contraction. Sometimes CCBs worsen or produce urinary incontinence by impairing detrusor contraction. A lower dose of calcium channel blocker could be tried, a different class could be tried, or incontinence products could be used.

36. Mrs. Jackson complains of urinary incontinence when she laughs or sneezes. What would be first line to treat her symptoms?

a. **Kegel exercises**
b. **Prescribe oxybutynin**
c. **Avoid caffeine and alcohol**
d. **Minimize fluids at nighttime**

37. Mrs. Lovely, an 84 year old complains of fecal incontinence. A likely cause is:

a. **inactivity.**
b. **constipation.**
c. **poor fluid consumption.**
d. **medication related.**

38. Which antibiotic should be with caution if an elderly patient has cardiac conduction issues?

a. **Amoxicillin-clavulanate**
b. **Trimethoprim-sulfamethoxazole**
c. **Ciprofloxacin**
d. **Macrodantin**

39. A 71 year-old female presents with a vesicular rash that burns and itches. Shingles is diagnosed. An oral antiviral:

a. **should be started within 72 hours of the onset of symptoms.**
b. **must be started within 96 hours of the onset of the rash.**
c. **can be started at any time after appearance of the rash.**
d. **will nearly eliminate the risk of post-herpetic neuralgia.**

40. A patient presents with hematuria, RBC casts, and proteinuria. What is a likely explanation?

a. **Acute renal failure**
b. **Chronic renal insufficiency**
c. **Glomerularnephritis**
d. **Prerenal disease**

36. ***a***
This patient has stress incontinence. The first line approach with these patients is to attempt to strengthen the pelvic floor muscles. Appropriate performance of Kegel exercises is key. Prescribing an anticholinergic might worsen incontinence because it will cause urinary retention. Avoiding caffeine and alcohol are especially helpful for people with urge incontinence, but could have a minimal benefit with this patient. However, this does not address the underlying problem, weak pelvic muscles. Minimizing fluids at nighttime will help if nocturia is a problem.

37. ***b***
Underlying constipation is a common cause of fecal incontinence in older adults. However, typically it is multifactorial. Risk factors include: age > 80 years, impaired mobility, and neurologic disorders including dementia. Inactivity and poor fluid consumption may contribute to constipation but are not causes of fecal incontinence.

38. ***c***
Quinolones such as ciprofloxacin and levofloxacin are often used to treat urinary tract infections, especially in older adults. All of the quinolones have been implicated in possible QT prolongation. Knowing this should cause prescribers to use care especially when using these or other quinolones in adults with underlying conduction defects. This is especially the case if a patient is on other drugs concurrently that can prolong the QT interval

39. ***a***
This patient has been diagnosed with shingles. This can be a painful neuritis. Shingles is treated with an oral antiviral agent preferably within 72 hours of onset of the symptoms. Treating shingles with an oral antiviral shortens the severity and duration of shingles. It may also help decrease the incidence of a post-herpetic neuralgia.

40. ***c***
This patient has blood and protein in his urine. Neither are substances that should be present. Additionally, RBC casts are present. A cast is a protein globule with red blood cells adhered to it. These findings are indicative of damage to the kidney. It is very likely that glomerulonephritis or other glomerular disease is present. Other considerations for these findings include renal vasculitis.

41. **Mrs. Brandy is having contrast dye next week for a heart catheterization. What drug does NOT need to be stopped prior to his catheterization?**

    a. **Naproxen**
    b. **Furosemide**
    c. **Metformin**
    d. **Losartan**

42. **An elderly adult with a complaint of shoulder pain has a positive "drop arm" test. What is his likely diagnosis?**

    a. **Peripheral neuropathy**
    b. **Shingles**
    c. **Broken clavicle**
    d. **Torn rotator cuff**

43. **A 72 year old patient complains of knee pain when she climbs stairs or walks long distances. Crepitus is palpable in the affected knee. What is the likely cause?**

    a. **Femoral tendinitis**
    b. **Patellar tendinitis**
    c. **Arthritis of the knee**
    d. **Patellar bursitis**

44. **The "pill-rolling" tremor that is typical in patients with Parkinson's disease is:**

    a. **an early manifestation of the disease.**
    b. **present only with movement.**
    c. **usually bilateral.**
    d. **worse when the patient sleeps.**

45. **A patient who had a stroke has recovered and is performing all of her activities of daily living. Taking aspirin for stroke prevention is an example of:**

    a. **primary prevention.**
    b. **secondary prevention.**
    c. **tertiary prevention.**
    d. **quaternary prevention.**

41. *d*

Naproxen and furosemide should be stopped for 24 hours prior to the catheterization. Metformin should be stopped 48 hours prior to the catheterization. Furosemide is stopped because it contributes to volume depletion. NSAIDs like naproxen are withheld because of the impact on renal prostaglandin production. Metformin has been implicated in lactic acidosis when combined with contrast dye in an impaired kidney.

42. *d*

A positive drop arm test should give the examiner a good idea of the diagnosis of torn rotator cuff. An MRI confirms the diagnosis. The drop arm test is performed by asking the patient to hold his arm on the affected side away from the body at 90 degrees. If he has a torn supraspinatus, he will not be able to do that. If the supraspinatus is torn, he will be able to hold his arm away from his body, but he will not be able to slowly lower it to his side.

43. *c*

This is probably osteoarthritis of the knee. Typical symptoms include the ones mentioned and also pain with standing up after sitting. She will report stiffness after sitting for long periods and after awakening in the morning. She can try many non-pharmacologic approaches to pain relief such as heat and exercise. Acetaminophen and NSAIDs may be used but with caution. X-rays will indicate the severity of the disease. She may be a candidate for knee replacement if severe disease is present.

44. *c*

The "pill-rolling" tremor is the earliest manifestation of the disease. It occurs at rest, but not with movement. The tremor is worse with emotional stress and gets better or ceases with sleep.

45. *b*

The patient is taking aspirin to prevent recurrent stroke. Research demonstrates that taking an aspirin daily can prevent subsequent strokes and MI significantly. Secondary prevention means that the intervention is performed to prevent another occurrence of the deleterious event. If she had never had a stroke but took an aspirin daily for prevention of stroke, that would be primary prevention. Taking an aspirin at home during the course of having an MI is an example of tertiary prevention. There is no reference in the literature to quaternary prevention.

46. When should medications be started in a patient diagnosed with Parkinson's disease?

a. **As soon as the disease is diagnosed**
b. **When symptoms interfere with life's activities**
c. **When non-pharmacologic measures have been exhausted**
d. **After MRI and CT have ruled out stroke or tumor**

47. Which factor listed below is NOT considered a risk factor for development of osteoporosis?

a. **Asian race**
b. **Infrequent physical activity**
c. **Alcoholism**
d. **Late menopause**

48. A 70 year old patient has had intermittent back pain for more than 3 years. In the last year, it is constant (pain scale is 2-3/10) and at times is sharp. She is not a surgical candidate. What class of medication would be a good choice for improvement of chronic pain in this patient?

a. **Naproxen**
b. **Codeine**
c. **Amitriptyline**
d. **Sertraline**

49. A patient who wrote a living will has changed his mind about the initiation of life-sustaining measures. What statement is true about this?

a. **He cannot change his mind regarding the content of the living will.**
b. **He can only change the content if he is of sound mind.**
c. **A healthcare provider is exempt from liability if they provide care outside the living will.**
d. **An attorney must be consulted if the living will is changed at any time.**

50. In a patient with end of life physical pain, constipation commonly occurs. What is the most common cause of this?

a. **Decreased activity**
b. **Decreased fluids**
c. **Opioid use**
d. **General slowing of body processes**

46. ***b***
The medications used to treat patients with Parkinson's disease do not prevent progression of the disease. Therefore, it is not necessary to start them until the patient's symptoms dictate that he desires more control of movements. The dose of medications is always the lowest one that achieves control of symptoms. It can be titrated upward as needed to control symptoms. Orthostatic hypotension is a common side effect of the medication and so should be monitored closely.

47. ***d***
Late menopause increases the patient's exposure to estrogen. Estrogen plays a role in development of hard, dense bones. Early menopause is a risk factor. Other risk factors include cigarette smoking, low body weight, female gender, low calcium and vitamin D intake.

48. ***c***
This patient's pain sounds neuropathic. It is typical of pain experienced by people who have radiculopathy or neuropathy. It may be treated with tricyclic antidepressants or topical anesthetics. Opioids will produce relief and so can physical therapies. Pain management is specific to the type pain a patient experiences.

49. ***b***
A living will is intended to allow a patient to provide instructions for his family and health care providers about how he would like his care directed if he is unable to make these decisions. He can change the content at any time. If however, he is determined not to be of sound mind, any changes that he attempts to make should not be followed. A healthcare provider is bound to carry out the living will provided it does not violate any laws or the ethics of the provider. In this case, the provider would be exempt from liability for not carrying these out. In the case of an ethical dilemma, the healthcare provider should identify another healthcare provider who is willing to carry them out. An attorney is not required to be consulted to change the content of a living will.

50. ***c***
Opioids can cause severe constipation. At end of life this can be a significant cause of discomfort for the patient. Measures for relief of constipation should be instituted.

51. A 70 year-old female has been in a mutually monogamous relationship for the past 33 years. She has never had an abnormal Pap smear, what recommendation should be made regarding Pap smears for her?

  a. They may be continued annually.
  b. They should be performed every 5 years.
  c. They can be discontinued now.
  d. They can be discontinued at age 75 years.

52. What recommendation should be made to a 70 year-old female regarding mammograms?

  a. She should continue to have them annually.
  b. She should have them annually until age 75 years.
  c. She should have them every three years.
  d. She should have them annually as long as she has a reasonable life expectancy.

53. What is American Cancer Society's recommendation for prostate screening in a 70 year-old male?

  a. He should be screened annually with PSA only.
  b. He should be screened annually with PSA and DRE.
  c. He should be screened until he has a life expectancy of less than 10 years.
  d. Screening can stop at age 75 years.

54. What are the recommendations for screening older patients for depression?

  a. Screen at each visit.
  b. Screen only if symptoms exist.
  c. Screen only patients who are at high risk.
  d. Screen every patient annually.

55. How often should lipids be screened in patients who are 65 years and older if they have lipid disorders or risk factors?

  a. Annually
  b. Every other year
  c. Every 3 years
  d. Every 5 years

51. c

Pap smears screen for cervical cancer. Cervical cancer is very *uncommon* in older women, especially those who have no risk factors. Most learned authorities agree that screening for cervical cancer can be discontinued in women aged 65-70 years unless there are risk factors (previous GYN cancer, HIV positive). This patient still needs to visit the nurse practitioner for an annual exam but sampling of cervical cells can be discontinued in a patient of this age.

52. ***d***

Breast cancer is more prevalent in older women. In fact, 85% of breast cancer occurs in women after age 50 years. Older women profit from screening with mammograms and should continue to receive screening. No age limit has been established for discontinuing mammograms.

53. ***c***

Prostate cancer screening at age 70 years includes both prostate specific antigen measurement (PSA) and digital rectal exam (DRE). Prostate cancer is typically a slow growing tumor, thus if life expectancy is < 10 years, screening is not cost-effective.

54. ***a***

Depression is very common in all adults, especially older adults. Screening can be accomplished easily and quickly in a primary care setting. Untreated depression leads to higher rates of mortality when other co-morbid conditions exist, especially heart disease.

55. ***a***

Screening should take place annually for patients who have coronary artery disease and other risk factors like diabetes, peripheral artery disease, or prior stroke. These patients are at very high risk and annual screening is economically justified. In a setting of a low risk patient who does have any of the abovementioned risk factors, United States Preventive Services Task Force recommends screening every 5 years.

56. A decrease in blood pressure can occur in men who take sildenafil and:

- **a. amlodipine.**
- **b. tamsulosin.**
- **c. metoprolol.**
- **d. any antihypertensive medication.**

57. 5-alpha-reductase inhibitors work by producing:

- **a. dilation of the detrusor vessels.**
- **b. a decrease in the size of the prostate.**
- **c. increase blood flow to the prostate.**
- **d. inhibition in the prostate tissue synthesis.**

58. A 76 year-old male presents with urethral irritation after voiding. If sexually transmitted diseases and urinary tract infection are ruled out, what is another etiology?

- **a. Acute bacterial prostatitis**
- **b. Chronic prostatitis**
- **c. Epididymitis**
- **d. Asymptomatic bacteriuria**

59. How long should a patient be treated with antibiotics if he has prostatitis secondary to an STD?

- **a. About 5 days**
- **b. 7-10 days**
- **c. 14 days**
- **d. Longer than 14 days**

60. A patient who is 65 years old states that she has "hayfever" and has had this since childhood. What agent could be safely used to help with rhinitis, sneezing, pruritis, and congestion?

- **a. Nasal steroid**
- **b. Ipratropium**
- **c. Antihistamine**
- **d. Decongestant**

56. ***d***

Any antihypertensive medication could have an additive effect with sildenafil (or other in the class). Caution is advised and should only be used if the male has stable blood pressure. A specific drug-drug interaction to be aware of is the one that can occur with sildenafil and alpha blockers like tamsulosin, alfuzosin, prazosin, doxazosin, or terazosin. This combination of medications may increase the risk of symptomatic hypotension because the effect of these two drugs is additive.

57. ***b***
The class of drugs known as the 5-alpha-reductase inhibitors reduces the size of the prostate gland but benefits are not usually realized for several months; maybe up to 6-12 months before a symptom decrease is realized. For men who need relief of symptoms related to prostate enlargement, an alpha-blocker will provide significantly faster symptom relief. These two drugs can be used in combination.

58. ***b***
Chronic prostatitis can produce these symptoms. Sometimes this is accompanied by perineal pain, but the patient may have a normal prostate exam. Acute bacterial prostatitis patients will present with fever, chills. Examination of the prostate gland reveals a tender, boggy prostate gland. Epididymitis can produce scrotal pain, not dysuria or irritation with voiding. Asymptomatic bacteriuria is asymptomatic. These patients don't know they have this because they have no symptoms.

59. ***d***
The prostate gland does not absorb antibiotics very readily. Consequently, antibiotics must be given for 4-6 weeks to enable the gland to achieve high enough concentrations to treat and effectively eradicate prostatitis. Treatment can be very expensive depending on the antibiotic used.

60. ***a***
A nasal steroid is considered the gold standard for improvement of all symptoms associated with allergic rhinitis (hayfever). Ipratropium helps with rhinitis only. An antihistamine helps will all symptoms listed but is not as effective at relieving symptoms of congestion as a nasal steroid. A decongestant is extremely effective at relieving congestion, but no other symptoms listed.

61. Mr. Daigle is an 80 year-old patient who takes warfarin for chronic atrial fibrillation. Today his INR is 6.0. His CBC is normal and there is no evidence of bleeding. The nurse practitioner should:

a. **stop warfarin for the next two days and repeat the INR on day 3.**
b. **admit to the hospital immediately.**
c. **administer Vitamin K and repeat INR tomorrow.**
d. **stop warfarin for one week and recheck INR.**

62. Which antihistamine is preferred for treating allergic rhinitis in an older adult?

a. **Diphenhydramine**
b. **Chlorpheniramine**
c. **Once daily, non-sedating**
d. **Long-acting, sedating**

63. Which long-acting antihistamine listed below is sedating?

a. **Loratadine**
b. **Cetirizine**
c. **Azelastine**
d. **Fexofenadine**

64. How should the class effect of the nasal steroids be described?

a. **There is a lot of variation among agents within the class.**
b. **There are no significant systemic effects with these.**
c. **There are high rates of nasal bleeding.**
d. **It is generally not well-tolerated.**

65. An elderly female with emphysema who has been treated with inhaled steroids for many years should:

a. **consider treatment for osteoporosis prophylaxis.**
b. **have oxygen at home for exacerbations.**
c. **use inhaled steroids and beta-agonists.**
d. **be watched for softening of teeth.**

66. The symptoms of asthma in an elderly patient:

a. **are more likely to be a cough.**
b. **are more likely to be characterized by wheezing.**
c. **have greater variability than in younger adults.**
d. **are distinct from chronic heart failure.**

61. ***a***
An INR of 6.0 is elevated and this patient could suffer a devastating bleed anywhere in the body. A patient with an INR of 5 – 9 without bleeding may have warfarin stopped temporarily and decrease the maintenance dose when it is safe to resume warfarin, i.e. when the INR is closer to the patient's therapeutic range. If the patient was at high risk for bleeding, was bleeding, or if the INR was higher, Vitamin K could be administered. This is not the case with Mr. Daigle. A good history should be completed to find out the reason for the increase in INR. A high risk client with an elevated INR would be admitted to the hospital and closely monitored, but a client with no co-morbidities (no bleeding history or thrombocytopenia) and considered low risk, may be monitored as an outpatient.

62. ***c***
The preferred antihistamines are the long acting (once daily dosing) and non-sedating. Long-acting is favorable for older adults because of ease of dosing. Non-sedating is important for safety. The first generation antihistamines are sedating and consequently not as favorable to use in older adults.

63. ***b***
Cetirizine (Zyrtec) is NOT non-sedating. In older patients, the usual dose is decreased from 10 mg daily to 5 mg daily. This is due to the sedative effect of cetirizine. It should be dosed at nighttime to minimize the initial sedative action. It has a prolonged geriatric half-life. Caution is advised. Fexofenadine is the least sedating of the oral agents listed.

64. ***b***
One reason these are preferred agents in older adults (and young children) is that there are very few systemic effects. The steroids are absorbed across the mucous membranes and are deposited in the area where they need to work. There is absolutely no sedation associated with their use. They are generally well-tolerated. The class is predictable. There is very little variation between agents.

65. ***a***
Elderly females are at higher risk than others for osteoporosis. A female with emphysema is likely small in stature and has a low body mass index, two additional risk factors. Additionally, she probably has emphysema because she smoked (or still smokes). If she is Asian or Caucasian, she has still another risk factor. Her risk factors for osteoporosis could be significant. Osteoporosis should be considered when managing patients long-term with inhaled or oral steroids.

66. ***a***
Asthma is usually diagnosed in children or young adults, but after age 65 years, 5-10% of newly diagnosed asthma patients are part of this age group. The most common presentation is cough, not wheezing. Exacerbations are much less variable than in younger adults. This is often not diagnosed initially because the patient presents with symptoms that seem more like heart failure or COPD.

67. An elderly patient with COPD receives a prescription for an inhaled beta agonist. What prescribing considerations must be made for this patient?

a. **Use this early in the morning**
b. **Use 2 puffs every 8 hours**
c. **Use 1 puff every 4-6 hours**
d. **Rinse your mouth well after using**

68. Restless legs syndrome is part of the differential diagnosis for Mr. Wheaton. What should be part of the laboratory workup?

a. **BUN/Cr**
b. **Serum ferritin**
c. **ALT/AST**
d. **Urinalysis**

69. A common complaint in older patients who have cataracts is:

a. **sensitivity to sunlight.**
b. **poor peripheral vision.**
c. **increased incidence of falls.**
d. **eye pain in the affected eye.**

70. An elderly patient who has a red eye with tearing was diagnosed with conjunctivitis. What characteristics below indicate viral conjunctivitis?

a. **Moderate tearing**
b. **Profuse tearing**
c. **Moderate exudate**
d. **Profuse exudate**

71. The Mini-Cog™ is helpful in screening patients with suspected:

a. **delirium.**
b. **dementia.**
c. **Parkinson's disease**
d. **stroke.**

67. ***c***
An example of an inhaled beta agonist is albuterol or bitolterol. These agents stimulate the beta-receptors in the lungs and in the heart. This helps the patient breathe better because it produces bronchodilation, but it potentially can produce arrhythmias or angina because beta-receptors in the heart can become stimulated too. The dose for a patient with underlying cardiac problems is half the dose (and used with caution). A common side effect of these agents is jitteriness, tremor, nervousness, and potentially hypokalemia if used on a regular basis.

68. ***b***
Restless legs syndrome (RLS) is the unrelenting urge to move the legs. This rarely affects the upper extremities. The symptoms are relieved by movement of the affected limbs and only occurs if the affected limbs are at rest. Iron deficiency has been considered as a cause of RLS. The exact mechanism of iron deficiency is not known, but many patients who exhibit symptoms of restless legs syndrome have low serum ferritin levels and have relief of symptoms when supplemented with iron. Even in patients with normal serum levels, a month long trial of iron may be helpful.

69. ***a***
Loss of peripheral vision and eye pain is typical in patients with glaucoma, not cataracts. Patients with cataracts may be at higher risk for falls because they have difficulty seeing, however, this is not a common complaint of patients who have cataracts.

70. ***b***
A patient with viral conjunctivitis typically has profuse tearing and minimal exudate. Patients with bacterial conjunctivitis have moderate tearing and exudate. Both are considered highly contagious. Patients should refrain from work or group activities for 48 hours until symptoms have subsided.

71. ***b***
The Mini-Cog is a screening tool for dementia. It is performed by telling the patient names of 3 unrelated items. The patient is distracted by being asked to draw the face of a clock; and to indicate two specific times by drawing the hands on the clock. Then, the patient is asked to repeat the names of the three objects. Scores are received for correct naming of the items and clock drawings.

72. A 74 year-old who retired as a store clerk last year would like to start an exercise program. She tells the nurse practitioner that she would like to start walking 15-20 minutes daily. Which statement is correct regarding the patient?

a. **She should have a stress test prior to initiating a walking program.**
b. **She should have an EKG performed in the clinic today.**
c. **She does not need any testing because she is asymptomatic.**
d. **She should have labs and EKG performed prior to starting.**

73. A 78 year-old adult who has a 50 pack year smoking habit asks the nurse practitioner about the benefits of quitting "at my age". What should the nurse practitioner reply?

a. **There is little benefit because you've smoked for so much for so long.**
b. **This would help decrease your risk of developing COPD.**
c. **This will decrease your risk of all cause mortality 5 years after stopping.**
d. **Your heart will benefit minimally from quitting smoking.**

74. What choice below would be beneficial to a 76 year old who takes daily oral steroids for COPD and now takes a daily aspirin for primary prevention of myocardial infarction?

a. **Screen for infection with *H. pylori***
b. **Daily proton pump inhibitor**
c. **Antacids PRN heartburn**
d. **Daily use of low dose famotidine**

75. The most common sequela of influenza in older adults is:

a. **sinusitis.**
b. **hepatitis.**
c. **pneumonia.**
d. **bronchitis.**

76. A 75 year old adult asks for the pneumonia vaccine. He states that he had one at age 65. What is the recommendation of CDC on revaccination after age 65 in an individual who has already received one at or after age 65?

a. **Revaccination is recommended now**
b. **Revaccination is recommended every 5 years after age 65 years**
c. **Do not revaccinate this patient at this time**
d. **He should have received one at age 70 years**

72. ***c***

The obvious risk of starting a new exercise program is the risk of cardiac events. Evidence does not support routine EKG or cardiac testing in patients who are asymptomatic. She should be told about symptoms to watch for and to stop immediately if chest pain or shortness of breath develops. A 74 year-old who retired last year will benefit from any type of exercise. She will develop improved conditioning, reduce her risk of many chronic diseases including cardiovascular disease, reduce the risk of falls, and decrease functional limitations. Exercises for older adults fall into 4 categories: aerobic, muscle strengthening, flexibility and balance.

73. ***c***

Smoking cessation at any age is beneficial to the person engaging in smoking cessation. Data demonstrates that after 5 years of smoking cessation, there is a significant decrease in the risk of death from coronary disease, cancer, and COPD. The patient already has COPD if he has a 50 pack year habit. All patients should be counseled to quit smoking regardless of age.

74. ***b***

Aspirin does increase the risk of gastrointestinal bleeding; especially if it is given in combination with oral steroids. Most learned authorities and ACOVE (Assessing Care of Vulnerable Elders) agree that when 2 or more risk factors for GI bleed are present, aspirin should not be added without some form of protection for the GI tract (misoprostol or a daily PPI). In considering all the risks for GI bleed, the most significant ones are age > 75 years, history of GI bleeding, warfarin use, daily NSAID use, and chronic steroid use.

75. ***c***

More than 90% of deaths associated with influenza occur in older adults. Pneumonia is the most common cause of death and most common reason for hospital admission in older patients with influenza. Annual immunization is recommended for all adults in the United States.

76. ***c***

The recommendation of CDC is NOT to revaccinate this patient. After initial vaccination at or after age 65 years, no revaccination is recommended. If initial vaccination occurred prior to age 65 years, and at least 5 years has passed since the initial immunization, revaccination can occur once.

77. What is true regarding the "shingles" vaccine given to adults at or after age 50?

a. **It is a weakened form of the chickenpox virus.**
b. **It is the same as the chickenpox virus.**
c. **It contains significantly more virus than the chickenpox vaccine.**
d. **It is not related to the chickenpox immunization at all.**

78. An older adult was screened for colorectal cancer and had a positive screen. She went on to have a colonoscopy that was normal. She does not have colorectal cancer. The screen was a:

a. **false negative.**
b. **false positive.**
c. **true negative.**
d. **true positive.**

79. A patient is 86 years-old and functions independently. He has hypertension, hyperlipidemia, BPH, and flare-ups of gout. His last colonoscopy was at age 76 years. What should he be advised about having a colonoscopy?

a. **Colonoscopy is the preferred method for screening in the elderly**
b. **Colonoscopy is ill advised in the elderly**
c. **The patient should consider an alternative screening method**
d. **Screening is not necessary after age 80 years**

80. An independent 82 year-old male patient is very active but retired last year. His total cholesterol and LDLs are moderately elevated. How should the NP approach his lipid elevation?

a. **He has reached an age where treatment holds little benefit**
b. **Treatment is not age dependent; he should receive niacin today**
c. **Treatment is based on expected length of life**
d. **He should receive a statin today until he is 85 years**

81. Women are commonly screened for osteoporosis at age 65 years. How should screening for osteoporosis be managed in a male this age?

a. **They should be screened starting at age 65 if they have risk factors.**
b. **They should be screened routinely at age 65.**
c. **They do not need screening since this is not prevalent in males.**
d. **They should be screened if they have prostate disease.**

77. *c*

The "shingles" (Herpes zoster) vaccine contains 14 times the number of plaque-forming units of virus than the varicella vaccine. The immunization has reduced the incidence of shingles and post-herpetic neuralgia in adults who received it. The vaccine is recommended by CDC for all immunocompetent adults who are 60 years or older. It is given once. The FDA has approved use of this vaccine at age 50 years. The vaccine is only used to prevent shingles. It is not used to treat shingles or post-herpetic neuralgia.

78. *b*

The screen was a false positive. Unfortunately, one of the hazards and great expenses of screening tests is the cost associated with false positives and false negatives. All screening tests have inherent costs associated with them.

79. *c*

Colonoscopy enables the examiner to visualize the entire colon and is a superior screening tool for colorectal cancer, but there are significant risks of bleeding and perforation in older adults. Additionally, the colon prep can produce massive shifts in electrolytes that can increase the likelihood of arrhythmias, weakness, and falls.
As a general rule, patients with a life expectancy of less than 5 years should forego colorectal cancer screening via colonoscopy. An alternate method such as stool for occult blood could be considered in this patient. Prior to any screening test such as colonoscopy, consideration must be given to the patient's overall health status, colorectal cancer risk, and desire to pursue treatment if cancer or disease is diagnosed.

80. *c*

Older adults have higher rates of coronary events than younger adults do. Treatment of elevated lipids in older adults has been shown to decrease overall mortality, decrease major coronary events, and is associated with relative risk reduction for subsequent coronary events. United States Preventive Services Task Force and American Heart Association recommend lipid-lowering therapy because it clearly benefits older adults. This patient should have a statin started if lifestyle modifications do not allow him to reach goal lipid values. Niacin is poorly tolerated and wouldn't be a first choice in older adults because of hypotension and flushing.

81. *a*

Men develop osteoporosis less frequently than women do. However, low bone density in the elderly is a common finding. If males have risk factors and are 65 years or older, most learned authorities agree with screening using DEXA scan. Common risk factors in men are systemic steroid use, low body mass index, hypogonadism, or primary hyperparathyroidism. They are treated with bisphosphonates and other interventions (calcium and Vitamin D supplementation, weight bearing exercises, etc.) just as females are.

82. **Besides hypertension, what risk factor contributes the most to development of an abdominal aortic aneurysm?**

   a. **Valvular dysfunction**
   b. **Elevated LDL values**
   c. **Cigarette smoking**
   d. **Alcohol consumption**

83. **How often should hearing be screened with audiometry in older adults?**

   a. **Annually**
   b. **Twice annually**
   c. **At each visit**
   d. **Only if symptoms exist**

84. **What is the value of Vitamin D supplementation in the diet of older adults?**

   a. **It decreases the risk of falls.**
   b. **It decreases the severity of hip fractures.**
   c. **There is no clear value unless a Vitamin D deficiency is identified.**
   d. **It helps to prevent fractures.**

85. **What is the recommendation for daily multivitamin supplementation in older adults?**

   a. **Supplementation reduces morbidity.**
   b. **Supplementation reduces mortality.**
   c. **It decreases the relative risk of dementia.**
   d. **It has no proven benefit.**

86. **Which factor listed below does NOT contribute to the risk of falls in older adults?**

   a. **Decreased vision**
   b. **Changes in cognition**
   c. **Decreased hearing**
   d. **Anticholinergic medications**

87. **What should the nurse practitioner assess in a patient who reports a fall but does not have serious physical injury?**

   a. **Blood pressure while the patient is seated**
   b. **Medications taken a few hours before the fall**
   c. **Visual acuity and ability to distinguish colors**
   d. **The ability to get out of a chair easily**

82. ***c***
Smoking clearly increases the risk for abdominal aortic aneurysm (AAA). The prevalence in women is far lower than in men; and the benefits associated with screening women for AAA do not justify the costs. However, United States Preventive Services Task Force and American Heart Association recommend one-time screening for males aged 65 to 75 who have ever smoked. Other learned authorities recommend screening between 65 and 75 if they have a first degree relative who required repair of a AAA.

83. ***a***
ACOVE authors recommend annual hearing screen for older adults. The screen should include a questionnaire and handheld audiometry. Screening annually resulted in greater adherence with using hearing assistive devices when hearing problems were identified.

84. ***a***
Vitamin D reduces the relative risk of falls by 22%. In older patients, daily intake of Vitamin D should be 800 IU. In addition to Vitamin D, 1200 mg of calcium is also recommended.

85. ***d***
No studies have demonstrated specific benefit to daily consumption of multivitamins in older adults. However, a daily multivitamin supplement ensures adequate intake of essential vitamins and so should be considered for older adults.

86. ***c***
Many factors contribute to falls in older patients. The annual incidence of falls in patients who are 80 years and older is near 50%. About 5% of falls result in serious consequences. Risk for falls should be assessed frequently in older adults.

87. ***b***
There are many things to assess when a patient reports a fall. The blood pressure should be compared in various positions: sitting to standing, lying to sitting, to assess for orthostatic hypotension. Assessing blood pressure only in a sitting position will not help identify orthostatic hypotension. Medication history in the last 72 hours would be important. Sometimes medications taken the night before will leave a patient with decreased alertness the following day. The circumstances surrounding the fall should be discussed. Visual assessment should be assessed, but color differentiation is not specific to the assessment. Gait and balance assessment as well as assessment of cognitive changes should be done.

88. What should the nurse practitioner recommend to any elder taking medications?

a. **Have someone check your medications prior to taking them**
b. **Never take your medicine on an empty stomach**
c. **Keep a list of all of your medications with you**
d. **Have a pharmacist review your list once a year**

89. What recommendation should be made to an elder who is diagnosed with mild dementia?

a. **Driving will probably not increase your risk of an accident.**
b. **The healthcare provider should recommend that the patient stop driving today.**
c. **The healthcare provider should recommend assessment of driving to determine risk of an accident.**
d. **The patient may continue to drive as long as he feels comfortable.**

90. An elderly male with moderately severe dementia presents with his caregiver daughter. His BMI is 18. His clothes have food stains on them and he looks as though he hasn't been bathed in days. How should the nurse practitioner handle this?

a. **The NP should comment to the daughter about his poor care.**
b. **The NP should report this as potential elder abuse.**
c. **The patient should be asked about his care.**
d. **The daughter should be asked about the type of care he receives.**

91. What is the simplest screen for nutritional adequacy in elderly patients?

a. **Measure their weight**
b. **Measure their BMI**
c. **Ask about food preferences**
d. **Obtain a 72 hour food recall diary**

92. What is the most common nutrition syndrome in elderly patients?

a. **Undernutrition**
b. **Over nutrition**
c. **Malnourishment**
d. **Vitamin B-12 deficiency**

88. ***c***
A list of current medications should be kept with each patient and carried with him especially when healthcare visits are scheduled. Many older adults are capable of taking medications without supervision and so choice one is not correct. Many medications should be taken without food (thyroid supplementation for example). A pharmacist can evaluate the list of medications for drug-drug interactions, but the pharmacist will not know the diagnoses and other reasons for choosing the medications.

89. ***c***
Dementia independently increases the risk of motor vehicle accident if the patient drives. The healthcare provider should discuss this with the patient and a family member, if a family member is present during the elder's evaluation. Depending on the degree of impairment, the healthcare provider could recommend stopping driving, or recommend that an assessment be done. The assessment is usually completed by either an occupational or physical therapist or someone trained to assess this.

90. ***b***
This patient presents as though he is being poorly cared for and mistreated. This occurs in about 3-8% of the adult population in the United States. There is no evidence that the patient has been physically abused, but he obviously suffers from neglect. This is a form of elder abuse just as physical, sexual, psychological, or financial abuse is. Elderly patients with dementia are those who suffer abuse most frequently.

91. ***a***
In older adults, serial weight is the simplest screen for assessment of nutritional adequacy. Weight loss in elderly patients is associated with greater mortality than weight maintenance.

92. ***a***
Some elderly patients have great challenges associated with eating and maintaining weight. They may be edentulous or have anorexia. Weight loss is associated with greater mortality in older adults than in patients who have not had recent weight loss. Clinically significant weight loss is usually considered to be about 4-5% of total body weight within 6-12 months. In older patients who do lose weight, they are less likely to gain it back than younger adults. This also increases risk of mortality.

93. Two common causes of weight loss in the elderly are:

a. anorexia and depression.
b. depression and malignancy.
c. malignancy and social isolation.
d. financial limitations.

94. Which disease listed below does NOT impact an elder's ability to eat?

a. Stroke
b. Parkinson's disease
c. Dysphagia
d. Hyperlipidemia

95. Many older adults have cachexia. What characterizes this?

a. Anorexia and weight loss
b. Weakness and fatigue
c. Illness and loss of muscle mass
d. Starvation and weight loss

96. A 95 year-old male has lost muscle mass as he has aged. He does not have any underlying disease that has caused this loss. What is this termed?

a. Hypoproteinemia
b. Sarcopenia
c. Cachexia
d. Dithering

97. An 84 year-old presents with a stated involuntary weight loss. He states that he's lost about 6 pounds in the last 6 or 8 weeks. What statement below is NOT part of the assessment?

a. The weight loss should be measured today and again in the next few weeks.
b. A laboratory evaluation should be performed.
c. Evaluate his dietary intake.
d. Evaluate his upper and lower extremity muscle mass.

93. *b*
Malignancy is the most common cause of weight loss in the elderly. Depression is the second most common reason. Other reasons that contribute to weight loss are social isolation. Many elders live alone and consequently eat alone. Many elderly patients have financial and mobility limitations that make eating and acquiring foods more difficult. Anorexia is not unusual in the elderly, but there are a number of reasons for this. Some are physical, social, and psychosocial.

94. *d*
Many, many diseases impact an elder patient's ability to eat. About 50% of patients who have had stroke have impaired ability to eat. This can include difficulty feeding self as well as difficulty swallowing. Parkinson's disease and many other neurological diseases have great impact on eating since coordinated muscle movement is needed for swallowing and feeding. Hyperlipidemia has no significant impact on a patient's ability to eat.

95. *c*
Cachexia is common in older adults and is associated with increased mortality. It is described as a syndrome of underlying illness that is accompanied by loss of muscle mass. Illnesses associated with cachexia are malignancies, renal disease, COPD, and chronic heart failure. Other matters are associated with cachexia and may contribute to loss of muscle mass. These include loss of appetite, insulin resistance, and increased catabolism of bodily proteins.

96. *b*
Sarcopenia is the term used to describe loss of muscle mass related to aging. The actual definition is a decrease in appendicular muscle mass that is measured as a two standard deviation decrease. It is associated with increased falls, disability, and impairment. In males, this is due to decreased production of testosterone.

97. *d*
Involuntary weight loss in older adults is often due to malignancy or disease. The initial assessment of an older adult who reports involuntary weight loss is to document the weight loss. If prior measurements are part of the patient's chart, this would be helpful. Laboratory assessment should also be performed. Consideration should be given to performing a CBC, TSH, metabolic panel. Also consider chest and abdominal x-rays. If all are normal, he should be monitored and re-weighed on the same scale for comparison. A dietary consult should be in order. However, even with negative initial findings, a significant number of patients are later found to have disease or malignancy.

98. Which of the following is NOT part of the prescription for management of weight loss in older adults?

a. **Increase carbohydrate intake**
b. **Increase the calories at each meal**
c. **Increase the frequency of meals**
d. **Consider liquid supplements**

99. What medication listed below could be used to increase appetite in an anorexic patient?

a. **Megestrol**
b. **Loratadine**
c. **Fexofenadine**
d. **Serum ferritin**

100. What is true regarding overweight states in older adults?

a. **This is clearly associated with increased mortality in older adults.**
b. **Mortality in the elderly related to overweight states declines over time.**
c. **BMI is a good way to assess nutritional states in the elderly.**
d. **There are no potential metabolic or functional benefits to weight loss in the elder.**

98. ***a***
When treating patients with weight loss, the goal is to increase the number of calories at each meal. Fats are more heavily laden with calories than carbohydrates. Carbohydrates (and proteins) provide only 4 calories per gram; fats provide 9 calories per gram. The addition of fats will increase calories much more quickly than increasing carbohydrate intake. All of the suggestions listed above will increase caloric intake. Daytime snacks should be offered too. Consider a Vitamin B supplement because this can stimulate appetite.

99. ***a***
Megestrol acetate has a positive effect on weight in patients who are trying to gain weight. It increases appetite and may improve quality of life. Weight gain may take up to 3 months before it is measurable. Megestrol has the potential to cause edema and so should be used cautiously (or not at all) in patients with chronic heart failure.

100. ***b***
Overweight and obese states are not as important in predicting mortality in the elderly as they are in their younger counterparts. After age 65 years (some studies demonstrate after age 70), weight is less significant in decreasing risk for mortality than in younger adults. There are some benefits to weight loss in the obese elderly. One of them is better balance and decreased risk for falls. Others include less sleep apnea, decreased risk of diabetes, decreased rates of shortness of breath with respiratory and cardiac diseases.

Pediatrics

1. **When is Osgood-Schlatter disease most likely to produce symptoms?**

    a. **Before a growth spurt**
    b. **During a growth spurt**
    c. **After vigorous exercise during adolescence**
    d. **Without regard to age or exercise**

2. **A 12 month-old is here today to be vaccinated with varicella. A patient's mother reports that her 12 month-old child was exposed to chickenpox about a week ago. The NP should recommend that he:**

    a. **be given the vaccine.**
    b. **wait 4 weeks to receive the vaccine.**
    c. **not receive varicella today because he is not old enough.**
    d. **receive MMR only today, not varicella.**

3. **A 6 day-old has a mucopurulent eye discharge bilaterally. What historical finding explains the etiology of the discharge?**

    a. **Infant is Hepatitis B positive.**
    b. **Infant received silver nitrate drops.**
    c. **Mother has chlamydia.**
    d. **Delivery was by C-section.**

4. **A child has 8-10 medium brown café au lait spots > 1 cm in diameter. The differential diagnosis should include:**

    a. **vitiligo.**
    b. **eczema.**
    c. **neurofibromatosis.**
    d. **neuroblastoma.**

5. **A 6 year-old is brought to your clinic because of behavior problems at school. DSM V criteria are used to diagnose attention deficit disorder (ADD). Which finding must be present for this diagnosis?**

    a. **Compulsivity**
    b. **Inability to follow directions**
    c. **Poor social skills**
    d. **Inattention**

1. *b*

Osgood-Schlatter disease occurs during a growth spurt when the knee is subjected to activities that place repeated stress at the superior tibia. The quadriceps, especially after certain activities (running, jumping, and bending of the lower leg), exert stress on the patellar tendon, which pulls on the tibial tuberosity. This produces swelling at the tibial tuberosity and pain, especially with running, jumping, and bending of the knee. Vigorous exercise during non-growth periods will not produce Osgood-Schlatter disease.

2. *a*

The patient who reports recent exposure to an infectious disease should be vaccinated today unless something else contraindicates the immunization. Since he is 12 months old, he is old enough to receive varicella and MMR. Varicella should be given on the same day as MMR or the two vaccines must be separated by at least 4 weeks.

3. *c*

Infants born vaginally to mothers who have chlamydia have a 60-70% risk of acquiring *C. trachomatis*. Newborns may present with pneumonia and/or conjunctivitis. The most common clinical feature is conjunctivitis that occurs 5 to 14 days after delivery. It is characterized by swelling of the lids and a watery discharge that becomes mucopurulent. The conjunctivae are erythematous. This must be treated orally because topical treatment is not effective. The drug of choice in infants is oral erythromycin 50 mg/kg/day in divided doses for 14 days whether treating pneumonia or conjunctivitis.

4. *c*

Neurofibromatosis (NF) is a common neurocutaneous disorder. The most common form is von Recklinghausen's NF. Approximately 85% of patients with NF have this type. The incidence is about 1 in 2600 individuals. Children with this disorder have cognitive deficits, learning disabilities and other neurological related problems. They should be referred for diagnosis and treatment.

5. *d*

There are three categories of symptoms: hyperactivity, inattention, and impulsivity. The diagnostic criteria have been defined by the American Psychiatric Association and can be found in the DSM V.

6. A one year-old patient's mother reports allergy to gelatin. The mother describes the reaction as "lips swelling and breathing difficulties which necessitated a trip to the emergency department". Which immunizations should be avoided?

a. **Varicella, DTaP, and MMR**
b. **Varicella and MMR**
c. **IPV, DTaP, and Hepatitis B**
d. **Hepatitis A and B, meningococcal**

7. A 2 month-old is diagnosed with thrush. An exam of this patient's saliva demonstrates all *except*:

a. **hyphae.**
b. **yeast.**
c. **spores.**
d. **a positive KOH.**

8. Medications considered first line to treat attention deficit disorder and attention deficit hyperactivity disorder are Schedule:

a. **I.**
b. **II.**
c. **III.**
d. **IV.**

9. A 7 year-old male presents with encopresis. The NP might expect:

a. **constipation.**
b. **delayed maturation.**
c. **urinary tract infection.**
d. **laxative abuse.**

10. A 6 year-old has been diagnosed with Lyme disease. Which drug should be used to treat him?

a. **Doxycycline**
b. **Amoxicillin**
c. **Azithromycin**
d. **Cephalexin**

6. ***b***

Varicella and MMR should be avoided until allergy testing can take place. However, according to CDC, this patient should be skin tested prior to administering either of these vaccines to establish sensitivity to gelatin. IF the skin tests are negative, the vaccine can be given as with non-allergic children. Other than MMR and varicella, there are no contraindications to any other US immunizations.

7. ***c***

The visualization of yeast, hyphae, pseudohypha in saliva usually indicates Candida species. The diagnosis of thrush is usually made on clinical presentation and there is no need for KOH. Spores are a form assumed by some bacteria and fungi that are extremely resistant to heat and consequently are very difficult to kill.

8. ***b***

Schedule II medications are those described as having a high abuse risk. These can cause severe psychological or physical dependence. Stimulants are used to treat patients with ADD/ADHD because they are thought to affect the dopaminergic and noradrenergic systems that cause the release of catecholamines in the synapses in the central nervous system. Stimulants are considered first line pharmacologic therapy. Specific medication types are methylphenidate, dextroamphetamine, and mixed amphetamine salts. They all have abuse potential and should be prescribed very cautiously.

9. ***a***

The underlying cause of encopresis, repetitive soiling of stool by a child who is 4 years of age or older who should be potty trained, is usually chronic constipation. The ultimate goal is to reverse the constipation and establish normal bowel habits by the child. Having the patient use daily laxatives reverses constipation. Once he is able to have one soft bowel movement daily and a routine has been established, the laxatives are slowly weaned off. Attention to dietary factors must be addressed so that the child's diet will support a daily bowel movement.

10. ***b***

Amoxicillin, doxycycline, and cefuroxime have all been shown to have equivalent efficacy for treatment of Lyme disease. However, because this patient is only 6 years old, he should not be given doxycycline as a first line treatment unless the other regimens are contraindicated. Macrolides, like azithromycin should not be used first line because they are poorly effective at eradicating infection. They may be used in patients who are intolerant of penicillins and cephalosporins and who cannot take doxycycline. First generation cephalosporins like cephalexin are not effective.

11. Hirschsprung's disease is characterized by:

- **a. intermittent constipation in the first year of life.**
- **b. inability to absorb carbohydrates.**
- **c. failure to pass meconium in the first 48-hours of life.**
- **d. chronic fecal incontinence.**

12. A pregnant patient is concerned because her 12 month-old needs an MMR immunization. What should the NP advise this patient?

- **a. The MMR is a dead virus; therefore, there is no risk to the mother.**
- **b. Have the child wait until Mom delivers.**
- **c. Have the child wait until Mom is in her 28th week or later before immunization.**
- **d. MMR immunization presents no risk to the child's mother. Immunize now.**

13. A 10 year-old female presents with a three-month history of abdominal pain. She has been diagnosed with recurrent abdominal pain. During the interview the nurse practitioner is likely to elicit a finding of:

- **a. nocturnal pain.**
- **b. change in bowel habits.**
- **c. school absenteeism.**
- **d. pain relief with ibuprofen.**

14. A 6 week-old male infant is brought to the nurse practitioner because of vomiting. The mother describes vomiting after feeding and feeling a "knot" in his abdomen especially after he vomits. The child appears adequately nourished. What is the likely etiology?

- **a. Gastroesophageal reflux (GER)**
- **b. Pyloric stenosis**
- **c. Constipation**
- **d. Munchausen syndrome by proxy**

15. A 4 year-old has been diagnosed with measles. The nurse practitioner identifies Koplik's spots. These are:

- **a. spots on the skin that are pathognomonic for measles.**
- **b. red rings found on the tongue that have a white granular area inside the ring.**
- **c. found on the inside of the cheek and are granular.**
- **d. blanchable areas on the trunk and extremities.**

11. ***c***
Another name for this condition is aganglionic megacolon. The affected segment of colon is absent of ganglia that are responsible for producing peristalsis. The diagnosis cannot be made in the first 48-hours of life, but a suggestion of the diagnosis can be made because meconium is not passed in a timely manner. Consequently, most children are diagnosed in the neonatal period. Patients usually present with emesis, abdominal distention, and failure to pass stool. An abdominal x-ray will demonstrate distal intestinal obstruction with dilated bowel loops. The patient should be referred for surgery to remove the diseased segment of colon.

12. ***d***
MMR immunization in the child presents no risk to the pregnant mother. MMR is actually attenuated, also thought of as an inactivated form of the virus. Therefore, there is no risk to her. If the mother were pregnant, she should not be vaccinated. If she is contemplating pregnancy, she should avoid MMR for 4 weeks following immunization.

13. ***c***
Recurrent abdominal pain can be diagnosed after three episodes of abdominal pain that severely affects the child's usual activities and occurs over at least a three month period. No acute cause can be identified. Fewer than one in 10 children with recurrent abdominal pain attends school regularly. The goal in treating these children is a return to normal function and activities, not necessarily relief of pain. Caregivers must be coached to avoid reinforcement of pain behaviors with the child.

14. ***b***
This scenario is typical of an infant with pyloric stenosis. It is more common in males (88%) and usually is diagnosed before the child is 12 weeks old. The classic presentation is an infant who vomits immediately after eating. The "knot" in the abdomen is the typical "olive-shaped mass" palpable at the lateral edge of the rectus abdominus muscle in the right upper quadrant of the abdomen. The mass is best palpated immediately after vomiting. The differential should include GER, but no mass is palpable. Munchausen syndrome by proxy is the fabrication or induction of an illness in a child in order for the caregiver to receive attention.

15. ***c***
Koplik's spots are found in the oral cavity, especially on the buccal mucosa opposite the first and second molars. The spots are white and granular and are circled by an erythematous ring. The spots are pathognomonic for measles. There is an exanthem associated with measles. It typically is described as cranial to caudal in progression. The lesions become confluent and last for approximately 4 days before fading begins.

16. What choice below is a risk factor for sudden infant death syndrome (SIDS)?

- **a. Maternal age > 19 years**
- **b. SIDS in a second degree relative**
- **c. Low birth weight**
- **d. Female gender**

17. A child is diagnosed with bronchiolitis. Which choice below would NOT be part of patient management?

- **a. Antipyretics**
- **b. Nebulized bronchodilators**
- **c. Oral steroids**
- **d. Antibiotics**

18. A definitive diagnosis of sickle cell anemia can be made:

- **a. by a CBC.**
- **b. by a hemoglobin electrophoresis.**
- **c. by a pathologist with visual examination of red cells.**
- **d. with a serum ferritin, iron level, and hemoglobin.**

19. A 4 year-old presents with fever, rhinorrhea, and a high pitched whooping cough. This is:

- **a. bronchiolitis.**
- **b. croup.**
- **c. foreign body aspiration.**
- **d. pertussis.**

20. The most common cause of pneumonia in very young children is:

- **a. *S. pneumonia.***
- **b. *S. aureus.***
- **c. *Mycoplasma.***
- **d. a viral infection.**

21. Which patient below is most likely to experience stranger anxiety during a physical exam?

- **a. A 6 month-old male**
- **b. A 12 month-old female**
- **c. A 3 year-old female**
- **d. A 4 year-old female**

16. c

Risk factors for SIDS are maternal age < 19 years, SIDS in a sibling, not a second degree relative. Male gender is a risk factor since more males have SIDS than females. Low birth weight babies are at increased risk of SIDS.

17. *d*

Bronchiolitis is a viral infection and antibiotics would be inappropriate for management. Since fever commonly accompanies bronchiolitis, antipyretics such as acetaminophen and ibuprofen are commonly used. Bronchiolitis is characterized by wheezing, and so bronchodilators, especially nebulized, are commonly employed to decrease respiratory effort. Oral steroids are controversial in bronchiolitis but are commonly used in infants and children when there is significant edema in the small airways.

18. *b*

Sickle cell anemia is initially suspected on visual exam of the red cells. They have a sickled-shape, hence the name sickle cell anemia. These cells can be identified as early as 3 months of age. Once a positive screen is identified, it is repeated using either hemoglobin electrophoresis or DNA analysis.

19. *d*

Pertussis, a bacterial infection, is extremely contagious. Transmission is via direct contact with respiratory droplets. The cardinal symptoms are fever, rhinorrhea, and a "whooping cough" which may last up to 100 days.

20. *d*

In children less than 5 years old, the most common cause of pneumonia is a viral pathogen. Rarely are studies performed to identify viral pathogens, however one of the most common viral pathogens is respiratory syncytial virus (RSV). *S. pneumoniae* is a common cause of pneumonia in very young children, it is also implicated in elderly adults as a causative agent in pneumonia. In adolescents, *Mycoplasma* is the predominant pathogen.

21. *b*

Infants younger than 6 months and children older than 3 years typically do not exhibit stranger anxiety when the examiner enters the room. There is no known difference between stranger anxiety in male and female children. The most specific time for stranger anxiety to develop is about 9 months.

22. **A 9 year-old female has presented to your clinic because of a rash on the left, upper area of her anterior trunk. She is embarrassed and very reticent to lift her blouse because her nipple will be exposed. How should the NP proceed?**

    a. **Examine the patient with the area covered as much as possible**
    b. **The NP should lift the blouse to expose the area for exam**
    c. **Ask the accompanying caregiver to expose the area for exam**
    d. **Examine all other areas of the trunk, then ask the child to lift her blouse**

23. **A healthy 7 year-old child is diagnosed with pneumonia. He is febrile but not in distress. What is the preferred treatment for him?**

    a. **Supportive measures, it is probably viral**
    b. **Amoxicillin, doses 80-90 mg/kg/d**
    c. **Azithromycin**
    d. **Doxycycline**

24. **A 4 year-old is being examined today in the NP clinic. He appears shy and does not make eye contact with the examiner. The mother does not make eye contact with the examiner either. The patient lacks animation and does not smile. What likely possibility must be considered?**

    a. **The patient is depressed.**
    b. **Sexual abuse is very likely.**
    c. **Neglect is possible.**
    d. **The child probably does not have medical insurance.**

25. **The chest circumference of a 12 month-old is:**

    a. **routinely measured on well-child visits.**
    b. **is 1-2 cm larger than head circumference.**
    c. **is smaller than head circumference.**
    d. **is equal to head circumference.**

26. **A child's resting heart rate can be expected to be between 60 and 100 beats per minute once he reaches:**

    a. **4 years of age.**
    b. **6 years of age.**
    c. **10 years of age.**
    d. **12 years of age.**

22. *d*
The NP must visualize the area during exam so that an appropriate diagnosis can be made. Since the child is 9 years old, she should be given the opportunity to remove her blouse before allowing another adult to do this. Allowing the child to do this will put "control" in her hands.

23. *c*
In this age group (> 5 years), the most common pathogen is an atypical one like *Mycoplasma* or *Chlamydia*, therefore a macrolide is the preferred agent. It is usually chosen first for its coverage of atypical pathogens. Doxycyline is not an appropriate choice because it is contraindicated in children younger than 8 years, however, it does provide coverage against the atypical pathogens. Amoxicillin provides no coverage of atypical pathogens and so it is a poor choice.

24. *c*
The possibility of neglect should always be given when a young patient and caregiver make poor eye contact with the examiner. Other clues to neglect are a lack of animation and no social smile. Additionally, the child should be observed for nutritional status, behavior, attitude, and physical appearance. Sexual abuse should also be considered, but there is nothing in the stem of the question to suggest this or a lack of medical insurance.

25. *b*
The head of infants and children up to 18 months of age is commonly 1-2 cm larger than chest circumference. The chest circumference is measured at the nipple line. This is not routinely measured at well-child visits, but is assessed if there is concern about the circumference of either head or chest. An exception to this observation can occur in premature infants where the head grows very rapidly.

26. *c*
Normal heart rate varies with age. Generally, as the heart becomes more efficient, the rate begins to decrease. This occurs with age. Four and six year-old children can be expected to have normal heart rates between 60 and 140 beats per minute. By age 10 years, the usual heart rate more closely approximates that of an adult, 60-100 beats per minute.

27. An early indication that a young patient has renal artery stenosis is:

- a. decreased urine production.
- b. increased blood pressure.
- c. decreased glomerular filtration rate (GFR).
- d. coarctation of the aorta.

28. How often should blood pressure be measured in a child who is 3 years old?

- a. Blood pressure measurement should begin at age 6 years, then every other year.
- b. It should be measured every other year.
- c. It should be measured annually.
- d. It should be measured only at well child visits.

29. The term caput succedaneum refers to:

- a. cradle cap.
- b. atopic dermatitis.
- c. scalp edema.
- d. asymmetric head shape.

30. The nurse practitioner is examining a 3-month old infant who has normal development. She has identified an alopecic area at the occiput. What should be done?

- a. Order a TSH
- b. Order a hydrocortisone cream
- c. Suspect child abuse
- d. Encourage the caregiver to change the infant's head position

31. An infant is brought to the nurse practitioner because his gaze is asymmetrical. Which finding indicates a need for referral to ophthalmology?

- a. He is 2 months of age.
- b. He is 3 months of age.
- c. He has persistent strabismus.
- d. His red reflex is normal.

27. *b*
Blood pressure is not routinely measured in children younger than 3 years of age unless an underlying abnormality such as coarctation of the aorta, tumor, nephrotic syndrome, renal artery stenosis, etc. is suspected or diagnosed. Routine blood pressure measurement usually begins at 3 years of age if the child is cooperative. Usually the first indication that a patient has renal artery stenosis is an elevated blood pressure. Changes in functioning of the kidney occur after damage to the kidney occurs.

28. *c*
Beginning at 3 years of age, blood pressure is measured annually. It continues to be measured annually through adulthood. Prior to age 3 years, blood pressure is not routinely measured. Blood pressure is assessed in all 4 extremities at birth to assess for coarctation of the aorta, patent ductus arteriosus (PDA), other cardiovascular abnormalities, or significant murmurs. If blood pressure is only assessed at well-child visits for older children, it will not occur annually.

29. *c*
Caput succedaneum is a common finding in newborns. It is a result of pressure over the presenting part. This results in some ecchymosis of the scalp. While this may be disturbing to new parents who observe this in their newborn, it will resolve in a few days and is harmless.

30. *d*
In a normally developing infant, an alopecic area at the occipital area is generally because the infant has been placed in the supine position during sleeping and waking hours. Prolonged pressure on the occipital area can restrict hair growth. This is normal and will resolve when the infant begins to have better head control and movement; and he begins to have less pressure on the occipital area. Sometimes coarse, dry hair can be indicative of hypothyroidism; not necessarily alopecia.

31. c
Strabismus may be completely normal in the first few months of life. Persistent strabismus at any age likely indicates eye muscle weakness, cranial nerve abnormalities or a number of other pediatric eye diseases. The infant with a normal red reflex probably does not have retinoblastoma or congenital cataracts, but both of these conditions can result in strabismus. This infant should be referred to an ophthalmologist for evaluation if he has persistent strabismus.

32. An adolescent takes isotretinoin for nodulocystic acne. She is on oral contraceptives. Both were prescribed by the dermatologist. The adolescent arrives in your clinic with a sinus infection. Her temperature is 99.5 degrees F and her blood pressure is 160/100. How should this be managed?

a. **Call the dermatologist to report the elevated BP**
b. **Treat the sinus infection and recheck the BP in one week**
c. **Discontinue the isotretinoin today**
d. **Discontinue the oral contraceptive today**

33. A tympanic membrane (TM) is erythematous. Which factor listed below is NOT the cause of an erythematous TM?

a. **Acute inflammation**
b. **Coughing**
c. **High fever**
d. **Crying**

34. How long should a 6 year old with acute otitis media be treated with an antibiotic?

a. **5 days**
b. **5-7 days**
c. **10 days**
d. **Until the erythema has resolved**

35. The most common cause of acute pharyngitis in children is:

a. ***S. pyogenes.***
b. ***H. influenzae.***
c. ***M. pneumoniae.***
d. **respiratory viruses.**

36. Epstein-Barr virus is responsible for:

a. **mononucleosis.**
b. **the most common cause of pharyngitis.**
c. **most teenage cases of pharyngitis.**
d. **viral pharyngitis in young children.**

32. ***a***

The nurse practitioner is responsible for treating the sinus infection but has also become aware of a potentially harmful situation involving the elevated blood pressure and oral contraceptive use. The safest and most professional action is to call the dermatologist to discuss your concerns regarding the elevated BP and concomitant oral contraceptive use since this potentially increases the risk of stroke in this adolescent. Care and professional courtesy should be exercised when discontinuing a medication that another provider has initiated. Professional courtesy is extended to the prescriber by calling them prior to discontinuing a medication they have ordered.

33. ***b***

An erythematous TM can be caused by the conditions listed above. Coughing does not produce an erythematous TM. The tympanic membrane (TM) can take on numerous colors depending on the condition or status of the patient. Under normal conditions, the TM is usually described as pearly gray or pink. When there is fluid behind the TM, it may take on a white, gray, or blue appearance. When pus is present behind the TM, it can appear white or yellow.

34. ***b***

The recommendations from the American Academy of Pediatrics are 5-7 days of an antibiotic for children 6 years and older who have mild to moderate acute otitis media (AOM). Children less than 2 years of age should be treated for 10 days. Children 2 years and older may be treated for 5-7 days for AOM if they do not have a history of recurrent AOM.

35. ***d***

The most common cause of acute pharyngitis is infection with viral agents. The most common viruses are adenoviruses, coxsackie A virus, and parainfluenza virus. The most frequent bacterial cause of acute pharyngitis is *Streptococcus pyogenes*. The most prevalent time of year for Streptococcus outbreaks is winter.

36. ***a***

Infectious mononucleosis is caused by Epstein-Barr virus (EBV). This commonly affects adolescents but can affect various age groups. The most prominent feature of mononucleosis is fever, fatigue and pharyngitis.

37. A 6 year-old patient with sore throat has coryza, hoarseness, and diarrhea. What is the likely etiology?

a. **Group A *Streptococcus***
b. ***H. parainfluenzae***
c. **Viral etiology**
d. ***Mycoplasma***

38. An adolescent complains of knee pain. He is diagnosed with Osgood-Schlatter disease. What assessment finding is typical?

a. **The pain is always bilateral.**
b. **Pain worsens with quadriceps contraction.**
c. **There will be an avulsion of the quadriceps tendon.**
d. **Assessments vary. An x-ray can be used for diagnosis.**

39. A 3 year-old has been diagnosed with acute otitis media. She is penicillin allergic (Type 1 hypersensitivity reaction). How should she be managed?

a. **Amoxicillin**
b. **Amoxicillin-clavulanate**
c. **Cefuroxil**
d. **Clarithromycin**

40. An 8 year-old has a painful limp. He reports that his knee hurts medially. On exam he has pain with internal rotation of the hip. How should the NP manage this situation?

a. **He should be immediately referred to orthopedics.**
b. **The NP should order a hip x-ray, CBC and ESR.**
c. **The NP should order a hip and knee x-ray.**
d. **He should be referred for synovial fluid aspiration.**

41. Which infant has feeding behavior NOT associated with an infant with congenital heart disease?

a. **Limited intake of volume of milk**
b. **Feedings that take "a long time" to complete**
c. **Feedings that are interrupted by sleeping**
d. **Infants that burp frequently when feeding**

37. ***c***
This constellation of symptoms is typical of a viral infection. Group A *Streptococcus* is usually not accompanied by coryza. *H. parainfluenzae* is not a common cause of pharyngitis. *Mycoplasma* usually is associated with lower respiratory tract infections.

38. ***b***
In patients with Osgood-Schlatter disease, pain can be unilateral or bilateral. What is obvious on assessment is a swelling of the tibial tubercle. X-rays are not needed for diagnosis. Pain worsens with squatting or crouching and with contraction of the quadriceps muscle against resistance. An avulsion of the quadriceps tendon should be part of the differential for patients who exhibit severe pain.

39. ***d***
This patient experienced a Type I allergic reaction to penicillin. This is characterized by hives, wheezing, or anaphylaxis. It is NEVER considered safe to prescribe a cephalosporin. Macrolides may be prescribed to patients with a true Type 1 reaction to penicillin. Since amoxicillin is a penicillin, it should not be prescribed.

40. ***b***
In an 8 year-old, there are several diagnoses in the differential. One must consider Legg-Calve Perthes, transient synovitis of the hip, a slipped capital femoral epiphysis (SCFE), and a septic hip. This could be as benign as transient synovitis that does not require referral. All of the others mentioned would need urgent orthopedic referral. Once the diagnostics were completed, the NP would have a better idea about whether orthopedic referral was essential.

41. ***d***
Infants who burp frequently probably are swallowing too much air with feeding. There are some red flags associated with feeding that should prompt the examiner to assess for congenital heart disease. Parents frequently report the situations that were described in the question as well as feedings that are interrupted by choking, gagging, or vomiting. Additionally, some infants will have fast breathing with feeding or a persistent cough or wheeze.

42. Hand-foot-and-mouth disease and herpangina:

- a. both produce pustules on oral mucous membranes.
- b. potentially can cause orchitis in infected males.
- c. are viral infections caused by Coxsackie viruses.
- d. will only occur in the spring and summer.

43. Which statement below best characterizes scoliosis in an adolescent?

- a. It is more common in males and is idiopathic.
- b. There can be unequal rib prominences or shoulder heights.
- c. The diagnosis can be made when the curvature is 8° or more.
- d. There is a strong familial component to this condition.

44. Many factors can contribute to the risk of congenital heart disease. Which maternal disease carries a higher risk of transposition of the great vessels (TGA), ventricular septal defect (VSD), and hypertrophic cardiomyopathy?

- a. Hypothyroidism
- b. Diabetes
- c. Lupus
- d. Hypertension

45. A young child has an audible murmur. The nurse practitioner describes it as a grade 4 murmur. How should this be managed?

- a. The child should be monitored for other abnormal findings.
- b. The child should be referred to cardiology.
- c. An EKG should be performed.
- d. The nurse practitioner should palpate to see if a thrill is present.

46. A positive Trendelenburg's test could be used to identify a child with:

- a. scoliosis.
- b. Osgood-Schlatter disease.
- c. nursemaid's elbow.
- d. slipped capital femoral epiphysis.

47. The nurse practitioner identifies satellite lesions in a 6 month-old infant. These are:

- a. worrisome in an infant this age.
- b. indicative of candidal infection.
- c. found in the axilla bilaterally.
- d. completely benign lesions present at birth.

42. ***c***
These two common viral exanthems are caused by Coxsackie A viruses. Sometimes herpangina is caused by Coxsackie A or B. Ulcerations are produced on the mucous membranes, not pustules. Orchitis can occur in males infected with mumps. Herpangina typically occurs during summer and fall; hand-foot-and-mouth disease (HFM) occurs in late summer and fall. Both produce oral symptoms, but only HFM produces blisters on the palms of the hands and/or soles of the feet. Both are self-limiting viral illnesses.

43. ***b***
Scoliosis is diagnosed when the degree of curvature is 10° or more. It is more common in girls because they have more rapid vertical growth than boys. There is not a strong familial component to this disease. Rather, it is idiopathic. It is assessed using the Adams Forward Bend test. There can be unequal scapula prominences and heights, waist angles, and chest asymmetry.

44. ***b***
Maternal diabetes increases the risk of the above named diseases. Congenital infections like cytomegalovirus, herpesvirus, rubella, or coxsackie virus can increase the risk of many cardiac structural abnormalities. In fact, TORCH is an acronym used to describe 5 maternal infections that are deleterious to the fetus. The acronym TORCH stands for Toxoplasmosis, Other (syphilis), Rubella, Cytomegalovirus (CMV), Herpes simplex virus (HSV).

45. ***b***
The child should be referred to pediatric cardiology. A grade 4 designation for a murmur indicates that a murmur is loud and has a thrill associated with it. The finding of a thrill is always an abnormal finding and requires referral. A thrill can be palpated with the examiner's hand over the anterior chest in the area of the point of maximal impulse (PMI).

46. ***d***
Asking a child with a complaint of hip pain to stand on the affected side is how the Trendelenburg test is assessed. A positive Trendelenburg test occurs when standing on the affected leg causes a pelvic tilt, such that the unaffected hip is lower. This can be assessed and observed in children with slipped capital femoral epiphysis, Legg-Calve-Perthes disease, or developmental dysplasia of the hip. Nursemaid's elbow is a common ligamentous injury in young children. The radial head becomes subluxed. Displacement is usually easy to reduce.

47. ***b***
Satellite lesions are common in the diaper area of infants with a candidal diaper infection. They generally are associated with a beefy red rash. The skin creases are more commonly affected, but satellite lesions can be found anywhere that Candida can be found.

48. A 3 year-old female had a fever of 102 degrees F for 3 days. Today she woke up from a nap and is afebrile. She has a maculopapular rash. Which statement is true?

- **a. This child probably has measles.**
- **b. The rash will blanch.**
- **c. This is a streptococcal rash.**
- **d. This could be Kawasaki disease.**

49. What advice should be given to a parent who has a child with Fifth Disease?

- **a. This commonly causes pruritis in young children.**
- **b. He can return to school when the rash has disappeared.**
- **c. Acetaminophen should be avoided in this child.**
- **d. A parent may experience joint aches and pains.**

50. When can a child with chickenpox return to daycare?

- **a. 24 hours after he is fever-free**
- **b. 48 hours after he is fever-free**
- **c. After all lesions have crusted over**
- **d. When he no longer itches**

51. A child with a sandpaper textured rash probably has:

- **a. rubeola.**
- **b. strept infection.**
- **c. varicella.**
- **d. roseola.**

52. A 3 day-old infant weighed 8 pounds at birth. Today he weighs 7.5 pounds. How should this be managed?

- **a. Assess the baby for a cardiac anomaly**
- **b. Add an extra feeding in the AM and PM**
- **c. Have the mother return to re-weigh the baby in 1 week**
- **d. Continue feeding every 2-4 hours**

53. At what age would it be unusual to see thrush?

- **a. At birth**
- **b. 2 months**
- **c. 6 months**
- **d. 8 months**

48. ***b***
This describes a patient with roseola or exanthem subitum. This is a common viral exanthem found in young children caused by the Human Herpes Virus 6B. It is characterized by high fever for 3 days followed by the abrupt cessation of fever and the appearance of a maculopapular rash. This usually resolves in a few days. The child may return to school or daycare when he has been fever free for 24 hours.

49. ***d***
Fifth disease, erythema infectiosum, is a common viral exanthem seen in children 5-15 years of age. This produces a maculopapular rash that blanches easily. This rash is not pruritic but may last for several weeks before it completely goes away. Children are allowed to attend school as long as they have been fever free for 24 hours. Discomforts of this illness (fever, body aches, etc.) may be treated with acetaminophen or ibuprofen. Adults who are exposed to children with Fifth Disease can complain of arthralgias and myalgias for several weeks.

50. ***c***
Chickenpox is highly contagious and can be spread via respiratory secretions from an infected individual or by direct contact from the vesicle fluid from lesions on the skin or mucus membranes. The usual incubation period is about 2 weeks but can be as long as 21 days or as short as 10 days. The greatest period of infectivity is 48 hours prior to the onset of the rash and until all the skin lesions have crusted over.

51. ***b***
Streptococcal infections can present as a sandpaper textured rash that initially is felt on the trunk. Rubeola, measles, produces a blanching erythematous "brick-red" maculopapular rash that begins on the back of the neck and spreads around the trunk and then extremities. Varicella infection produces the classic crops of eruptions on the trunk that spread to the face. The rash is maculopapular initially and then crusts. Roseola produces a generalized maculopapular rash preceded by 3 days of high fever.

52. ***d***
Babies will lose about 10% of their birth weight in the first 3-4 days of life. This baby has lost about 8 ounces; this is about 10% of his birth weight. This is an appropriate weight loss in this time. He should rapidly gain this weight back. When children begin losing weight and growth slows, one consideration should be given to congenital cardiac anomalies. There is no need for the mother to return in one week to re-weigh this infant. The infant should be asked to return for his 2 month check.

53. ***a***
Thrush is an infection in the oral cavity caused by yeast. Yeast grow in a warm, dark, moist environment. It is not unusual to see thrush in young infants who are breast or bottle fed. It would be unusual to see thrush in a newborn. In fact, this should cause concern regarding an immunocompromised state in the infant or hyperglycemia in the mother.

54. Cranial nerve II could be assessed in a young infant by:

a. assessing squinting response to bright light.
b. feeling for squeezing of fingers.
c. observing response to loud noise.
d. assessing rapid eye movement.

55. Which reflexes might a one month-old infant be expected to exhibit?

a. Moro, stepping, rooting
b. Stepping, rooting, tonic neck
c. Babinski, Moro only
d. Fencing, stepping, rooting

56. A 2 month-old infant has an asymmetric Moro reflex. What statement is true?

a. This is normal. It develops bilaterally later.
b. This indicates a side of dominance.
c. The infant could have a hearing problem.
d. The infant could have a birth injury.

57. What would be age appropriate anticipatory guidance for the parent of a 9 month-old infant?

a. Keep syrup of ipecac in case of accidental poisoning
b. Stranger anxiety will develop by a year of age
c. Your baby should be able to say 10 words before a year
d. Discuss weaning from a bottle

58. When does a child's vision approximate 20/20?

a. 2 years
b. 3 years
c. 4 years
d. 5-6 years

59. Conjunctivitis:

a. produces blurred vision in the affected eye.
b. usually begins as a viral infection.
c. produces anterior cervical lymphadenopathy.
d. is common in patients who are nearsighted.

54. ***a***

Cranial nerve II is the optic nerve. It is responsible for vision. In a young infant, shining an ophthalmoscope light into each eye and observing the infant squint or close his eyes can be used to assess vision. Vision is usually assessed more formally when the infant is cooperative, usually about 3-4 years of age. If vision problems are suspected in an infant, referral to an ophthalmologist is recommended.

55. ***a***

A one month old infant would be expected to exhibit the Moro, stepping, rooting, and Babinski reflexes. The tonic neck, or "fencing" reflex isn't exhibited until about 2-3 months of age. This is assessed by lying the baby on his back and turning his head to one side. If the reflex is present, he should extend his arm on the side that his head is turned. The opposite arm assumes a flexed position. This pose mimics a fencer and thus, the name.

56. ***d***

The Moro reflex is a startle reflex. Observation of the reflex is confirmed if the infant symmetrically flings his arms away from his body followed by an immediate flexion of both arms in response to simulating falling. If this is asymmetrical, it could indicate an injury during or after birth (more likely during birth) such as a brachial plexus palsy, hemiplegia, or even a fractured clavicle. The Moro reflex usually disappears between 3-6 months. The significance of this reflex is for evaluation of integration of the central nervous system.

57. ***d***

Weaning from the baby's bottle takes place about a year of age. This should be discussed at the visit prior to the time this would take place. 9 months is an appropriate time to discuss this. Syrup of ipecac is no longer recommended. Parents and caregivers should be instructed NOT to use this. Stranger anxiety develops about 9 months of age. The average 12 month old says about 2-5 words.

58. ***d***

A child's vision should be screened beginning at age 3 years if he is cooperative. The vision of a 3 year-old should be about 20/50. A 4 year-old's vision is usually 20/40. By 5 years of age, vision is usually 20/30. By 6 years of age, a child's vision should be approximately normal, 20/20.

59. ***b***

Conjunctivitis or "pink eye" usually begins as a viral infection. As the conjunctiva becomes irritated, the eye is rubbed and fingers introduce bacteria. A secondary bacterial infection develops. Conjunctivitis produces a red (or pink) eye, but should never produce blurred vision. A patient with a red eye and blurred vision should be referred to ophthalmology. The pre-auricular nodes may be palpable when a patient has conjunctivitis, not the anterior cervical ones.

60. A patient has suspected scarlet fever. He likely has a sandpaper rash and:

a. negative throat swab.
b. a positive rapid strept test.
c. diarrhea with abdominal cramps.
d. petechiae on the trunk.

61. Which reflex may be present at 9 months of age during sleep?

a. Moro reflex
b. Rooting
c. Stepping
d. Tonic neck

62. A child who is 15 months old is referred to as a(n):

a. infant.
b. toddler.
c. preschooler.
d. youngster.

63. A child who can stack a maximum of 5 blocks is probably:

a. 1 year.
b. 15 months.
c. 2 years.
d. 3 years.

64. A young female has breast buds bilaterally. This represents Tanner Stage:

a. 1.
b. 2.
c. 3.
d. 4.

65. The age at which a child can first walk backwards is:

a. 12 months.
b. 15 months.
c. 18 months.
d. 24 months.

60. ***b***

A patient with scarlet fever (scarlatina) has a common childhood disease that is characterized by sore throat, fever, and a scarlet "sandpaper" rash. The causative organism is Group A beta hemolytic *Streptococcus pyogenes*. The patient's rapid strept test will likely be positive. If the rapid Strept test is negative, the throat swab should be positive. Diarrhea with abdominal cramps is not specific to scarlet fever. Petechiae represent an extravasation of blood under the skin and are not present with scarlet fever unless some other disease process is present. Petechiae should be considered to be a very serious finding.

61. ***b***

The rooting reflex disappears about 2-3 months of age but may be present during sleep up to 12 months. The Moro reflex disappears somewhere between 3 and 6 months, usually 4-5 months. The tonic neck, or "fencing" response, generally disappears about 6 months of age. The stepping response disappears about 9 months. Interestingly, this is usually when infants are beginning to take the first steps with assistance.

62. ***b***

Infant is the term given to a child from one month of age up to 12 months of age. The term toddler is given to children starting at 12 months of age to three years. Four and five year-olds are referred to as preschoolers.

63. ***c***

Common developmental tasks for a 2 year-old include: stacking 5 blocks, following 2 step commands, using 2 word phrases, kicking a ball, saying at least 20 words, and walking up and down stairs one step at a time.

64. ***b***

Tanner Stage II is characterized by the formation and presence of breast buds, small areas of surrounding glandular tissue, and widening of the areola.

65. ***c***

Common developmental tasks for an 18 month old include: walking backwards, throwing a ball, saying 15-20 words, pointing to multiple body parts, pointing and naming objects in a book, and stacking 3-4 blocks.

66. When is a child first able to stand on one foot?

a. 18 months
b. 2 years
c. 3 years
d. 4 years

67. At what age should initial blood pressure screening take place?

a. 3 years
b. 4-6 years
c. 6 years
d. 6-10 years

68. What is the usual age for vision screening in young children?

a. 2 years
b. 3 years
c. 4 years
d. 5 years

69. What is the earliest age that an average child would appropriately receive construction paper and a pair of scissors with rounded points?

a. 3 years
b. 4 years
c. 5 years
d. 6 years

70. What is the earliest age that an average child would be able to copy a triangle, know his colors, and count on his fingers?

a. 3 years
b. 4 years
c. 5 years
d. 6 years

71. What Tanner stage corresponds to an average 8 year-old?

a. Stage 0
b. Stage 1
c. Stage 2
d. Stage 3

66. ***c***
Common developmental tasks for 3 year-old include: standing on one foot, riding a tricycle, saying his name, gender, and age, copying a circle, and recognizing some colors.

67. ***a***
Blood pressure should be measured immediately after birth and anytime there is a suspected cardiac problem. After this time, blood pressure screening should begin at 3 years of age and then, annually. A pediatric blood pressure table must be used because normal blood pressure varies with age, gender, and height. A pediatric blood pressure table will display the maximum systolic and diastolic blood pressure expected for the child. Taller and heavier children will have higher blood pressures.

68. ***b***
Initial vision screening should take place at 3 years of age. If the child is not cooperative, screening should be attempted 6 months later. If the child is still not cooperative at 3.5 years, it should be attempted at 4 years. Generally, children are cooperative at 4 years of age. The usual vision of a 3 year-old is 20/50.

69. ***b***
A 4 year-old should have the dexterity to cut and paste. Therefore, this is the most appropriate age. A 5 or 6 year-old may also use these items, but these would be appropriate as early as 4 years. Pointed tips represent hazards especially in a classroom with multiple children moving simultaneously.

70. ***c***
Common developmental tasks for a 5 year-old include: ability to draw a person with a body, head, arms, and legs, recognize most letters and can print some, know his address and phone number, dress self without help, able to skip and tiptoe, and play cooperatively and enjoy a playmate's company.

71. ***b***
The Tanner scale indicates the stages of sexual development of males and females. The development of sexual characteristics is described based on the Stage. An average 8 year-old would be expected to be pre-pubertal. This is characterized as a Tanner Stage 1. Pubertal changes can occur as early as 9-10 years in males or females. If changes occur prior to this, precocious puberty should be considered.

72. A pregnant mother in her first trimester has a 5 year-old who has Fifth Disease. What implication does this have for the mother?

- **a. She does not have to worry about transmission to the fetus.**
- **b. She may get a mild case of Fifth disease.**
- **c. There is a risk of fetal death if she becomes infected.**
- **d. The mother should have a fetal ultrasound today.**

73. The average age of pubertal growth spurt in North American boys is:

- **a. 9.5 - 11.5 years.**
- **b. 10 - 12 years.**
- **c. 12 - 14 years.**
- **d. 14 - 16 years.**

74. A 15 year-old female has been sexually active since she was 12 years old. She presents today with concerns of pregnancy. How should this be managed?

- **a. Pregnancy test should be performed today.**
- **b. A parent or guardian is needed for permission for the pregnancy test.**
- **c. She should have a pelvic exam.**
- **d. She should have a Pap smear and a pelvic exam.**

75. An adolescent male reports that he has dysuria. He admits that he is sexually active. How should this be managed?

- **a. Prescribe azithromycin**
- **b. Prescribe azithromycin and ceftriaxone**
- **c. Urethral/urine cultures should be collected and screening done for STDs**
- **d. Collect a urethral culture and schedule a return appointment**

76. A 6 month-old male has a palpable cystic mass in his scrotum. His mother states that sometimes the size of his scrotum seems larger than today during the exam. How should this be managed?

- **a. Referral to urology as soon as possible**
- **b. Referral to urology if this has not resolved in 6 months**
- **c. Scrotal ultrasound should be ordered**
- **d. Order a urine specimen to rule out infection**

77. A 9 year-old has been diagnosed with chickenpox. A drug that should be avoided in him is:

- **a. penicillin.**
- **b. aspirin.**
- **c. ibuprofen.**
- **d. sulfa.**

72. ***c***

Pregnant mother should avoid exposure to patients with known Fifth disease. However, the risk of transmission is very low. She should avoid exposure to aplastic patients who are infected because they are highly contagious. Infection during pregnancy is associated with 10% fetal death. There is no need for an ultrasound today. This pregnant patient does not have evidence of disease. She should be monitored for a rash which could indicate infection.

73. ***c***

Growth spurt in girls takes place earlier than boys. In girls of North American origin, the growth spurt occurs between 10 - 12.5 years. Completion of the growth spurt occurs later in boys but not usually before 16 years of age. In girls, completion of the growth spurt can occur as early as 14.5 years.

74. ***a***

A serum pregnancy test is highly sensitive even early in pregnancy and is prudent today. If the serum pregnancy test is negative, it is unlikely that this patient is pregnant. This patient should be counseled regarding issues of safe sex and STDs. Because she presents for an exam and requests a pregnancy test, a parent or guardian is not needed for consent because parental consent is not required for a reproductive issue in a sexually active adolescent.

75. ***c***

This patient has dysuria. Dysuria could represent infection with an STD like chlamydia, gonorrhea, or trichomonas. Less likely, this patient could have a UTI or some other irritation of the urethral meatus. Cultures should be collected to establish a diagnosis and other STDs should be assessed (HIV, hepatitis B and C, syphilis etc.).

76. ***b***

This situation describes a hydrocele. It is very common in young males and usually resolves by a year of age. If it has not resolved by 12 months of age, the patient should be referred to urology. A cystic mass in the scrotum with a description of changing in size of the scrotum supports the finding of a communicating hydrocele. A scrotal ultrasound is not indicated at this time.

77. ***b***

Aspirin is always avoided in the case of viral infections in children and adolescents. The incidence of Reye syndrome is increased if aspirin is given. This is especially true with varicella and influenza infections. The typical constellation of symptoms occurs during a bout of chickenpox and includes nausea, vomiting, headache, excitability, delirium, and combativeness with progression to coma. Since aspirin use has declined sharply, Reye syndrome has too.

78. Children with an inguinal hernia:

a. have a history of an intermittent bulge in the groin.
b. are usually symptomatic.
c. have a mass that is always present on exam.
d. are usually irritable and often constipated.

79. An infant is diagnosed with diaper dermatitis. Satellite lesions are visible. This should be treated with a:

a. moisture barrier like zinc oxide.
b. topical anti-fungal agent.
c. topical anti-bacterial agent.
d. low potency steroid cream.

80. A 14 year-old patient has an acute, painless groin swelling. What tool would yield the most information to identify the etiology of the swelling?

a. Abdominal radiographs
b. Ultrasound of the abdomen
c. Ultrasound of the scrotum
d. MRI of the scrotum

81. A nurse practitioner has successfully reduced a nursemaid's elbow. How can the NP know that it was successful?

a. X-rays
b. Child moves the affected arm at the elbow
c. A click is heard
d. The deformity has resolved

82. Which of the following is true regarding metatarsus adductus?

a. This is another term for clubfoot
b. Mild flexible metatarsus usually spontaneously corrects
c. X-rays are usually necessary to diagnose this
d. Infants frequently require casting to correct

83. A congenital heart abnormality often discovered during the newborn period is coarctation of the aorta. How is this assessed?

a. By comparing right and left femoral pulses
b. By comparing right and left pedal pulses
c. By comparing upper and lower extremity blood pressures
d. By auscultating a audible bruit in the carotid arteries

78. ***a***
Inguinal hernias are usually asymptomatic and absent on exam but can sometimes be elicited by increasing intraabdominal pressure such as occurs with straining or crying. The "silk sign" is infrequently appreciated but represents a silky thickening of the cord. If it is able to be palpated, it is done by placing a single finger next to the inguinal canal at the level of the pubic tubercle and gently moving the finger from side to side. Children with an incarcerated mass are often irritable but not constipated.

79. ***b***
The finding of satellite lesions associated with diaper dermatitis indicates a Candidal infection. This patient will be most effectively treated with a topical anti-fungal agent, allowing the lesions to be exposed to air for periods of time (like during a nap). A moisture barrier like zinc oxide is more beneficial when the diaper dermatitis is due to irritants like prolonged exposure to urine or feces. A low potency steroid cream should be used with caution in an infant with a fungal infection. A low potency cream in conjunction with an anti-fungal can be helpful if there is a great amount of underlying inflammation but has the potential to worsen the infection.

80. ***c***
The patient has an acute swelling of the groin. Since the etiology could include several scrotal problems (inguinal hernia, hydrocele, or varicocele), an ultrasound will yield quick reliable information with a diagnostic accuracy of 93% for acute groin problems. The definitive treatment for inguinal hernia is surgical repair.

81. ***b***
Successful reduction occurs when the child moves the affected arm at the elbow. Normal range of motion is established immediately if done correctly. X-rays are not needed. There is no visible deformity when subluxation occurs. The examiner's clue is clinical history and position in which the child holds his arm. When the examiner performs the reduction, the examiner may feel a click over the radial head when the arm is hyperpronated.

82. ***b***
Metatarsus adductus (MA) is the most common congenital foot deformity. It is not related to clubfoot. In MA, the forefoot deviates medially, the hindfoot remains in a neutral position. This is a common cause of in-toeing gait and usually spontaneously corrects. This can be diagnosed on clinical presentation. An x-ray is not necessary. Casting is usually reserved for severe MA characterized by a rigid forefoot.

83. ***c***
Coarctation is frequently missed on initial assessment. This disorder is characterized by elevated blood pressures in the upper extremities and diminished blood pressures in the lower extremities. It can be assessed by measuring and comparing blood pressures in the upper and lower extremities.

84. Clubfoot:

a. **always requires an urgent neurosurgical referral.**
b. **involves the foot and lower extremity.**
c. **involves the foot only.**
d. **can be corrected with casting and exercises.**

85. A 12 year-old male with hip pain presents to the NP clinic. Hip pain has occurred with activity for the past 4-6 weeks but his pain is worse and now involves the knee. There is no history of trauma. How should the work-up be initiated?

a. **Order a hip and knee x-ray**
b. **Order a hip x-ray and a sed rate**
c. **Perform Trendelenburg's test in the office**
d. **Have the child squat in the office to assess the hips**

86. The nurse practitioner sees a child who presents with fatigue and purpura on his lower extremities. His temperature is normal. The differential includes:

a. **anemia.**
b. **hypothyroidism.**
c. **acute leukemia.**
d. **Kawasaki syndrome.**

87. A 12 month-old was screened for iron deficiency anemia and found to be anemic. The nurse practitioner ordered oral iron. In one month, the child's hemoglobin was re-assessed. It increased greatly. What choice might account for this?

a. **The mother administered it with his bottle of milk.**
b. **The child is drinking apple juice.**
c. **The child received his iron as prescribed.**
d. **The child experienced a growth spurt.**

88. A mother presents with her one-month old infant. She reports that he cries inconsolably every evening after his first evening feeding. She asks for help. What should be done?

a. **Order stool specimens**
b. **Order ranitidine for the infant's bottle**
c. **A different formula should be tried**
d. **Education, parental reassurance, and encouragement**

84. *b*
Clubfoot is also known as talipes equinovarus. The foot is plantar flexed and the forefoot and sole are thrust medially. This involves the foot and lower extremity. It is an urgent orthopedic referral, not neurosurgical referral. Casting and splinting usually takes place initially with surgical treatment delayed if needed until 3-6 months if necessary. However, the majority of patients will be successfully corrected with taping, splinting, and/or casting when early intervention occurs.

85. *c*
There are several diagnoses in the differential. The assessment of this child should begin in the office. Asking the child to stand on the affected leg performs the Trendelenburg's test. If there are weak adductor muscles in the affected hip, a pelvic tilt will be visible in the unaffected hip. This can be found in children with a slipped capital femoral epiphysis, Legg-Calve-Perthes disease, or developmental dysplasia of the hip. After assessment of the hip, knee, and gait in the office, a hip x-ray to include AP and lateral should be ordered. The advantage of a sedimentation rate or C-reactive protein is that it will be elevated in patients with the aforementioned hip problems. It will be elevated in septic arthritis and other inflammatory causes of hip pain.

86. *c*
The presence of purpura must make the nurse practitioner consider platelet problems. Fatigue should prompt consideration of anemia. Both are seen in patients with leukemia. Acute leukemia must be considered because of the combination of fatigue and purpura. This child needs a CBC as soon possible. Kawasaki syndrome is an autoimmune disease that produces vasculitis of the mid-sized arteries. Henoch-Schonlein purpura could also be considered as part of the NP's differential, but this was not a choice.

87. *c*
This child's hemoglobin should have increased if he is receiving the iron as prescribed, and there is no other disease process occurring. If the child's hemoglobin is not increasing, the instructions for administering the iron should be reviewed with the caregiver and the dosage should be re-calculated. If the hemoglobin does not improve despite this, further assessment is needed.

88. *d*
This describes colic. Colic is a symptom complex characterized by episodes of inconsolable crying accompanied by apparent abdominal pain. It typically occurs between 1-3 months of age and usually in a very predictable pattern, typically in the evening after feeding. Many different approaches are tried, but medication like ranitidine is not indicated, changing formula is not indicated either. Parents need education regarding colic, comfort measures like rhythmic rocking or frequent burping, much reassurance, and encouragement.

89. A 4 year-old female is brought in to the clinic by her mother who reports that she is constantly scratching "her private part". The patient states that it itches. On exam, the vagina is red and irritated. How should the NP proceed?

a. Call child protection for suspected sexual abuse
b. Prescribe a cortisone cream
c. Collect a vaginal swab of the external vagina for microscopic evaluation
d. Prescribe a topical antifungal

90. A 3 day-old full-term infant has a bilirubin level of 16 mg/dL. How should this be managed?

a. Monitor only
b. Increase fluids and stop breastfeeding
c. Increase breastfeeding
d. Order phototherapy for the infant

91. An adolescent has acne. The nurse practitioner prescribed a benzoyl peroxide product for him. What important teaching point should be given to this adolescent regarding the benzoyl peroxide?

a. Don't apply this product more than once daily
b. This often causes peeling of the skin
c. Photosensitivity of the skin can occur
d. Hypersensitivity can occur with repeated use

92. A 15 year-old male has worked this summer as a lifeguard at a local swimming pool. He complains of itching in the groin area. He is diagnosed with tinea cruris. The nurse practitioner is likely to identify:

a. swelling of the scrotum.
b. macular lesions on the penis.
c. well marginated half moon macules on the inner thigh.
d. maceration of the scrotal folds with erythema of the penis.

93. A 4 month-old infant has thrush. The mother is breastfeeding. She reports that her nipples have become red, irritated, and sensitive. What should the nurse practitioner advise the mother of this baby to treat thrush?

a. Have the mother exercise good hygiene of her nipples
b. Administer an oral anti-fungal suspension to the mother
c. Administer an oral anti-fungal suspension to the infant
d. Treat the infant with an oral anti-fungal suspension and the mother's nipples with a topical anti-fungal agent

89. ***c***
This child has a vaginitis. There are many diagnoses in the differential including pinworms, yeast, contact irritants from soap or bubble bath, etc. Since the diagnosis is not clear, some evaluation must occur in order to determine the diagnosis so proper treatment can be initiated. Since the description of the problem does not indicate what the diagnosis is, it is inappropriate to treat with a cortisone cream or topical antifungal.

90. ***d***
There are several ways to determine how elevated the bilirubin level is. One measure is to use the Bhutani nomogram. It predicts bilirubin levels based on post-natal age. A level of 16 mg/dL is considered high intermediate. Since the bilirubin probably will rise a little more, phototherapy is probably appropriate.

91. ***c***
Benzoyl peroxide can produce sensitivity to the sun and so adolescents should be informed of this. This product can be used twice daily. It can cause peeling of the skin, but this is not a frequent occurrence. Hypersensitivity can occur with any topical product and is not specific to benzoyl peroxide.

92. ***c***
Tinea cruris, "jock itch" is common during warm months and in humid areas. It is a fungal infection that affects the scrotum and inner thighs, but never affects the penis and is never evidenced by scrotal swelling. He is probably at increased risk because he is working as a lifeguard and may wear damp or wet swim trunks during work. He should be treated with a topical antifungal cream, advised to dry off after swimming and put on dry swim trunks.

93. ***d***
If the infant has thrush, he should be treated with an oral anti-fungal suspension like nystatin. This is given 4 times daily after feedings. Since the mouth of the infant is in contact with the mother's nipples during breastfeeding, and they sound infected too, the mother and infant should be treated simultaneously. Care should be given so that the mother gently washes her nipples and dries them before breastfeeding. This will minimize or eliminate ingestion of the topical anti-fungal in the infant.

94. An adolescent male has had a sudden onset of severe scrotal pain following a kick in the groin earlier in the day in a soccer game. How should this be managed?

a. A urine specimen should be collected.
b. A scrotal ultrasound should be ordered.
c. He should be referred to the emergency department.
d. He should be examined carefully for a low riding testicle.

95. A 2 year-old has a sudden onset of high fever while at daycare. The daycare attendant describes a seizure in the child. The child is brought to the clinic; neurologically he appears normal. His body temperature is 99.9 degrees F after receiving ibuprofen. He is diagnosed with otitis media. How should the nurse practitioner manage this?

a. Assess the child and refer to the ER
b. Treat the otitis media and give education about fever management
c. Start the child on seizure precautions
d. Have him admitted to the hospital for observation

96. A 6 month-old infant has a disconjugate gaze. The nurse practitioner observes that the 6 month old tilts his head when looking at objects in the room. Which statement is true?

a. Nystagmus will be present.
b. The infant will have an abnormal cover/uncover test.
c. The patient's vision is 20/200.
d. He needs a CT to rule out an ocular tumor.

97. A young child has developed a circumferential lesion on her inner forearm. It is slightly raised, red and is pruritic. It is about 2.5 cm in diameter. This is probably related to:

a. a genetic disorder.
b. the child's new cat.
c. juvenile rheumatoid arthritis.
d. a psoriatic lesion.

98. A sexually active adolescent male has a warty growth on the shaft of his penis. It is painless. This is likely:

a. trichomonas.
b. syphilis.
c. herpes.
d. human papilloma virus.

94. ***c***

There are two important differential diagnoses with the development of scrotal pain: testicular torsion and epididymitis. Because of the history of this occurring following groin trauma, and the fact that he is an adolescent, testicular torsion must be excluded. If testicular torsion is the cause of his pain, getting this patient into the ER/hospital so that torsion can be reversed must be paramount to the treatment decision. Obtaining an ultrasound will delay treatment and that decision should be deferred to the urologist. Reversal of the ischemia should take place within 4-6 hours of the onset of pain in order to protect the viability of the testicle.

95. ***b***

The child may have had a febrile seizure at the daycare related to a sudden elevation of body temperature. The sudden rise (or even fall) of body temperature can precipitate a seizure in young children. The most common diagnosis associated with febrile seizures is otitis media. The mother should be advised about behavior to watch for that could indicate the child is having a seizure. If this behavior occurs again, the child should be brought for neurological evaluation. Information should be provided to the caregiver regarding management of elevated body temperature in the child.

96. ***b***

The cover/uncover test is used to assess strabismus, a common cause of disconjugate gaze. Strabismus represents a nonparallelism of the visual axis of the eyes. This results in the inability of both eyes to focus on the same object at the same time. At 6 months of age, a disconjugate gaze and tilting of the child's head is a red flag. This child needs referral to ophthalmology. While an ocular tumor could be present, this is unlikely and not the action that should be taken today.

97. ***b***

This describes ringworm. It is a fungal infection that is common in children. A typical precipitant is a new animal like a cat. Since it appears on the inner forearm, it is likely the child got this from holding the cat. It should be treated with a topical anti-fungal agent.

98. ***d***

This is not a clinical presentation of trichomonas because this produces a discharge. Syphilis produces a painless lesion but it presents as an ulceration with a hard edge and clean, yellow base. Herpes produces lesions, but these are painful and produce burning. HPV, human papilloma virus, produces warty growths as described above.

99. At what age should screening for oral health begin?

- **a. At birth**
- **b. 3 months**
- **c. 6 months**
- **d. 1 year**

100. Risk assessment for dyslipidemia should begin at:

- **a. 2 years.**
- **b. 6 years.**
- **c. 10 years.**
- **d. 18 years.**

99. ***c***

Examination of the mouth may begin at birth, but oral health screening should begin at 6 months of age. Part of the screening should be for the need for fluoride supplementation. Oral health risk assessment should take place at 6 months, 9 months, and referral to a dental home should take place by one year of age. Oral health risk assessment should continue periodically at health screening visits at 18, 24, and every 6 months until a dental home is established.

100. ***a***

Dyslipidemia assessment does not necessarily mean a lipid profile, though these are recommended between 18 and 21 years of age. Dyslipidemia assessment refers to assessing family history of dyslipidemia, premature cardiovascular disease, or diabetes, body mass index > 85% for age and sex, or history of other systemic diseases like Kawasaki Disease or treatment, or renal disease.